Valuation in Criticism

VALUATION IN CRITICISM
and other essays

by
F. R. LEAVIS

collected and edited
by
G. SINGH

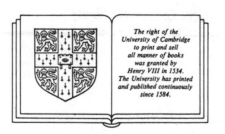

The right of the
University of Cambridge
to print and sell
all manner of books
was granted by
Henry VIII in 1534.
The University has printed
and published continuously
since 1584.

CAMBRIDGE UNIVERSITY PRESS

Cambridge
London   New York   New Rochelle
Melbourne   Sydney

Published by the Press Syndicate of the University of Cambridge
The Pitt Building, Trumpington Street, Cambridge CB2 1RP
32 East 57th Street, New York, NY 10022, USA
10 Stamford Road, Oakleigh, Melbourne 3166, Australia

First published 1986

Printed in Great Britain at
the University Press, Cambridge

British Library cataloguing in publication data
Leavis, F. R.
Valuation in Criticism and other essays.
1. English literature – History and criticism
2. Criticism
I. Title II. Singh, G.
820.9   PR57

Library on Congress cataloguing in publication data
Leavis, F. R. (Frank Raymond), 1895–1978
Valuation in criticism and other essays.
1. English literature – History and criticism
Addresses, essays, lectures. 2. American literature –
History and criticism – Addresses, essays, lectures.
3. Criticism – Addresses, essays, lectures. I. Singh, G.
II. Title.
PR99.L358   1986   820.'.9   85–25475

ISBN 0 521 30966 2 hard covers
ISBN 0 521 31210 8 paperback

Contents

2296501

Contents

Sources and acknowledgments

'T. S. Eliot – a reply to the condescending', 'D. H. Lawrence', and 'William Empson: intelligence and sensibility' appeared in *The Cambridge Review* (8 February 1929; 13 June 1930; 16 January 1931); 'The influence of Donne on modern poetry' in *The Bookman* (March 1931); 'Marxism and cultural continuity' was the prefatory statement in Leavis's first collection of essays, *For Continuity*, 1933; 'Under which king, Bezonian?', 'Restatements for critics', 'Dr Richards, Bentham and Coleridge', 'Henry James's first novel: *Roderick Hudson*', 'The responsible critic', and '"Scrutiny": a retrospect' appeared in *Scrutiny*, vols. I, III, XIV, XIX and XX; 'Literary studies: a reply' in *Universities Quarterly* (II, 1, November 1956); 'The literary discipline and liberal education' in *Sewanee Review* (vol. 55, 1947), 'Felix Holt, the Radical' appeared as an introduction to George Eliot's novel (Dent, Everyman's Library, 1966). 'George Eliot's Zionist novel' originally appeared in *Commentary* (October 1960) and was reprinted as an introduction to *Daniel Deronda* (Panther, 1970); '*Nostromo*: a foreword' appeared as an introduction to the novel published by New American Library (A Signet Classic, 1960); 'Yeats: the problem and the challenge' appeared in *Lectures in America* (1969; now out of print). 'Shaw against Lawrence' and 'Genius as critic' appeared in *The Spectator* (1 April 1955 and 24 March 1961 respectively). 'Lawrence after thirty years' – the text of a lecture delivered at Nottingham University, 17 June 1960 – appeared in *D. H. Lawrence: a critical anthology*, ed. H. Coombes (Penguin, 1973; out of print); 'Valuation in criticism' in *Orbis Litterarum* (21, 1966); and 'T. S. Eliot and the life of English literature' – Cheltenham Festival Lecture given in October 1968 – in *The Massachusetts Review* (vol. 10, 1, winter 1969). 'Reading out poetry' – the transcript of a lecture given at Queen's University, Belfast, 10 May 1972 – was published by Queen's University, together with the proceedings of a Commemorative Symposium on F. R. Leavis, in 1979; 'T. S. Eliot's influence', 'Standards of criticism', 'Thought, meaning and sensibility: the problem of value judgment' and 'Notes on Wordsworth' are published here for the first time.

Editor's introduction

This volume is almost certain to be the last collection of F. R. Leavis's essays to include previously unpublished material. It also gathers together essays, reviews, articles and lectures which have not appeared in volume form before, or which are now relatively hard to find. An additional interest is that the contents range from his very first published articles to the things he was engaged in writing immediately before his final illness. This material, from the whole span of a long writing career, shows both the continuity of his preoccupations and important respects in which his judgments changed. This is especially the case with T. S. Eliot and D. H. Lawrence. Leavis wrote more about Eliot than about any other writer, and he moved from a simple conviction of Eliot's greatness and importance to a more troubled sense that discriminations had to be made. The process can be traced in the essays reprinted here. With Lawrence the movement was in the other direction: from an obscure sense of challenge to a final conviction of unalloyed admiration.

The earliest essays are naturally placed first, in a group. The three articles in *The Cambridge Review* are fresh, challenging and entirely positive (compare, for instance, the remarks on Empson in the later essay 'The Literary Discipline and Liberal Education'). As Leavis said later, *The Cambridge Review* was a 'very institutional journal which is owned and, one hears, watched over, by an innominate committee of Dons'; he came to think that the publication was 'a Quixotic folly (I don't regret it)' – presumably because he thought it marked him out early as an anti-establishment troubler of the academic peace. Certainly the reputations of Eliot and Lawrence were not then the assured values that they are now, and it took some courage to champion them. In the piece on Eliot can be seen the first statement of Leavis's views about poetic language and the 'alteration of expression', and an adumbration of his later concept of 'The Third Realm'. This had its first explicit formulation in the celebrated Richmond Lecture on C. P. Snow, but it can be seen restated in several essays in this volume. The article on Lawrence is notable for the first statement of the parallel with Blake. Compare, however, the retrospective glance at this article in the later 'Lawrence After Thirty Years'.

1

The second group of essays is chosen from *For Continuity*, Leavis's first collection, of 1933. 'Marxism and Cultural Continuity' has not been reprinted since; nor has 'Restatements for Critics'. They need to be read alongside 'Under Which King, Bezonian?'. The three articles together show Leavis engaging in the 1930s with the Marxist theory of culture, which he shows to have been at that time incoherent and insufficiently disengaged from the system it thought it was attacking: it was 'in the matter of values, too bourgeois, too much the product of the material environment'. 'The process of civilization that produced, among other things, the Marxian dogma, and makes it plausible, has made the cultural differences between the "classes" inessential. The essential differences are indeed now definable in economic terms, and to aim at solving the problems of civilization in terms of the "class war" is to aim, whether wittingly or not, at completing the work of capitalism [that is, modernization of society via its industrialization] and its products . . . ' That kind of utopianism was in the 1930s like the 'exaltation' of H. G. Wells and in the 1960s like the scientism of C. P. Snow: another aspect of the 'vast and increasing inattention' which was part of the plight of the industrial system, and where the offered nostrums were the undiagnosed symptoms of what Leavis later comprehensively summed up as technologico-Benthamism. The expressions of his distress at the blindness, and consciousness of his own Cassandra-role can be felt in the later essays as a real anguish.

In the third section, the Introductions to *Felix Holt*, *Daniel Deronda* and *Nostromo* offer readings of the novels in question – novels characterized by moral and artistic maturity, psychological acumen, imaginative humanity and social responsibility: things which for Leavis were the constitutive characteristics of 'The Great Tradition'. *Felix Holt* acquired classic status for this reason, while *Daniel Deronda* brings out George Eliot's greatness 'at its most Tolstoyan'. If the Zionist part of the novel is, as Henry James said, 'at bottom cold', it is not merely because it was 'done from the outside', but because it has its origin in 'an unreduced enclave of immaturity', where it is not so much the great intellect that is in control as something emotional – 'something that, in part at least, is a paradoxical immaturity'. *Nostromo*, on the other hand, dealing with 'the tormenting conscience' of the dedicated craftsman, invokes and exemplifies 'the conviction of a subtle rightness of expressive form to be achieved'. Leavis compares Conrad with Flaubert (whose conception of the art of the novel strongly influenced Conrad's) and finds that *Nostromo*, though the most Flaubertian of Conrad's works, attests to 'a full engagement in life, and (whatever the intensity of concern for "form") an art of which *that* can be said is radically unlike Flaubert's'. (The definition of the

Flaubertian fear of life can be seen crystallizing itself in several of the other essays in this volume.) In claiming 'classical currency' for Henry James's first novel *Roderick Hudson*, Leavis emphasizes its 'distinctly Jamesian' qualities; its technical preoccupation, the choice and treatment of the theme, and the characteristic felicities of style. Even though it is a minor work, Leavis finds it 'more worth reading and re-reading than the greater number of Victorian fictions that are commonly offered us as classics'.

The essay 'Yeats: the Problem and the Challenge' is a late revaluation of Yeats, and so a reconsideration of Leavis's own position *vis-à-vis* what he had written in *New Bearings* some thirty years before. Yeats's stature as a major twentieth-century poet is assessed from the point of view of the critic who asks: 'How much of the fully achieved thing *is* there in Yeats's *œuvre* – what proportion of the wholly created poem that stands there unequivocally in its own right, self-sufficient?' Leavis's unequivocal answer is that it is not large.

'Shaw Against Lawrence', 'Lawrence After Thirty Years' and 'Genius as Critic' were published between Leavis's book *D. H. Lawrence: Novelist* (1955) and the later full-length treatment of Lawrence: *Thought, Words and Creativity* (1976). The two essays state Leavis's position on aspects of Lawrence's work and art, including his preoccupation with sex and how it 'transcends anything that the word "sex" suggests'. In 'Lawrence After Thirty Years', Leavis tells us that the theme 'slips for me, to begin with, into another: myself thirty years ago' (when he wrote the first piece on Lawrence in *The Cambridge Review*). Leavis's conviction that Lawrence was a profoundly original genius, 'a creative genius of the greatest kind', someone who imposed 'an extremely difficult adjustment', and who had to be 'lived with and lived into', grew steadily but consistently – a process in the course of which he came to see Lawrence as 'the great anti-Flaubertian', 'a radical and potent counter-influence to the aesthetic, the esoteric and the sophisticated' and, in the age of Marxizing, 'an essential enemy of the didactic'.

In 'Genius as Critic' Leavis is reviewing *Phoenix*, which contains 'immeasurably the finest body of criticism in existence' – the criticism of that 'rare being who is alive in every fibre and has the centrality and easy swiftness of genius' and which makes Lawrence so 'un-Eliotic in [his] utterance'. This essay may be regarded as a foil to Leavis's essay on 'Eliot as Critic' (in *Anna Karenina and Other Essays*).

'T. S. Eliot's Influence' was found among Leavis's papers as a typescript (possibly the text of a lecture, although I have not been able to establish when and where it was given; but it was written some years after the 'Retrospect' for the reprinted *Scrutiny*). This and 'T. S. Eliot and the Life of English Literature' complement each other in that both undertake to evaluate Eliot's achievement in the light of his influence – more 'a matter of mere fashion' than 'a profound or vital influence' – and his classical status examined by one who is not an 'uncritical admirer of T. S. Eliot'.

In the last section of the volume Leavis is expounding his concept of, his approach to and his convincingly exemplified views on criticism, literary studies, value judgment and the reading out of poetry. 'Dr Richards, Bentham and Coleridge' (a review of I. A. Richards's *Coleridge on Imagination*) brings out the fundamental difference of approach between Richards and Leavis – not only to Coleridge, but also to poetry and to literary criticism. One origin of Leavis's 'anti-philosophical' approach to criticism and the ground on which he was, in subsequent years, to call himself an 'anti-philosopher' may be traced to this essay, in which he takes Richards to task for 'heading away from the concrete' and for being 'the happy servant of a set of abstract terms'. (But the same resistance to abstraction is seen in 'Marxism and Cultural Continuity' and 'Restatements for Critics'.)

In 'Literary Studies: a Reply', Leavis is responding to what Professor W. W. Robson had written under the heading 'Literary Studies' (*Universities Quarterly*, vol. 10, no. 2, February 1956). Leavis's comment challenges Robson's views on the 'separation' between the literary historian and the literary critic; between training intelligence (which Robson advocates) and training sensibility; between knowledge as such, and judgment, as well as Robson's use of the word 'aesthetic'.

Some years earlier, in 'The Literary Discipline and Liberal Education' – Leavis's contribution to the symposium on the teaching of literature organized by *Sewanee Review*, in which the contributors were Mark Van Doren, Rosemond Tuve, Austin Warren and René Wellek – Leavis had already developed some of these views while defining literature as a discipline of intelligence. He also commented on the working of what he called 'the institutional mind on the "humane" side of the universities', and put us on our guard against 'inert acquiescences, concessions to social amenity, tacit agreements to take the form for the reality and the running of the machine for the movement' – formulae that sum up what was increasingly to be the ethos of Leavis's subsequent writings and criticism.

'The Responsible Critic' – a polemical exchange with F. W. Bateson – has both an 'occasional' character and a permanent validity and relevance, like Leavis's exchange with René Wellek ('Philosophy and Literary Criticism'). On both occasions the challenge gave Leavis the opportunity of saying 'some obvious but important things by way of reply' as well as of redefining his own views on the nature and function of a responsible critic. The essay comes closest to expounding one part of Leavis's theoretical position as a critic – his attitude to the role of 'scholarship' in literary criticism. Himself a trained historian, he could well appreciate the value of knowledge and scholarship, but what was of primary importance to Leavis was the criterion of relevance, and the logic with which he demolished Bateson's case is as effective as the critical acumen.

'*Scrutiny*: a Retrospect', another 'occasional' piece written when Cambridge University Press brought out the 20-volume reprint of *Scrutiny* in 1963, is a landmark in twentieth-century literary criticism. Writing about *Scrutiny* – its origin and ethos, the odds it had to fight against in order to survive, and the revolutionary impact it made – Leavis recapitulates an important period in his own life and career as well as in his wife's, and documents *Scrutiny*'s role in establishing what is new, unconventional and original in twentieth-century literature. The hostility *Scrutiny* aroused in some circles is for Leavis a proof of its decisive role in altering twentieth-century literary taste and sensibility, as well as in establishing 'a new critical idiom and a new conception of the nature of critical thought'. '*Scrutiny*: a Retrospect' is at once a piece of cultural and literary autobiography, the critique of an epoch, and the summing up of an ethos. Having come through the battles he and his wife had to fight in order to keep *Scrutiny* going, having established a new approach to the criticism of the novel as well as of poetry, Leavis – protagonist turned chronicler – could affirm what his journal had achieved with courage and frankness as well as with impassioned disinterestedness. A comment on what Leavis says in '*Scrutiny*: a Retrospect', came from Q. D. Leavis herself. She meant to use this quotation from Sydney Smith as one of the epigraphs for her proposed Memoir of her husband:

To set on foot such a journal in such times, to contribute towards it for many years, to bear patiently the reproach and poverty which it caused, and to look back and see that I have nothing to retract, and no intemperance or violence to reproach myself with, is a career of life which I must think to be extremely fortunate.   (Preface to his *Collected Works*,
on his founding and editing *The Edinburgh Review*)

Both the desirability and the difficulty of setting on foot such a journal as *Scrutiny* was, was further examined by Leavis in his seminar paper on 'Standards of Criticism' given at York University, probably in 1965. In analysing what constitutes those standards, and their dependence on the existence of an educated public, Leavis makes some key formulations of a theoretical nature. As for instance when he argues how 'few even of the respectable admired writers of a given time are original in the important sense' and how the critic 'helps to form the contemporary sensibility' which Leavis defines as 'a practised readiness of response over a certain selective range, a habit of implicit reference and expectation'. Such a habit was exemplified by 'the play of criticism on intellectual life and on the contemporary scene in general' in the nineteenth century, which saw the existence of so many established reviews, magazines and journals addressing 'a calculated, informed and morally responsible public'.

'Reading Out Poetry' is the text of a lecture Leavis gave in 1972 at Queen's University, Belfast. Starting from the premise that 'the mere reader of poetry who doesn't do a great deal of full reading out won't be able to read out in imagination', Leavis went on to demonstrate his own way of reading poetry out by quoting from Shakespeare, Pope, Hopkins, Hardy and Eliot, with critical comment on what he quoted. His lecture is based on the belief that one's way of reading out poetry determines and is determined by one's critical response to the text – to its rhythm, cadence and inflexion, which enact the subtlety and delicacy of thought and feeling. The drift of the lecture, of course, very much hinged on Leavis's voice and practical demonstration, but the accompanying commentary is of sufficient critical interest to merit inclusion in this volume. There is a special interest in that the text is a transcript of Leavis's partly extempore performance. It is only very lightly edited, and more than any other printed text gives a direct sense of him as speaker.

In 'Valuation in Criticism' Leavis formulates and sums up what criticism meant to him and how one arrives 'at intelligent and sensible judgments in the concrete' by means of *real* critical experience, which he characterizes as 'the most disturbing and inescapable way to a radical pondering, a new and profound realization, of the grounds of our most important determinations and choices'.

That the nature of value judgment continued to exercise his mind till the end is manifest from the last essay in this volume – part of what Leavis had been writing in his last two years. It bears moving and convincing testimony to his moral, intellectual and critical concerns, and shows him grappling with the problems and concepts that had long preoccupied him, with a depth of insight and complexity as well as originality of thought and perception which remained vigorously operative till the very end. One of the subjects that concerned Leavis in his last years was Wordsworth, whose 'profoundly original' genius, he said, enabled him 'to think vitally, that is profitably, about the *sui generis* nature of life' and 'to achieve articulate thought about meaning, value and art-speech'. 'Notes on Wordsworth' attributes a peculiar importance to Wordsworth, whose distinctive characteristics bring out for Leavis 'the sense in which creative genius pushes forward the frontiers of language and in the perception which is thought achieves the new'.

The essay is representative of Leavis's last phase, and brings us into contact with a man engaged in the revaluation of his life's work, and struggling with the complex distinctions and definitions arising out of it. It conveys the urgency of a man defining with poignant dignity and finality the meaning of his existence as a critic.

I

T. S. Eliot – a reply to the condescending

Under the title 'For Mr T. S. Eliot', there appeared in a recent number of the *New Statesman* a review of Mr Eliot's last book.

'Mr Eliot's great reputation among the young', pronounced the reviewer, 'is due to two facts: that, of those men who practise and criticize the more recent fashions in literature, he has some acquaintance with the past – an acquaintance that strikes with awe the young men whose reading begins with the Edwardians; that he holds very distinct and reasonably dogmatic opinions, and evidently writes from his mind rather than from his "dark inwards" or "the red pavilion of his heart." ' One recognized the note. It tends to recur when the consciously adult, especially in the academic world, speak and write of Mr Eliot. One remembered the distinguished scholar who, reviewing not long ago some work of Mr Eliot's, spent a good deal of his column pointing out how much better it had been done by another distinguished scholar, a friend of the reviewer, but nevertheless conceded that Mr Eliot, though 'not a critic of the first trenchancy', was not wholly without critical gifts. Those of us who are aware of our debt to Mr Eliot have learnt not to be too provoked by this kind of condescension. It offsets the snobism attendant, inevitably, upon the vogue that Mr Eliot enjoys, and suffers from. But the challenge quoted above does seem to give one who still counts himself among the young, and who discusses literature a good deal with others of the young, a fair opportunity to acknowledge the debt and to define its nature.

First of all, we recognize in Mr Eliot a poet of profound originality, and of especial significance to all who are concerned for the future of English poetry. To describe him as 'practising the more recent fashions' is misleading, and betrays ignorance and prejudice. It suggests that he is one of a herd of 'modernist' poetasters. But there is no other poetry in the least like Mr Eliot's: he is an originator, and if he has his mimics, he could be confused with them only by the malicious or the incompetent. Nor is it his fault if he is included in the Sitwellian 'we'. 'Profound originality' were considered words. Mr Eliot says in *The Sacred Wood* that the historical sense is 'nearly indispensable to anyone who would continue to be a poet beyond his twenty-fifth year; and the historical sense involves a perception, not

11

only of the pastness of the past, but of its presence; the historical sense
compels a man to write not merely with his own generation in his
bones, but with a feeling that the whole of the literature of Europe
from Homer and within it the whole of the literature of his own
country has a simultaneous existence and composes a simultaneous
order. This historical sense, which is a sense of the timeless as well as
of the temporal and of the timeless and of the temporal together, is
what makes a writer traditional. And it is at the same time what makes
a writer most acutely conscious of his place in time, of his contem-
poraneity.' Mr Eliot is now well beyond his twenty-fifth year, and his
latest poetry has a new vitality. 'Salutation', which appeared in *The
Criterion* for January, last year, and 'Perch' io non spero', which
appeared in the last 'Printemps' number of *Commerce*, have a power
and a beauty that might, one would think, compel recognition even
from an anthologist. The poet bears out the critic. His poetry is more
conscious of the past than any other that is being written in English
to-day. This most modern of the moderns is more truly traditional
than the 'traditionalists' – and he is a poet.

'By losing tradition,' he says in *The Sacred Wood*, 'we lose our hold
on the present.' It is because of his hold on the present that he has his
great reputation among the young. Poetry tends recurrently to confine
itself by conventions of 'the poetic' which bar the poet from his most
valuable material, the material that is most significant to sensitive and
adequate minds in his own day; or else sensitive and adequate minds
are barred out of poetry. Something of this kind has clearly been
wrong with poetry in this century, and efforts at readjustment, those,
for instance, of Mr Masefield, Mr Binyon, and Mr Squire, have commonly served only to call attention to its plight. Mr Eliot is so important because, with a mind of very rare sensitiveness and adequacy, he
has, for himself, solved the problem, and so done more than solve the
problem for himself. His influence will not be measured by the
number of his imitators, but will manifest itself in indirect and subtle
ways of which there can be no full account. In any case, the academic
mind charting English poetry a century hence will not be tempted to
condescend to Mr Eliot.

His influence has made itself so profoundly and so widely felt in so
short a time because he is a critic as well as a poet, and his poetry and
his criticism reinforce each other. One would hardly guess from the
description of him as 'criticizing the more recent fashions in literature'
that his criticism had been almost wholly confined to writers of the
past. If Dryden and Donne are in fashion Mr Eliot may have had
something to do with their being so; it is he alone who has made them
more than fashions. 'The important critic', he says in *The Sacred*

Wood, 'is the person who is absorbed in the present problems of art, and who wishes to bring the forces of the past to bear upon the solution of these problems.' We who are aware of our debt to Mr Eliot find his criticism so important because it has pursued this aim with such indubitable success. The present writer, having undertaken to lecture on contemporary poetry, looked through several years of the likely journals, and found that the helpful review or critique almost always showed the influence of *Homage to John Dryden*.

Mr Eliot's acquaintance with the past, then, has impressed us so much because it has illuminated for us both the past and the present. We find commonly that the erudition of the constituted authorities does neither. His acquaintance with the past is profound enough to have reshaped the current effective idea of the English tradition. If no serious critic or poet now supposes that English poetry in the future must, or can, develop along the line running from the Romantics through Tennyson, this is mainly due to Mr Eliot. But for him we certainly should not have had this clear awareness; and for this debt alone – it is a very great, though incalculable debt – the histories of English literature will give him an important place.

All this might suggest that Mr Eliot's criticism is pervaded by the propagandist spirit. It is not so. 'English criticism', he has remarked, 'is inclined to argue or persuade rather than to state'; but his own is the last against which such a charge could be brought. It is so entirely controlled by the will to 'see the object as in itself it really is' that some people reading it, and missing the non-critical that they expect to find in criticism, think (or so they report) that it contains nothing at all. It makes some of us feel that we never read criticism before. At any rate Mr Eliot represents for us the essentially critical, and when, intimidated by the insinuation of priggishness, we are told that criticism is 'any kind of writing about books', we are stiffened by the thought of him as by a vicarious conscience. Those of us who are giving a good part of our lives to the study of literature are especially grateful to him. For no one has set forth for us our justifying ideas so clearly and cogently, and no critic has served them in his practice with such austere integrity.

The critic, he concludes in an essay on 'The Function of Criticism', must have 'a very highly developed sense of fact'. This suggests well enough where, in his account of criticism, the stress falls. The critic must cultivate this sense of fact in regions where there are no facts that can be handed round or brought into the laboratory. He must aim, in so far as he is a critic, to establish the work of art as a fact, an object existing outside of, and apart from, himself. Actually, of course, this cannot be done, and there is no one demonstrably right judgment. But a critic is a critic only in so far as he is controlled by these ideals. And their inaccessibility leads, not to arbitrariness, but to askesis, not to assertiveness, but to docility. He seeks help, confirmation, and check from as many qualified minds as possible. 'For the kinds of critical work we have admitted,' writes Mr Eliot, 'there is the possibility of co-operative activity, with the further possibility of arriving at something outside of ourselves, which may provisionally be called truth.' All this may be both old and obvious to the adult, but we who admire Mr Eliot had never before had it made obvious to us; and we are grateful to him for the clearness and force with which he has set forth the idea of criticism, and for the athletic rigour with which he has verified his principle in his practice.

We have learnt from Mr Eliot what is meant by 'an interest in art and life as problems which exist and can be handled apart from their relations to the critic's private temperament'. And it seems to us the only kind of interest that can justify a prolonged study of literature. But there will always be people who find Mr Middleton Murry's kind of interest more exciting (though we ourselves acknowledge a debt to Mr Murry for stimulus, derived mainly from his early work). It is not, however, only those who prefer prophecy, exaltations, and the ardours of the private soul who find Mr Eliot's criticism unrepaying. There are others, sober enough, who are baffled and repelled by the very purity of its devotion to literature, by its very rigour. For Mr Eliot never forgets that poetry is made of words. His approach is commonly by way of technique, and his dealings with 'content' are always rigorously controlled and disciplined. He is not (to adapt some words of his own) one of those who, in writing about Hamlet, forget that their first business is to study a work of art. So those who are accustomed to think of Hamlet as a man with a life antecedent to, and outside of, the play, a subject for psychoanalysis, feel that Mr Eliot induces cerebral corrugations to no end. 'To the member of the Browning Study Circle,' he says, 'the discussion of poets about poetry may seem arid, technical and limited. It is merely that the practitioners have clarified and reduced to a state of fact all the feelings that the member can only enjoy in the most nebulous form; the dry technique implies, for those who have mastered it, all that the member thrills to; only that has been made into something precise, tractable, under control. That, at all events, is one reason for the value of the practitioner's criticisms – he is dealing with his facts, and he can help us to do the same.'

Although Mr Eliot never forgets to see poetry as a texture of words, he is as much concerned with what lies behind as other critics, and more effectively. 'Their words', he says, comparing Shakespeare, Donne, Webster and Tourneur with Jonson, 'have often a network of tentacular roots reaching down to the deepest terrors and desires. Jonson's most certainly have not . . . ' This suggests fairly well the manner of Mr Eliot's approach to the more inward critical problems, and the kind of control he maintains. And with this continence he is, we find, as fertile in generalizations, explicit and implied, as any critic we know. 'Ériger en lois ses impressions personnelles, c'est le grand effort d'un homme s'il est sincère': it is not for nothing that he set this sentence from Remy de Gourmont at the head of the first essay in *The Sacred Wood*. For instances of his generalizing one may adduce his elucidation of impersonality, of the relation between the work of art and the personality of the artist, and the account which he gives in *Homage to John Dryden* of the relation between thought and emotion in poetry. Such things as these we find in the essential structure of our thinking about art. They seem to us to be among those ideas which, says Mr Eliot, 'stand forth luminous with an independent life of their own, so true that one forgets the author in the statement'.

And among such ideas, for some of us, is Mr Eliot's conception of order. The more we brood over the critic's problem of making his judgment something more than an assertion of personal like or dislike the more inevitable we find the conception of European literature as an organic whole, and within it, English literature as an organic whole, an order – an order in which each new thing must find a place, though the existing order is modified all through by the addition. Here we come to the wider implications of Mr Eliot's 'classicism', and about these there is, naturally, less certain agreement than about statements of principle that arise immediately out of considerations of technique. And, of course, the 'classicism' involves things outside of literature.

These other things are to the fore in Mr Eliot's last book. The 'very distinct and reasonably dogmatic opinions' that he holds concerning these things, whether we agree with them or not, seem to us to give 'For Lancelot Andrewes' the 'coherent force' that we have always found in Mr Eliot's work. The reviewer's judgment to the contrary[1] seems to us so perverse as to call for something other than ordinary critical incompetence to explain it. In any case, to liken Mr Eliot's 'dogmatic opinions' to Dr Saintsbury's 'predilections' will not do. Dr Saintsbury's high Toryism appears mainly as accidental to his writings on literature. And whoever found in the expressions of it anything more than traits of a personality, racy and assertive, a Character? Mr Eliot's 'predilections' are central to all his work; they are its structure and articulation, its organization, and if we leave them out we leave out everything. This is not to intend any disrespect to Dr Saintsbury; we know the debt that we owe to scholarship. But the mention of his name serves to bring out the peculiar nature of the debt we owe to Mr Eliot.

It is because of Mr Eliot that such erudition as Dr Saintsbury's does not merely overwhelm us, and make us feel that life is not long enough to take literature seriously. For if Mr Eliot has told us that erudition is 'useless unless it enables us to see literature all round, to detach it from ourselves, to reach a state of pure contemplation', he has also given us inspiring, if chastening, examples of erudition being used to such end. It is he who has heartened us and shown us the way to a study of literature that may hope to produce something other than mere accumulation.

In his latest utterances, now that he has passed on 'to the problem of the relation of poetry to the spiritual and social life of its time and of other times', we may not always follow him, in either sense of the word. But we await eagerly the promised statements of his position. And we believe that, whatever this may be, it is compatible with the completest intellectual integrity. Meanwhile we are much impressed by his way of stating the problem – the problem of preserving civiliz-ation. At any rate, we feel that we must consider very seriously his view of civilization as depending upon a strenuously achieved and traditional normality, a trained and arduous common sense, a kind of athletic poise that cannot be maintained without a laborious and criti-cal docility to traditional wisdom.

Even were the problems that Mr Eliot is concerned with less urgent to us he would be notable for the spare and sinewy scrupulousness of his writing. It is this that has enabled him to exert so much influence with a bulk of published work that would fill no more than a middling-sized book. 'When there is so much to be known,' he says, 'when there are so many fields of knowledge in which the same words are used with different meanings, when everyone knows a little about a great many things, it becomes increasingly difficult for anyone to know whether he knows what he is talking about or not.' There could be no more effective awakener of the intellectual conscience than Mr Eliot: he has made it less easy to shirk.

D. H. Lawrence

I have repented a great deal my undertaking to write on D. H. Lawrence: it was rash. There have been many warnings. Eminent critics have shown by example how difficult and perilous it is. To make Lawrence an occasion for asserting one's superiority over Bouvard and Pécuchet, Babbitt and Sir William Joynson-Hicks is easy, but it is hard to be critical without getting oneself confused with Mr J. C. Squire. And although one does not mind being called 'highbrow', it is painful to remember that someone whom one respects has been provoked to endorse the term with his authority. It is a delicate business. Mr Eliot, for instance, in *The Nation*, replied to a challenging letter of Mr Forster's by asking some very pertinent critical questions, and Mr Forster, to our surprise – Mr Forster of all people – dismissed them with an angry retort.

I start by assuming that 'genius' is the right word for D. H. Lawrence, though Mr Eliot did this, and it did not save him. Perhaps the ascription has been too long a commonplace. 'In the early days,' says Lawrence, in 'An Autobiographical Sketch' printed in *Assorted Articles*, 'they were always telling me I had got genius, as if to console me for not having their own incomparable advantages.' So I had better say at once what I mean by ascribing genius to Lawrence. I have in mind the same kind of thing as when I say that Blake obviously had genius. Lawrence had it as obviously. He had the same gift of knowing what he was interested in, the same power of distinguishing his own feelings and emotions from conventional sentiment, the same 'terrifying honesty'. The parallel might be worked out in considerable detail, starting from the book of squibs that is the occasion for this article.[1] They remind one of the similar verse in which Blake sought relief, and they also are interesting mainly because of their author, though they show again and again an amusing and effective idiosyncrasy, as, for instance, in the lines on the *London Mercury*, or here:

> Oh what a pity, oh! don't you agree
> that figs aren't found in the land of the free!
>
> Fig-trees don't grow in my native land;
> there's never a fig-leaf near at hand

when you want one; so I did without;
and that is what the row's about.

Virginal, pure policemen came
and hid their faces for very shame,

while they carried the shameless things away
to gaol, to be hid from the light of day.

And Mr Mead, that old, old lily
said: 'Gross! coarse! hideous!' – and I, like a silly

thought he meant the faces of the police-court officials,
and how right he was, and I signed my initials

to confirm what he said; but alas, he meant
my pictures, so on the proceedings went.

The content of these lines reminds us of the community between Blake's and Lawrence's preoccupations: they may both be said to have been concerned with the vindication of impulse and spontaneity against 'reason' and convention. The difference between them is the more interesting in that it is more than the difference between individuals. In the background of Blake are Rousseau and the French Revolution. In the background of Lawrence are the social transformations of the nineteenth century, Darwin, the war, and an age of psychoanalysis and anthropology. So his search for the inner reality, for the hidden springs of life, took Lawrence a good deal further:

He turned away. Either the heart would break or cease to care. Best cease to care. Whatever the mystery which has brought forth man and the universe, it is a non-human mystery, it has its own great ends, man is not the criterion. Best leave it all to the vast, creative, non-human mystery . . . The eternal creative mystery could dispose of man, and replace him with a finer created being. Just as the horse has taken the place of the mastodon.

It was very consoling to Birkin to think this . . . The fountain-head was incorruptible and unsearchable. It had no limits. It could bring forth miracles, create utterly new races and new species in its own hour, new forms of consciousness, new forms of body, new units of being. To be a man was as nothing compared to the possibilities of the creative mystery. To have one's pulse beating direct from the mystery, this was perfection, unutterable satisfaction. Human or inhuman mattered nothing.

Blake, if he could have thought this, would not have found it consoling. Birkin, of course, though one of Lawrence's obvious self-dramatizations, is not to be taken as completely representative, but it is fair to make this passage an opportunity for noting that Lawrence's preoccupation with the primitive fosters in him a certain inhumanity: the context gives the judgment the appropriate force.

His originality asserts itself in his earliest books. In *Sons and Lovers*, his third novel, he is mature, in the sense of being completely himself. It is a beautiful and poignant book, showing a sincerity in the record of emotional life, such as is possible only to genius. There we find the complexities of personal relations – the tangled attractions and repulsions, self-abasements and tyrannies, of love in particular – exposed with the fanatical seriousness characteristic of Lawrence. According to Mr Middleton Murry (in the current *New Adelphi*) it was quickly discovered 'that in *Sons and Lovers* Lawrence had independently arrived at the main conclusions of the psychoanalysts, and the English followers of Freud came to see him.' Besides this psychological subtlety the book (like *The White Peacock* and all the early work) is remarkable for a sensuous richness of a kind that leads one to talk loosely of the author as a 'poet'. (He did indeed write verse, but not much of it is poetry, though it is very interesting in various ways: he rarely attained the level of the *Ballad of a Second Ophelia*.) This richness may be seen at its best in the lovely passage at the opening of *The Rainbow*. It derives from his poignant intuition of the common flame in all things that live and grow; from his sense of the mysterious intercourse of man with the world around him.

Sons and Lovers bears obviously a close relation to Lawrence's own history. *The Rainbow* deals with three generations, yet it seems to bear much the same kind of relation to personal experience. In fact, Lawrence seems here to be exploring his own problems, to be living them through in the book. *Sons and Lovers*, for all its beauty and poignancy, everyone I have discussed it with agrees with me in finding it difficult to get through. *The Rainbow* is a great deal more difficult. We do not doubt the urgency for the author of these shifting tensions of the inner life, this drama of the inexplicit in personal intercourse, but for us the effect is one of monotony. Lawrence's fanatical concern for the 'essential' often results in a strange intensity, but how limited is the range! And the intensity too often fails to come through to us. Behind these words we know that there are agonies of frustration, deadlock and apprehension, but we only see words.

In a sense Lawrence is exploring his problems, living them through, in all his novels, but from *The Rainbow* onwards we are aware of certain conclusions. Indeed, he insists on our being aware of them, for, not content to leave them implicit, he enforces them by illustration, comment and symbolism. He becomes, in fact, a prophet, and imposes on the critic the same kind of task as Blake does. His conclusions involve a great deal of declaiming against 'ideas', 'ideals' and 'mind-knowledge'. For Lawrence arrived at a passionate conviction that man is destroying himself with consciousness, with self-consciousness. Health – life – depends upon complete emotional spontaneity, he believed, and this has been made impossible for us by self-consciousness, by 'mind-knowledge'. ('Blake too', he says, 'was one of these ghastly, obscene "Knowers".') The aim, then, is to throw off all ideas of how we ought to feel, all will to feel one way rather than another, 'so that which is perfectly ourselves can take place in us'. Now these conclusions, so stated, are not very new, and it is in any case not the literary critic's business to discuss them in the abstract. The manner of the critic's concern with them Lawrence himself has indicated: 'Art speech is the only speech,' he said in *Studies in Classic American Literature*. And in *Lady Chatterley's Lover*:

It is the way our sympathy flows and recoils that really determines our lives. And here lies the importance of the novel, properly handled. It can inform and lead into new places the flow of our sympathetic consciousness, and it can lead our sympathy away in recoil from things gone dead. Therefore the novel, properly handled, can reveal the most secret places of life – for it is in the *passional* secret places of life, above all, that the tide of sensitive awareness needs to ebb and flow, cleansing and refreshing.

When, so authorized, we consider as a work of art a novel, say *Women in Love*, in which the 'conclusions' are embodied, our judgment cannot be altogether favourable to them. For *Women in Love* hardly 'informs and leads into new places the flow of our sympathetic consciousness.' To get through it calls for great determination and a keen diagnostic interest. One of the reasons for the difficulty is indicated by this passage:

He [*i.e.*, Birkin-Lawrence] was not very much interested any more in personalities and in people – people were all different, but they were all enclosed nowadays in a definite limitation, he said; there were only about two great ideas, two great streams of activity remaining, with various forms of reaction therefrom. The reactions were all varied in various people, but they followed a few great laws, and intrinsically there was no difference. They acted and reacted involuntarily according to a few great laws, and once the laws, the great principles, were known, people were no more mystically interesting. They were all essentially alike, the differences were only variations on a theme. None of them transcended the given terms.

Lawrence's main interest lay much lower than personality, and the characters in *Women in Love* tend to disintegrate into swirls of conflicting impulses and emotions. It is difficult to keep them apart. A more radical criticism is suggested by this passage from *Studies in Classic American Literature*:

I always remember meeting the eyes of a gypsy woman, for one moment, in a crowd, in England. She knew, and I knew. What did we know? I was not able to make out. But we knew.

It is this kind of 'knowledge' that Lawrence is pervasively concerned with in *Women in Love*: if it can be conveyed at all it is only by poetic means. But Lawrence uses for the purpose a specialized vocabulary of terms that he tries to invest with a new potency by endless reiteration: 'dark', 'pure', 'utter', 'inchoate', 'disintegrate', 'uncreated', 'violated', 'abstract', 'mindless', 'lapse out', 'loins of darkness', and so on. This method is, to use one of Lawrence's own terms of reprobation, mechanical:

> 'Gerald,' he said, 'I rather hate you.'
> 'I know you do,' said Gerald. 'Why do you?'
> Birkin mused inscrutably for some minutes. 'I should like to know if you are conscious of hating me,' he said at last. 'Do you ever consciously detest me – hate me with mystic hate? There are odd moments when I hate you starrily.'

The great part of the book gets no nearer to concrete particularity than that. Failure of this kind, in a man of Lawrence's genius, would seem to throw doubt on the project of recovering pure spontaneity by getting rid of mind-knowledge. Lawrence himself clearly had misgivings: he tried to settle them by putting them into the mouths of characters:

> 'What is it but the worst and last form of intellectualism, this love of yours for passion and the animal instincts.'

and

> 'You *don't* trust yourself. You don't fully believe yourself what you are saying. You don't really want this conjunction, otherwise you wouldn't talk so much about it, you'd get it.'

But even in *Women in Love* the genius of Lawrence is apparent in passages of description, and passages evoking subtle shades of consciousness, strange stirrings of emotion, intuitions of 'unknown modes of being'. In the short stories of such volumes as *The Ladybird*, *England my England*, and *The Woman who Rode Away*, where he has no room for prophecy and is not tempted to dwell upon his 'conclusions', his genius triumphs again and again. In critical equity these should receive close attention, but there is not space enough. His novels, as he wanders from country to country – Italy, Australia, Mexico – looking for a new mode of consciousness, exhibit in varying measure the kind of defect indicated above. They are fascinating, exasperating, and very difficult to read through – at least, at the risk of being included under Mr Forster's 'highbrows whom he bored', I must confess to having found them so. *The Plumed Serpent* describes an attempt to restore the ancient religion of Mexico. The descriptions of the country and the evocations of 'the dark power in the soil' are marvellous, but Lawrence's efforts to persuade himself that he takes the Mexican religion seriously invite the application to himself of certain comments that, in *Studies in Classic American Literature*, he makes on Melville:

At first you are put off by the style . . . It seems spurious. You feel Melville is trying to put something over you. It won't do.

And Melville really is a bit sententious: aware of himself, self-conscious, putting something over even himself . . . He preaches and holds forth because he's not sure of himself. And he holds forth, often, so amateurishly.

His last novel, however, is not open to this kind of criticism. *Lady Chatterley's Lover* shows that where sex is concerned he knew what he meant. So far as artistic success can validate his teaching about the relations between man and woman, the book does so: it is beautifully poised and sure. It magnificently enforces the argument of *Pornography and Obscenity* – and so cannot expect free circulation. It is a masterpiece of a rare order. Criticism of it must take the form of the question: How comprehensive or generally valid is this solution?

There is no room to argue the question here, even if I thought myself competent. I will only say that it seems to me too easily assumed that *Lady Chatterley's Lover* represents greater health and vitality than *A Passage to India* (this is not the same as the question of the authors' relative genius). We ought to ask ourselves: if we accepted the first without reserves, how much of what is represented by the second should we have to abandon?

The question is a tribute to both authors.

The influence of Donne on modern poetry

Those who are seriously interested, whether as poets or readers, in modern poetry (I might almost say in poetry at all), feel themselves closer to the seventeenth century than to the nineteenth. The qualities that make the seventeenth century so congenial are represented above all by the Metaphysical poets. And of these Donne was the undisputed chief.

Metaphysical poetry is a byword for erudite obscurity, metaphorical extravagance and cerebral corrugation. But, as Doctor Johnson conceded, 'to write on their plan, it was at least necessary to read and *think*' (the italics are mine). In the tradition established by Donne it was assumed that a poet should be a man of distinguished intelligence, and that he should bring into his poetry the varied interests of his life. This, to put it briefly, is the importance of Donne to modern poetry. For the tradition coming down to us from the nineteenth century is very different, and we have begun to realize that this tradition has something to do with the plight revealed by the anthologies of contemporary verse – by any anthology indeed covering the last two or three generations.

This tradition took its rise in the period of the great Romantics. It involved a prejudice against recognizing as poetry anything that was not in the most obvious sense of Milton's formula, 'simple, sensuous and passionate'. Poetry, it was assumed, must be the direct expression of simple emotions. The 'poetical' emotions were of a limited class: the tender, the exalted, the noble, the poignant – in general, the sympathetic. (It is still quite common to hear it questioned whether satire can be poetry.) Wit, play of intellect, stress or cerebral muscle had no place; they could only hinder the correct response, which was to be 'moved'. And there is something further to be noted of 'the poetical' in the nineteenth century which comes out if we consider these half-dozen well-known poems: 'La Belle Dame Sans Merci', 'Mariana', 'The Lady of Shalott', 'The Blessed Damosel', Morris's 'Nymph's Song to Hylas', 'A Forsaken Garden' and O'Shaughnessy's 'Ode'. Nineteenth-century poetry, we realize, was characteristically preoccupied with the creation of a dream-world.

If anyone finds it difficult to see why such a set of habits and preconceptions should have become more and more disastrous as the century went on, that is further evidence of their malign strength. It means that they have charmed out of sight the very function of poetry. For poets are not merely men with a gift for making verbal melodies, or writing on the consecrated themes in consecrated manners, or singing new songs about old, unhappy, far-off things. Poetry matters because of the kind of poet who is more alive than other people – more alive in his own age. He is, as it were, at the most conscious point of the race in his time. The potentialities of human experience in any age are realized only by a tiny minority, and the poet is important because he belongs to this, and has moreover the power of communication. We should go to poetry, not for a kind of emotional thrill we know beforehand to be 'poetical', but for the response to life of unusually sensitive and adequate minds. And we should expect to find modern poetry quite 'unpoetical', for the urgencies and stresses incident to a sensitive modern will not be mainly associated with dawn, dew, flowers or country place-names, or dreams of old romance. They will be associated with the unescapable environment of urban civilization and its background of modern thought.

This account of poetry could not have been drawn from *The Oxford Book of Victorian Verse*. And this is proof enough that the nineteenth-century tradition was disastrous. For the habits and ideas current at any time matter much more than we easily realize. At this point I must add to the account of poetry that I have given that it is a craft, an art of using words. A young poet learning his craft has to start somewhere, and he naturally starts in his own period, from current models. And a poet starting from the Romantics, or Tennyson or the Pre-Raphaelites would have had to have a very unusually powerful genius to develop into the kind of poet I have described. He would tend to express successfully in his poetry only those of his interests which were 'poetical'. Indeed we should hardly expect such a tradition to attract the kind of mind that constitutes the consciousness of an age. And if we look through any anthologies covering the last fifty years, it becomes impossible to doubt that distinguished minds that should have gone into poetry have gone elsewhere. It is hard to explain otherwise the dearth of original talent.

To make a fresh start under such conditions is a desperate matter. That is why Mr Eliot is so important. Having unquestionably a mind of rare distinction, he has solved his own problem as a poet, and so done more than solve the problem for himself. His influence has been the more effective in that he is a critic as well as a poet, and his criticism and his poetry reinforce each other. And it is not for nothing that his criticism has been mainly directed upon the seventeenth century. One might say that the effect of his poetry and his criticism together has been to restore the seventeenth century to its proper place in the English tradition. In his Hogarth pamphlet, *Homage to John Dryden*, he says: 'A thought to Donne was an experience; it modified his sensibility. When a poet's mind is perfectly equipped for its work, it is constantly amalgamating disparate experience; the ordinary man's experience is chaotic, irregular, fragmentary. The latter falls in love, or reads Spinoza, and these two experiences have nothing to do with each other, or with the noise of the typewriter or the smell of the cooking; in the mind of the poet these experiences are always forming new wholes.' This passage suggests well enough the importance of Donne, the supreme representative of Metaphysical poetry, to the contemporary poet. Donne in his poetry could be intellectual and lyrical, cynical and serious, witty and intense at the same time. A modern's ways of feeling will be different, but are likely to be similarly complex.

Except in exhibiting a complex sensibility of the kind just described, Mr Eliot's poetry is not like Donne's. And the poetry of future poets (if there are any) will not be like Mr Eliot's. But it is probable that they will owe enormously to him (bearing to him the same kind of relation as the later Romantics bore to Wordsworth and Coleridge); and what they will learn from him will be, as much as anything, how to learn from Donne. For an example of what I mean I would point to *Cambridge Poetry, 1929*, where Mr William Empson has half a dozen remarkable poems.

> 'Twixt devil and deep sea, man hacks his caves;
> Birth, death; one, many; what is true, and seems;
> Earth's vast hot iron, cold space's empty waves.
>
> King spider walks the velvet root of streams;
> Must bird and fish, must god and beast avoid;
> Dance like an angel on pin-point extremes.

When he opens a poem in this way he is a modern poet; but he would not have written in this way but for Donne.

If I do not adduce a number of modern poets, that is because modern poets are very rare.

William Empson:
Intelligence and sensibility

This book [*Seven Types of Ambiguity*] is highly disturbing. Here is a man using his intelligence on poetry as seriously as if it were mathematics or one of the sciences. And Mr Empson's is clearly a mind qualified for distinction in fields of thought where serious standards hold. He seems to think that such standards will be tolerated in the field of criticism. How, then, shall the amateur of belles-lettres defend the Muses and himself? There is the well-tried argument against analysis. Mr Empson glances at this – in a kindly way, it is true, but it becomes very difficult to use. There is an amusing passage that I should like to quote, but, as Mr Empson says (producing an ambiguity of his own), 'the position of a literary critic is far more a social than a scientific one', and I prefer to take no risks. It ends (this much is quite proper): 'the reasons that make a line of verse likely to give pleasure, I believe, are like the reasons for anything else; one can reason about them; and while it may be true that the roots of beauty ought not to be violated, it seems to me very arrogant of the appreciative critic to think that he could do this, if he chose, by a little scratching.' Elsewhere he says: 'however wise the view may be that poetry cannot be safely analysed, it seems to me to remain ignoble; and in so far as people are sure that their pleasures will not bear thinking about, I am surprised that they have the patience not to submit them to so easy a destruction.'

But at any rate the analysis of poetry demands something more than intelligence. Mr Empson's is not in question; but what about his sensibility? Well, as we read through Mr Empson's book we become less confident about separating sensibility from intelligence. Is it merely because we have not had a scientific or a mathematical training that we have so often failed to see what was before our eyes? For as Mr Empson again and again convicts us of not having really read familiar passages of poetry we cannot often contend that what we have missed doesn't matter. He has, in short, a very fine sensibility, and is, in every way, an uncommonly adequate reader of poetry. The objector to analysis may take what comfort he can from the sympathy Mr Empson shows him in the last chapter: 'The object of life, after all, is not to understand things, but to maintain one's defences and equilibrium, and live as well as one can; it is not only maiden aunts who are placed like this.' But the objector will hardly have got so far. *Seven Types of Ambiguity* is only for those who believe that they can afford to understand.

We are so unaccustomed to meeting with a first-class mind in criticism that we are apt to lose touch with serious standards. *Seven Types of Ambiguity* is that rare thing, a critical work of the first order; literary criticism that makes a difference to the reader, that increases his efficiency, that improves the apparatus for the future critic. Its range is wider than the title might suggest. Under the head of 'ambiguity' Mr Empson examines many of the most important things about the use of language in poetry. If one feels sometimes that he is apt to be a little too ingenious in detecting ambiguities, one ends by agreeing that it is difficult to exaggerate the subtlety and complexity of English as used by its masters. And if one finds it hard to hold on to his classifications, one is more than satisfied by this modest reply: 'Thus I think my seven types form an immediately useful set of distinctions, but to a more serious analysis they would probably appear trivial and hardly to be distinguished from one another. I call them useful, not merely as a means of stringing examples, but because, in complicated matters, any distinction between cases, however irrelevant, may serve to heighten one's consciousness of the cases themselves.'

In the course of his inquiries he deals with samples of verse of most periods from Chaucer to the present day, and throws out by the way general suggestions about differences between period and period and type and type that are of the highest value. Indeed, there is more of the history of English poetry in this book than in any other that I know.

I will make no pretence of discussing the main topics that Mr Empson raises. I will merely try and fortify my self-esteem by differing with him upon a minor point or two. '... Browning and Meredith, who did write from the world they lived in, affect me as novel-writers of merit with no lyrical inspiration at all' – I should have thought that Browning's power was lyrical or nothing. 'Wordsworth frankly had no inspiration other than his use, when a boy, of the mountains as a totem or father-substitute.' – Mr Empson does not take this kind of approach (it is not characteristic of the book) too seriously, and in a like spirit I would point questioningly to *The Prelude*, Book II, lines 233–84. This passage, I think, makes it plain that, if we substitute 'mother' for 'father', Mr Empson's suggestion thus emended finds support in Wordsworth's own avowal.

Then it is possible to comfort oneself by pointing out that Mr Empson's memory, which he appears to have trusted a good deal in quoting, is not perfect. Particularly, he has introduced an ambiguity of his own into Milton. The Mulciber passage as he quotes it runs:

> flung by angry Jove
> Sheer o'er the crystal battlements: from dawn
> To noon he fell, from noon to dewy eve,
> A summer's day; and with the setting sun
> Dropped into Lemnos the Aegean isle –

'Milton is extremely cool about the matter,' comments Mr Empson. But – 'dropped into', as if to supper – no, not so cool as that. There's clearly something more than that 'dawn' for 'morn' wrong with the quotation. And then, on pages 217–18, he puzzles us by quoting from Marvell:

> And all the jewels that we prize

and telling us that 'which' (which should have been printed) suggests more than 'that' would have done.

And then there is the further resource of taking up and developing some of Mr Empson's suggestions. When, for instance, he remarks that 'an insensitivity in a poet to the contemporary style of speaking, into which he has been trained to concentrate his powers of apprehension, is so disastrous' I should like to make the application to Milton. But there would be no end to such a commentary, for the book contains like provocations on every page.

Mr Empson's equipment is remarkable, and still more remarkable is the mastery with which he uses it. We have met with critics who could refer lightly to the sciences, to mathematics, to anthropology, to psychology, and this capacity has not appeared a strength. It is impossible to question Mr Empson's command of his resources. His erudition is always relevant, his instruments are always appropriate. His work is so mature that it is difficult to refrain from impertinent references to the year in which his name appeared in the class-lists of the English Tripos. Perhaps it will not be impertinent to remark that he draws many of his examples from books set for that tripos, and to claim for it that it gave him suitable opportunities and did not get in his way. Now had it been any other university school of English – . Yes, Cambridge may pardonably take some credit for him.

His book is the work of a mind that is fully alive in this age, and such a book has a very unusual importance. This is brought home particularly in the last chapter. It is an event to have the response of a younger generation to the problems envisaged by Mr Eliot and Mr Richards, for Mr Empson is as alive as they to the exciting strangeness of the present phase of human history. He implies more than he says, so that we are left expecting.

And, immediately, there is that book of poems which he has given us a right to demand.

II

Marxism and cultural continuity

Of the following book [*For Continuity*] the first component piece, *Mass Civilisation and Minority Culture*, appeared as a pamphlet three years ago. If I had rewritten it this year the only change would have been that I should have found for it some more recent illustrations; the reasons for insisting on the case it presents are not less strong now than before. The rest of the book, but for the longer essay on D. H. Lawrence, appeared in *Scrutiny* as articles and reviews, and I do not think it is merely author's vision – parental bias – that makes me see them, reprinted together with the first piece, as forming more than a collection. For they all illustrate, develop and enforce, in ways more and less obvious, the same preoccupation and the same argument – the preoccupation and the argument of *Mass Civilisation and Minority Culture*; and, moreover, misunderstanding possible, it seems, when they were separate will be less easy in the book.

I have not eliminated the repeated mention of *Scrutiny*; that, without a good deal of rewriting, would have been impossible. Indeed, the reminder of the occasional circumstances of production seemed appropriate, since 'occasional' in this case intimates not a lack of seriousness and intensity, but the reverse of an academic and purely theoretical spirit, and such a reminder may, for some readers, complement positively the admission, made at the end of this prefatory note, of disabilities on the plane of theoretical exposition.

But perhaps the most common criticism will not be that the preoccupation of the following pages is insufficiently consistent, intense and intent upon practice.

Where something like inconsistency may be fairly charged, and the effects of time found manifest in such ways as to suggest that, here at least, there should have been rewriting rather than reprinting, is in the treatment of D. H. Lawrence. And if I were to rewrite the long essay on him it would certainly be different. But I shall never again, I suppose, be able to give the body of his works the prolonged and intensive frequentation that went to the preparing of that essay, whatever its crudities. It records a serious attempt at stabilizing and defining a reaction, and since his, I believe, is pre-eminently a case in which the attitude of those who find him important is likely to be a developing one, and not simple, I feel justified in leaving the reprinted pieces, of changing tone and stress (and it is these chiefly which change), to convey together my sense of Lawrence's significance. At any rate, the procedure is not merely self-indulgence: I cannot read some parts of the early set appraisal without wincing.

About one most important matter I shall certainly (to judge from the latest signs) be told that I am out of date. Discussing, in an article reprinted in this book,[1] the Marxian doctrine of culture, I remarked that it was extremely difficult to determine what precisely orthodoxy was. In the immediate future, I gather from Mr Edmund Wilson (whom I take to be a good index), the answers to one's questions are going to be different from those of a year ago. Writing on 'Art, the Proletariat and Marx' in the *New Republic*[2] for 23 August of this year, Mr Wilson tells us that the views that anti-Marxists attribute to Communists are attributed erroneously:

It cannot be insisted too strongly . . . that the great Communists have been men who fully understood the importance of art and literature and whose primary idea about them in connection with the revolution was that they wanted to make it possible for more people to get the benefit of them. Nor did they deny the value of the literature and art produced while the bourgeoisie were in the ascendant. On the contrary, they credited to the bourgeoisie the main cultural achievements of the period when the bourgeoisie had been the rising and revolutionary class. They were aware that they themselves derived from the bourgeois culture. And they attacked it only in so far as it was used to defend and cover up the iniquities of the capitalist system.

This is very encouraging. All that we contend for seems to be conceded here. It still, of course, remains to be seen what consensus about these propositions will reveal itself among Communists. Mr Wilson himself notes that Mr Granville Hicks continues to advance hardly consonant ones, and that whereas Engels, 'in pointing out how Goethe's work was influenced by his social position, expresses for him high admiration and speaks of him invariably with respect', Mr Clifton Fadiman, 'in the interests presumably of Marxism, is prepared not without impatience to bury Goethe forever'. Still, Mr Wilson is not speaking without book: he refers in his article to his authorities, *Voices of October* and a report on *Art and Literature in Soviet Russia*; and it seems likely that he represents what is to be the common explicit attitude.

But it would be rash to conclude, nevertheless, that we – those of us who, from a view of culture like that attributed by Mr Wilson to the true Marxist, deduce the need to work very actively for cultural continuity – are going to find Marxists very actively sympathetic. That is not the way, one fears, in which advantage will be taken of the vagueness in which theoretical orthodoxy is still left. 'Neither Marx nor his

followers', says Mr Wilson, clearing things up, 'believed that there
was nothing more in literature and art than the expression of economic
appetites; they thought that philosophy and art were part of what
Marx called a "super-structure" which rested on the base of the "social
relations" of the prevailing system of society – social relations which
derived their peculiar characteristics from the "methods of production". Marx was not a crude mechanist of the kind who used to talk
about consciousness as a "phosphorescence" which ran parallel to,
without affecting, physical processes.' Marx as a Marxist, one ventures, was not really concerned about literature and art; his concern
was for a simplification involving, as an essential condition, the
assumption that literature and art would look after themselves. However this may be (and I plead guilty to the familiar charge – I have not
minutely studied the Bible), it is certain that for most Marxists the
attraction of Marxism is simplicity: it absolves from the duty of wres-
tling with complexities; above all, the complexities introduced if one
agrees that the cultural values – human ends – need more attention
than they get in the doctrine, strategy and tactics of the Class War.

   What, as a matter of fact, one commonly finds in Marxists is that
oblivion of, indifference to, the finer values which is characteristic of
a 'bourgeois', 'capitalist' or Rotarian civilization – the civilization produced by a century of the accelerating modern process. Exposing Mr
Granville Hicks's muddle, Mr Wilson says: 'The best American novel
about the class struggle I have ever read is Dreiser's *American Tragedy*,
which deals with the effects of big bourgeois ideals on a middle-class
boy and a country girl: the class struggle is the struggle in the soul of
Clyde Griffiths between his desire to get away from his proletarian
occupation and up into the world of his rich relatives, and his purely
human solidarity with Roberta.' The *American Tragedy* may be about
class struggle; what it is most remarkable for is the complete unawareness it betrays of any possible ideals other than those of the crude,
completely unleavened 'bourgeois' world that Dreiser, himself completely of it, exhibits. Mr Wilson, one does not question it, knows of
other values, but it would be difficult to illustrate more aptly than by
his comment, which bears no reference to them and could not have
been offered if they had been present to his mind, the point made in
'Under Which King, Bezonian?' regarding the tendency of a preoccupation with the Class War.

   Of course the economic maladjustments, inequities and
oppressions demand direct attention and demand it urgently, and of
course there is a sense in which economic problems are prior. But concentration on them of the kind exemplified by Mr Wilson works to the
consummation of the cultural process of capitalism. What Mr Wilson

forgets in commenting as a Marxist on the *American Tragedy* the world, by the time all the Clydes have been given economic security in which to cultivate their 'purely human solidarities' (for comment on this 'value' of Dreiser's it is fair to refer to Miss Dudley's book on him), is likely to have forgotten for good.

This fear will, no doubt, be countered with the example of Russia. In Russia Marxism has been rigorously applied, and the result, we are told, is cultural regeneration. Terms as well as facts need evaluating; but it does seem as if the change of attitude registered by Mr Wilson corresponds to actual developments in Russia. After years of rigorous practice in the spirit of the doctrine preached by Mr Granville Hicks and his friends, authority in Russia to-day (see, for instance, Mr Maurice Hindus's *The Great Offensive*) favours the fostering of cultural values that would be recognized as such by one interested in tradition. And practical Marxism in Russia does appear to have released an impressive volume of energy in cultural directions.

All this one can have no desire to ignore or belittle: the world does not offer so much elsewhere for hope to feed upon that one is tempted to reject what is fairly offered by the great Russian experiment. But no sound conclusion can be drawn that does not take account of the ways in which the conditions of the experiment are unique. It is as dangerous to argue from its development as it would be to deduce from the initial revolutionary success the possibility of a repetition elsewhere. Russia is the country in which Trotsky's hope (as summarized by Mr Wilson) could be: 'By the time the people at large had learned to read and write well enough to produce a real culture, the proletariat would have disappeared in the classless socialist society.' In such a country, illiterate, inert and economically primitive, a drive for literacy, economic efficiency and social righteousness together might well be expected to bring, along with mechanization, a cultural awakening.

In England and America conditions are very different: that simple statement hardly needs elaborating. Literacy and mechanization it is not suggested we need crusade for; and it is certainly not safe to assume that, in these countries, if we concentrate upon social-economic righteousness, the cultural values will assert themselves appropriately in their own good time. They need all the relevant concern of all those who know what they are. But Marxian preoccupations (however enlightened one may be about the relations between culture and the 'methods of production') are otherwise directed. And a thousand observers will note with Mr Wilson the 'closing of the literary market to writers who had come out a little too outspokenly on the wrong side of the economic fight' for one capable of insisting that this, after all, doesn't represent the main forms of thwarting and starvation that literary talent and literature suffer today.

The reply will come that nevertheless the root-causes are economic. But there is not, explicit or implicit, any tendency here to deny the need – an urgent need – for direct attention to economic and political problems. There are people, says Mr Wilson, 'who, due to an absorption in some special pursuit or study, have the illusion that the intellectual or the aesthetic or the moral activity of man takes place in some sort of vacuum. And there are also people who will admit that literature and art are affected by race, nationality, climate, sexual tendencies and physical constitution, but will not admit that they can be affected by the way in which the author and his readers make their livings or the sources from which they derive their incomes.' The attitude of this book is very different, whether it is literature that is being discussed, or the conditions of literature. It is one that appears to be sanctioned by Mr Wilson when he says that Marx and Engels were 'certainly not proletarians (Engels helped run his father's factory and Marx lived on Engels' money), and they did not attempt to become proletarians . . . They were aiming at a point of view and a culture beyond those of their bourgeois education; but it was a point of view above classes, not a proletarian point of view – they were trying to develop an intellectual discipline which should lay the foundations for the "first truly human culture".'

There *is*, then, a point of view above classes; there *can* be intellectual, aesthetic and moral activity that is not merely an expression of class origin and economic circumstances; there *is* a 'human culture' to be aimed at that must be achieved by cultivating a certain autonomy of the human spirit. That the point of view is difficult of attainment makes it the more incumbent on *les clercs* to insist on the possibility and the necessity. The 'activity', it is agreed, must be a matter of discipline: one's comment on the Marxian attitude is that, whatever Marx may have intended, it seems positively to discourage the kinds of discipline without which 'culture' will indeed be something like a mere function of the economic conditions, of the machinery of civilization.

The Marxist, in fact (whatever orthodoxy may be), seems both to under- and to over-rate the possible 'autonomy' spoken of above. About the present, and the future thought of as relevant to action, he is toughly sceptical: he admits no reality but the Class War (and the only real differences between classes today are economic). About the millennial future, when the classless society shall possess the earth, he is full of the naïvest faith in the capacity of the human spirit for self-direction.

But this is to misrepresent the case: 'faith' suggests something far too positive. Actually, in this matter, the (type) Marxist is a good 'bourgeois': the essential problem is not present to him, and he shares the incapacity to realize the issues that is characteristic of the civilization developed under capitalism. It is this incapacity – this 'vast and increasing inattention' – that is the enemy in this book; if Marxism figures a good deal as its representative, it is for reasons that may be found not altogether unflattering. The positive preoccupation throughout is, in various ways, with the conditions and function of the extra-individual mind – consciousness, sense of value and memory – that a living culture is; to insist that, in a civilization of which the machinery becomes more and more overwhelming, the life and authority of this mind must be worked for consciously. The inadequacies and possible mis-suggestions of the term 'mind' here are perhaps sufficiently provided for in the pages discussing D. H. Lawrence.

That the insistence is not superfluous I am reassured by (among other things) the comments of critics on an article, reprinted in this book, in which I discuss the part of literary criticism in the creation and defining of a 'contemporary sensibility'. To be so serious about so trivial a matter! To arrive, as the result of earnest thought on the problems of our time, at desiderating (*ridiculus mus*) an authoritative 'centre of real consensus', involving such agreement as that 'Mr Eliot and D. H. Lawrence both (however one may "place" them relatively) demand serious attention, and that the supersession by Book Society standards of the standards that compel this judgment will, if not fiercely and publicly resisted, be a disaster for civilization' – it is too fatuous, these critics feel, for serious comment.

But for others it will not be so much the intrinsic triviality of the ends in view that provokes derision: even sympathetic critics will ask how they are to be attained. To the questions of the resolute sceptic there is no very impressive answer that can be given. In the context adduced above the suggestion of answer (bearing, there, specifically upon literary criticism) is in no more coercive terms than these: 'where there is a steady and responsible practice of criticism a "centre of real consensus" will, even under present conditions, soon make itself felt'. When one passes to the extra-literary implications and refers to education the sceptical questions are as difficult to answer convincingly.

Obviously, in the nature of the case, radical doubt at this point will not be shifted by argument. Whether or not one responds positively to such suggestions as those put forward here depends ultimately upon one's sense of realities; a positive response is a readiness to act as if certain kinds of expectation were reasonable. 'Ultimately' in the last sentence is not mere padding: it acknowledges, or rather asserts, the function of critical scrutiny. It may perhaps be retorted that expectations are harboured in this book along with critical findings that make them look not very reasonable. But those who believe in a potential autonomy of human nature such as is implied in the Marxian view of the future should take thought before dismissing as patently futile such initiative and response as are contemplated here – such measure of reliance on intelligence, sanity and humane sense. There is no question (the reminder is not, perhaps, superfluous) of offering an alternative to Marxism – a self-sufficient prescription. The form of the insistence is that, whatever else must be done or attempted (and the simple formula should be suspect), *this* is necessary; and 'this' is something that still seems in no danger of being too much attended to. If such modesty and such aims appear ineffective, it might be asked in what ways they are more so than, for instance, incitements to the Class War that are likely to be effective, if at all, in precipitating some Fascist *coup d'état*, with the attendant advance of brutalization.

'Under which king, Bezonian?'

Pistol – *Under which king, Bezonian? speak, or die.*
King Henry IV, Part II. Act V, Sc. 3.

It would be very innocent of us to be surprised by the frequency with which we are asked to 'show our colours', but the source of the command does sometimes surprise us. Indeed, this very formulation came first from Mr George Santayana, and others whom we respect have repeated it, in substance, since. We should have thought that we had amply made out our case (if that were needed) for holding the assertion and application of serious standards in literary criticism to be an essential function, and one disastrously inoperative now.

Not that we suppose the service of this function to be the whole duty of man, or our own whole duty. The more seriously one is concerned for literary criticism the less possible does one find it to be concerned for that alone. *Scrutiny* has not, as a matter of fact, confined itself to literary criticism. But to identify *Scrutiny* with a social, economic or political creed or platform would be to compromise and impede its special function. This, in its bearing on the challenge now in view, has already been glossed by: 'the free play of intelligence on the underlying issues'. More, of course, needs saying. What is immediately in place is to insist that one does not necessarily take one's social and political responsibilities the less seriously because one is not quick to see salvation in a formula or in any simple creed. And it is unlikely that anyone actively and sympathetically interested in *Scrutiny* (whether as a reader or otherwise) will exhibit this kind of quickness. On the other hand, those of us who are particularly engrossed by the business of carrying on *Scrutiny* should perhaps resolve (though it seems unnecessary) to warn ourselves now and then against making the perception of the complexity of problems an excuse for complacent inattention: special duties are not ultimately served by neglect of the more general. But the special function of *Scrutiny* is an indispensable one, and there appears to be no danger of its being excessively attended to.

Sympathizers, then, may be, and, no doubt, are, of varying social, political and economic persuasions. But the function indicated would

38

hardly have been fully realized if its bearing on such persuasions were left at this, no more immediate and particular than has yet been suggested. If there seems to be no reason why supporters of *Scrutiny* should not favour some kind of communism as the solution of the economic problem, it does not seem likely (there is no thought here of Mr Middleton Murry) that they will be orthodox Marxists. The efficiency of the Marxist dialectic, indeed, makes it difficult to determine what precisely orthodoxy is (we do not find even Mr Maurice Dobb, whom Mr Eliot singles out for commendation, very lucid). But there can be no doubt that the dogma of the priority of economic conditions, however stated, means a complete disregard for – or, rather, a hostility towards – the function represented by *Scrutiny*.

Why the attitude expressed in the varying formula that makes 'culture' (a term to be examined) derivative from the 'methods of production' – why this attitude must be regarded as calamitous Trotsky himself brings out in his *Literature and Revolution*. This book shows him to be a cultivated as well as an unusually intelligent man (which perhaps has something to do with his misfortune). But he too, unhappily, like all the Marxists, practises, with the familiar air of scientific rigour, the familiar vague, blanketing use of essential terms. He can refer, for instance, to the '2nd of August, 1914, when the maddened power of bourgeois culture let loose upon the world the blood and fire of an imperialistic war'. This, however, is perhaps a salute to orthodoxy. And it would not be surprising if he had thought it wise to distract attention, if possible, from such things as the following, which uses 'culture' very differently, and is hardly orthodox: 'The proletariat is forced to take power before it has appropriated the fundamental elements of bourgeois culture; it is forced to overthrow bourgeois society by revolutionary violence, for the very reason that society does not allow it access to culture.' The aim of revolution, it appears, is to secure this accursed bourgeois culture for the proletariat. Or, rather, Trotsky knows that behind the word 'culture' there is something that cannot be explained by the 'methods of production' and that it would be disastrous to destroy as 'bourgeois'. To assert this un-Marxian truth is the aim of his book. 'The proletariat', he says, 'acquires power for the purpose of doing away with class culture and to make way for human culture.' And he insists that the necessary means to this consummation is to maintain continuity. That is, he knows, and virtually says, that 'human culture' at present is something covered by 'bourgeois culture', the Marxian blanket.

But even Trotsky, although he can speak of the need to 'turn the concept of culture into the small change of individual daily living' and can say that 'to understand and perceive truly not in a journalistic way but to feel to the bottom the very section of time in which we live, one has to know the past of mankind, its life, its work, its struggles, its hopes', cannot (or may not) realize the delicate organic growth that 'human culture' is. Otherwise he could not so cheerfully contemplate fifty years of revolutionary warfare, during which everything must be subordinated to proletarian victory, and assume, without argument, that the result will be a society in which 'the dynamic development of culture will be incomparable with anything that went on in the past'. But perhaps, and 'dynamic' strongly suggests it, 'culture' again means something different.

Indeed, Trotsky at this point in the argument, like all the Marxists, becomes indistinguishable from Mr Wells. Neither of them has faced the problem, though Trotsky, unlike Mr Wells, appears capable of seeing it if it is put. A Marxist intelligent enough and well-enough educated to speak of a 'human culture' that must, if it is to exist at all, carry on from what orthodoxy dismisses as 'bourgeois culture', can hardly have failed to divine that, if he thought too much, not only his orthodoxy but his optimism would be in danger. Nothing brings out more strongly that orthodox Marxists (like most other publicists) use the word 'culture' uncomprehendingly than their failure even to perceive the problem – the problem that their dogma concerning the relation between culture and the 'methods of production' confronts them with in a particularly sharp form.

It confronts us all. For it is true that culture in the past has borne a close relation to the 'methods of production'. A culture expressing itself in a tradition of literature and art – such a tradition as represents the finer consciousness of the race and provides the currency of finer living – can be in a healthy state only if this tradition is in living relation with a real culture, shared by the people at large. The point might be enforced by saying (there is no need to elaborate) that Shakespeare did not invent the language he used. And when England had a popular culture, the structure, the framework, of it was a stylization, so to speak, of economic necessities; based, it might fairly be said, on the 'methods of production' was an art of living, involving codes, developed in ages of continuous experience, of relations between man and man, and man and the environment in its seasonal rhythm. This culture the progress of the nineteenth century destroyed, in country and in town; it destroyed (to repeat a phrase now familiar) the organic community. And what survives of cultural tradition in any important sense survives in spite of the rapidly changing 'means of production'.

All this seems fairly obvious, and what should be equally obvious is the new status and importance of leisure. Leisure (however much or little there might be) mattered less when work was not, as it is now for so many, the antithesis of living. (See, e.g., George Bourne, *Change in the Village*, pp. 200–16.) Now, unless one is unusually lucky, one saves up living for after working hours, and for very few indeed can the breadwinning job give anything like a sense of fulfilment or be realized as in itself a significant part of a significant process. Marxists do not contemplate any reversal of this development; nor is enthusiasm for Five Year Plans, the sense of a noble cause, or romantic worship of mechanical efficiency, to be permanently the sanction of labour in itself unsatisfying. 'The Revolution,' writes A. L. Morton, a Marxist, in the October [1932] *Criterion*, 'neither creates nor is intended to create a new leisure class. It is intended rather to create a leisure community.' The Marxist, then, who offers his Utopia as anything better than Mr Wells's, must face the problem that we should all be facing. For any reasonable hope for civilization must assume that the beneficent potentialities of machine-technique will be realized, and there seems no reason to doubt that the material means of life might be assured to all at the cost of small labour to each.

The problem is suggested by Mr Morton here: 'The state of poetry is largely dependent upon the connection of the leisure class with the productive powers. The connection must be close and vital, though that of the individual poet need not be, since he expresses less himself than his social environment. The great ages of poetry have been those in which the poetry-producing class was young and vigorous and was breaking through existing productive relationships. Conversely, a class without social functions tends to produce decadent poetry.' Without being uncritical of Mr Morton's generalizations one may ask: What will 'social functions' be in a leisure community – a community, that is, in which the 'productive process' is so efficient as no longer to determine the ordering of life? Mr Morton speaks of a 'leisure community integrally associated with the productive forces in a way in which no one class has ever been before'; but there is surely no particular virtue in being 'associated' with productive forces so mechanically efficient that 'integrally', here, seems to mean very little? No doubt when we are all leisured the special moral disadvantage of belonging to a leisure class will be gone, but 'social function', it is plain, means so much more in the generalizations about culture and the productive process that it is inapplicable here, or, if applied, becomes a mere arbitrary counter. It is a comment on the Marxian dialectic that it can take a man in this way up to the problem and leave him unable to see it.

The problem faces us all, and not hypothetically, but practically and immediately. It is a more difficult one than Trotsky, that dangerously intelligent Marxist who has some inkling, suggests in his statement of it: 'The main task of the proletarian intelligentsia in the immediate future is not the abstract formation of a new culture regardless of the absence of a base for it, but definite culture-bearing, that is, a systematic, planful, and, of course, critical imparting to the backward masses of the essential elements of the culture which already exists.' The problem is, rather, not merely to save these 'essential elements' from a swift and final destruction in the process that makes Communism possible,[1] but to develop them into an autonomous culture, a culture independent of any economic, technical or social system as none has been before. Whether such a rootless culture (the metaphor will bear pondering, in view of the contrast between the postulated Communist society – in constant 'dynamic' development – and any that has produced a culture in the past) can be achieved and maintained may be doubtful. If it cannot, we have nothing better to hope for than a world of Mr Wells's men like gods, and have rather to fear that the future has been forecast in California.[2] If it can, it will be by a concern for the tradition of human culture, here and now, intenser than Trotsky's (the Marxist excommunicate); a concerted and sustained effort to perpetuate it, in spite of the economic process, the triumphs of engineering and the Conquest of Happiness, as something with its own momentum and life, more and more autonomous and self-subsistent. And in its preoccupation with this effort *Scrutiny* does not find itself largely companied.

This plea, however, will not bring us off; we have no illusions. There is a choice; we must speak or die: Stalin or the King by Divine Right? And the Marxist dialectic, with its appearance of algebraic rigour, stern realism and contemptuous practicality, has great advantages – in dialectic – over those who are pusillanimous enough to let themselves be bothered by the duty and difficulty of using words precisely. The rigour, of course, is illusory, and, consequently, so are the realism and the practicality. 'In general', says Mr Edmund Wilson approvingly in *The New Statesman and Nation* for 15 October, 'it is surprising how promptly the writers are lining up in one or other of the camps, and how readily their antagonisms are developing.' When people line up so promptly one suspects, not only that the appeal of the *chic* has something to do with it, but that the differences are not of a kind that has much to do with thinking; and the ready development of antagonisms among those whose differences are inessential should surprise only the very innocent.

Trotsky's use of the term 'culture' has already been noted. It is part of what Mr Wilson calls the 'Marxist technique'; he himself speaks of the 'old bourgeois culture' and the 'culture of Marxism'. 'Bourgeois' and 'class', likewise, are primary indispensables of the technique. Prince Mirsky, in his celebrated essay in *Échanges* (December 1931), dealing with 'la poésie bourgeoise', takes as 'le poète bourgeois' Mr T. S. Eliot. He exhibits less acuteness – or (and very naturally) more orthodoxy – than Trotsky, who would hardly have been naïve enough to pronounce (though he does contradict himself, and is capable, he also, of sentimentality): 'La bourgeoisie est vide de valeurs, toutes les valeurs vivantes sont du côté de la classe ouvrière.' The 'values' of the working class (though, of course, one never knows what definitions the Marxist, when challenged, will produce from under the blanket) are inevitably those induced by the modern environment – by 'capitalist' civilization; essentially those, that is, of the 'bourgeoisie' and of most Marxists. Mr Wilson (to illustrate this last point), a critic intelligent enough at his best to have written the best parts of *Axel's Castle*, was capable of resting the structure of that book on the values of the 'man who does things', and, seeing that he had thus proclaimed himself a contemporary of Dr John B. Watson, we ought not to have been surprised when he came out as an admirer of Kipling and inno-cently assumed that Lytton Strachey was a great writer.

Prince Mirsky, although, presumably, he does not enjoy Mr Wilson's advantage of having been born to the English language, has over Mr Wilson the advantage of living in London. He would not, as Mr Wilson has (see *The New Statesman and Nation*), have solemnly endorsed the collocation of 'Dostoevsky, Cervantes, Defoe and E. E. Cummings . . . ' And he may have a good critical sensibility. But that is not proved by his exposition, intelligent and adroit as it is, of Mr Eliot's poetry. What he certainly shows is unusual skill in applying the 'Marxist technique', and the way in which in explaining 'The Waste Land' he seizes on the 'structural symbols', *l'humide, le sec et le feu*, and overstresses their function, paying little attention to the essential organization, betrays the influence of the Marxian training. But the significantly betraying thing is the footnote: 'les lecteurs d'Edith Sitwell sont en grande partie les mêmes que ceux de Bertrand Russell dont les *Principles of Mathematics* sont l'évangile des logistes.' Mathematicians are often illiterate, and Bertrand Russell wrote *The Conquest of Happiness*, and Prince Mirsky might as aptly have said that the readers of Edith Sitwell are in great part the same as those of Ernest Hemingway.

The relevance of this further appeal to performance in literary criti-cism should not need urging. To be concerned, as *Scrutiny* is, for liter-ary criticism is to be vigilant and scrupulous about the relation between words and the concrete. The inadequacies of Mr Wilson and Prince Mirsky as literary critics are related to their shamelessly uncritical use of vague abstractions and verbal counters. What is this 'bourgeois culture' that Mr Eliot represents in company, one pre-

sumes, with Mr Wells, Mr Hugh Walpole, *Punch*, *Scrutiny*, Dr Marie
Stopes and the *Outline for Boys and Girls*? What are these 'classes', the
conflict between which a novelist must recognize 'before he can reach
the heart of any human situation'? (See 'Literary Criticism and the
Marxian Method' by Granville Hicks in *The Modern Quarterly* for
summer 1932.) The Marxist, of course, is pat with his answer: he will
define class in terms of relation to the 'productive process'. The concept so defined – how usefully and how adequately to the facts this is
not the place to discuss – will, at any rate, engage with its context. But
when one comes to talk of 'bourgeois culture' the context has changed,
and only by virtue of the Marxist dogma and the Marxist dialectic is it
possible to introduce the concept here and suppose one is saying anything. Class of the kind that can justify talk about 'class-culture' has
long been extinct.[3] (And, it might be added, when there was such
'class-culture' it was much more than merely of the class.) The process
of civilization that produced, among other things, the Marxian
dogma, and makes it plausible, has made the cultural difference
between the 'classes' inessential. The essential differences are indeed
now definable in economic terms, and to aim at solving the problems
of civilization in terms of the 'class war' is to aim, whether wittingly or
not, at completing the work of capitalism and its products, the cheap
car, the wireless and the cinema. It is not for nothing that Trotsky's
prose, when he contemplates the 'dynamic development of culture'
that will follow the triumph of Revolution, takes on a Wellsian exaltation, and that, when he descends to anything approaching particularity, what he offers might have come from *Men Like Gods*. And the
title of Prince Mirsky's essay, 'T. S. Eliot et la Fin de la Poésie
Bourgeoise', should have been one word shorter.

The rigour of the Marxian dialectic, then, is illusory, and the brave
choice enjoined upon us the reverse of courageous, if courage has anything to do with thinking. Must we therefore take the other alternative
offered us: 'si le poète – l'idéologue – bourgeois veut opposer à la
Révolution quelque chose de positif et de convaincant (de convaincant
pour son propre esprit) il ne peut avoir de recours qu'à la résurrection
de quelque revenant médiéval . . . ? Must we be Royalists and Anglo-
Catholics? In the first place, reasons have been advanced for doubting
whether those who find Marxism convincing, for their own minds, are
applying minds in any serious sense to the problems that face us and
them. So if, while agreeing that the recovery of religious sanctions in
some form seems necessary to the health of the world, we reply that
they cannot be had for the wanting, the Marxist had better not start to
think before he twits us with ineffectiveness. And as for Anglo-
Catholicism and Royalism, those who may find these, *pour leurs*

propres esprits, convincing do not convince us that they are taking up an effective attitude towards the problems. The impressive statement, in the abstract, of a coherent position is not enough. And the main reply to the gesture that bids us, if we respect ourselves, line up there, as the logical and courageous alternative, is not that *The Principles of Modern Heresy* and *The Outline of Royalism* have not yet, after all, been given us, but: 'look at *The Criterion*.'

The editor's spare – too spare – contributions almost always exhibit the uncommon phenomenon of real thinking turned upon the 'underlying issues', though, in their bearing on concrete problems, they show no signs of coming any nearer than before to effective particularity. But we must not, under Marxian incitement, suggest unfair tests. The effective particularity we can fairly demand would involve maintaining in *The Criterion* high standards of thinking and of literary criticism. The point that it is necessary to make is, in view of our own enterprise, a delicate one, but only the more necessary for that. Let us suffer the retort when, and as much as, we may deserve it, and express now the general regret that the name of *The Criterion* has become so dismal an irony and that the editor is so far from applying to his contributors the standards we have learnt from him.

The relevance of the point may be enforced by remarking the particular weakness of *The Criterion* for the dead, academic kind of abstract 'thinking', especially when the 'thinker' (incapable of literary criticism) stands in a general, abstract way for 'order', 'intelligence' and the other counters, all of which are worth less than nothing if not related scrupulously to the concrete.

The Marxist challenge, then, seems to us as heroic as Ancient Pistol's and to point to as real alternatives. And we do not suppose that, in *Scrutiny*, we, more than anyone else, have a solution to offer. But, looking round, we do think that, without presuming too much, we can, since there seems no danger of too great an intensity of concern for them, make it our function to insist on certain essential conditions of a solution. Nor, inadequate as our insistence may be, does it appear superfluous to insist that the essential problems should be faced.

Nothing more (if it lived up to this account) should be needed to justify *Scrutiny*. But if some more immediate engaging upon the world of practice would reassure, then we can point to it. We have a special educational interest, and the association of this with the bent already described is unprecedented and has already shown its strength.

Restatements for critics

Critical attention is something to be grateful for, even when it is as pettish in animadversion as 'Ille Ego's' review of *Scrutiny* in *The New English Weekly* for 5 January. This is not to be ungrateful for the generous notice that we have been so widely accorded: warm acknowledgements are due. Nor is it to flatter 'Ille Ego' with the suggestion that his comments are very subtle or profound: his pettishness betrays itself, in the familiar ways, as one of the familiar manifestations of uneasily ambitious immaturity. But the misunderstandings he exhibits in naïve forms have, we know, from spoken criticism and from correspondence, a fairly representative quality, and we tender him thanks for the occasion he provides.

Scrutiny, he complains, refuses to be committed. Instead of giving honest and undivided allegiance to its true 'god', T. S. Eliot, from whom it 'obviously derives' (like most else in 'literary Cambridge these past ten years') it goes whoring after D. H. Lawrence. Worse than that, it was conceived in sin, and it has from birth onwards denied its god: 'It has its origin in a desire not to be committed to Mr Eliot,' or to any other god or prophet. 'It is very definitely not-committed. Indeed, its primary concern appears to be precisely that: to avoid being committed.'

To what, it might be asked, is 'Ille Ego' committed? Anyway, 'very definitely', to knowing the antenatal history of *Scrutiny* and the 'reality' of Blake, D. H. Lawrence and T. S. Eliot. Under three of these heads, at least, we admit to being much less 'committed'. But the more naïve self-committals of 'Ille Ego' may be left to themselves. When he is usefully representative is when he puts his fundamental incomprehension in so plausible a form as this: 'The distinction is suggested in the title. *The Criterion* judges; *Scrutiny* scrutinizes. Compared to judgment, scrutiny is a non-committal occupation'.

We stand self-condemned, then, by the modesty of our title, by our very lack of pretension. Yet title and pretension are not everything. Forbearing the inquiry whether *Scrutiny* has committed itself less often and less decisively than any other journal in particular judgments, let us ask what, where judgment is in question, the criterion is: what are the standards? The values of intelligence, tradition and orthodox Christianity? But judgment is not a matter of abstractions; it involves particular immediate acts of choice, and these do not advance the business of judgment in any serious sense unless there has been a real and appropriate responsiveness to the thing offered. Without a free and delicate receptivity to fresh experience, whatever the criterion alleged, there is no judging, but merely negation. And this kind of negation, persisted in, with no matter what righteous design, produces in the end nullity: the 'criterion', however once validated by experience, fades into impotent abstraction, the 'values' it represents become empty husks. The safety sought in this way proves to be the safety of death.

Of course there is more to be said; there is another side. It is not wisdom that stops at advocating the free play of individual sensibility. Indeed, the truly living sensibility cannot be content to be merely individual and merely free. One cannot suppose it either possible or desirable to go on 'experiencing' as if there had been nothing before. And with the beginnings of maturity the problem of organization becomes one for serious effort; taken seriously, it leads to a discipline and a training, emotional and intellectual, designed to 'preserve the individual from the solely centrifugal impulse of heresy, to make him capable of judging for himself, and at the same time capable of judging and understanding the judgments of the experience of the race'. But this is no matter of simple acceptance or conformity. It is part of our great debt to Mr Eliot that he has made it so plain that there can be no easy way or simple solution. Of tradition he wrote: 'It cannot be inherited, and if you want it you must obtain it by great labour.' But it is just our criticism of *The Criterion* that so many of its writers are condemned by the spirit of this dictum. Judgment cannot be a matter of applying the accepted (or 'inherited') standards, any more than thinking can be a matter of moving the recognized abstractions according to rule.

Again, in his essay on Massinger, Mr Eliot wrote: 'What may be considered corrupt or decadent in the morals of Massinger is not an alteration or diminution in morals; it is simply the disappearance of all the personal and real emotions which this morality supported and into which it introduced a kind of order. As soon as the emotions disappear the morality which it ordered appears hideous. Puritanism itself became repulsive only when it appeared as the survival of a restraint after the feelings which it restrained had gone.' The bearing of this upon (say) a grave and persistent lack, in a journal standing for order, intelligence and orthodoxy, of criticial sensitiveness to contemporary literature – to literature and art in general – does not need elaborating, perhaps.

Our criticism, then, is no repudiation of our debt to Mr Eliot (and *The Criterion*), but the reverse. Nor when we suggest that D. H. Lawrence should have been a test is it necessary, or intelligent, to conclude that we have transferred our allegiance to D. H. Lawrence. 'But to *use* Eliot to escape the reality of Lawrence,' pronounces 'Ille Ego', 'and to use Lawrence to escape the reality of Eliot, is to insult both of them.' To suggest that one should 'accept' Mr Eliot or D. H. Lawrence is to insult both of them, it might be retorted, by gross incomprehension, for, whatever the 'reality' of either may be, it is certainly such that to contemplate 'accepting' it is to repudiate it. The reality of Mr Eliot in one sense is just what is in question. And to propose Lawrence as a test is not to suggest that Lawrence's reality is simple, a matter for allegiance, loyalty or acceptance. An intelligent, that is, a respectful, attitude towards him must necessarily be a discriminating one; for though 'Ille Ego' speaks of Lawrence's 'philosophy' as something to be accepted or rejected, those who have read what Lawrence wrote know that he was inconsistent, and inconsistent in such ways that to think of systematizing him is to betray a complete obtuseness to his significance.

What Lawrence offers us is not a philosophy or an *œuvre* – a body of literary art – but an experience, or, to fall back on the French again, an *expérience*, for the sense of 'experiment' is needed too. In him the human spirit explored, with unsurpassed courage, resource and endurance, the representative, the radical and central problems of our time. Of course he went into dangerous places, and laid himself open to reprehension as setting dangerous examples and inciting to dangerous experiments. But if he earned reprehension, we owe him gratitude for earning it.

More than one summing-up is possible, and it would be absurd to demand agreement with one's own; the stress will fall here for some and there for others. But especially by those who stand for 'order' should he have been recognized as a test: a refusal on their part to consider him seriously must appear a very bad sign indeed. And to take the easy recourse of dismissing him in a plausible, too plausible, bracket with Rousseau, or to use Mr Murry against him, amounts to such a refusal. The reluctant conclusion is at last compelled that the insidious corruptions attendant upon 'classicism' have not been sufficiently guarded against; that 'order' and 'tradition' have ceased to be a living tension, a strenuous centrality, and have become something very different.

'Ille Ego' complains that we desert 'at the point where Eliot becomes the orthodox Christian. That, as might have been expected, is too much for Cambridge.' But what *is* orthodox Christianity? (And is 'Ille

Ego' 'committed' to it?) If it means the kind of rejection of life implicit in Mr Eliot's attitude towards sex, then we do certainly dissociate ourselves at that point. Lawrence's preoccupation with sex seems to us much less fairly to be called 'obsession' than Mr Eliot's, and very much preferable. And we know that many who profess Christian sympathies share this view.

If we go on to say that it does not follow that we accept any Laurentian religion we shall, perhaps, not now be taunted with cowardly evasiveness. What, indeed, was Lawrence's religion? 'Curse the Strachey', he wrote during the war, 'who asks for a new religion – the greedy dog. He wants another juicy bone for his soul, does he? Let him start to fulfil what religion we have.' To talk of the 'religious sense' that he represents may sound weak, but it should not to those who have read the *Letters*. For many today the essential thing is to meet such a sense in the concrete, dominating ('I am a passionately religious man'), and unmistakably an expression of health, courage and vitality. And we meet it, we find, in Lawrence – in the Lawrence who has the right to exclaim as he does against 'glib irreverence', because all his writing exhibits reverence as a fact, a fact of honesty, strength and sensitiveness; the Lawrence who disturbs complacency about 'sex reform' so much more potently than Mr Eliot.

This is not to pronounce against the ultimate necessity of theologies, creeds and rituals: it is probable that *Scrutiny* enjoys, and will enjoy, support from readers who profess and practise. But most, we imagine, who respond to Lawrence's 'one must speak for life and growth, amid all this mass of destruction and disintegration' find the possibility of adhesion to any formal religion a remote one – as remote as a satisfying answer to the question, What does such adhesion mean in effect? Does, for instance, a declaration of 'faith in death' mean a negative acquiescence in the drift of things here below, or, as it might, the opposite?

We have at any rate some notion of the test. And we know that, in such a time of disintegration as the present formulae, credos, abstractions are extremely evasive of unambiguous and effective meaning, and that, whatever else may be also necessary, no effort at integration can achieve anything real without a centre of real consensus – such a centre as is presupposed in the possibility of literary criticism and is tested in particular judgments. But 'tested' does not say enough; criticism, when it performs its function, not merely expresses and defines the 'contemporary sensibility'; it helps to form it. And the function of *Scrutiny*, as we conceive it, is (among other things) to help to persuade an effective 'contemporary sensibility' into being – for that, rather, is what the critical function looks like when decay has gone so far.

The peculiar importance of literary criticism has by now been suggested; where there is a steady and responsible practice of criticism a 'centre of real consensus' will, even under present conditions, soon make itself felt. Out of agreement and disagreement with particular judgments of value a sense of relative value in the concrete will define itself, and, without this, no amount of talk about 'values' in the abstract is worth anything. And it is not merely a matter of literature ('It would appear that "literary appreciation" is an abstraction and pure poetry a phantom' – T. S. Eliot, *Selected Essays*): there is hardly any need to illustrate the ways in which judgments of literary value involve extra-literary choices and decisions. It should at any rate be enough to suggest that those who differ philosophically and theologically – who differ about religious 'beliefs' – may agree that Mr Eliot and D. H. Lawrence both (however one may 'place' them relatively) demand serious attention, and that the supersession by Book Society standards of the standards that compel this judgment will, if not fiercely and publicly resisted, be a disaster for civilization.

Such consensus can, and must, test and justify itself in action. Above all there are, or we should determine that there shall be, immediate consequences in education: at any rate, the determination, resolutely pursued, would provoke real agreement and real differences. This (need it be said?) is not to show contempt for creed and theory, or to suggest that the function represented by, for example, *The Criterion*, is unnecessary. But what we propose does seem to us certainly necessary if creed is not to be merely debilitating and theory a relapse upon the wrong kind of abstraction, inert and unprofitable.

The Marxist, however, will still protest that (as one correspondent puts it) we are invoking education in order 'to escape the urge to political action'. It is of no use, it would seem, while he remains a Marxist, to reply that we do not offer education as an alternative. We cannot, it is true, look forward with any hope to bloody revolution, but we are not (again, need it be said?) politically indifferent. It seems appropriate here to speak in the first person. Let me say, then, that I agree with the Marxist to the extent of believing some form of economic communism to be inevitable and desirable, in the sense that it is to this that a power-economy of its very nature points, and only by a deliberate and intelligent working towards it can civilization be saved from disaster. (The question is, communism of what kind? Is the machine – or Power – to triumph or to be triumphed over, to be the dictator or the servant of human ends?)

When I add that I believe one cannot reasonably pretend to lay down what are the right immediate steps without consulting specialists, and that one of the functions of *Scrutiny* is to provide criteria, from the realm of general intelligence, for determining which specialists can be trusted, and how far, the Marxist will smile. I can only reply, by way of earnest, that a serious educational movement will inevitably, and, as far as I am concerned, explicitly, aim at fostering in schools and in education generally, an anti-acquisitive and anti-competitive moral bent, on the ground (there are others) that the inherited code is disastrously and obviously inappropriate to modern conditions.

But this is not said in any hope of conciliating the Marxist, for he it is who insists on the one thing, the one necessary preoccupation: to confess to a sense of complexities is to play the bourgeois game. Thus our correspondent complains: 'you refuse to admit that "art" and "culture" are among the chief instruments of oppression – a form of dope. Or if you recognize this . . . you are scornful at the idea that Eliot *and* Walpole, Wells, *Punch*, *Scrutiny*, Stopes and the *Outline for Boys and Girls* are all manifestations of bourgeois culture. I contend that they are – and Eliot seems to me as typical as *Punch*, but "at a different level of appeal" (or "sensitiveness" or "intelligence").' Marxism is indeed, to adapt Lenin's adaptation of the 'dope' formula, the alcohol of the intellectual, warming and exalting, obliterating difficulties, and incapacitating for elementary discriminations. After the passage just quoted, one is not surprised to get a defence of Prince Mirsky's 'toutes les valeurs vivantes sont du côté de la classe ouvrière', for to include Mr Eliot and *Punch* under 'bourgeois' is to empty the term 'value' of all serious meaning.

It is true that one might call not only *Punch* and Mr Walpole, but also Mr Eliot and D. H. Lawrence 'products' of capitalist civilization, in that the use made by these last two of their talents was determined by the environment into which they were born. But rejection, after all, is not the same as acceptance, and it is a bourgeois incapacity that cannot recognize the human values that Mr Eliot and Lawrence, in their different ways, are asserting against the environment – very different ways, and if the values are different too, they are alike in being equally not generated in the modern economic process. Indeed, this is our criticism, that in the matter of 'values' the Marxist is too bourgeois, too much the product of the material environment. It is impossible to believe that he who is so obtuse to essential distinctions means anything when he speaks of the 'culture' that will supervene upon a politico-economic revolution: the finer human values have, so far as his sense of them goes, been left behind for good in capitalist Progress.

The simplifying dialectic itself works like a machine. 'You are quite right,' says the correspondent already quoted, 'in stating that "the dogma of the priority of economic conditions means a complete disregard for – or hostility towards – the functions represented by *Scrutiny*". Orthodox Marxists (i.e. Leninist Marxists) would be hostile to *Scrutiny* . . . ', and he goes on to stigmatize as a '*contresens*' our talking of a culture that will have a 'momentum and life of its own' when we have admitted that 'the economic process must profoundly affect existence'. Yet, by anyone not trained in the Marxian dialectic, the nature of the complexity is not hard to recognize. There seems no reason for repeating the argument of 'Under Which King, Bezonian?' that the dialectic itself brings the Marxist to the point at which he must contemplate a quite different relation between culture and the economic process from that of the past. To put it simply, instead of dictating to the mass of mankind their uses of time, the economic process will free their time, in large measure, for uses dictated by inner human nature, if there should be one capable of dictating.

But is there such a thing as 'inner human nature'? The Marxian theory (and historical forecast) would seem to leave little room for it, though implicitly postulating the need for a very potent one, to take over when the Class War ends and the economic process recedes into unobtrusiveness; and that is why the Marxian future looks so vacuous, Wellsian and bourgeois. That mechanical efficiency should be a religion for Russia, and ever more ambitious engineering a sufficient future, is, in the present phase, understandable and perhaps necessary. But, however badly civilization may work, the West can imagine a 'technocratic' or 'planned economy' America too easily to find it an inspiring vision; a more adequate incitement to devoted activity is needed, and needed at once.

We assume an 'inner human nature',[1] and our recognition that it may be profoundly affected by the 'economic process' persuades us that it must rally, gather its resources and start training itself for its ultimate responsibility at once. A cogent way in which the human spirit can refute the Marxian theory and the bourgeois negative lies open in education. 'L'éducation pourra tout,' the correspondent referred to above credits us with believing: that, perhaps is answered. '*Scrutiny* will, no doubt, offer destructive analyses of education as it is – there are precedents enough – but the Scrutineers will effect no change.' If we do not make the obvious and modest response, that is not because we rate our own powers or importance high, but because we know that we speak (having the luck to be in a position to do so) for a formidable and growing body of conviction. Whether or not we are 'playing the capitalist game' should soon be apparent, for a serious effort in education involves the fostering of a critical attitude towards civilization as it is. Perhaps there will be no great public outcry when it is proposed to introduce into schools a training in resistance to publicity and in criticism of newspapers – for this is the least opposable way of presenting the start in a real modern education. Yet the inevitable implications, accompaniments and consequences of such a training hardly need illustrating.

The teaching profession is peculiarly in a position to do revolutionary things; corporate spirit there can be unquestionably disinterested, and by a bold challenge there, perhaps the self-devotion of the intelligent may be more effectively enlisted than by an appeal to the Class War.

III

III

Felix Holt, the Radical

To study George Eliot's development from *Scenes of Clerical Life* (1857) to *Daniel Deronda* (1876) is to form a sharper sense of the inevitability with which the novel achieved that rapid rise to primacy which makes the Victorian age in literature so impressive. I am thinking of the inevitable way in which potential creative writers of the kind that make literature important as 'criticism of life' were drawn into prose fiction. George Eliot had not the irrepressible creative spontaneity of Dickens, the great initiating genius. In fact, it seems safe to conclude from the history that she wouldn't have been a creative writer at all – certainly not a great one – if the novel hadn't, when circumstances led her to attempt fiction, been already there, a dominant presence on the literary scene, and in forms commanding serious attention from the cultivated. She didn't start to be a novelist till she was close on forty.

When, having started, she found herself (there was an economic motive – fiction sold) committed to going on, her problem, she being not merely a matured Maggie Tulliver, but a woman of distinguished intellect, immense knowledge and high cultivation, was to discover ways of bringing all her living interests – the whole of her experience, in which disciplined thought and study and wide reading had played so large a part – into the new art of creative expression she was developing for herself, and in the preoccupation with which she was herself developing.

The novel that preceded *Felix Holt* (1865–6) was *Romola* (1862–3), which brings to an end the first phase of her novel-writing. *Romola* is heavy going, and represents something like a defeat. In it she had with heroic laboriousness tried a mistaken way (mistaken, in the light of what her genius proved itself to be) of integrating the intellectual who had translated Strauss and Feuerbach and was the 'strong woman of the *Westminster Review*' with the novelist: with immense concern for strict, detailed and documented accuracy she wrote a historical novel. She gave much thought to psychological analysis, but the prevailing moral and emotional ethos of the book is that which we think of as focused in the Maggie Tulliver of *The Mill on the Floss* (1860), or the Dorothea Brooke of *Middlemarch* (1871–2).

Romola, in the material reward and the esteem it brought, was a great success: George Eliot's genius appears in her implicit adverse judgment. Her well-known comment to the effect that she began it a young woman and finished it an old one conveys her sense of energy and life spent in grinding painfully towards a dead end. The actual sequel was new development: her next work, appearing three years after *Romola*, was *Felix Holt*.

Felix Holt has for subtitle 'The Radical'. Perhaps title and subtitle together do something towards explaining why so remarkable a novel doesn't seem to enjoy the recognition it deserves, representing as it does a decisive growth of major power in George Eliot. In it she becomes one of those we call with full intention the great novelists. But Felix Holt himself is not one of her successes; from his first appearance he bores in return for the attention he demands, rather than persuades us of his reality. And if we thought of *Felix Holt* the novel as having Felix for its central character, and of its political interest (for it is a 'political novel') as represented by his 'radicalism' should we, while entertaining these preconceptions, form a fair idea of the book's nature or strength? But then who, once embarked on a serious reading, *could* entertain such preconceptions for long?

Felix Holt has its faults; it is no more a perfect work than any other novel she wrote. Her advances – and with each work (even with *Romola*) she in some sense advanced – were qualified, incomplete and uneven. Her greatest achievement, I think, is the strong half of *Daniel Deronda*, her last novel; but it is accompanied by the other half, to which the title more obviously applies, and the *longueurs* of which, after her first vogue, got in the way even of so impressive an achieved creation: for decades the book lay virtually unread and unknown. There are weaknesses, then, in *Felix Holt*; but the presence of a political interest is not among them. Rather it has to be recognized as essentially associated with the advance.

'These social changes', writes the author in chapter 3, 'are comparatively public matters, and this history is chiefly concerned with the private lot of a few men and women; but there is no private life that has not been determined by a wider public life.' The social changes she describes are those which, in political terms, we think of in connection with the Reform Bill of 1832. And the sentence quoted intimates the way in which the inevitable commitment, once she had embarked on fiction, to developing the novel into something justifying Lawrence's claim for it[1] made her a great creative writer – which, as her work in verse, *The Spanish Gypsy* and *The Legend of Jubal* sufficiently testify, she wouldn't otherwise have been. Inevitable commitment, because the creative – the real poetic – impulse in her, her inherent genius, needed for its congenial expression the art in which the new civilization was learning to discover itself. She needed to find the way to bring into the novel as she herself was faced with developing it the whole of herself, her understanding, her powers and her experience.

Romola must have left her knowing in her inner consciousness that *this* – the translation of Dorothea Brooke to Savonarola's Florence, reconstructed with immense and appallingly conscientious erudition and exhausting labours of the higher navvying – was not the way to bring together the earnest conscience, the imaginative humanity, the psychological insight, the trained and equipped intellect and the strong social responsibility. The novel proposed for her by her nature, her gifts and her experience would deal with life as lived in the England in which she was rooted, in which her own personal problems had been wrestled with, and about which she knew so much and cared so much.

She could hardly have realized this with the fullness that completes itself in the achieved creation if so much had not already been done by others. For she hadn't the astonishing originative genius of Dickens, who, plunged in young manhood into a professional writer's career by way of a journalist's immersion in the world of the hustings, political meetings, criminal trials and social evils, started, where his art was concerned, at the beginning, and created the modern novel almost on his own. When George Eliot was moving uncertainly from *Romola* to *Felix Holt*, and thinking of herself as possibly a poet, *Dombey and Son*, *Little Dorrit* and *Great Expectations* were all there to testify, in face of ambitions that were to produce *The Spanish Gypsy* (1868), and in a positive way very relevant to her own need and essential poetic impulse, that poetry was no longer (in Arnold's phrase) the 'crown of literature'.[2] *Bleak House* (1853), with its use of a political theme in the course of its treatment of the social changes brought about by the development of industry, is even more obviously relevant to her undertaking in *Felix Holt*. Of course, the political-social novel was well established when Dickens wrote *Bleak House. Coningsby* and *Sybil* had appeared in 1844 and 1845, *Mary Barton* in 1848, and *Alton Locke* in 1850.

Felix Holt is very much a work of the great George Eliot, a product of her distinctive genius in its maturity. One is apt, dismissing Felix Holt the titular hero, to think of it as memorable – as classical – for the Transome drama it evokes with such force and penetration. And the Transome drama one thinks of as one of Hubris, the tragic irony and Nemesis enacted between Mrs Transome, the handsome solicitor Matthew Jermyn, and their son Harold, in a context of county society. And certainly, while it expresses George Eliot's characteristic moral sensibility at its maturest, and her surest insight into character and motive, it makes us reflect that this is the George Eliot who knew Greek tragedy intimately: Harold pressing in blind confidence to the exposure of Jermyn, his mother's impotent horror, and Jermyn's hate, uttering itself at the catastrophe in 'I am your father' – the Greek affinity is plain. But the art, the observation and the sensibility are modern, and intensely George Eliot. And of Mrs Transome one reflects that, unlike as she is to the feminine type we have in Dorothea Brooke and yet done with so sure a sympathetic insight, she testifies to George Eliot's achievement of a major artist's impersonality.

The Transome drama, however, cannot be separated off in the way such a commentary suggests. George Eliot's treatment, with its cogency of major art, enforces her dictum that 'there is no private life that has not been determined by a wider public life'. The long introduction that opens the book – and it is beautifully justified by what follows – tells us how the knowledge, intelligence and ranging interests of the intellectual are to enter into the poetic conception and inspiration of the novelist; to become one with it, and make clear the nature of the new art. 'Posterity may be shot, like a bullet through a tube, by atmospheric pressure from Winchester to Newcastle: that is a fine result to have among our hopes; but the slow old-fashioned way of getting from one end of the country to the other is the better thing to have in the memory.' What, with the aid of the stage-coachman's commentary, we see and learn does more than establish a picturesque décor for the drama of the individual actors. 'In these midland districts the traveller passed rapidly from one phase of English life to another': coexistent phases – what we are given is a conspectus of the interplaying forces and inertias, the old, the new and the emergent, that were turning pre-industrial England into modern.

The personal drama opens in chapter 1; we see the proud and bitter Mrs Transome awaiting with confident eagerness the return from the Levant of her son, who is to restore the fortunes of Transome Court, and enable her to take again her proper place in county society. But not only has county society been affected by changes of civilization; Harold himself, though socially ambitious, is ambitious in a new spirit of the age that makes him, kindly as he is, cruelly blind to his mother's hopes and fears. It is a conflict of egotisms, a theme congenial to George Eliot's genius, and done with all her insight and power, and it entails in an essential way a political interest: Harold – it is in the character made so clearly manifest to us, and in the role the character has cast him for – decides to put up for Parliament. That he should do so accords with his mother's plans for him, but she had not conceived that it would be as a Liberal: Harold, well-informed and shrewd, knows that times have changed.

What the inconceivable, but inexorable, means, the developing novel brings home to us. All the hints of the introduction are taken up; what they portend is seen as inseparable from the central drama of personal wills and hopes and hatreds. This is a drama of social individuals; inescapably social and shown to be that in the fullest sense, in a given society at a given moment of civilization. And the moment chosen is patently felt by the novelist to have the most poignant relevance to any concern for England entertained by a responsible person at the moment at which she writes. She treats the political interest fully, giving proof of an impressive mastery of all the aspects: the background of economic development and class; the realities of persuasion, motive, campaigning and the hustings.

We remember Disraeli's brilliant performance in this field; she was not the pioneer, and the example was there. But her knowledge is her own acquisition, and fully possessed; the distinctive note of her fine and robust intelligence is everywhere and the observation is first-hand. Moreover, she has an advantage over Disraeli in dealing with the working class, the rustics, the tradesmen, and the provincial middle class in general: her knowledge is from much closer.

Yet Felix Holt, the working-class Radical, is not a success. He is done, not from observation (whatever she may have thought), but from idea, and the idea comes too much and too obviously from the Dorothea Brooke in George Eliot – from the nobly idealistic feminine imagination. It isn't that the intention wasn't an intelligent one, but that the carrying out was more difficult than she permitted herself to realize: her nobility was too much for her. Her presentment of practical politics is convincingly and very intelligently realistic: it brings out how little we can expect from a pure disinterested devotion to ideals and avowed policies. To enforce that truth, and, at the same time, disclaim any suggestion there might seem to be of resigned acquiescence, by having fearless and consistent disinterestedness represented by a central character – one can conceive that such an intention might be successfully carried out. But the character would have to be, not only credible, but real, and Felix is not real; he has been conceived too easily and self-indulgently. And the reader enjoys his talk almost as little as the Reverend Rufus Lyon's: if not real, he is certainly a bore.

Felix's relations with Esther only confirm the diagnostic reference to Dorothea Brooke: they clearly belong to the world of Dorothea's imagination. Esther, being a woman, is not as complete a failure as Felix. But one finds oneself saying that she doesn't know whether she is Gwendolen Harleth or Dorothea Brooke. George Eliot, of course, meant her for a complex potentiality, the emergence and triumph of the latent good in whom is brought about by Felix. In so far as we feel

her to be real we feel that she ought to have married Harold Transome.
But all that intricate and exacting part of the plot which is needed to
prove her an heiress, and put her in a position to reject Harold and
renounce Transome Court nobly for Felix, must be for most readers
merely a nuisance. It represents a Victorian prompting that couldn't
be felicitously taken up into the art her genius was developing.

But the novel as a whole is – or should be – a classic.

George Eliot's Zionist novel

Daniel Deronda (1876) was George Eliot's last novel. It is also, of all her novels, that which presents her most massively and compellingly as a great novelist – one of the greatest – and shows her greatness at its most Tolstoyan (for, peculiarly among the novelists of her language she has qualities prompting that description). All through her novelist's career, in fact, she continued to develop her powers, achieving the art that reveals them at their most impressive in the immense effort of the close. This is not, of course, to say that she achieved a perfect art (*Daniel Deronda* is more obviously not perfect than any other of her novels), or that her development manifested itself in a simple steady progress. She offers us, as a person, and in the creative genius her life nourished, a case of very interesting complexity. She never – except (I think one may fairly say) in *Silas Marner*, which tale, among her novels, recommends itself to us as a product of triumphant and unlaboured inspiration, yet is not the less a major classic – achieved perfection. The intimately related constatation is that she went on developing, though she left behind her neither the Maggie Tulliver (of *The Mill on the Floss*) in her make-up (for all the advance of maturity), nor the George Eliot who wrote *Silas Marner* – and nothing of that kind again.

She is among those great writers any one of whose works makes us, as we focus on it, think of its relation to the other works in the *œuvre* and (it virtually follows) to the 'case'. I am not saying that the *Daniel Deronda* I am exalting is not, as a classic of major art, self-sufficient. The book stands in and as itself. The duly responsive reader cannot but see what it is that he has in front of him. Both the nature of the greatness and that there are distinctions to be made – discriminations between what represents its varied strength and what does not – must be plain. Yet no one can fail to divine that there is a 'case' – a person and a life – behind the art, the oddities, and the failures. And with the relating of the given work to the *œuvre* and the life, critical understanding becomes surer, more intelligent, more inward. I say 'critical understanding', thinking strictly of the business of the literary critic as such, there being about the kind of diagnostic inquiry I have in mind when I talk of a 'case' nothing impertinent. For, reversing T. S. Eliot's famous Flaubertian dictum, one can say that, where truly great art is in question, there is never a separation between the life that suffers and experiences and the mind that creates. To be intelligent about the personal significance of *Daniel Deronda*, the relation of the book to George Eliot's peculiar 'case', is to have a surer appreciation of the characteristic impersonality of the art she has created, on so large a scale, in the massive strong part of the book.

That part, I have elsewhere suggested,[1] might, by way of getting for George Eliot more of the recognition she deserves, be called *Gwendolen Harleth* and printed by itself (it would make a very substantial novel). The actual title, *Daniel Deronda*, is certainly a misdirection; it insists, as pointing to the *raison d'être* of the book, on the also very substantial part of it that does not come from the great creative George Eliot. But, in the re-reading that preceded the present note, my already growing sense that the surgery of disjunction would be a less simple and satisfactory affair than I had thought has been reinforced. And I have here given my reasons for holding that the admirer of George Eliot's genius, intent on a full appreciation, will demand the whole book that she wrote, and will be right. My own insistence now must be that, for such an appreciation, it is important to be clear just in what way the Zionist part (I may call it – all, I mean, of *Daniel Deronda* that is portended by the title) fails to justify the place given it by George Eliot in her total conception: what are the nature and significance of the failure and what is the relation of the characteristics manifested in the Zionist part to her creative greatness?

At this point I find it helpful to make a reference to Henry James's criticism. As a critic of George Eliot he seems to me unsurpassed, and everyone interested in her ought to know his commentaries – I am thinking in particular of the article written as a review of the John W. Cross *Life*, and of '*Daniel Deronda*: a Conversation', both of which are to be found in James's *Partial Portraits*. His fine intelligence shows to great advantage in them (it is not for nothing that he owes so much to George Eliot), and the sum of what he says conveys an appreciation that is perceptive and pretty just. Yet his criticism, distinguished as it is, is not altogether satisfactory: it contains a great deal in the way of fallacious proposition and dubious suggestion, and can be quoted in the furtherance of critical unenlightenment, the analysis it embodies being inadequate. For instance, faced, in considering *Daniel Deronda*, with making the major discrimination called for, James says: 'All the Jewish part is at bottom cold.'

We know what he means. The Jewish part was – inevitably – done from the outside. It was an achievement of those intellectual energies – the power of acquiring immense erudition with indefatigable labour

(James speaks of 'her exemption from cerebral lassitude'), and of applying it with an unremitting concern for factual and historical truth – which had gone to the working-up of the historical setting in *Romola*. One may be struck not only by the immense capacity for intellectual acquisition, but by the intelligence about the world of her time that had enabled George Eliot to forecast how the passion of nationalism would affect the Jews. And one may feel that at this date it is not James who, with his jibe (thrown out in the 'Conversation' through the mouth of Pulcheria) about 'tea-parties at Jerusalem', shows to advantage. The point I have to make, however, is that the whole case of George Eliot is more complex than James suggests.

The provincial girl, of lower middle-class origin, who by sheer ability established herself as a figure of the English intellectual world while still in young womanhood *was* a woman. She was fully a woman, with a woman's needs. When, at thirty-seven, she published her first fiction, she had already had a distinguished career as an intellectual. It was not till several years later that she wrote *The Mill on the Floss*, yet one's criticism of that novel must be that it is too much the work of Maggie Tulliver. It is too much written from inside Maggie, whose yearnings and exaltations and spiritual intensities are offered just as Maggie felt them and might have offered them; out of relation, that is, to any maturer experience. The clear autobiographical identity of Maggie with George Eliot is peculiarly poignant in the earlier part of the book, in the rendering of the stresses suffered by the sensitive and gifted child in that bucolic milieu – notably of the girl's flinching sense, continually played on by obtuse adult comment and allusion, that she decidedly lacks beauty and attractiveness by the criteria of the immediate community that is decisive for her. The significance is not less poignant when we note that there is one great difference between Maggie and the actual George Eliot: Maggie enacts in adolescence the ugly duckling transformation; the deplored 'gypsy' traits (her Dodson kin are blond) turn into the commanding beauty of a magnificent brunette.

There is warrant enough for finding here, in so autobiographical a novel, an element of daydream – self-indulgent, self-compensatory – on the part of the author (for George Eliot's unhappy sense of her lack of any obvious feminine charm there is plenty of evidence from her life). And there is a significance for the critic in the association of this daydream element with the uncritical presentment of Maggie's yearning for a steady spiritual exaltation, an intensity that, with the potency of being in love, shall transfigure life and give it an irresistible purpose. The genius of the great George Eliot manifests itself in the power and intransigence of her sense of the real (I called her, above,

Tolstoyan). The disconcerting thing about her is the way in which, after she has achieved what one can only call the full possession of her genius, there should still remain in her an unreduced enclave of immaturity. It is there in *Middlemarch*, sorting oddly with the strength of that novel – there in the heroine Dorothea. Considering the valuation of Dorothea's idealism we are expected to endorse, and the relations with Ladislaw we are expected to find convincing and touching, a sense of the real, we tell ourselves, is precisely what *this* George Eliot is deficient in:

'No, I don't think that,' said Dorothea. 'I have no longings . . . But I have a belief of my own, and it comforts me.'

'What is that?' said Will, rather jealous of the belief.

'That by desiring what is perfectly good, even when we don't quite know what it is and cannot do what we would, we are part of the divine power against evil – widening the skirts of light and making the struggle with darkness narrower.'

The nobility is tainted with self-indulgence.

There is no dangerous heroine in *Daniel Deronda*. There is, however, a significant agreement that the hero is not a man. This judgment, in its negative intention, is a denial that Deronda can be credited with any reality, let alone the convincingness necessary to a major *dramatis persona*. But it registers something positive at the same time: the constatation that Deronda, though he cannot be called a creation, is very positively feminine – very positively a feminine expression. Who, contemplating the ardours, the emotional intensities, the idealistic exaltations that are focused in him can think 'cold' an apt word for this failure of the creative writer? The high-powered intellectual, with her disinterested and clearsighted humanity, is certainly very much engaged in the Zionist part, but when we contemplate Deronda we cannot ignore the presence in it of something strongly, and very questionably, emotional; a powerful, but equivocal, element of inspiration (as it must have seemed to the author, for it brought with it a drive of energy).

The nature of the inspiration is given us when we are told (characteristically) of Deronda's 'sweet irresistible hopefulness that the best of human possibilities might befall him – the blending of a complete personal love in one current with a larger duty'. Deronda here indulges himself in a more inclusive hopefulness than Maggie or Dorothea in their exalted moods – or Deronda himself – tends to cultivate in full consciousness. In his capacity of spiritual adviser he tells Gwendolen, 'the refuge you are needing from personal trouble is the higher, the religious life, which builds an enthusiasm for something more than our own appetites and interests', and the essential – the sufficient – 'enthusiasm' he proposes for himself is that which he acquires when he discovers he is a Jew, and, having made the acquaintance of his mother, comes back from the interview 'with something better than freedom'. This 'larger duty', a permanent intoxication, all-sufficient and transfiguring, is the 'religious' exaltation longed for by Maggie and Dorothea. But Deronda himself is shown as realizing his 'sweet hopefulness' to the full: he wins his Mirah, and so is able to identify 'the larger duty', the 'enthusiasm', with a 'complete personal love'. This imagined life of sustained and wholly satisfying intensity George Eliot now conceives as a man's (we are to take him as the beau ideal of masculinity). We clearly haven't here the direct simplicity of auto-biographically personal expression, but the George Eliot predominant, all the same, is not the great genius, with her command of creative impersonality – nor creative at all: the attempt to dramatize the less creative 'inspiration', these dubiously emotional and idealistic impulsions, in a hero could produce only unreality. But George Eliot is oddly, and significantly, unaware of the difference between this and the wonderfully vital art of which there is such a wealth in *Daniel Deronda*. The fact that her intellectual powers have been so strenuously and congenially engaged in the development of the Zionist theme of which Deronda is the focus is a strongly favouring condition of this unawareness.

The point I have been coming to is that one must not, as Henry James with so many other critics tends to do, make her possession of these intellectual powers responsible for the defeat, or abeyance, of the great novelist in the Zionist part. It is not the great intellect that is in control there, but something emotional – something that, in part at least, is a paradoxical immaturity, and uses the intellectual powers for its own purposes. Properly, these powers belong with the superb intelligence that (carrying with it an inwardness of self-knowledge and a fine mastering sense of the real) is to the great artist wholly a strength, an essential manifestation of the novelist's genius. And one cannot but recognize that as present in the part of the novel we judge to be unsuccessful they compel admiration. The failure, in fact, though the upshot of one's critical notes is clear and unequivocal, is not the altogether simple case I have perhaps suggested. There is something in what, in the 'Conversation', Henry James suggests through the mouth of Constantius:

Gwendolen's history is admirably typical – as most things are with George Eliot: it is the very stuff that human life is made of . . . The universe forcing itself with a slow, inexorable pressure into a narrow, complacent, and yet after all extremely sensitive mind, and making it ache with the pain of the process

– that is Gwendolen's story. And it becomes completely characteristic in that her supreme perception that the world is whirling past her is in the disappointment not of a base but of an exalted passion. The very chance to embrace what the author is so fond of calling a 'larger life' seems refused to her. She is punished for being narrow, and she is not allowed a chance to expand. Her finding Deronda pre-engaged to go to the East and stir up the race-feeling of the Jews strikes me as a wonderfully happy invention. The irony of the situation, for poor Gwendolen, is almost grotesque, and it makes one wonder whether the whole heavy structure of the Jewish question was not built up by the author for the express purpose of giving its proper force to this particular stroke.

Certainly George Eliot intended such a tragic irony. And the peculiar quality of her genius asserts itself in her conceiving the climax of Gwendolen's tragedy in those terms – as enacted in that situation. We cannot miss the intention, or fail to be impressed by the conception. Impressed; but we are not convinced with the conviction brought by great art. The conception remains an intention, and no amount of the exalted emotional energy brought up by George Eliot with the Zionist theme can generate the kind of reality we have in the Gwendolen–Grandcourt part. It will not after all do to say that she 'built up' the 'whole heavy structure of the Jewish question' solely in order 'to give its proper force to this particular stroke': Constantius offers to credit her with an impersonal wholeness of creative impulse and conception that is certainly lacking here. She expanded herself on the 'Jewish question' because (partly, at least) of a personal emotional need working in ways of which she is not sufficiently aware, and in this the whole Deronda function is involved. Even when, in her presentment of the Zionist theme, she seems most impersonally the nobly earnest intellectual – and there is a great deal that is very impressive – the truly noble Victorian by whom we are impressed is the character and the powerful mind, but not the genius. George Eliot would not have found the Zionist 'enthusiasm' she offers to imagine as the all-sufficient life-significance for Deronda of any avail for herself – nor would she, in actuality, any equivalent religion of race or heredity. She cannot, in fact, really do the imagining she undertakes; she is not (for all her illusion to the contrary) engaged in her wholeness – not engaged as an artist must be in order to create. The living intelligence that goes with her creativity would have told her that, in finding it possible to enlist her intellectual powers in the proposing of such substitutes for religion (her poetic drama, *The Spanish Gypsy*, in which the heroine, informed unexpectedly by a stranger that she is his, a gypsy's daughter, realizes thereupon that it is her life's purpose and meaning to serve the gypsy people, is another document), she was showing herself – conscientious, but profoundly religious agnostic as she was –

too much a Victorian, too much the product of a local and limiting climate.

The failure of creativity, the absence of the great novelist, is very apparent at the tragic climax, the parting between Deronda and Gwendolen, where it is calamitous. Too often we have had to comment that Deronda, in so far as he is anything, is a prig. What are we to say about his valedictory offer of consolation to Gwendolen (see the close of chapter 69), to whom it has just been broken that he is about to marry Mirah? Yet what else could he have said? What intimate and poignant relation could be convincingly shown between a mere emotionalized postulate, which is what Deronda is, and a concrete individual who is as real to us as Gwendolen? Yet we cannot eliminate the postulate from an account of the superlatively successful rendering of Gwendolen's tragedy – George Eliot's greatest achivement. Nevertheless, that he is not a created reality hardly matters, hardly constitutes a serious qualification, when we are admiring a great novel, *Gwendolen Harleth*, that we can't help thinking of trying to separate off: it merely has a rough edge.

One might be inclined to call the prepotence, more or less subtle, in the Deronda part, of the element of nobly feminine self-indulgence the price paid, the self-compensation, for the sustained impersonality and maturity of the rest. But to do so would be to imply that one feels suggestions of strain, or of difficult achievement, about that triumph of the artist. The contrary is true: there is an effect of creative freedom and inevitability; the complete genius in its wholeness is here; the born novelist, possessed by her themes and in full possession of them, and drawing on an inexhaustible charge of relevant experience and observation. It can be said that Gwendolen did not, as heroine, present George Eliot with any tempting opportunity for insidious self-identification. It must at the same time, then, be said that in George Eliot's treatment of this girl so different from herself there is no lack of the inwardness given by sympathy. Her power to achieve tragic art through the impersonality of imaginative insight was shown impressively in *Felix Holt*, in the Transome drama, where Mrs Transome is highborn, handsome, imperious, and not in the least idealistic. The nature of George Eliot's genius in its creative wholeness is perhaps best brought out by a comparative reference back from Gwendolen to Rosamond Vincy of *Middlemarch*. In some ways the likeness between them might appear very close. Both are spoilt beauties, exhibiting an extreme narrowness of feminine egoism. The most characteristic physical gesture attributed to them, an expression of proud elegance and grace, is the same for both: they 'turn' their long necks. But the charming Rosamond in her pretty self-centred complacency is merely stupid, unteachable, and destructive. George Eliot, while not absolving Lydgate from responsibility for his fate, sees Rosamond, whose potent attraction for him she presents with an intelligent woman's exasperation, as the snare into which he falls. Rosamond has no potentiality but to continue to be her trivial self – that is, to be destructive to a talented man. Gwendolen, on the other hand, not merely 'has a root of conscience in her'; she is capable of being made, as an individual study, the focus of a study of a whole society. It is above all of this part of *Daniel Deronda* that James's Constantius is speaking when he says: 'I delighted in its deep rich English tone, in which so many notes seem blended together.' The envious admiration felt by the author of *The Portrait of a Lady* was natural; George Eliot's rendering of English life has an obvious advantage in intimacy over his – which came later. But hers is more than a matter of providing the drama of Gwendolen's fate with a 'deep rich' background: the intimacy, the inwardness, the apparently free abundance, are necessary for the development of the moral-psychological – or spiritual – theme. What is Tolstoyan about George Eliot is the way her preoccupation with the individual conscience and her intense conviction of its responsibility go with an insight, not only into the part played by social pressure in such a case as Gwendolen's, but into the extent to which what in the individual passes as a moral sense may itself be the representative of mere convention, the superficial but robust product of a climate or environment:

She had only to collect her memories, which proved to her that 'anybody' regarded illegitimate children as more rightfully to be looked shy on and deprived of social advantages than illegitimate fathers. The verdict of 'anybody' seemed to be that she had no reason to concern herself greatly on behalf of Mrs Glasher and her children.

Gwendolen, beautiful and self-willed, is shown as commanding at home, from her charming and diffident mother and her sisters, the deference of the spoilt child. Nothing in the 'county' society in which they move tends, at any rate by inducing a growth of moral perception, to correct or counter the spoiling. Its tendency may be fairly represented by the rector, Mr Gascoigne, Gwendolen's uncle and acting father. It would be easy to assemble quotations to make it seem that George Eliot's presentment of him was satirical. Actually it is essential to her purpose that she should make us share her sense of him as a fine figure of a man and an admirable person, and she beyond any question does. The social historian of the English nineteenth century must be able to appreciate that there may be snobbery that isn't merely ignoble, and George Eliot's presentment of the rector – she performs the novelist's historical function supremely well – deserves to be a classical illustration:

> This match with Grandcourt presented itself to him as a sort of public affair; perhaps there were ways in which it might even strengthen the Establishment. To the Rector, whose father (nobody would have suspected it, and nobody was told) had risen to be a provincial corn-dealer, aristocratic heirship resembled regal heirship in excepting its possessor from the ordinary standard of moral judgments. Grandcourt, the almost certain baronet, the probable peer, was to be ranged with public personages, and was a match to be accepted on broad general grounds national and ecclesiastical.

There is irony here, but this is not satire – not the satirizing of hypocrisy. Nor is it when, as the upshot of his admonition to his oddly hesitant niece, he tells her:

> Then, my dear Gwendolen, I have nothing further to say than this: you hold your fortune in your own hands – a fortune such as rarely happens to a girl in your circumstances – a fortune in fact which almost takes the question out of the range of mere personal feeling, and makes your acceptance of it a duty. If Providence offers you power and position – especially when unclogged by any conditions that are repugnant to you – your course is one of responsibility, into which caprice must not enter.

The educative potency of the conventional moral climate as well as its pressure is powerfully evoked. In this environment, against this background, takes place the fatal convergence that seems to rob Gwendolen of choice. To escape service with the bishop's wife she confidently seeks her interview with Herr Klesmer, and gets her crushing humiliation. The whole painful scene (chapter 23), poignant in its personal drama and illustrating the intelligence of George Eliot's critical attitude toward English society and civilization, is wonderfully done. The place of the arts and the artist in England – in Klesmer, who is so much more than a successful figure of comedy, that theme is brought up by a novelist who shows herself admirably qualified to deal with it. I am pretty sure, in fact, that James found in *Daniel Deronda* the subject and the background of *The Tragic Muse*.

Shattered and at a dead end from this interview, Gwendolen receives Grandcourt's request for permission to call on her. How can she fail to be elated?

> But no! she was going to refuse him. Meanwhile, the thought that he was coming to be refused was inspiriting: she had the white reins in her hands again; there was a new current in her frame, reviving her from the beaten-down consciousness in which she had been left by the interview with Klesmer. She was not now going to crave an opinion of her capabilities; she was going to exercise her power.

The subtleties of her psychology are done with a compelling inward-

ness. But when we come to such things as the scene between
Gwendolen and Grandcourt (chapter 27) we see that it is unequivocally on the *novelist* that the stress must fall: the artist with the specific
genius and a complete command of her art. I am thinking not only of
the consummateness of the dialogue, rendering as it does with such
perfect delicacy and precision of dramatic power the play of the
opposed forces beneath it, and having for upshot Gwendolen's almost
involuntary acceptance of Grandcourt's adroit proposal; I am thinking
too of the immediate reality of the whole drama, the way in which the
movements and gestures of the actors are *seen*.

For other notable examples I would specify the interview (chapter
30) at Gadsmere between Grandcourt and Mrs Glasher when he goes
to get the diamonds, and the successive scenes between Grandcourt
and Gwendolen and Gwendolen and Lush in chapter 48. But it would
be a mistake to suggest that there could be any separating off of the
directly dramatic from the other modes that a novelist of George
Eliot's scope has to use. It is time to insist that as an artist and tech-
nician she has a flexibility, and in her command of the varied resources
of her native language a felicity with which she doesn't always get
credited. To say 'analysis' in connection with *Daniel Deronda* is
perhaps to suggest the abstract and Germanic prose that one may find
in the less successful parts of the book. But this is analysis:

Had Grandcourt the least conception of what was going on in the breast of his
wife? He conceived that she did not love him: but was that necessary? She was
under his power, and he was not accustomed to soothe himself, as some cheerfully disposed persons are, with the conviction that he was very generally and
justly beloved. But what lay quite away from his conception was, that she
could have any special repulsion for him personally. How could she? He himself knew what personal repulsion was – nobody better: his mind was much
furnished with a sense of what brutes his fellow-creatures were, both mas-
culine and feminine; what odious familiarities they had, what smirks, what
modes of flourishing their handkerchiefs, what costume, what lavender-
water, what bulging eyes, and what foolish notions of making themselves
agreeable by remarks which were not wanted. In this critical view of mankind
there was an affinity between him and Gwendolen before their marriage, and
we know that she had been attractingly wrought upon by the refined negations
he presented to her. Hence he understood her repulsion for Lush. But how
was he to understand or conceive her present repulsion for Henleigh
Grandcourt?

There is much of this kind in *Daniel Deronda*, and to remind ourselves
as we read that the author has a great mastery of living dialogue is to
have no sense of paradox: this analysis is in the most sensitive touch
with the perception and the intuition. They seem, in fact, to be
present, and the prose that renders them is (to use James's distinction)

the 'poet's' rather than the 'philosopher's'. It is the prose of the novelist who can do Gwendolen's flights and sallies and high-spirited femininities so supremely well.

What, one may ask, is the great advantage this novelist has over the Henry James who admired her, testifying to his admiration with *The Portrait of a Lady*? One can answer that she knows her English world better than James knows any world, and has a corresponding advantage in respect of her heroine. But that is not all. It is time to make again the point that she was the author of *Silas Marner*, which had come out fifteen years before. *Silas Marner* was written by one whose youth and upbringing were very different from James's, and not in any world of sophisticated manners and brilliant conversation. Its classical quality is bound up with that; it lies in her grasp of basic human need, the essential conditions of maintaining a distinctively human life, the fundamentals of civilized human society as seen and felt in a traditional rustic community. From *Silas Marner* Hardy got his prompting to the Wessex novels.

The art is very different from that in which George Eliot sets forth the tragedy of Gwendolen Harleth; but there is a continuity. Or rather, to revert to my earlier way of putting it, in *Daniel Deronda* the author of *Silas Marner* is still there: there is no incongruity in the suggestion that the Hardy who owed so much to *Silas Marner* could be very positively in resonance with the later book too. And he actually did, I think, take the use of the name of the old West Saxon kingdom, Wessex, from *Daniel Deronda*, where also (a congruous fact) he would find that manifest influence of Greek tragic thought which undoubtedly played its part in the suggestiveness that George Eliot's work in general had for him. Hubris and Nemesis can be clearly felt in Gwendolen's tragedy, and the kind of implicit creative response to the pondered impact of Greek religious drama exemplified here was as natural to George Eliot when she was presenting the fate of the young lady in sophisticated society as when she was dealing with the lives of the actors in *Silas Marner*. It is an intimately related point that she felt her sophisticated society – felt it in a charged and realizing way – as belonging to and dependent on the full context of life, traditional, economic, unsophisticated, and necessary, evoked by the name 'Wessex'.

The clinching touch may fitly be a reference to the importance of George Eliot for D. H. Lawrence, who studied her closely. He recognized the intimate bearing of her work on that to which he himself was committed – he the pioneering novelist whose own exploration of the individual psyche was inseparable from a preoccupation with the changing historic society to which it belonged, and whose interest in the finer creative expressions of civilized man was that of one who knew, by birth and upbringing, the world of the basic labour, traditional and industrial, by which civilization was sustained.

Nostromo: a foreword

Joseph Conrad started writing his first novel, *Almayer's Folly*, on the flyleaf, margins, and inside covers of his copy of *Madame Bovary*. He told his friend and collaborator Ford Madox Ford, besides this, that he had conceived the idea of becoming a writer when, looking through a porthole of his ship, which was then at Rouen, he saw, on the quay, the inn at which Emma Bovary had had one of her assignations with Rodolphe. He gave, at other times, other accounts of the decisive moment. But, of course, we need see here no essential contradiction, and my first two sentences convey pregnantly one of the distinctive aspects of Conrad's place in English literature. He spoke French before he spoke English, and it was French masters he studied when forming his sense of the art to which he aspired to devote himself: he thought of the novelist's business as strictly and exactingly an art – an art demanding dedication and devotion; and his conception of the art was strongly influenced by Flaubert.

And actually, in the idea – or ideal – of art his work represents, he is equally unlike Dickens, the great truly national artist who thought of himself as a great national entertainer, and George Eliot, the decidedly intellectual, and yet very English, great novelist. In Conrad's work we sense beyond question the tormenting conscience of the dedicated craftsman, the conviction of a subtle rightness of expressive form to be achieved: we sense a spirit of dedication that we may reasonably describe as deriving from Flaubert's quest of *le mot juste*, the right cadence, and a final perfection in part and whole.

But Conrad the man was very different from Flaubert – as the second sentence of this introduction, in registering his admiration for *Madame Bovary*, recalls at the same time. A seaman in the British merchant service, with a history of exile, action, and varied adventure behind him, and apparently keen on becoming a master mariner – what could be more unlike Gustave Flaubert, who, always afraid of life (by his own confession), spent his allotted span for the most part in his comfortable Norman retreat above the Seine, free in his luxurious security for a martyred addiction to 'art' and to hatred of the bourgeois. The paradoxes, improbabilities, and total wonder of Conrad's career are well known; but they have so much significance for one's appreciation of him as a great writer that they must be briefly rehearsed. To have been born the son of a conspiratorial Polish aristocrat, to have conceived in boyhood in his landlocked native country the ambition to become a British master mariner, and then to have achieved it – that is remarkable enough. To have been at the same time a British master mariner and a highbrow novelist (for Conrad began writing while still following the sea) – that is more remarkable: it sounds indeed improbable in the extreme. But the improbability grows when one realizes that, though it was an English novelist the Polish British seaman set out to be, his first 'other language' was not English but French: before taking a berth on a British merchant ship and committing himself to the daily use of English, he had, in fact, been (among other things) a *lieutenant de torpilleur* in the French navy.

Yet when, not far short of forty, he gave up the sea for the profession of letters, having (unlike Flaubert) married, and being (again unlike Flaubert) faced with earning a living and supporting a family, the career he embraced was that of a creative writer in the English language. We have his own word for it that, where the language was concerned, there was no choice: he didn't adopt the English language, but was adopted by it, and (he affirmed) if he hadn't written in English he wouldn't have written at all. True, Ford suggests that such pronouncements must be discounted in the light of the circumstances (the 1914 war), and Conrad's ardour of devotion to his adopted country. Ford says that French, he thinks, always retained a certain priority for Conrad: for expression in speech, and so, presumably, for thought, it came to him with a more 'native' readiness. And we have to grant that Gallicisms can be found on almost every page of Conrad's writing. Nevertheless, his best prose, that in which his great work is written, must for most of us give a convincing force to his own attestations: we cannot think of it as anything but the prose of a very distinguished creative writer whose living, feeling, and remembering have been done in English – the Gallicisms go for nothing. Consider, for instance, the opening of *The Shadow-Line* – or any other passage of that tale. I pick on the tale because it is one of Conrad's supreme things, and it lends itself peculiarly well to use for corrective illustration when one is dealing with various current misconceptions about Conrad. Its prose is idiomatic, unrhetorical, livingly sensitive in rhythm and nuance, and, while free from any touch of 'style' or fine writing, intensely personal, so that you could tell any paragraph of it for Conrad at a glance.

If the prose of *Nostromo* strikes one as more formal, that is not because it doesn't in essentials answer to the description I have just given, but because *Nostromo* represents a different kind of undertaking from *The Shadow-Line*. This latter is one of his *nouvelles* – I use the French term to denote those tales of Conrad's which are long enough to be printed and bound separately, but which are really long short stories rather than novels. The distinction is an important one. Conrad was a great master of the *nouvelle*; some of his finest work is in that form. But he was also a very great novelist, and his standing as one of the great creative writers in the language rests mainly upon the massive achievement represented by five major works that can be described as classic novels. They are *Nostromo* (1903), *The Secret Agent* (1907), *Under Western Eyes* (1911), *Chance* (1913), and *Victory* (1915). Of these, *Nostromo* is in formal organization the most elaborate, and represents the most ambitious undertaking. Conrad, I think, was right in regarding it as his greatest creation, and it seems to me one of the world's great novels.

As for *The Shadow-Line*, not only is it a *nouvelle*; it has (while being a superb work of art) a clear autobiographical quality – it comes directly out of Conrad's personal life, and records a critical experience in his own development. The effect of a comparatively informal freedom not suggesting any Flaubertian spirit of 'art' goes with this autobiographically – or confessionally – personal directness and inwardness. The tale seems to me the best of Conrad's *nouvelles*, and I underline it because it provides an admirable criterion for discriminating among his tales in general. Those who perceive the kind of masterpiece it is will not be inclined to offer us *The Nigger of the 'Narcissus'* or *Youth* as giving us a representative idea of Conrad's genius. That they *are* so often offered us as such illustrates the power of one of the misconceptions from which Conrad has suffered: he is thought of as a 'writer about the sea'. The characteristic that made me pick on *The Shadow-Line* is not there in *The Nigger of the 'Narcissus'*, which is wholly about simple seamen as such, the much played-up mystery of the protagonist imposing no qualification of this account. *The Shadow-Line*, on the other hand, gives the subtle drama of thought and feeling in the young ship's captain who is the narrator. This young captain is introspective, highly sensitive, and an intellectual. In fact, he gives us immediately and pretty fully the complex Joseph Conrad.

One could hardly, however, have divined from the tale the range of interests and the power to present them in a closely organized work of impersonal art that are demonstrated in *Nostromo*. This book gives us with astonishing vividness the picturesque and violent drama of a South American state. It is Conrad's supreme triumph in the evocation of exotic life and colour, and he must have known that, as such, it was qualified to have won envious praise from Flaubert. As a whole, in fact, *Nostromo* is the most Flaubertian of Conrad's works. But Conrad's art serves a full engagement in life, and (whatever the intensity of concern for 'form') an art of which *that* can be said is radically unlike Flaubert's.

Nostromo has a public, or political, theme, which is represented by the Gould Concession, and the part that it plays in the revolutionary politics of Sulaco: the relation between material and moral interests. Charles Gould, the 'Costaguana Englishman', states the idealistic, or sanguine, view of this relation: 'What is wanted here is law, good faith, order, security . . . Only let the material interests once get a firm footing, and they are bound to impose the conditions on which alone they can continue to exist. That's how your money-making is justified here in the face of lawlessness and disorder.' But the theme as acted out in the total drama is a profound irony. The idealizing Charles Gould has for associate in his enterprise the American financier Holroyd, who, by seeing them as subserving the promotion of a 'pure form of Christianity', makes a virtue out of the profitable use of his millions. At the end of the book, when the revolution has taken place and brought about the triumph of order and ideals, the people are nursing a sullen grudge against the 'liberal' regime (identified with privilege and exploitation), and the workers of the silver mine, as Doctor Monygham ironically points out, could most certainly *not* be counted on to rise and march (as they had done in furtherance of the revolution) to the defence of their *señor administrador*, Charles Gould. Further, at the personal level, Gould's idealistic devotion to the mine has led him insidiously into a kind of infidelity to his wife, whom we see spending her days in starved loneliness.

The Gould Concession, in fact, is in the first place the personal history of its inheritor Charles Gould (and the tragedy of his wife). And here we have an instance of the way in which *Nostromo* is organized: the public theme is presented in terms of a number of personal histories, each one of which gives us what can be called a private theme. These histories are of the main characters, each of whom enacts a particular answer to the question: what do men find to live *for* – what kind of motive force or radical attitude can give life meaning or direction? Charles Gould's antithesis (and contemptuous critic) is the French Martin Decoud, 'dilettante in life', and the voice of sceptical intelligence. He scorns the self-deceiving sentimentality of the Anglo-Saxon, dupe of ideals – if sometimes, oddly enough, seeming to get a mysterious strength from them. Marooned for a few days on the small island in the gulf, he discovers that his own presumed self-sufficiency was an illusion. Believing in nothing but the 'truth of his sensations', he feels *that* turning into illusion as his identity slips away from him. His sensations cease to be *his*. As his aloneness continues, he feels his identity merging into the surroundings – a sensation he cannot bear:

he blows his brains out. The whole thing is done with disturbing power. It is the most sharply focused instance in Conrad's work of that theme which he deals with so often: isolation, and the collaborative nature of the individual life even when its most intimate inner aspects are in question. Here we have the insight and the testimony of the deracinated exile, who had learned from deprivation and strain and suffered by himself.

Along with this poignant mastery of the theme of isolation (it recurs in different forms in *Nostromo*) goes Conrad's intense imaginative interest in the varying role of ideals, and of the importance for the individual life of what, for himself, was most vividly represented by the ship, and the code of the merchant service. Readers of *Nostromo* will note that, seaman though he (Conrad) may have been, his attitude is not a simple one, and that in the matter of 'ideals', for instance, his wisdom – and he strikes one as wise – cannot be easily summed up. The total irony of the book undoubtedly conveys a criticism of Charles Gould. On the other hand, Gould's critic, Decoud, the man without ideals, can by no reader be taken as charged with Conrad's approval. The idealist who is consistently impressive and shown in a wholly sympathetic light is Giorgio Viola, the old Garibaldino. But he, monumental survivor of the old heroic days, belongs to a world that clearly has little bearing on the conditions we are confronted with in *Nostromo*. Nostromo himself is another simple figure. Picturesque man of action and popular hero, he knows that he lives 'to be well spoken of' – that is, in and for his reflection in the eyes of others. His theft of the silver, committing him to furtive ways, takes the force out of his mainspring. His opposite, Doctor Monygham, cares, as only an idealist could, for nothing but his reflection in his own eyes. And he is self-contemptuous, having, under torture, offended against his ideal ('officer and gentleman'). His success in the desperate venture that saves the situation depends on his being ready to be ill-spoken of and ill-thought of – on, that is, his reputation for 'unsoundness' and a shady past. It is certainly a triumph of idealism, and the irony doesn't diminish it.

These notes sufficiently suggest the nature of the whole patterned interplay of theme, and the only other theme-actor I will mention is Captain Mitchell ('Fussy Joe'). If he represents an ideal, it is the merchant service, and irony plays a large part here. Like Captain MacWhirr of *Typhoon*, he is unimaginative, sane, and stable to the point of stupidity. These qualifications qualify him for the essential part he plays in the total irony, as the eloquently reminiscent, triumphant, and uncomprehending eye-witnesses of the revolution. (Conrad's reversal of the time-order in thus disclosing the success of the revolution to us will be seen to be an essential condition of the total irony.)

No other of Conrad's five classic novels, which are all very different, has anything like this close patterned structure, or this range. At the other extreme from *Nostromo* is *Victory*, presenting the case of the dominant character, Heyst the 'English-speaking Swede', who is clearly very close to Conrad the cosmopolitan intellectual. The whole book gives us an intensive and profound study of the isolation theme. The theme is central again to *Chance*, where it appears in the moral isolation of the financier-convict's child, Flora de Barral. The isolation theme has again a searching and poignant treatment in *Under Western Eyes*, where it is represented by the student Razumov. In this book, the 'western eyes' of a Pole are turned upon Czarist and revolutionary Russia. *The Secret Agent* can be described as a melodramatic thriller, and it is perhaps the supreme ironical novel in the language.

In justice to Conrad it will be well to be explicit about the inferiority of both his earliest and his latest books. The two early ones, *Almayer's Folly* and *An Outcast of the Islands*, are certainly not among the classics of the language, and will hardly be found very interesting by most admirers of *Nostromo*. The novels written – or finished (for there was work that had been on the stocks many years) – after the 1914 war came from a very tired man. *The Arrow of Gold* contains some interesting autobiography, but is not one of Conrad's great novels. *The Rescue* and *The Rover* hardly matter.

Henry James's first novel: *Roderick Hudson*

Mr John Lehmann is to be thanked for putting *Roderick Hudson* into circulation. Perhaps it will now be read. And if it is read – really read – it will cause some surprised enjoyment. For its reputation has not been of a kind to get it picked out from among the shelf-fulls of Henry James in the library. The current impression since James began to 'come in' has been, I think, that *Roderick Hudson* is at best no better than negligible – just what you would expect a first novel to be. After the war of 1914, sampling some lecture courses for the English Tripos, I went to one on 'The Modern Novel', given by the young advanced intellectual, the intransigent anti-academic, of the day and a good index of what 'the few who can talk intelligently' (etc.) were saying, and he told us how James, in revising, had changed Roderick's exclamation' 'It's like something in a novel', into 'It's like something in a bad novel'. Nothing more, one gathered, needed saying: here was the authoritative dismissal.

Actually, that reading of the revision is utterly unwarranted. As Mr Michael Swan, adducing evidence, tells us in the introductory note to the present edition, Henry James, looking back, thought highly of this early work. This is not surprising: *Roderick Hudson* is an extremely interesting and extremely distinguished novel. For a first novel it is very remarkable indeed – remarkable in its maturity and in its accomplishment. And it was written in the mid-Victorian age – begun in 1874, when *Daniel Deronda*, which was to influence James so profoundly, had not yet appeared. Of the English novelists of his time, his seniors or coevals, George Eliot alone can be thought of as having much in the way of instruction and incitement to give a writer bent, as James was, on making the writing of novels a completely serious art, and there is no reason for seeing *Roderick Hudson* as markedly indebted to her. The debt that can, as I shall show later, be noted is to Dickens, in whom no one will suppose James to have found the model or the inspiration for an art addressed consistently and calculatingly to the adult mind, and demanding its sustained critical attention. In *Roderick Hudson*, when all criticisms have been urged, we have such an art, so that James's first novel has better claims to classical currency

– is more worth reading and re-reading than the greater number of Victorian fictions that are commonly offered us as classics.

James has a real theme – a theme qualified to engage the full powers of a highly intelligent mind, widely experienced and profoundly interested in human potentialities. What is astonishing is that, in his first 'attempt' (his own words), he should have been able to show so sufficient an answering mastery of art. For, in spite of shortcomings that he himself notes in the late Preface, *Roderick Hudson* is, substantially, an achieved work. It exhibits no crudities, no redundancies, and no uncertainties of purpose. The technical preoccupation is already most distinctively Jamesian. It is true that what particularly strike one as characteristic felicities in the writing turn out again and again to have come in with the late revision, yet it didn't need this to make the writing wonderfully intelligent, brilliant and sensitive.

If one took one's cue from the title – and it is remarkable what persistent anaesthesias can plead no better excuse – one might judge that James had been overweening in his choice of theme. Imagine a sculptor-born, but born in a small town of pristine New England. Transported in early manhood to Europe, to Rome, how will he respond to the sudden impact of 'an immemorial, a complex and accumulated civilization', with all its visible witness, its overwhelming revelation, of art. (In Rowland Mallet's praise 'he had heard absolutely for the first time in his life the voice of taste and authority'.) It is an interesting idea, but how, one might comment, could it conceivably be *done*, seeing that to *do* the postulated genius is obviously impossible – postulated is all it can, in the nature of things, be? Isn't it a mark of the young James's callowness that he shouldn't have seen the disqualifying force of this objection? He was indeed in later years, in some of his best *nouvelles*, to deal successfully with the writer as writer; but writing was something he knew from the inside – *that* was his genius, and it had a major part in his life. But what did he know about sculpture or the visual arts? Wasn't his very ignorance, or naïvety, about them a condition of the confidence with which he committed himself to the undertaking? This is the best he can do by way of evoking one of Roderick's masterpieces (the bust of Christina Light):

The bust was in fact a very happy performance – Roderick had risen to the level of his subject. It was thoroughly a portrait, – not a vague fantasy executed on a graceful theme, as the busts of pretty women in modern sculpture are apt to be. The resemblance was close and firm; inch matched inch, item with item, grain with grain, yet all to fresh creation. It succeeded by an exquisite art in representing without extravagance something that transcended and exceeded.

Even as strengthened in the revised phrasing – it ran earlier: 'there was extreme fidelity of detail, and yet a noble simplicity. One could say that, without idealization, it was a representation of ideal beauty' – this kind of thing hardly helps our conventional assent to the postulate. And isn't James disablingly romantic in his notion of creative genius? Isn't he merely offering us in his Roderick Hudson – incontinently 'spontaneous' and, when the afflatus comes, an inspired *enfant terrible*, but otherwise childish in irresponsibility, moody and inflammable – a conventional 'artistic temperament', and asking us to believe that great works of art can issue out of that?

But to criticize the book on these lines is to ignore what it actually offers. As James himself says in the late Preface, 'the centre of interest throughout . . . is in Rowland Mallet's consciousness' – 'and this in spite of the title of the book'. What he tells us he aimed at doing is what, with an art already extraordinarily Jamesian and mature, he has done. Rowland's consciousness was to be not 'too acute', but 'a sufficiently clear medium to present a whole'. 'This whole was to be the sum of what "happened" to him, or in other words his total adventure; but as what happened to him was above all to feel certain things happening to others, to Roderick, to Christina, to Mary Garland, to Mrs Hudson, to the Cavaliere, to the Prince, so the beauty of the constructional game was to preserve in everything its especial value for *him.*'

James in telling us this is explaining how it should be that the weakness he remarks in the treatment of Roderick, whose break-up under exposure to Europe occurs too rapidly, isn't fatal to the book. The same considerations explain why the offer to make creative genius, in the person of a sculptor, a major actor in the drama wasn't disastrous. What had to be conveyed was the impression on Rowland Mallet – *his* conviction confirmed by that of the world in general that peoples Rowland's drama; and that one must judge to be sufficiently *done*. Nor is any crudely romantic notion of genius endorsed by James or by Rowland. In fact, to explore the nature of genius is one of the aims of the book, and a questioning of the relation of creative power to the 'artistic temperament' constitutes one of Rowland's central preoccupations. He is surprised, disconcerted and shocked by the progressive exposure of Roderick's lack of ballast and excess of egotism and irresponsibility. He had believed in the 'essential salubrity of genius', and we have every reason for associating him with Mary Garland when we learn about her that she 'had supposed genius to be to one's spiritual economy what a large balance at the bank is to one's domestic'. Such an assumption clearly doesn't strike James as merely a revelation of naïvety.

There is characteristic Jamesian art in the way in which Roderick is played off on the one hand against Sam Singleton, developing a small talent with conscientious and pedestrian industry, and, on the other, against Gloriani, who represents 'art with a mixed motive, skill unleavened by faith, the mere base maximum of cleverness' – represents the sophistication and corruption of cosmopolitan Europe. 'He had a definite, practical scheme of art, and he knew at least what he meant. In this sense he was almost too knowing.' (There is, too, paired against Singleton, another kind of accomplished limitation: mere academic industry, in the person of the innocent and skilful Miss Blanchard.) By his dramatic and poetic methods James is clearly working towards the suggestion of a positive idea of genius that agrees pretty much with Mary Garland's. Again and again the critical and constructive intention becomes explicit in dramatic utterances or reported reflections, as for instance the letter to his cousin Cecilia in which Rowland writes: 'I think it established that in the long run egotism (in too big a dose) makes a failure in conduct; is it also true that it makes a failure in the arts?'

But we have here only part of the theme or system of interests that gives *Roderick Hudson* its life, organization and significance. The 'drama' of 'Rowland Mallet's consciousness' enacts, in James's first novel, that critical-constructive preoccupation with the 'international theme' which is so radically and persistently characteristic of James's own genius. Rowland Mallet, with the significantly mixed ancestry of which we are so carefully told, has been 'brought up to think much more intently of the duties of our earthly pilgrimage than of its privileges and pleasures'. Become a man of independent means, with no need or call to work, he devotes himself to his un-Puritanic interest in art, but suspects all the same that 'he wholly lacks the prime requisite of an expert *flâneur* – the simple, sensuous, confident relish of pleasure'. He is 'for ever looking for the uses of the things that please and the charm of the things that sustain'.

As even these brief quotations suggest (especially the second), James's attitude towards America – here, of course, it is New England in particular – isn't a simple one. Nor is his attitude towards Europe. What he dramatizes in this novel, as in later ones, is a complex process of comparative appraisal, out of which emerges the suggestion of an ideal positive that is neither Europe nor America. Of the aspect of American civilization represented by Mr Leavenworth James may be said to be simply critical; the satire 'places' unambiguously, and there is little suggestion of any compensating entry to be made on the other side of the account:

Mr Leavenworth was a tall, expansive, bland gentleman, with a carefully-brushed whisker and a spacious, fair, well-favoured face, which seemed somehow to have more room in it than was occupied by a smile of superior benevolence, so that (with his smooth white forehead) it bore a certain resemblance to a large parlour with a very florid carpet, but without mural decoration. He held his head high, talked impressively, and told Roderick within five minutes that he was a widower travelling to distract his mind, and that he had lately retired from the proprietorship of large mines of borax in the Middle West. Roderick supposed at first that under the influence of his bereavement he had come to order a tombstone; but observing the extreme benevolence of his address to Miss Blanchard he credited him with a judicious prevision that on the day the tombstone should be completed a monument of his inconsolability might appear mistimed. Mr Leavenworth, however, was disposed to give an Order, – to give it with a capital letter.

'You'll find me eager to patronise our indigenous talent', he said. 'You may be sure that I've employed a native architect for the large residential structure that I'm erecting on the banks of the Ohio. I've sustained a considerable loss; but are we not told that the office of art is second only to that of religion? That's why I have come to you, sir. In the retreat that I'm preparing, surrounded by the memorials of my wanderings, I hope to recover a certain degree of tone. They're doing what they can in Paris for the fine effect of some of its features; but the effect I have myself most at heart will be that of my library, filled with well-selected and beautifully-bound authors in groups relieved from point to point by high-class statuary. I should like to entrust you, can we arrange it, with the execution of one of these appropriate subjects. What do you say to a representation, in pure white marble, of the idea of Intellectual Refinement?'

'Whose idea, sir?' Roderick asked. 'Your idea?'

But at this question, and especially at a certain sound in it, Mr Leavenworth looked a little blank. Miss Blanchard artfully interposed. 'I wish I could induce Mr Hudson to think he might perhaps do something with mine!'

It immediately relieved the tension and made Mr Hudson consider her with great gravity. 'If your idea resembles your personal type, Miss Blanchard, I quite *see* my figure. I close with you on Intellectual Refinement, Mr Leavenworth, if this lady will sit for us.'

I have quoted this passage at some length, because it illustrates well James's debt to Dickens. Dickens couldn't have written it; it comes from a more cultivated mind. ('Whose idea, sir?' Roderick asked. 'Your idea?'.) Yet the debt to *Martin Chuzzlewit* is unmistakable, and it is plain that what James got from Dickens was not merely a manner, but a cue for 'placing' critically certain aspects of the American scene. (Much could be written on this debt in relation to James's later work.)

But mostly what James sees in America calls for more complex and delicate attitudes than that of *Martin Chuzzlewit*, even when it calls for the satirically critical note. Mr Striker, for instance, (see chapter 3) is a different case from Mr Leavenworth:

'An antique, as I understand it,' the lawyer continued, 'is an image of a pagan deity, with considerable dirt sticking to it, and no arms, no nose and no clothing. A precious model, certainly!'

*   *   *

'Now this study of the living model,' Mr Striker pursued. 'Give Mrs Hudson a sketch of that.'

'Oh dear, no!' cried Mrs Hudson shrinkingly.

'That too,' said Rowland, 'is one of the reasons for studying in Rome. It's a handsome race, you know, and you find very well-made people.'

'I suppose they're no better than a good tough Yankee,' objected Mr Striker, transposing his interminable legs. 'The same God made us!'

It might seem that the entry was to be made all on one side here too. But by the time we have read Mr Striker's closing speech we are aware that the business of appraisal is not so simple as that:

I didn't go to any part of Europe to learn my business; no one took me by the hand; I had to grease my wheels myself, and such as I am, I'm a self-made man, every inch of me! Well, if our young friend's booked for fame and fortune I don't suppose his going to Rome will stop him. But, mind you, it won't help him such a long way neither. If you've undertaken to put him through there's a thing or two you had better remember. The crop we gather depends upon the seed we sow. He may be the biggest genius of the age: his potatoes won't come up without his hoeing them. If he takes things so almighty easy as – well, as one or two young fellows of genius I've had under my eye – his produce will never gain the prize. Take the word for it of a man who has made his way inch by inch and doesn't believe that we wake up to find our work done because we have lain all night a-dreaming of it: anything worth doing is plaguy hard to do!

Rowland makes the credit entry for us; he, we are told, 'could honestly reply that this seemed pregnant sense, and he offered Mr Striker a friendly hand-shake as the latter withdrew'.

But it is when we come to Mary Garland, the counter-figure to Christina Light, *femme fatale* and product and representative of corrupt and corrupting Europe, that we have the separating out of the American elements that James peculiarly values. 'Miss Garland,' says Mr Striker, introducing her, 'is the daughter of a minister, the grand-daughter of a minister, the sister of a minister.' That is, she is meant to give us the essential New England ethos, and her presentment expresses a positive and warmly sympathetic appreciation that fore-casts *The Europeans*. It was not long after the introduction before Rowland had 'passed from measuring contours to tracing meanings', for 'she appealed strongly to his sense of character'. She is very intelli-gent, and not at all incapable of developing an interest in art, as she proves when Roderick's collapse brings her, with his mother, to Rome. She concludes finally that 'man wasn't made to struggle so much and miss so much, but to ask of life as a matter of course some beauty and some charm'. But she is incorruptible. And James clearly admires with Rowland 'the purity and rigidity of a mind that had not lived with its door ajar upon the high-road of cosmopolite chatter, for passing phrases to drop in and out at their pleasure, but that had none the less looked out, from the threshold, for any straggler on the "march of ideas", any limping rumour or broken-winged echo of life, that would stop and be cherished as a guest'. For James she clearly represents a cherished possibility – a distinctively American possibility: 'She might have been originally as angular as he had, on the other scene, liked her for being; but who was to say now what mightn't result from the cultivation in her of a motive for curves?'

Mary Garland may not be as positively a triumph as Christina Light, yet she is not a failure. Her part in any case isn't to hold the limelight. James himself in the Preface questions the convincingness of her relations with Roderick. Wasn't it too convenient that Roderick just at that improbable moment (as James sees it) should imagine himself to fall in love with such a girl, and so effectively, with ironic consequences for Rowland? But, whatever weaknesses may be detected in it, *Roderick Hudson* is a most interesting success. It is a minor work in the Jamesian *œuvre*; but even in comparison with the great things it deserves better than to be spoken of slightingly.

Yeats: the problem and the challenge

Yeats, for all his conviction of an essential affinity, was radically unlike Blake. I have marked a score or two of places in the collected poems where that comment has occurred to me. I start with it because it is certainly something that needs to be said, and because in an attempt to define Yeats's poetic character it must be a key emphasis. Not that I am going to develop it, or shall treat the theme systematically in any part of this lecture. Having introduced it in this way I shall be able to pick it up from time to time and it will be all the while implicitly present; at least, I mean it to be.

An undertaking of the kind to which I am committed has its own necessities of approach and procedure. I am committed, I had been inclined to say, to some rashness; but 'rashness' suggests irresponsibility, so I withdraw the word. What I must aim at is a quintessential economy, and it demands that I should be peculiarly responsible. The invitation I accepted to give this lecture came to me as a challenge, and I accepted it, not merely because of the flattering terms in which it was framed, but because I had already myself issued the challenge. I had told myself more than once that all those years (now a third of a century) having passed since, in the earliest beginnings of the recognition of Yeats as a major twentieth-century poet, I had with some care expressed my sense of what he had achieved and where he stood, I ought, now that his work had been long completed, and my notes and hieroglyphs had thickened in the margins, to attempt a *compte rendu* – something both bold and precise – once again. The precision aimed at entails economy, and the economy entails hazards – or, at any rate, in a world where there are many Yeats specialists (a portentous change since I first wrote on Yeats) one will necessarily seem to be 'asking for it'. There must be bold judgments, but they will have to rest on a minimal and highly selective presentation of the grounds.

We *have* now all the *œuvre*. That itself affects one's sense of Yeats – for there are significant developments. I have re-read him a good deal in recent years; I have discussed him this past academic year with keen and well-read undergraduates at my new university; and I have gone through and pondered the whole body of poems. My sense of Yeats and of his place in English literature hasn't changed much. But I now lay more emphasis on the question: How much of the fully achieved thing *is* there in Yeats's *œuvre* – what proportion of the wholly created poem that stands there unequivocally in its own right, self-sufficient? I have in mind the period of his work in which he challenges us to think of him as a major poet. And it seems to me that the proportion is not large.

And there is the problem I had in view in my title. It is a problem of critical statement that is (which is why it matters) one of critical *compte rendu* – the problem of arriving at a clear critical recognition of just what Yeats's achievement was. For confusion is very possible, and confusion is a bad thing. It tends, I think, to prevail – which is bad (shall I say) for the causes to which Yeats devoted his life. To have started as a belated Victorian Romantic poet, to have won a distinctive place as such, and then to have developed a poetic as decidedly twentieth-century and post-Edwardian as Eliot's – that is a great achievement. Expression is only altered by a man of genius – Eliot's own dictum, as you know: Yeats too had genius. To describe the alteration he effected isn't a simple matter, and to say this is a compliment. The poetic he created for himself has considerable variety, range and flexibility. In touch with the spoken living language and the speaking voice, it admits of many tones and the expression of complex and subtly changing attitudes. There is no element of a man's experience in the twentieth century that, of its nature, it excludes.

Yet one couldn't in 1919, when I began to read seriously in contemporary literature, have attributed any such achievement to Yeats, who had then been writing through three full decades, and was forming the habit of presenting himself in his verse (an un-Blakelike characteristic) as an aging man. He had already been going a long while, and was an established name, when I first began reading poetry as a boy – say seven or eight years before the war. The poems by which he was known were congenial to the late Victorian taste of that Edwardian–Georgian period, and, in spite of the suggestion of ancient and obscure Irishness, presented no difficulty. In their hypnoidal vaguenesses ('dim', 'dream-pale') and incantatory rhythms they exemplify that preoccupation with creating a dream world, or poetic otherworld, which Eliot in a famous essay noted as a characteristic of Victorian poetry.

In 1919, from when my continuous cultivated interest in modern poetry dates, I read *The Wild Swans at Coole*, and I read Middleton Murry's review of it in the *Athenaeum*. I thought it, and still think it, a very good review (it is to be found in *Aspects of Literature*). It is entitled 'Mr Yeats's Swan Song' and in it Murry says: 'He remains an artist by determination, even though he returns downcast and depressed from the great quest of poetry', and 'His sojourn in the world of the imagination, far from enriching his vision, has made it infinitely tenuous'. Contemplating such poems as 'I am Worn Out with Dreams' and 'The Collar-Bone of a Hare', Murry says 'Not even the regret is passionate; it is pitiful . . . It is pitiful because, even now in spite of all his honesty, the poet mistakes the cause of his sorrow. He is worn out not with dreams, but with the vain effort to master them and submit them to his own creative energy. He has not subdued them nor built a new world for them; he has merely followed them like will-o'-the-wisps away from the world he knows. Now, possessing neither world, he sits by the edge of a barren road that vanishes into a no-man's-land, where there is no future, and whence there is no way back to the past.' Murry doesn't say anything about developments, in the collections leading up to this latest, towards a new art of poetic expression, post-Victorian and post-nineties, but who at that date would, or could, have done? For who could then have seen in Yeats the potentiality of a major poet?

It was *The Tower*, coming – most remarkable fact – when Yeats was over sixty, that made the difference. The hindsight then became poss-ible with the advantage of which one saw point – in fact, a decided critical interest – in tracing the development of Yeats's poetic from *The Wind Among the Reeds* onwards; for one saw that there had been a development into such command of expression as implied, for con-summation and *raison d'être*, a modern major poetry. It isn't essential for my inevitably limited purpose to attempt the tracing. That purpose entails an insistence, very necessary (may I be allowed to say?) now that the study of Yeats as a major poet has become an academic insti-tution, on the firm and clear recognition without which such an inquiry can't be undertaken intelligently, and with critical profit.

It is important to insist, then, that Yeats's great poems aren't many. It doesn't follow that only they are worth having. But the interest of the total *œuvre*, an intelligent appreciation of the significance and genuine value, depends on one's being clear about the restrictive effect of the most essential kind of evaluative judgment. Yeats's great poems are a very small proportion of the whole. It is an immediately relevant point – and I speak with the emphasis of personal experience when I say this – that it was the appearance of *The Tower* in 1928 that made it possible to think of claiming for Yeats the status of a modern poet who demanded to be considered along with Eliot.

I remember vividly the impact of *The Tower*, of which I have a first edition, acquired in the way in which I have acquired such first editions as I have had – I bought it when it came out. There, at the very beginning of the book, was one of Yeats's major successes; there was one of his great poems – the first that one was to know: 'Sailing to Byzantium'. I see that, troubled as I am by the problem of economy, I must give this poem some particular attention. The troubling force of the problem immediately is that I know I can't find time to read out the uninterrupted whole either first or finally, but must confine myself to reading the poem in bits, with breaks for commentary. But I can assume that, as an organically knit whole, it is familiar enough to prevail against the disruptive process. Before starting I will make some general observations that would not have been preliminary if there had been time for me to read the poem out first.

The distinctively post-Victorian kind of organic complexity that Yeats has here achieved is suggested when one says that 'Sailing to Byzantium' lends itself as little to paraphrase as Eliot's almost contemporary 'Marina' does. It one tries to render the sense in prose one finds very soon that one is committed to exegesis and the description of an organization that is utterly unproselike. The impulsions and interests out of which the poem comes are those which we know as the inveterate Yeatsian themes – these form the thematic material (for, in emphasizing the essentially unproselike mode – which nevertheless demands the full waking attention of the thinking mind, one can't help invoking the musical analogy).

There are, given added poignancy by the nostalgia for lost youth, the compelling values represented by the words 'love' and 'life'; there is the recoil from transience and age; and there is the preoccupation with the eternal – an escape from transience and an assurance of a real reality that shall transcend time. The poem is an organic structure of the motions, the impulsions, the recoils and contradictions and incompatibles, suggested by that account. The contradictions and incompatibles are reconciled only in that they make a compelling, or convincing poem; problems are evoked with intensity, but there is no solution. The poem is convincing; it satisfies as a tense and vital tonality. Nothing could be less like Johnson's conception of an acceptable poem – or, to take a distinguished and sophisticated mind of a nearer age (I as an editor had the honour of printing him once), George Santayana's. For them the poet should know beforehand what his thought is to be and what his conclusions. But Yeats in such a poem as 'Sailing to Byzantium' discovers, or determines (for 'discover' suggests a kind of conscious recognition there may never have been), where he stands in relation to thought, conclusion and belief as he composes – in the composing: the process of composition, a matter of much piecing, patching and redrafting, is the process of discovery or determination.

And this is the moment at which to say that too often Yeats, working at a poem, lets his extra-poetic habits get in the way of poetic success. 'Poetic success' here means a kind of convincingness and inevitability that comes of, that *is*, a complete sincerity – the sincerity that is of the whole being, and not merely a matter of conscious intention. To explain what I mean by 'extra-poetic' habits I need only point to *A Vision*, that representative of a lifelong quasi-creative addiction which was not sharply or surely distinguished by Yeats from his real creative concern. That Yeats had this addiction, and the addictions to the occult and the esoteric that went with it, is an important datum; the evidence is there in various ways in his poetry. And I am not saying anything so simple as that they are all to be regretted and wished away. But I do say that there is no good reason for supposing that one need study the schematisms, the diagrammatics, the symbolical elaborations to which Yeats devoted so much of his energy. At a time when the professional study of literature has grown so portentously there is point in putting aside the refinements and qualifications possible in a fuller statement and insisting, with emphasis, that a close critical appreciation of a successful poem of Yeats doesn't require that one should bring up any special knowledge or instructions from outside. One can invoke Coleridge's well-known dictum to the effect that a poem should contain within itself the reason why it is so and not otherwise. To suppose that Yeats is a special case to which this doesn't apply is a mischievous delusion – a point to which I shall revert.

I will now read the opening stanza of 'Sailing to Byzantium':

> That is no country for old men. The young
> In one another's arms, birds in the trees,
> – Those dying generations – at their song,
> The salmon-falls, the mackerel-crowded seas,
> Fish, flesh, or fowl, commend all summer long
> Whatever is begotten, born, and dies.
> Caught in that sensual music all neglect
> Monuments of unaging intellect.

The poet is so clearly drawn to what in that stanza he evokes with such force and poignancy that when one comes to the 'Monuments of unaging intellect' one can't help taking them with an ironical effect of *pis-aller*. And a sardonic irony will indeed be found to have had a determining part in the total effect of the poem. Nevertheless the second stanza makes it plain that the concern for the eternal has not, after all, been summarily 'placed':

> An aged man is but a paltry thing,
> A tattered coat upon a stick, unless
> Soul clap its hands and sing, and louder sing,

> For every tatter in its mortal dress,
> Nor is there singing school but studying
> Monuments of its own magnificence;
> And therefore I have sailed the seas and come
> To the holy city of Byzantium.

The very frankness of the opening – 'An aged man is but a paltry thing . . . *unless*' – serves to emphasize the positiveness of the belief, or emotional investment, represented by 'monuments' while this mood prevails. The stanza, as one can't but illustrate in reading it out, moves forward with a lift the significance of which is unmistakable. The 'singing' of 'singing school' invests the 'studying', paradoxically, with the evoked gladness and life-affirmation of the first stanza, so associating the 'monuments' with a suggested higher life that shall transcend the disadvantages fated to the generations of 'whatever is begotten, born, and dies'. 'Byzantium', a symbol both pregnant and indeterminate, has for its clear immediate function to suggest the antithesis of the world of nature – the world of 'those dying generations'. Why the poet should have found the indeterminateness congenial to his need comes out in the next stanza:

> O sages standing in God's holy fire
> As in the gold mosaic of a wall,
> Come from the holy fire, perne in a gyre,
> And be the singing-masters of my soul.
> Consume my heart away; sick with desire
> And fastened to a dying animal
> It knows not what it is; and gather me
> Into the artifice of eternity.

We know by now that, whatever the total effect of the poem may turn out to be, it will hardly be affirmation. The poet's heart 'knows not what it is' nor what it wants, and the theme (if that is the word) or burden of the poem is the given kind of poignant, and humanly representative, indeterminateness. Intensely the soul interrogates itself and its images of fulfilment and finds no answer that doesn't turn into an irony.

> . . . sick with desire
> And fastened to a dying animal

– the ambiguity is essential and undeniable: Which is it – nostalgia for that country which is not for old men, or nostalgia for the eternal posited as the antithesis? The poet couldn't, I think, have said, and in any case the question isn't his but ours. The poem gives us the ambiguity; and then, we note, the invocation of the sages completes itself and the stanza with the appeal to

> . . . gather me
> Into the artifice of eternity,

about which the important thing to say is, not that it's a resolution, but
that it's the ambiguity turning into an irony. The ironical force of
'artifice' is developed in the last stanza. It is a felicity of surprise that
illustrates well the 'metaphysical' suppleness of Yeats's mature poetic
art:

> Once out of nature I shall never take
> My bodily form from any natural thing,
> But such a form as Grecian goldsmiths make
> Of hammered gold and gold enamelling
> To keep a drowsy emperor awake;
> Or set upon a golden bough to sing
> To lords and ladies of Byzantium
> Of what is past, or passing, or to come.

The 'monuments of unaging intellect' with all the impressive associ-
ations of Byzantium – esoteric wisdom, metaphysico-theosophical cult
and mystery, hieratic art – have been reduced to a clockwork toy, and
the song of this now (after the promise of the 'singing school' in stanza
III) represents the higher life or reality that was to compensate for the
lost song of those 'dying generations'. The duplicity of the last line
gives the completing touch to the irony:

> Of what is past, or passing, or to come.

This retains, inevitably, something of the solemn vatic suggestion that
emanates from the foregoing poem. But what in its immediate context
of the closing half-stanza it evokes is court gossip.

I am not saying that the irony is the irony of one who passes an
ironical verdict and mocks (that stage comes later in Yeats). It is the
irony of a tormenting complexity of experience – a complexity that
entails an irreducible and tormenting contradiction of impulsions or
imperatives or verdicts. In the poem Yeats attains a tense and tentative
poise, but, as is intimated by the irony (unforeseen when he started,
we have reason from the drafts for guessing) in which the poem does
nevertheless in a natural way come to rest, this is no index of an
achieved stability. I open here what should be a major critical theme
for the student of Yeats, but obviously I can't do much by way of
developing it.

Something I can with economy do is to look comparatively at
'Byzantium', the closely related poem from *The Winding Stair*. I shall
at the same time be able to enforce and carry further another point I
have already made: 'Sailing to Byzantium' is (as a poem *should* be) self-

sufficient; it doesn't demand for its appreciation that one should bring up from outside any knowledge of special intentions on Yeats's part, or of the elaborate systems that form their context. When I first read the poem *The New English Dictionary* didn't help me with 'perne' ('perne in a gyre'), but I wasn't seriously troubled; the poetic context charged the word sufficiently for its function. Now that I *know* what 'perne' literally means the poem has gained nothing. On the contrary, not only would the pre-Yeatsian meaning be a nuisance in itself if thought of; the loaded 'perne' added to 'gyre' makes it more difficult for the reader to repress the movement of irritation aroused in him by the Yeatsian technicality of the phrase, which stands out from the poem, and proposes another context. But the major temptation to the exegete is 'Byzantium', though that symbol pretty obviously needs no commentary, since, for any educated person who can read poetry, it works without help as the poem requires. I say 'obviously', but the point I have to make is that the habit of specialist exegesis doesn't favour the recognition of a truth of that kind, critically important as it is.

This may be illustrated by the way in which the poem 'Byzantium' from *The Winding Stair* is commonly exalted above 'Sailing to Byzantium' – that, at least, is the impression I have brought away from the books on Yeats I have read. The accepted view, I gather, is that 'Byzantium', the later poem, is the 'richer' – I have seen that word used of it by more than one Yeatsian. It is a view that only the habit of the Yeats specialist can explain – the habit of taking the opportunities offered by the text to invoke Yeats's prose elaborations and bring into the poem what isn't there, and what one wouldn't take to be there if one were 'trusting' the poem (I invoke Lawrence). Respect for Yeats's genius dictates that one should if possible read his poems as poems. And if one reads 'Byzantium' as a poem one sees that the total attitude is, beyond question, comparatively simple.

One might very well say bluntly of this poem that its mood is sardonic bitterness. On the one hand, what is so irresistibly given in the opening stanza of 'Sailing to Byzantium' – 'the young in one another's arms', the sensual music – is virtually absent, and, on the other, where the eternal is concerned, there is no suggestion of soul's clapping its hands and singing. I will again read stanza by stanza, making the minimal commentary. Instead of the opening stanza I have just recalled we now have this:

> The unpurged images of day recede;
> The Emperor's drunken soldiery are abed;
> Night resonance recedes, night-walkers' song
> After great cathedral gong;

> A starlit or a moonlit dome disdains
> All that man is,
> All mere complexities,
> The fury and the mire of human veins.

The tone is given in that dominating rime-word 'disdains', which entails the following emphasis on 'All'. Ostensibly it defines the relation as now conceived or felt between 'all that man is' and the eternal. And all that man is reduces to:

> mere complexities,
> The fury and the mire of human veins.

The disdain goes with the bitterness that is a strong element in the poem. The one like the other is, in whatever way conveyed, Yeats's, and they relate to the other unBlakean characteristic, the pride that figures so much in the attitudes of Yeats's poetry.

This poem no more than 'Sailing to Byzantium' starts with a given foreseen balance of tones and stresses, a calculated total economy, in view. Its organization has nothing of the expository about it, and is not to be explained by reference to any supposed Yeatsian scheme in the background. It has the livingness of enacted self-discovery, brought by the technical skill of the poet to the satisfyingness of a completed poem – analogically a musical satisfyingness, and for us an index of sincerity. Yeats's poetic mastery appears in the delicate shifts of distance, tone and attack. So at the second stanza we have the change to the hushed, intent and personal; we are with Yeats at a séance, some experiment in magic and the occult, an invocation of the dead. Given in dramatic immediacy, there is the questioning of ontological status that greets, and takes stock of, the apparition:

> Before me floats an image, man or shade,
> Shade more than man, more image than a shade;
> For Hades' bobbin bound in mummy-cloth
> May unwind the winding path;
> A mouth that has no moisture and no breath
> Breathless mouths may summon . . .

Then, from the note of generalizing consideration into which the questioning has passed, the poet, as if arrived at a sudden resolution of doubt, breaks into action – for the effect on us is that:

> I hail the superhuman;
> I call it death-in-life and life-in-death.

Which is it? There is surely a difference. To 'hail the superhuman' as 'death-in-life' *and* 'life-in-death' with that air of ecstatic assurance is to transcend the balancing of doubt and belief in irony; to drop thought in an act, the act being an expression of intense sardonic bitterness.

This prevails through the rest of the poem. It is attributed in the next stanza, paralogically but the more significantly, to the golden toy, whose mechanical singing it is that now replaces that of the 'dying generations'. In a quasi-musical way the opening of the stanza echoes, with an effect of pointless ironic dryness, the ontological opening of the previous stanza:

> Miracle, bird or golden handiwork,
> More miracle than bird or handiwork,
> Planted on the star-lit golden bough,
> Can like the cocks of Hades crow,
> Or, by the moon embittered, scorn aloud
> In glory of changeless metal
> Common bird or petal
> And all complexities of mire or blood.

The great temptation to fully equipped commentators comes with the next stanza. But we don't all need the help they bring from Yeats's reading about Byzantium. In fact, in my own observation it serves only to distract the commentator from the actuality of Yeats's poetry, which is here not obscure. It doesn't matter from what reading, what tradition about spirits, purgation and the Emperor's pavement the memory came; the poetry that came of the memory is self-sufficient, and its significance clear. The 'flames that no faggot feeds' are the 'holy fire' from which the sages of the earlier poem are bidden to come and 'be the singing masters of my soul'. 'Flames begotten of flame', independent of matter, they represent a purely spiritual potency. The spirits *suffering* purgation are 'blood-begotten' – it is that body–soul antithesis which Yeats (unlike Blake in this too) finds so troubling. What, in the face of the exegetical habit, needs to be emphasized if one is concerned with poetic significance, is the evoked sense of agonized futility in which the stanza ends. This is what, in this self-imposed ordeal of self-questioning and self-realization (a major poem for Yeats *was* that), the hope of escaping from time and the complexities of mire and blood has become for him.

I have anticipated with my own comments in this way in order that I may go on to read the rest of the poem – two stanzas – to the close:

> At midnight on the Emperor's pavement flit
> Flames that no faggot feeds, nor steel has lit,
> Nor storm disturbs, flames begotten of flame,
> Where blood-begotten spirits come
> And all complexities of fury leave,
> Dying into a dance,

An agony of trance,
An agony of flame that cannot singe a sleeve.

Astraddle on the dolphin's mire and blood,
Spirit after spirit! The smithies break the flood,
The golden smithies of the Emperor!
Marbles of the dancing floor
Break bitter furies of complexity,
Those images that yet
Fresh images beget,
That dolphin-torn, that gong-tormented sea.

The nature and significance of the bitterness come out in the offer to reduce the 'dolphin' itself to mire and blood – for the traditional association of the dolphin, friend of man, with a vitality and a grace that are at the same time both physical and more than that is strong enough to insist on itself decisively here: there is discord.

The two 'Byzantium' poems, in their likeness and their difference, associate very closely and form together an impressive achievement. The quasi-musical way in which they treat their thematic material, organize their complexities of impulse and attitude, and bring together their tensions, contradictions and irreconcilables into satisfying totalities makes them triumphs of a wholly original art of creative expression that is contemporary with Eliot's. The originality is of the order that we know as the mark of genius; they are major poetry. Yet they stand apart; I know of no other successes of that kind in the collected volume of Yeats.

Why this should be so isn't hard to understand. 'Sailing to Byzantium' doesn't come out of any wholeness of being or mastery of experience; its poetic or quasi-musical satisfyingness as a totality is not an index of any permanent stability achieved by the poet in life. The contradictions, uncertainties and shifting stresses that, exploratorily, wondering what he is ('sick with desire, he knows not what he is'), Yeats for once succeeds – astonishingly at sixty – in dealing with creatively, don't favour the repetition of that kind of success. The energy that achieved it has become in 'Byzantium' unmistakably the energy of desperation, intense with the 'bitter furies of complexity'. He is ready to hand over to Crazy Jane and Jack the Journeyman, who represent the abandonment of all concern for the resolution, or paradoxically creative management, of the complexity.

It is characteristic of Yeats to have had no centre of unity, and to have been unable to find one. The lack is apparent in his solemn propoundings about the Mask and the Anti-self, and in the related schematic elaborations. It is there, an essential theme for the critic, in that habit of cultivating attitudes and postures which makes one – if an

Englishman, at any rate – remark that Yeats is a fellow-countryman of
Wilde, Shaw and Joyce (I am thinking of that photograph of Joyce
with his walking-stick outside Shakespeare and Co.). It is not a simple
theme; that is why it presents an essential interest for the critic. We
have something that is at least intimately associated with the habit in
Yeats's attainment of a poetic that enables him to be both noble and
distinctively twentieth-century. With the valid and impressive
nobility of *tenue* –

> Beauty like a tightened bow, a kind
> That is not natural in an age like this

– go the devotion to the ideal beauty here personified in Maud Gonne,
and the importance assigned to patrician 'civilization' as represented
by Coole Park and Lady Gregory. We may think that the relative
value-affirmations aren't, a mature scale of value and a mature experience being in question, altogether acceptable, but nevertheless we
have to testify that in Yeats's poetry certain genuine validities are, with
a poet's realizing force, presented creatively so as to be compelling in
themselves. But with the nobility goes the habit of aspiring to

> dine at journey's end
> With Landor and with Donne.

He owes something to both poets, but with the addiction to Landor
and the odd coupling go his talk about the élite of great Irishmen to
which he belongs – Swift (an Englishman who hated Ireland),
Berkeley, Burke, Goldsmith, Grattan – and his proud conviction that
he had no blood of any huckster in his veins. Closely related, the significance being enforced by the 'Hard-riding country gentlemen' and
the 'Porter-drinkers' randy laughter' that come in the same paragraph
of 'Under Ben Bulben', is his choosing to close that valedictory poem
(but for the epitaph and the brief prelude to it) with a self-gratulatory
salute to the 'indomitable Irishry'. And the epitaph itself:

> Cast a cold eye
> On life, on death.
> Horseman, pass by!

– belongs, surely, to the category of attitudes that are struck.

Perhaps by now I have made it plain why, prompted by Yeats's own
contrary suggestion, I started by saying that he is very unlike Blake. I
don't myself believe that Blake had a comprehensive guiding wisdom
to offer, but it was his genius to be capable of a complete disinterestedness, and therefore of a complete sincerity. He had a rare integrity,
and a rare sense of responsibility as a focus of life. His experience was

his because only in the individual focus can there *be* experience, but his concern to perceive and understand was undeflected by egotism, or by any impulse to project an image of himself. He was not tempted to form one. 'Beauty like a tightened bow' – such a phrase couldn't have come from Blake, the artist and poet who speaks so characteristically of the 'wiry bounding line'. He couldn't have produced the portentous nonsense about 'number' that Years offers us in 'The Statues', that solemn parody of his esoterico-metaphysical vein. The 'wiry bound-ing line' is a living line, alive with the energy it conveys and defines, 'energy' in Blake's idiom being a spontaneous organic creativity that is the essence of life. His awareness of terrible complexities, and of prob-lems for which he has no solutions, doesn't entail any protest against the essential conditions of life. The insistent emphasis on 'dying generations' and the obsessed raging against inevitable age – these for Blake were sicknesses to be diagnosed.

I have been leading up in these last remarks to a mention – it can, now, be only a mention, or little more – of the poem of Yeats's which I like more than any other: 'Among School Children'. Its relevance at this point is that it presents, and implicitly proposes, the criteria I have been invoking in my comparative references to Blake. The charac-teristic Yeatsian themes are there, but the prevailing tone and the total attitude are different; the sardonic bitterness and the Swiftian note are absent – there is no hint of them. There is indeed a faint wryness about the touch of dramatized self with which the opening stanza closes; he sees himself for a moment through the children's eyes, which

> In momentary wonder stare upon
> A sixty-year-old smiling public man.

But the note is one of matter-of-fact acceptance, and Yeats clearly takes a natural satisfaction in his public standing as Senator Yeats. The 'I dream' with which the next stanza begins –

> I dream of a Ledaean body, bent
> Above a sinking fire, a tale that she
> Told of a harsh reproof, or trivial event
> That changed some childish day to tragedy –
> Told, and it seemed that our two natures blent
> Into a sphere from youthful sympathy

– introduces a retrospective survey, or audit, of a life's main preoccu-pations, which is developed as if it were in reverie. But the conclusion has a force of convinced and irresistible truth, coming as it does with (to use the analogy again) a perfect cogency of musical logic:

                              O Presences
          That passion, piety or affection knows,
          And that all heavenly glory symbolise –
          O self-born mockers of man's enterprise;

          Labour is blossoming or dancing where
          The body is not bruised to pleasure soul,
          Nor beauty born out of its own despair,
          Nor blear-eyed wisdom out of midnight oil.
          O chestnut-tree, great-rooted blossomer,
          Are you the leaf, the blossom or the bole?
          O body swayed to music, O brightening glance,
          How can we know the dancer from the dance?

There is nothing else like that in the collected poems. So far from its
being the proof of an achieved stability and wholeness in the poet, the
ugliest and most disturbing expressions of inner discord and rebellion
or despair to be found in his *œuvre* mark his final phase. And about the
significance of Crazy Jane and her accompaniments I will say no more;
it is surely plain.

  What I must do in closing is to revert to the question of where, in
sum, Yeats stands among the poets – or, more generally, of what place
he holds in English literature. The volume containing 'Sailing to
Byzantium' and 'Among School Children' impressed one – and
impresses – as coming from a major poet. And yet even that volume is
disappointing; for how much in it can be placed with those two poems?
I know of persons of judgment who think highly of 'Leda and the
Swan', but it seems to me to have too much of Parnassian art about it
to be thought of as coming from the great original poet who 'altered
expression'. I mention it because, in the range of Yeats's art, it represents something of a foil to the very characteristic mode we have in
the reverie poems: I am thinking of the title poem, 'The Tower',
'Meditations in Time of Civil War', 'Nineteen Hundred and Nineteen', and 'All Souls' Night'. And what I want to say about *them* is that
though they represent in diction and manner a creative habit without
which we shouldn't have had the great poems and though, with the
body of verse that associates with them in technical ethos, they count
immensely in our sense of Yeats as a major poet, they are not themselves among the great poems. They aren't closely enough organized
and they haven't, as wholes, an intense enough life.

  This is neither doing them critical justice nor suggesting their
interest. Still less is it possible to illustrate representatively the kinds
of interest that make the collected volume a book to read through from
time to time. The point I've been wanting to make can be put in a comparative way; the sense one has of Yeats's major status is differently

constituted from that which one has of Eliot's. Where Eliot is in question it is the economy, concentration, perfected art and assured creative purpose of the body of achieved poetry that tells. 'Perfected' is perhaps not altogether the right word for *The Waste Land*; but *The Waste Land* leads on to the succession of poems in the different perfected modes – from *Ash-Wednesday* to *Four Quartets* – that seems, in its unpredictable but consistent development, like one quintessential poetic work. And that, for us, *is* Eliot. But where Yeats is in question, while it is because of the poet that we are concerned with the man and the life, we *are* concerned with them – inescapably. The most resolutely literary-critical study of his poetic career entails biography, personalities, public affairs and history.

Yeats's status as a major figure in English literature is bound up with that truth, and to insist that a poem is to be judged as a poem and that literary criticism is a discipline for an exacting kind of relevance in response and comment is not to contradict it. You can't discuss the development by which Yeats finally achieved the poetic of 'Sailing to Byzantium' and 'Among School Children' without going into a great part of the literary history of half a century, and, as you ponder the amount of reference that that involves both to Yeats's personal life and to the civilization he lived in, you will find yourself once again asking (it is a salutary exercise): 'But what *is* literary history?' That is not, of course, asked to be answered. The point regards the way in which Yeats's career poses the insistent questions of the place, part and possibility of the major artist in modern civilization.

Lawrence after thirty years

Lawrence after thirty years – I hope I shall not, at any rate for more than a moment, be thought to be merely exhibiting my egotism when I say that my theme, when I contemplate it, slips for me, to begin with, into another: myself thirty years ago. After all, if I have been honoured with the invitation that brings me here it was in part, I suppose, because of my presumed ability to bear a certain kind of testimony. And in what I want to record first I shall, I hope, seem modest enough. It is that when I look back, when I read what I wrote thirty years ago, I am struck by my unintelligence about Lawrence – a given kind of unintelligence. This should sound modest enough as I said. Modest *enough*: I have not said that I was stupid; that would imply a relative judgment of myself that I can't honestly pretend to think just. In fact, it seems to me that, to go by the printed evidence, as a critic of Lawrence I was less unintelligent than T. S. Eliot, than E. M. Forster (see his treatment of Lawrence in *Aspects of the Novel*), or than Middleton Murry (see *Son of Woman* or anything else he wrote about Lawrence). I have adduced, you will have noted, three distinguished names – the names, may I not say, that represented critical authority at the time of Lawrence's death? What other names can one put with these?

I have now, in order to make the point I have had in mind, to observe further of my own unintelligent treatment of Lawrence that it showed a conscious inability to arrive at a convinced judgment – to arrive at the kind of critical conviction I remember speaking of here at Nottingham, some weeks ago, as its being the critic's business to aim at. I was sure Lawrence's work was of great interest, I had long been convinced that he was a genius, and as I had read and re-read him in that conviction I had been more and more impressed; but, characteristically, when I wrote about him I had no conviction that I understood what was in front of me – that I understood as a critic ought. The element of uncertainty, I say, was conscious; it was, at any rate implicitly, avowed; but it didn't prevent me from passing adverse judgments (as well as observations not meant to be adverse) that I now see to be unintelligent. Indeed, I will say that, in the intensity of my present conviction of Lawrence's irresistible success as a great original artist, I do, after all, now see them as stupid.

Yet, I repeat, I don't really think that the right thing to say is that I was stupid. Having adduced the three distinguished intellectuals who also were impressed by Lawrence, but who were not less unintelligent than myself about him, I needn't be afraid to tell you what representative meaning for criticism I see in the phenomenon, the chapter of personal history, I have recorded. For I do see a meaning – something more than just my stupidity: it is that Lawrence was a creative genius of the greatest kind. He is so profoundly original, and original in such important ways, that he imposes – he certainly imposed – an extremely difficult readjustment. He had to be lived with and lived into. And that in this testimony I am not merely recording a distinctive personal impercipience, insensitiveness or inflexibility in myself the notable cases I have reminded you of – the critical performances of Forster, Eliot and Middleton Murry – seem to me to warrant my assuming with some confidence.

The assertion that Lawrence was a creative genius of the greatest kind doesn't today seem especially daring or scandalous or paradoxical. And *that* is a great change from thirty years ago. Think of the scorn expressed by Eliot when Forster, at the time of Lawrence's death, wrote in a letter to the *Nation and Athenaeum*: 'he was the greatest imaginative novelist of our generation'. I recall this episode, not merely because I should not wish to have referred to the odd (and – I insist – significant) inadequacy of Forster's critical treatment of Lawrence without reminding you also of the generous felicity of that obituary salute, but because of the special value of Eliot as a witness – the special value of his self-commitments as evidence of the literary climate in which Lawrence died. Eliot had earned immense authority and influence in the world of literary culture; he was, as poet and critic, truly distinguished; and yet (though describable, I remember, by Middleton Murry in the earlier 1920s as 'intransigent') he was in 1930 not at all given to critical pronouncements likely to cause indignation or scandal among the cultural élite. The title of *The Criterion*, indeed, was an implicit claim to institutional status and responsibility, as the Editor's general conduct of that quarterly showed him to be very conscious, and when I remind you that *The Criterion* printed no obituary of Lawrence (though it did the honour to Bridges and Harold Monro), the significance I point to is not lonely perversity or moral heroism in the editor. If there was anything in the nature of moral heroism it was Forster's, who himself, like Eliot, belonged to Bloomsbury. The significance I point to is the transformation in Lawrence's standing. Things have changed since 1930 – changed so immensely that the occurrence of such adverse discrimination as *The Criterion* needed no audacity to commit itself to is today hardly credible.

Today, thirty years after, Lawrence, beyond possibility of question, *exists*, a major fact of English Literature, and would be assumed to exist as such by the most institutional *Criterion* and the most philosophically or temperamentally unsympathetic of editor-critics. Lawrence, we can say, is one of the accepted glories of our heritage, an English classic. An ambitious lecturer in a university English School can as judiciously bring out a book on *him* as on the Romantics, or Joyce, or George Moore. I can't, you see, help slipping into an ironic note. All the same, though I have my inevitable scepticisms, I do feel a lift at the heart when I think of the change. Scepticism gets its nourishment when, without a qualm, and actually without any danger of being made to feel ridiculous, a modish intellectual, paying his tribute to the fact of D. H. Lawrence, says that in his judgment the supreme work is *The Plumed Serpent*. But I am sure that the acceptance of Lawrence, his established recognition as a great writer, has been a real and immense gain, and that the creative works making so essentially and potently for life cannot, in our civilization, have been read so widely without good, not measurable, but major in mind and scale, coming of it.

Yet I don't the less think it important that the nature of the genius and the achievement should have a better recognition than, thirty years after Lawrence's death, one has any excuse for supposing one can count on even in the intellectual weeklies and the books that will be written up in the Sunday papers. Or let me put it this way: my own positive sense of the nature of genius – I mean, the sense that I am prepared to express in confident critical terms with the necessary freedom from what *The Times Literary Supplement* calls 'humility' – has been formed since 1930, in years of re-reading, and in the thinking and reformulation entailed in answering accounts of Lawrence I didn't like, and I think it in place that I should try and convey briefly some of the main notes of that sense now.

Forster's obituary tribute I did like, and I liked it, I've indicated, not merely because it was generous, but because of a certain felicity: 'the greatest imaginative novelist of our generation' – that, though the implicit relative valuation isn't high enough to satisfy me now, put the stress applaudably, it seemed to me; that is, to convey well the right intention. My own emphasis of those days, I will permit myself to add, still seems to me a happy one: Lawrence, I insisted (with my eye on Eliot), was essentially a great artist. I have confessed that my understanding of his work was then – and consciously – very defective. But the change, as understanding has left its bafflements behind, and judgment has become confident (in the way, I have reminded you, a critic's should aspire to be), has merely been my coming to realize that Lawrence was both a more triumphantly successful and a greater *artist* than I had seen.

By way of vindicating this insistence on 'artist' – my suggestion that there is point in it as a significant and pregnant emphasis – let me now say that an essential manifestation of Lawrence's greatness is his compelling us to revise, re-inform and re-realize our conception of 'art'. 'Art' is a word that is used very freely, with an assurance that it carries its meaning with it, and has a sufficiently clear value; and yet, as you know, there is more than one value, more than one corresponding conception. I suggest that the most important issues for a civilization may be entailed in these differences, and I hope I give force to the suggestion when I say that the difference in the conception of art represented by Lawrence and by Eliot seems to me to matter in that way. And here is ground enough for reverting on the present occasion to the lack of sympathy, the antithesis, between the two writers. Lawrence (may I not say?) we now see as the great creative genius of the 1920s. Eliot, in 1930, was the prepotent influence in higher literary taste and in critical thought and fashion. Lawrence, I have reminded you, was not in high repute critically; in the intellectual-literary world he enjoyed no high consideration. More is in question than brute 'literary history': there is essential significance that it would be odd not to adduce on such an occasion as this.

Eliot himself, as you know, was a decisive original creative force, and knew at first hand something of the resistance and blindness with which real originality, defeating expectation and habit, must count on being met. 'Sensibility alters from generation to generation in everybody, whether we will or no, but expression is only altered by a man of genius.' Again: 'they have not the sensitiveness and consciousness to perceive that they feel differently . . . and therefore must use words differently'. Eliot *had* the consciousness; it was he who 'altered expression', and that gives him his sure place in the history of English poetry. 'Poetry', one repeats for emphasis, pondering his rejection of Lawrence – the confident refusal to grant him the name of 'artist' – the tradition of formal poetry was a stream of itself, very much apart, and Eliot's sensibility and intelligence were narrowly specialized. But that is not all there is to be said. The profound antipathy Eliot undoubtedly had to Lawrence has a significance that can be seen plainly enough in the critical theorizing of *The Sacred Wood*. The antipathy of temperaments went with an opposition of conceptions of 'art'. I say 'conceptions' because I can't find another word; but in *Tradition and the Indi-*

vidual Talent, the essay that of course I have in the front of my mind, the suggestions of intellectual position, beneath an ostensible trenchancy, are too inconsistent and incoherent to come together in anything we can comfortably call a 'conception'. Yet there *is* a dominant and characterizing ethos; it is the ethos of Flaubert, for whom art is the justifying perfection, the higher reality, paradoxically engendered by the dedicated and martyred artist, hater of *la platitude bourgeoise*, out of the meanness and insignificance of life. The Flaubertian conception or attitude is of its intrinsic nature self-contradictory. What can a devotion to art be that is a contempt for life? Where, if not out of life, can the creative drive come from? It is all in the case that Flaubert's intensity of martyred devotion to art through a lifetime should have produced that exiguous *œuvre*. Lawrence is the great anti-Flaubertian, the complete, profound and wholly conscious representative in and for our own time of anti-Flaubertian art. He knew that his creativity came directly out of his living, and the spirit of Mallarmé's dictum, 'Au fond, voyez-vous, le monde est fait pour aboutir à un beau livre', he would have judged to be not only stupidly perverse but sterile: his art was for him the servant of life. There was nothing esoteric about it, and no more mystery than about life itself – towards which his attitude was one of reverent wonder, the antithesis of Flaubert's.

It is this attitude, or note, I have called 'wonder' which, more than anything else, I suppose, has prompted the description of Lawrence as a 'Romantic' – 'the last of the Romantics', I remember, a colleague of mine called him a quarter of a century ago, in a highly respectable academic work. But if 'Romantic' implies an imaginative or emotional or wilful irresponsibility in respect of the actual conditions of life, then the description has less than no felicity.

There is no doubt that the influence of *Tradition and the Individual Talent* encouraged such critics as the academic I have instanced to feel that one might place Lawrence reassuringly by calling him 'Romantic'; with the undisguised directness and freedom of his use of personal experience in creation he was, to admirers of Eliot, obviously *not* a classicist. But, as Lawrence with a quiet passing finality said, 'This classiosity is bunkum; still more cowardice.' The 'cowardice', clearly, regards the way in which 'impersonality', as Eliot expounds it, plays down the need for the artist to be a person with the courage of life and the responsibility of his experience in its living wholeness. 'There is never', Lawrence might have said, replying to Eliot's famous aphorism, 'a separation between the man who lives and the mind that creates.' And the verb 'live' takes on a fresh force in connection with Lawrence. 'An average man with those lungs,' said a doctor who examined him towards the end, 'would have died long ago, but with a *real* artist no normal prognosis is ever sure; there are other forces involved.'

It doesn't in the least follow that, as the 'impersonality' doctrine would suggest, Laurentian art is 'romantic', the servant of the author's 'personality' and devoted to expressing it. There is no paradox in the fact that the individual whose genius it was to be so uncompromisingly himself as an individual impressed his fellow-men by his unique *impersonality* – a power (it impressed them as power) that in many ways, explicit and implicit, is testified to by a host of varied witnesses assembled by Mr Nehls in that vast 'composite biography' which came out early last year. We can see that what they found so irresistible in him was not merely an intense vitality and a marvellous sympathetic insight, and not at all a dominating ego, but a profound and unquestionable disinterestedness, the manifestation of a rare kind of responsibility: they couldn't but register in his very disconcerting-ness a deeply impersonal sense and habit, of responsibility – responsi-bility towards life. The man who made this impression, so that 'Strangely enough, most people acknowledged Lawrence's right to rebuke them', was the *artist* who, questioned about the nature of the creative drive, answered: 'You . . . write from a deep moral sense – for the race as it were.'

'Moral,' to judge by the heavy weather made of it, is a difficult word. I will not try to say anything about the difficulties here. I need, I think, only say that, while in this Laurentian use it seems to me irreplaceable, unmisleading and justified, Lawrence in it is essentially the *artist*; he is speaking as the creative writer, the great original artist who, wonderfully inventive technically (he did more than 'alter expression'), wrote as a young author in 1915, with a confidence the justice of which is not yet, I believe, properly recognized: 'Tell Arnold Bennett that all rules of construction hold good only for novels which are copies of other novels. A book which is not a copy of other books has its own construction, and what he calls faults, he being an old imitator, I call characteristics.' Lawrence, of course, is taking up the word handed him by Arnold Bennett: 'its own construction' – with 'construction' go all the originalities of Laurentian art, back to what answers most obviously to Eliot's 'altered expression', the 'different use of words'.

About the 'deep moral sense' to which Lawrence referred as the creative drive in himself I can, after all, say this: the use of the formula has a clear significance as repudiating the conception of 'art', or the confusions of thought about art, represented in Eliot's essay, by the word 'aesthetic' – a word for which Lawrence has no need: he has no

such work for any word as Eliot gives to that. In Eliot it registers, not
a coherent conception, but a lack of unity and wholeness in the artist
and critic, and a consequent distrust of the life in himself. It is impossible to think of Lawrence saying about the art of anyone the equivalent
of what Eliot said of Pound's *Cantos*: that he was interested, not in
what Pound said, but in the way he said it. For Lawrence such a distinction was meaningless – certainly not one that could be reconciled
with an intelligent doctrine of art. He had no impulse to separate the
man who lived and experienced from the mind that created, and he
diagnosed it, where it appeared (for example, in Flaubert and his
descendants), as a malady – a malady that had its manifestations in the
artist's inner division and disharmony and his accompanying fear of
life.

I am not imputing any peculiar conception of art to Lawrence. What
I am saying is that he was both central and profound in this matter. It
is the aestheticisms and Flaubertianisms and esotericisms that were off
the centre, and (if you like) abnormal, being the outcome of the rapid
new development of nineteenth-century civilization. That the poet,
Lawrence's contemporary, who succeeded in 'altering expression' in
his own art did not, nevertheless, get clear of them, must, I think, be
seen as a fact in keeping with the general truth that formal poetry, for
all Eliot's achievement, did not reverse the upshot of the Victorian
age, which was that *that* stream of creative tradition had ceased to be
at the creative centre: the creative, the poetic strength of the English
language went, in the age of Tennyson and Swinburne, into the novel.
The great, the unequivocally major art – and what does 'major' mean
when we call, as we do, Eliot and Yeats 'major' poets? – is there. It is
in the work of the great novelists that we see those creative developments which keep the nature of major art, its function in respect of
human consciousness, its importance for life, plainly before us.

If with the criteria represented by a great novel, or (shall I say) by
the *œuvre* of a great novelist (for it is characteristic of the major artist
that he is fertile and that one of his works leads us back to the others –
we are drawn, wherever focused, to consider them in relation) we
approach Eliot or Yeats, we see something equivocal, something to
question, in his 'major' status. I pick on Eliot or Yeats, of course,
because both of them, each on his own, proved the possibility of
escaping the 'climate' or spell of Victorian poetic, and writing a distinguished and vital modern poetry. I had better, in the very limited
time left me, confine myself to Eliot. The point I had in mind is that
Eliot showed what stringent limitations could attend an impressive
success at 'altering expression' in poetry. The 'alteration' was triumphantly effected; the 'consciousness' (Eliot's word) that made it

possible makes him 'major'. But I have to insist that the impressiveness of the success against that nineteenth-century past as a
background should not lead us to credit the poet with a higher order
of creative achievement than is there. Perhaps I shall make my meaning plain enough if I say that, while I know that *The Waste Land* could
not have been the important historical fact that it is if it had not, for this
reader, built up sufficiently into a poem – if it had not, that is, actually
been with sufficient convincingness something of what it offers to be
– it is not, I think, as a poem of some length, a very compelling organic
whole. It is not in kind one of the world's major creations – as (I will
make the force of the proposition plain by saying) *Women in Love* is,
in kind and in achieved actuality.

I have been using Eliot (and I might equally have used Yeats) by
way of bringing out the full force of my constatation that Lawrence was
the greatest kind of artist – a truth that one may now, after thirty years,
utter without an effect of paradox, if not, perhaps, with the assurance
of a fully realizing reception. He said – he brought out from time to
time different formulations of the same conviction – that the novel was
'the highest form of human expression so far attained', and gave his
reasons in terms that amount to a definition of major art; in terms, that
is, of the artist as the supremely qualified and responsible explorer of
human experience. It is clear that his technical inventions have been
dictated by life – by the need to convey perceptions and realizations
that have come to him in his experience as a full human being, fully
committed to life. He can be so clear about the subordinate, ancillary,
decidedly *not* supreme status of art, and so free from aesthetic nonsense and esoteric confusions, because he is a whole integrated being.
('He was', says Catherine Carswell, 'the most harmonious man I have
known.') If his novels and tales have perplexed and baffled readers,
that has not been because of metaphysical or mystical obfuscations or
human eccentricity. On the contrary, a piercing clarity of intelligence
and a deep human centrality have been the marks of Lawrence's
genius, and the difficulty for the reader has come of these. He has compelled readjustments.

Let me finally remind you that if Lawrence, in the age of Eliot and
Joyce and Paul Valéry and Clive Bell, was a radical and potent
counter-influence to the aesthetic, the esoteric and the sophisticated,
he was equally, in the age of Marxizing, an essential enemy of the
didactic. He stood unequivocally for the integrity of art, and the
integrity of art was for him the inviolability of the human spirit. The
use of art to impose 'will' and 'idea' was an offence against life.
Positively, his work everywhere conveys and engenders a life-
reverence, civilization's extreme need of which the Marxisms and

didacticisms are not the only reminders and manifestations. By life-reverence I mean not something inculcated, but something that is his basic habit and of the essence of his art and that is manifested in the wonderful sensitive livingness of his prose. Let me finish by reading a piece, so as not to end with a generality and an abstract term; it comes in a letter to Lady Ottoline Morrell:

> The death of Rupert Brooke fills me more and more with a sense of the fatuity of it all. He was slain by bright Phoebus' shaft – it was in keeping with his general sunniness – it was the real climax of his pose. I first heard of him as a Greek god under a Japanese sunshade, reading poetry in his pyjamas, at Grantchester – at Grantchester upon the lawns where the river goes. Bright Phoebus smote him down. It is all in the saga.
>   O God, O God, it is all too much of a piece: it is like madness.

This is from a letter – a letter unmistakably written *as* a letter, yet in that brief *prime-sautier* passage standing alone we recognize immediately the genius of a great writer. We should know of course that it was Lawrence: no one else could have written it. What I called the sensitive livingness is manifested in the play of changing tone – a play that reveals itself in so short a space as, with all the penetration, and the irony that, isolated, would have been astringent, the expression of a profound human sympathy. Towards the evoked affectations of King's Hellenism there is neither the tone of 'insufferable' nor any indulgence. The 'sunniness' that balances the 'pose' is the appreciative recognition of a human realness – a recognition that, deepening, imparts the sense of a tragic imminence to the comedy of the vivacious and pregnant following sentence. And 'Bright Phoebus smote him down' isn't in sum satiric irony; it gives us a potent resonance of the tragic Greek. The passage, in all its diversity, is indeed 'all of a piece'. It is the appalled sense of the engulfing human disaster that prevails in Lawrence. What our literary intellectuals would do well to note in Lawrence, and study – but they won't – is the way in which he is never superior.

Shaw against Lawrence

Certainly an occasion for some applause: 'À Propos of Lady Chatterley's Lover' can at last be got. But (I am afraid I shall seem ungracious) I wish the manner of its reprinting – along with pieces from *Phoenix* (and other sources) and the promise of a companion volume of *Selected Literary Criticism* which will draw on *Phoenix* again and on *Studies in Classic American Literature* also – had not suggested that we are never to have a reprint of *Phoenix*, all of which we need. And we need the whole of *Studies in Classic American Literature*. The greatest writer of the twentieth century has been dead for twenty-five years; but essential works of his, works that should have been widely current and fulfilling their function, have remained unobtainable – some of them for decades.

Again, I wish that this volume had not been called *Sex, Literature and Censorship* – the title shrieks from the hideous dust-jacket. Eliot in *The Waste Land*, Joyce in *Ulysses*, Wyndham Lewis in *Tarr* – these, I am moved to comment, are concerned with sex; Lawrence is concerned with the relations between men and women. Of course, the 'ugly little word', as Lawrence called it, has to be used; he uses it himself. But associated in a title with 'censorship', under Lawrence's name, it plays up to all the misconceptions and misrepresentations from which Lawrence has suffered – all the subtly obstinate resistances that have made it so hard to get the nature of his work, and the meaning and scope of what he stood for, recognized. The point of my misgivings is enforced by Mr H. F. Rubinstein's introductory essay.

In the opening of it we read: 'D. H. Lawrence, a determined Shaw-hater . . . ' Determined hating, one comments, was as alien and impossible to Lawrence – as contrary to his nature and the profoundly considered ethic that he *lived* – as determined loving. No one who had in any serious sense read him could have used the phrase. Still, one tells oneself, Mr Rubinstein is only a lawyer, writing as a lawyer; his theme, 'The Law versus D. H. Lawrence', safely limits him, and his disability will hardly need to be obtruded. But on the next page we find him volunteering that 'the author of *St Joan* understood Lawrence better than Lawrence understood him'. And, though he refers modestly to 'mere lawyers', he considers it within his com-

112

petence to measure Lawrence for us against Shaw: they are comparable magnitudes (we gather); geniuses who 'sought essential truth, the
one through reason, the other through sex'. Both, he tells us,
'succeeded, in their supreme moments, in touching – as it were, at
opposite ends of a circumference – fringes of the same garment'.

Thus, in introducing this volume, Mr Rubinstein dismisses, lightly
and confidently, the whole meaning of Lawrence's work. For
Lawrence isn't accidentally or marginally anti-Shavian. Shaw represents as well as any writer the disorder of modern life that it was
Lawrence's genius to diagnose so unanswerably (for his depreciators
don't answer, they merely misrepresent, or as Mr Rubinstein does,
ignore him). And Shaw's case illustrates well how immensely
Lawrence's preoccupation, where sex is concerned, transcends anything that the word 'sex' suggests.

What repels Lawrence in Shaw is what Mr Rubinstein acclaims as
the triumph of reason. It is the automatism, the emptiness, and the
essential irreverence – all that makes Shaw boring and cheap; the
emotional nullity that when, as in *St Joan*, he confidently invites us to
respond to depth and moving significance makes him embarrassing
and nauseating. What Lawrence comments on in 'À Propos of Lady
Chatterley's Lover' is Shaw's treatment of sex:

He has a curious blank in his make-up. To him all sex is infidelity and only
infidelity is sex. Marriage is sexless, null. Sex is only manifested in infidelity,
and the queen of sex is the chief prostitute. If sex crops up in marriage, it is
because one party falls in love with somebody else, and wants to be unfaithful.
Infidelity is sex and prostitutes know all about it. Wives know nothing and are
nothing, in that respect . . . Our chief thinkers, ending in the flippantly cock-
sure Mr Shaw, have taught this trash so thoroughly that it has almost become
a fact.

This truth about Shaw is so plain that it didn't take a Lawrence to
perceive it. Where the genius appears is in the way in which Lawrence
illuminates the significance of the trait and of the whole Shavian
phenomenon, and justifies his own particular kind of insistence on the
crucial importance of a right attitude to sex. To say that his own
attitude is a religious one is not to say that he makes sex his religion.
How much more than sex (the 'sex' of Mr Moore's title) is in question
the great passage about the 'body' in 'À Propos of Lady Chatterley's
Lover' makes manifest – 'body' standing for all that spontaneous life
which the conscious mind, with its attached ego and 'personality', and
its instrument of will, can thwart, but cannot command. The body's
life, says Lawrence, is the life of *real* feelings; but 'our education from
the start has *taught* us a certain range of emotions, what to feel and
what not to feel, and how to feel the feelings we allow ourtselves to

feel', and today we are 'creatures whose active emotional life has no real existence, but all is reflected downwards from the mind'. The 'higher emotions' have to be faked:

And by higher emotions we mean love in all its manifestations, from genuine desire to tender love, love of our fellowmen, and love of God: we mean love, joy, delight, hope, true indignant anger, passionate sense of justice and injustice, truth and untruth, honour and dishonour, and real belief in anything: for belief is a profound emotion that has the mind's connivance.

What we have here is no matter of 'intuitive' shots and flashes, but pondered insight developed into articulated and ranging thought – thought that presents, in Lawrence's writings, a coherence and a consistency over its whole remarkable compass. For in spite of Mr Rubinstein's way of distinguishing him from Shaw, it is Lawrence who represents intelligence. And the criterion of intelligence we bring from Lawrence exposes Shaw's 'reason' as clever, conceited stupidity. The stupidity, the conceit and the irreverence are of a mind that has no real vital relations with a body: there is a clear aptness, as applied to Shaw, in the formulation that Lawrence prompts us with.

Mr Rubinstein rebukes Lawrence for pride. He adduces the 'boast that "being a novelist, I consider myself superior to the saint, the scientist, the philosopher, and the poet, who are all great masters of man alive, but never go the whole hog" ', and he tells us solemnly that Lawrence 'never became the equal – let alone the superior – of a saint'. Anyone who reads the 'boast' in its context will see that Lawrence, writing in a vein of free colloquial vivacity, is explaining why he holds the *novel* to be 'the highest form of human expression so far attained': it insists on the presence of the whole complex man ('It won't *let* you tell didactic lies, and put them over'). He is enforcing the characteristic Laurentian maxim: 'Never trust the artist; trust the tale.' Mr Rubinstein, of course, may still judge it a good occasion for testifying that *he* thinks a saint superior to any conceivable novelist. It is a pleasing preference in a lawyer.

The other major pieces in the volume besides 'À Propos of Lady Chatterley's Lover' are 'Pornography and Obscenity' and 'Introduction to These Paintings', one of the most impressive of all Lawrence's essays. It brings home to us the astonishing *reality* of his immense knowledge; his perceptions and judgments are always first hand. Here is an account of the essential development of European painting, with some amusing and devastating comments on Clive Bell and Roger Fry. The shorter pieces exemplify the extremely free colloquial manner that Lawrence used for the admirable journalism of which he wrote so much in the later years (his superb tales being so little in request).

Genius as critic

Since, in 1936, the year of its original publication, I first read *Phoenix*[1] through, it has seemed to me immeasurably the finest body of criticism in existence (and Lawrence left a good deal more critical writing than is included here). I am not, of course, claiming to speak out of a knowledge of all the criticism there is, but expressing my conviction that no collection as valuable can be found. The interest and profit it yields seem to me inexhaustible. I still find, every time I open it, new things to remember and to use. What a difference it would have made to me as an undergraduate, I tell myself! And I have done my best to promote its currency: a best that has not been as good as it might have been, since the volume has been for years out of print. Now at last it is obtainable again, and every undergraduate reading English can properly be urged to buy it: he needs his own copy.

Nor does its use start there. It can, in its astonishing variety, have an invaluable educational function at an earlier stage. For Lawrence's criticism, subtle, penetrating and individual as it is, has qualities that make it a peculiarly good initiation. These are suggested in the account of criticism and the critic that opens the essay on Galsworthy:

We judge a work of art by its effect on our sincere and vital emotion, and nothing else. All the critical twiddle-twaddle about style and form . . . is mere impertinence and mostly dull jargon.
A critic must be able to *feel* the impact of a work of art in all its complexity and its force. To do so, he must be a man of complexity and force himself . . . A man with a paltry, impudent nature, will never write anything but paltry, impudent criticism. And a man who is *emotionally* educated is rare as a phoenix . . .
More than this, even an artistically and emotionally educated man must be a man of good faith . . . A critic must be emotionally alive in every fibre, intellectually capable and skilful in essential logic, and then morally very honest.

That, in its un-Eliotic freedom of utterance, may sound a little naïve. But plainly, what we in fact have is the vital and sure intelligence of the actual phoenix, the rare being who is alive in every fibre and has the centrality and easy swiftness of genius. The naïvety is that habit of complete honesty which it has never occurred to him to suspect that he can't afford. To be introduced so potently to this con-

ception of intelligence is of the utmost value to the young. It is inseparable, of course, from a conception of art – a conception the antithesis
of that represented by Mallarmé's dictum: 'Au fond, voyez-vous, le
monde est fait pour aboutir à un beau livre.' The Laurentian conception is more properly to be called one in that it is wholly coherent, and
capable of being held – and lived – with complete consistency. It is
invoked quotably in many places in *Phoenix*, and is stated with some
insistence in the essay called 'Why the Novel Matters', the burden of
which can be represented by the brief sentence: 'Nothing matters but
life.'

Life, it may be commented, is a large term – too large to be of much
use in criticism. Actually, of course, it is a term that we cannot do without. And to have it brought home to one how essential a term may be
that cannot be defined is a major part of an education. That is what is
done for us in *Phoenix*. It ceases to be a mere large term: impossible as
definition may be, we need a word suggesting something analogous to
definition to denote the giving to 'life' of the force of significance it gets
in Lawrence's criticism. 'Alive in every fibre' (to read him is to have
that phrase charged with meaning), he has an incomparable sensitiveness and penetration of responsive percipience over a seemingly limitless range: his response to art is a response to life.

This way of putting it must not be taken as suggesting that he was
not strictly a literary critic, with the sureness of judgment of poetry
(for instance) that only a trained literary intelligence can have. There
is endless evidence of this in *Phoenix*, but for the sake of economy in
enforcing the point I will quote a convenient illustration from the
Letters. Writing to Eddie Marsh on Ralph Hodgson's 'Song of
Honour' he says:

There's the emotion in the rhythm, but it's loose emotion, inarticulate, common. It's exactly like a man who feels very strongly for a beggar, and gives him
a sovereign. The feeling is at either end, for the moment, but the sovereign is
a dead bit of metal. And this poem is the sovereign. 'Oh, I do want to give you
this emotion,' cries Hodgson, 'I do.' And so he takes out his poetic purse, and
gives you a handful of cash, and feels very strongly, even a bit sentimentally
over it.

It may be suggested that to arrive at this judgment on Hodgson's
poem was no very remarkable feat. But the letter was written in 1913.
To take this line with the creator of the Georgian vogue – and Marsh
was also Lawrence's own generous patron – Lawrence required a complete conviction (one he would have got no help towards forming), and
the formulation is still very strikingly that of a rarely gifted critic. The
relevant criteria, it will be noted, are implicitly invoked in the

judgment: what we have is, unmistakably, *literary* criticism of a compelling and very exceptional quality.

Where Lawrence is criticizing novels he may be thought of as the observer of life and civilization who has a marvellous insight into the human psyche in all its varieties. He is, we know, that. And in being that he is at the same time a literary critic – the supreme literary critic: a truth (it is, of course, no paradox) that can be effectively insisted on by pointing to his review of Mann's *Der Tod in Venedig*. He writes an admirable critique of that book, and in the course of it he deals with the author's case as man and artist, and relates him (a *locus classicus*, it should be) to Flaubert. His versatility as a critic is very remarkable. He was ready, it seems, to take on any book that might be sent to him – novel, memoir, psychology, poetry, H. G. Wells, Baron Corvo, Cunninghame Graham, Rozanov, Eric Gill – and he always justifies his readiness: he exhibits everywhere the same directness, subtlety and penetration. That is, the astonishing versatility presented in *Phoenix* is far from exemplifying what one thinks of as the almost inevitable limitations of brilliant and wide-ranging opportunism: he always writes from a deep centre (how utterly different from our versatile pundits of the Sunday papers!). From this centre he does all his thinking; for, though he disclaimed any bent for the thinking of the philosopher, he was a most powerful original thinker, preoccupied always with fundamentals, and it is this depth and this coherence of preoccupation that tell so impressively in his occasional work.

We see them (to insist on the value of the book as initiation for the literary student) in his use of the word 'moral' when there is question of the critic's basic criteria.

For the bourgeois is supposed to be the fount of morality. Myself, I have found artists far more morally finicky.

This will be found in the opening of the essay called 'Art and Morality'. Conveniently in view just opposite on the previous page we find the passage indicating the criteria he brings to novels:

Supposing a bomb were put under the whole scheme of things, what would we be after? What feelings do we want to carry through into the next epoch? What feelings will carry us through? What is the underlying impulse in us that will provide the motive power for a new state of things, when this democratic-industrial-lovey-dovey-darling-take-me-to-mamma state of things is bust?

These passages are sufficient intimation that though the term 'moral' has a special context and force in his use of it, his use is both legitimate and inevitable, and in full continuity with the normal uses. When he uses it most insistently, the term 'religious' is very close. ('At the maximum of our imagination we are religious'.) In the Hardy study he speaks of the 'vast unexplored morality of nature'. Of Clym Yeobright he says: 'He did not know that the greater part of life is underground.' That is, his critical thought is immensely more subtle and deep-going than Arnold's, the other great critic who challenged a basic critical function for the word 'moral'.

The 'Study of Thomas Hardy' is Lawrence's most sustained piece of constructive exploratory thinking. It is difficult, but will amply repay the young student's trouble – not primarily as a critique of Hardy, but as an emancipating and vitalizing exemplification of the nature of creative thought (which, of course, it could hardly be if the ideas were not themselves of high value). It is not Nietzschean, but in method it may, I think, be fairly taken to register an indebtedness to Nietzsche.

And this is an opportunity to remark on the extraordinary range and comprehensiveness of Lawrence's culture and intellectual equipment. Not only was he at home in English literature, and could read (and speak) French, German, Italian and Spanish; he was inward with all the intellectual forces – Nietzsche, Tyler, Frazer, Bergson, Freud and so on – that were active in the contemporary European mind. He was most emphatically an Englishman, but if any great writer of this century may be said to have written out of Europe – as *of* Europe – it was Lawrence.

Phoenix contains the long 'Introduction to These Paintings'. I don't know what art critics and art historians may say about it (it discusses the history of painting in Europe), but the genius, the marvellous intelligence, is most certainly there too. And those who still believe (having perhaps read it in the accounts of the expert evidence given recently in court) that Lawrence had no sense of humour will do well to look at the passage on Significant Form.

T. S. Eliot's influence

By some accident (it must have been a review, but I remember nothing about it) I bought *The Sacred Wood* when it came out. I hadn't then – with the war of 1914 in the immediate past – heard of T. S. Eliot; but who had? The war years had been years of distraction. Having come up originally a Scholar in History, I had, now back at Cambridge, gone over to the English Tripos, which, founded towards the end of the war, had just produced its first class-list. When I give my reasons for this opening it may be commented that my estimate of Eliot's influence promises to be not only personal but parochial. Well, in being the one (as, to be a real estimate, it had to be), it had necessarily, I think, to be in some sense the other: one must, if one is really to judge, be somewhere, and have a given set of more than theoretical interests and involvements – which should, of course, be relevant. How far I am exposed to the pejorative suggestions of 'parochial' others will judge.

I have indicated my reasons, in the 'Retrospect' I wrote for the reprinted *Scrutiny*, for holding that the foundation of the Cambridge English Tripos has proved to be an important fact in history. I won't discuss here the concurrence of accidents by which, at that ancient university, literary study was emancipated from Anglo-Saxon and a study of literature made possible (for undergraduates, and so for properly disposed and qualified 'teachers' or collaborators) that should foster approaches and habits of discussion tending to the establishment of an idea of literary criticism as, in its unschematic and anti-academic way, an essential and central discipline of thought. I will merely make the point that a coincidence favouring the efforts of those who saw the new possibilities – saw how the university might be made more like the centre of cultural life and educational influence it ought to be – was that the opening decade of the English Tripos started with the first impact of Eliot.

Without there having been any statement (or, I think, clear realization) of central issues involved, the English Tripos put no hither-limit in time to the English literature prescribed for study (whereas at Oxford there is a date, moved forward not long ago, but still falling within the nineteenth century, at which English literature, for academic purposes, ends). The importance of this abstention for the

119

English Tripos was not that it authorized candidates to hope for questions on *Ulysses* and young graduates to propose research on *Work in Progress* or the symbolism of Yeats, but that if you set a hither-limit you declare insidious war on any intelligent idea, or sense, of what a literature – a living literature – is, and impose an academic (that is, unintelligent and dead-safe) approach.

That, in those early years, the given Cambridge advantage became in large – in decisive – measure realized profit was ensured by the fact of T. S. Eliot. His attaining to general acceptance and academic respectability was not as easy and rapid as certain admiring institutionalists would now have us believe. There were years of confident resistance on the part of their predecessors. This was good for the young English School; for by 1922, when *The Waste Land* appeared in the first two numbers of *The Criterion*, the fact and nature of his genius were plain enough to a sufficient number of the alert, and they were immensely helped in the critical discussion of his aims and achievement by the criticism that he had published by 1924 (the new essays on the seventeenth century having come out in the Hogarth pamphlet, *Homage to John Dryden*). To have got its start in a decade when all intelligent students (teachers and undergraduates) could not but feel that, while working for the English Tripos (a university examination!), they were taking part in a decisive change of taste and renovation of critical thought, these entailing a new sense of the relation of the present to the past – what could more effectively have promoted the association in the new developing school of literary studies with an unacademic vitality?

I come now to a paradox about Eliot's influence. He is widely credited with having been a profound and subtle advocate of the idea of Tradition, and if one asks on what that reputation is based one must expect to be directed to 'Tradition and the Individual Talent', the essay that appeared in *The Sacred Wood*. Actually, if one is to judge by that essay, he was not only without any discussable idea of tradition, but incapable of sustained thought. 'Tradition' for him is a mere word, and the attitudes he offers to recommend with his use of it are such that those who have a serious concern for what, in intelligent use, it portends can only exclaim: 'How can such a mind be a poet's or critic's? What intelligent thought about art, or civilization, or life can come from a literary man who can speak of tradition as something to which the artist has continually to *sacrifice* himself?'

The essay as a whole is incoherent – or empty, except of unpleasant intentions (conscious and unconscious). And the fact is that all pretentious intellectuality of his to which he owes his reputation as an influence on intellectual fashions is in the same unpleasant way intellectually null. It couldn't have real influence; its influence could only be on fashion – fashion at the level of that contemptible literary world which (as Eliot loyally did) took Wyndham Lewis for an influential thinker. The irony is that those who now (it seems to be the correct thing in England, at any rate) see classical profundity and finality in 'Tradition and the Individual Talent' commonly talk as if there were an irresistible consensus that Eliot had recanted a youthful brashness about Milton, and profess an amused conviction that 'dissociation of sensibility' is an exploded myth.

The pregnant asides about Milton represent his real influence; they belong to the field of his strength in criticism – his strength in thought. His strength is not *there* when his thought is not in close and vital touch with his technical preoccupation, that of the poet who, in 1920 or thereabouts, was successfully 'altering expression' – learning how to 'use words differently'. He showed that something *could* be done after Swinburne. In the associated criticism, intent on his sharply focused 'practitioner's' themes and interests, he brought out pregnantly and with a vitalizing suggestive force the nature of essential literary history, and, in so doing, contributed the impulsion for unending creative thought. Those who 'read English' in my time, compelled to recognize the disconcerting stir of the live and real in contemporary poetry, recognized critically for the first time the nature of the Victorian taste in which they had been brought up – and that recognition led to historical inquiries, realizations and revisions. Eliot himself said little directly about the nineteenth-century background to the 1920s, but the virtues of his essays on the seventeenth century are – there is no need to argue – inseparable from their intense and pregnant relevance to the problems posed by his own situation in the twenties. We had, as we read this criticism and Eliot's own poetry, brought home to us the force of the truism that life is always here and now, and only out of the living present is there any access to the past.

It is a truism that, pondered, turns into a number of corrective and not easily statable truths – truths that Eliot, in his unsatisfactory 'theoretical' way, is pointing to when, in 'Tradition and the Individual Talent', he says of the 'historical sense' that it is 'a sense of the timeless as well as of the temporal and of the timeless and the temporal together', positing that this sense is 'what makes a writer traditional'. Impressive as this kind of thing may perhaps sound, the nullity that characterizes the thought of *this* Eliot thrusts itself on our attention when he sums up as follows: 'Someone said: "The dead writers are so remote from us because we know so much more than they did." Precisely, and they are that which we know.' We are forced to put the obvious and damning interpretation on this by the context and the essential aim (a matter for diagnosis) of the whole essay, which, under cover of a stern doctrine of disciplinary rigour and an ascetic posture (it is not a conception) of 'impersonality', is to absolve the artist from responsibility towards life. 'They are that which we know'! – this from the poet who, genius enough to be 'conscious' of the demands of a twentieth-century 'sensibility' and to attempt successfully a poetry growing out of it that should be vital modern art, 'altered expression'!

But the essays on the seventeenth century do really come from the poet. Since the mind engaged is the practitioner's, it inevitably, in a matter of course way, assumes the creative drive behind all successful 'expression' – the drive of urgent new life, and refers thus, in the pregnantly suggestive observations on Donne, the Metaphysicals, Marvell, Milton and Dryden, to changing actualities, and glimpsed potentialities, of a given civilization. Here, in living touch with the concrete, the supremely intelligent selective attention guided by the creative interests of the 1920s, his criticism gives us a very different Eliot from the would-be impressive enunciator of those unpleasant period intellectualities. He is too genuinely engaged to be portentous about 'tradition', but no better incitement to thought about those relations of poet to poet and to cultural change and continuity which are portended by the word could be offered the student than these essays, which, with their method of tact and quintessential economy, are (another way of describing the same vitality) a pregnant incitement to the kind of close reading that issues in 'practical criticism'.

The fact that, though in the century following Dickens's début the creative life of the English language had manifested itself to immensely greater effect in the prose of the novel than in formal poetry, Eliot had no critical competence at all there (so far as any intelligence about it on his part was concerned the novel might as well not have existed) doesn't entail as drastic a qualification of the indebtedness that has to be acknowledged to his influence as might perhaps seem to follow. His genius ('expression is only altered by a man of genius') started a new life of critical thought the manifestations of which far transcend the limits of his own field of interest – or desire to appreciate.

That last phrase, of course, lays a heavy emphasis on the limits – on Eliot's limitations and disqualifications. There is no avoiding this in any sincere account of his achievement and influence. All indebtedness of the kind I have been describing comprehends, of course, some element of the provocation to say 'no'; to realise (that is) that one judges emphatically otherwise – to receive the energizing impulse in that form. But Eliot's is a special case in a degree that makes the necessary insistence on limitations perhaps a delicate matter. Necessary, though: after forty years of pondering Eliot I have no doubt about what has to be said. His strength was peculiarly associated with weakness, so that if holding back from the harsh judgments that come to one's lips, one finds oneself saying that his weakness was his strength, it is only to recognize at once the corollary: his strength was weakness.

That gives the form of one's critical summing-up of his creative achievement. The 'pressure' that, in his curious and revealing account of the artist's 'impersonality', he recognizes with a passing ('scrupulous') after-glance to have a necessary part in the creative process (Eliot's emphasis falling on the 'poet's mind' as a 'receptacle for seizing and storing up numberless feelings, phrases, images, which remain there until all the particles which can unite to form a new compound are present together') is, in his own case, of a kind that he prefers not to contemplate – or that successfully evades the challenge of his intelligence: consider the implications of the essay on *Hamlet*, which throws more light on *Family Reunion* than on Shakespeare's play. As manifested in the phase culminating in *The Waste Land* it reveals an Eliot who belongs to the spiritual line of Flaubert. The creative ethos is of Flaubert's paradoxical kind; the 'Art' that goes with it won't yield any but an incoherent account. The 'pressure' that occasions 'fusion' in Eliot's 'receptacle' plainly derives in very large measure from the frustration of life in himself – the attitudes of disgust and cynical ('sophisticated') rejection-cum-nostalgia expressing emotional disorders that disable intelligence in him.

It is a drastically qualified kind of creativeness. It sufficed for his 'alteration of expression', a creative achievement that compelled from us the acclamation due to a man of genius. Here, in this intensely vital anti-Georgian poetic, the charged substance and nervous rhythmic life, of this compellingly contemporary verse was the tissue, it seemed, that would unfold its full organic significance in major creation. To put things retrospectively in this way, of course, is to give implicit expression to the subsequent disappointment. *The Waste Land* was, as the ambitious offer of a sustained complexity of organization that should justify itself by a 'major' significance conveyed, a sufficiently impressive whole to make it a convincing manifesto – a proof that something decisive had happened. The newly awakened consciousness couldn't but work rapidly, the change of taste be consummated, and – the Georgian fashion seen for what it was – a long and depressing chapter of literary history ended. But, for an admirer in the 1930s there was no evading the constatation compelled by an exposure of the poem to the full rigour of the relevant criteria, these having been allowed to exercise that authority which a real – that is, a truly respectful – criticism is intent on bringing to bear: the organization that had made *The Waste Land* a whole was not organic in the way promised by the local life of the parts, so irresistible in their diversity. When, later, we were told that the arrangement of the constituents into a poem was Pound's work there seemed no reason for incredulity.

To the reply that it is precisely the theme of *The Waste Land* that the world, the modern plight, of which Eliot offers his quintessential summing-up, doesn't permit of wholly organic creation on any comprehensive scale, and it was his achievement to make an impressive enough poetic success out of that plight – there is an obvious rejoinder: 'that doesn't dispose of the criticism'. To the question why, seeing the diversity of compelling life presented to us in the body of poems that Eliot did actually produce from *Gerontion* to *Four Quartets* – why dwell critically on what he didn't produce, there is a clear answer: we are prompted to a full clarity of critical recognition and registration not merely by the nature and strength of the actual product, but – and very insistently – by the extra-poetic modes of 'influence' that made Eliot an institutional major presence for the English-speaking world at the level of what may be called the higher culture. I put 'influence' in inverted commas for reasons I have already intimated: it was not a profound or vital influence that Eliot the intellectual exerted; any appearance to the contrary was a matter of mere fashion – fashion of a kind that deserved nothing but contempt. It was a fashion at a level at which T. E. Hulme could be made a distinguished mind and an intelligent force of historical importance, at which intellectually negligible British and American exponents of authoritarianisms (to use an inoffensive word for an ugly thing) could be – by way of assurance that the organ really had a philosophy – presented to the readers of *The Criterion* (of whom, it is immediately relevant to remark, there were very few).

To mention *The Criterion* is to enforce the point about the paradox that confronts anyone committed to discussing Eliot's influence. The editor was the Eliot of 'Tradition and the Individual Talent' and 'The Function of Criticism'. Regarding the latter it can be said that the difference between it and Arnold's essay is given in the omission from Eliot's title of 'at the Present Time': this discussion proceeds in terms of a generality the impressiveness of which (it is very consciously impressive) is a blankness about the here and now. The account he offers of the function fails ludicrously to suggest any conception such as an 'engaged' critic, one (say) starting a review that really had for *raison d'être* the strengthening of criticism in modern England, would have to form for himself and strive to realize. *The Criterion*, in fact, seemed to be edited by a foreign, very provincially cosmopolitan, academic. Instead of a vitally functional relation to the British scene and to the culture it offered to serve, it had its show of a philosophic basis of principle and its doctrinal bent: Anglo-Catholic in religion, Classicist in literature, and Royalist in politics.

No doubt the astonishing naïvety of his manifesto was quickly borne in upon him; he didn't reprint *For Lancelot Andrewes* in the preface to which it appeared. But for doctrinal formulation of the Criterionic ethos he had nothing better to supply. The actual published expressions of *The Criterion*'s Rightishness one remembers as being decidedly more unpleasant, if only because they were, at any rate in the 1930s, more closely related to contemporary actualities.

Nevertheless, they didn't, I think, matter much as influence. What *was* influential was the support Eliot gave the dominant literary movement of the Left; Faber and Faber on his advice published its poets (products of Eliot's influence, but – alas! – a 'renaissance' only for coterie purposes, fashion and publicity), and *The Criterion* offset its own bias of principle by letting them and their friends make it their organ. Does this mean that Eliot had at any rate some belief in criticism as an interplay of diverse judgments, a vitally formative clash of opinions? No, it means rather that he believed in nothing; or that he had no belief strong enough to make him resist social pressures. He was taken up in the early twenties by Bloomsbury, then at the height of its power, and found nothing questionable in its pretensions to be both an intellectual and a social élite. Apart from that special limited field I have particularized, he never showed much critical judgment; indeed, he again and again displayed an astonishing ineptitude. If he ever had an impulse to assert a bold independence of Bloomsbury, or of any later derivative social-literary milieu to which he belonged, he had no difficulty in suppressing it.

His very significant antipathy to Lawrence was clearly genuine, and he expressed it boldly when the world that mattered to him was with him. When that world changed its tune about Lawrence he changed too – but not in any recantation. He saved the posture of recantation for Milton: I am thinking of the British Academy lecture of some fifteen years ago. I say 'posture', because while the audience of *bien pensants* found itself enabled, with respectful triumph, to acclaim a recantation, anyone who brings to the reading of the lecture an innocence of the desire to see *that* in it must see that Eliot concedes nothing. He was certainly not given to any tactless intransigence of sincerity – his status as an institution mattered very much to him; but how could he recant about Milton? He knew that to deny the force and validity of those early references to Milton, so potent in their context and their relation to the 'alteration of expression' he had achieved, was to deny the achievement. He didn't, however, mind the institutionalists taking the excuse he gave them for acclaiming a recantation.

To say this is not to pronounce on what degree of calculating consciousness there might be in this exercise of his practised tact – or
civilized duplicity – of formal utterance. 'Surely,' he once wrote in
reply to a naïve protest of mine, 'you must have seen that I was at least
half-ironical'. There is no irony in the British Academy lecture; but if,
turning to the other end of the scale, one looks at his obituary note in
The Criterion on Robert Bridges (Lawrence didn't get one) one can't
blink the clear purpose of playing up to both of two discordant valuations of the Poet Laureate (who had been in so distinguished a social-
cultural way institutional). Another good (in the clinical sense)
example is to be seen in his commentaries, in *The Criterion* and in *The
Use of Poetry and the Use of Criticism*, on A. E. Housman's once famous lecture, 'The Name and Nature of Poetry'. The command of this
kind of urbane equivocation, in fact, can't but be recognized when we
ponder a few assorted illustrations together, as being rather, in its
essential significance, a manifest and humiliating weakness that
betrays deep-seated malady.

   Without courage, without conviction, without faith – that, for a
criticism that pays him the tribute of full explicit severity in judgment,
is how the weakness asks to be summed up. Which again brings us face
to face with the paradox, this time confronting us as *Four Quartets*. It
came, that truly paradoxical creative achievement, when one had been
settling down to the conclusion that there was nothing more to be
expected, and, actually, it turned out to be the close of Eliot's creative
life. And to what a rare kind of courage, what resolution and stamina,
it after all testified! I am thinking of the completeness with which it is
not what its Anglo-Catholic expositors take it to be. They can have
Ash-Wednesday if they like – which is not to say that I take it to be just
what they do, or that I don't still feel the spell of those beautiful poems
or that I utter the concessive phrase in the spirit in which I leave to the
expositors and fellow-Anglicans *Murder in the Cathedral*.

   But what has to be noted is that *Murder in the Cathedral* followed on,
and that it *is* just what it was taken to be and was meant to be taken to
be. It was a real success with the Church of England, and Anglican
clergy thronged the theatre at its performances; it established firmly
Eliot's institutional status. On the other hand, it was not a work for the
poet who had 'altered expression' to think of as a product of his genius,
and one could only hope, without confidence, that Eliot himself recognized that unequivocally. But *Four Quartets* gave us the unexpected:
a wonderful new product of the genius; a sustained creative work of
astonishing originality in which the 'weakness' – that which might
seem to be essentially anti-creative – presented itself as strength. It is
a more remarkable paradox than *The Waste Land*. All the resources of

the poet's genius are devoted to *not* affirming – to maintaining as complete an abstention from affirmation as can be achieved.

It would have been out of place for him here to speak of himself as 'having to construct something upon which to rejoice'. What of positive there is in the inner situation producing the work is, together with the courage to carry this supremely difficult and testing kind of exploration through to the limit, the hope that a religious affirmation will be felt to have affirmed itself by the close. The exploration is analytic, but it is of a kind that entails a creative use of language – one that only a very remarkable poet could command. 'What do I believe?' Eliot asks, a question that is at the same time and inseparably, 'What is believing?' 'How, using as I must in some measure, the conceptual currency, can I do so without implicitly taking over its illusory constatations and finalities, thus essentially closing the exploration and frustrating the aim?' There will be economy (I say this with my eye on my theme, Eliot's influence) if I allow myself to quote from what I wrote on *The Dry Salvages* when it appeared:

In the poetry, of course, there is no pretence that the sensibility is not Christian; but it is not for nothing that D. W. Harding [in *Scrutiny*] described 'Burnt Norton' . . . as being concerned with the creation of concepts. The poet's magnificent intelligence is devoted to keeping as close as possible to the concrete of sensation, emotion and perception. Though this poetry is plainly metaphysical in preoccupation, it is as much poetry, it belongs as purely to the realm of sensibility, and has in it as little of the abstract and general of discursive prose, as any poetry that ever was written. Familiar terms and concepts are inevitably in sight, but what is distinctive about the poet's method is the subtle and resourceful discipline of continence with which, in its exploration of experience, it approaches them.

I had the examination of the first three 'Quartets' from which this comes included, as an appendix, in *Education and the University*. My having it reprinted there intimates, I think, the kind of testimony to Eliot's influence I should like to close on. I prefer not, in such a context as the present, to count as 'influence' that which is usually associated with Eliot's religious poetry – the proud possessiveness with which the Anglo-Catholic literary-academic coterie regards it. This coterie, not discouraged by Eliot, made its possession of the great poet and intellectual (discouraging – inevitably – intelligent criticism of him) a distinction and a strength for the ordinary kinds of coterie purposes. But the influence I should like to leave Eliot credited with is to be thought of as an impulsion to life and growth. And that, I meant to suggest by reprinting my critique where I did, is notably there in *Four Quartets* – there in that astonishing exploratory creative achievement, which lends itself so potently to one's needs when one is faced with having to enforce one's insistence that the distinctive discipline of literary studies is to be conceived as a discipline of intelligence that is as much a discipline as the mathematical, but antithetically other.

The nature of 'thought' is what is in question, and it is there that Eliot helps as only so paradoxically gifted a genius could. And, for us, it is a peculiarly urgent need to get what effective recognition *can* be got for the truth that in a technology-dominated civilization there must be, if our *humanitas* (our full humaneness) is to be saved, a sustained corrective insistence on the kind of disciplined thought of which the rigour is a methodical distrust of the abstract, logically definable and schematic. The special responsibility rests on the artist, the creative writer in especial, and I suggest, pointing to the literary critic as my transition to the intentional theme (or 'idea'), that an adequate conception of criticism and its function 'at the present time' leads towards the university.

If I could feel that I had made the intention and relevance of this commentary on *Four Quartets* plain, then I should know that I had conveyed the tribute that, in a note on Eliot's influence, I should wish to end on. And my sense of the paradox he presents would I hope have been decently communicated.

T. S. Eliot and the life of English literature

I am not an uncritical admirer of T. S. Eliot; I hope that is well understood. I do indeed admire him as poet and critic, and think his work in sum of great importance – obviously of the first importance for those who today are troubled over the questions: What *is* English literature? where is it and how is it there? how does it have its life – which must be in the present or not at all (and I indicate here how troubling and urgent the questions are)? But the importance is essentially bound up with the fact that intelligent appreciation of Eliot's work entails radical criticism. Of course, the intelligent appreciation of any writer entails critical limitations and adverse judgments; that is clearly so, for instance, of that very great writer, Charles Dickens, but I shouldn't have said about him what I've just said about Eliot, regarding whom the insistence on the challenge to radical criticism takes a special emphasis.

I am not, then, an idolator of Eliot. I do all the same think him unquestionably a great poet; he is our last great poet – I mean, the last great poet we have had: that, whatever differences there may be regarding later claims and reputations, will hardly be disputed. There has in fact been in our literature no manifestation of major creativity since that which, culminating in *Four Quartets*, gives classical status to T. S. Eliot (I don't expect that to be disputed either), and, seeing that Eliot died only the other day, when he was not old compared with Bertrand Russell, who is still with us, there is nothing paradoxical even on the face of it in saying that he is the poet of our age. And actually he *is* major, and demands to be recognized as that, in terms of his immediate profound and poignant relevance to the world we live in – his modernity being (let me add at once) of a more interesting kind than the long-established account credits him with.

He is not so great a creative power as D. H. Lawrence, who died in 1930 – which datum doesn't all the same explain why, with my general themes in mind, it's Eliot I choose to discuss. It's by reason of the limitation attendant on the achievement that he lends himself to my purpose. You don't, where the Victorian age is in question, go to poetry for the kind of major significance that, as I've just suggested, characterizes Eliot the poet; we go to the novel, where the creative, or poetic, strength of the English language manifests itself. Eliot restores to poetry the capacity for major significance, and in doing it invites, in direct and pregnant ways that favour demonstrative economy, the discussion of those questions I've raised: In what sense has the past its life in the present, and what and where are the life and reality of English literature? He has here, for my purpose, an advantage over Lawrence – he offers me one that Lawrence doesn't. This distinctive characteristic of Eliot as a great innovating poet is associated with the fact that his creative achievement bears a peculiarly close relation to his criticism.

Lawrence is a critic too – a greater critic than Eliot, just as he is a greater creative power. He is much more freely a critic – infinitely more, and a critic over an unlimited range. Eliot is not freely a critic at all; in fact, he lacks most of the gifts one thinks of as making a critic. He is a distinguished critic only over an extremely narrow range; his good criticism bears immediately on the problems of the 'poetic practitioner' (his own phrase) who, in the years around 1920, when Swinburne pervaded the atmosphere and the Georgians were undertaking to occupy the field, was intent on proving that there might again be an important English poetry. He proved it – whether there has been any of importance since is another question.

You can't – this is the associated fact – be intelligent about Eliot's achievement without sharpening your sense of the relation of the present to the past. You bring from a study of the poetry a strengthened and subtilized apprehension of the truth that if you eliminate the past from the present – that is, if you break that continuity which of its nature is unceasingly creative – you destroy the essential human achievement, that which makes civilization a spiritual reality. To say as I've done that only in the present can the past live is not to deny that the past *is* the past. This may sound like a paradox, but it answers to what we all know. Past, present, time and change are necessary words and so, as words, familiar to us, but they cover irreducible complexities of experience, shifting indefinables and uneliminable equivocations. I might seem to be offering here a summary of Eliot's preoccupation in that astonishing work, *Four Quartets*. But the point I myself want to emphasize is this: there is something – I will call it 'cultural continuity' – that has its life in time, and, transcending 'present' and 'past', gives time its meaning and humanity its grasp of a real. It is maintained in a world of change – maintained responsively – by a process of collaborative re-creation in life and use that keep it constantly renewed.

The force of what I say can be made plain by a brief reference to the fact of language. Intimating the nature of my theme in opening, I threw out, among others, the question: Where *is* English literature? I will now ask: Where is the English language? You can't point to it. It is 'there', concretely 'there', only in so far as I utter the words, phrases and idioms, charged with the meanings and impulsions that put them in my mouth, and you take them. Or if this had been a colloquy discussion I should have said: 'There you have it; there it is, in the play, the criss-cross of utterance, taking place between us.' I won't say more by way of reminding you what is the nature of the life of the English language at any time, and in what sense life entails creative response to change. And I will make the point, in order that I may take it up again in a moment, that where in these matters we find ourselves talking, with a necessary emphasis, of 'continuity', the word 'creative' is in close attendance.

The language we speak doesn't merely provide an analogy of cultural continuity; it very largely *is* it; it is the essential core of it. Having written this, I came, in a review, on a very relevant sentence actually quoted from me, and, so prompted, I'll use it again. 'A language is more than such phrases as "means of expression" or "instrument of communication" suggest; it is a vehicle of collective wisdom and basic assumptions, a currency of criteria and valuations, collaboratively determined; itself it entails on the user a large measure of accepting participation in the culture of which it is the living presence.' This truth pressed urgently on Eliot (the pressure being an essential part of the creative pressure) when he wrote his profoundest poetry, *Four Quartets*, that intensely characteristic product of his genius. It is in one of its aspects an inquiry, conducted not theoretically but in the concrete and creatively, into the relation of words – verbal expression – to experience and thought, the inquiry being directed by an intense need to establish a sure apprehension of the real – the real that isn't to be found in the world he evokes in 'Difficulties of a Statesman' or the passage from the third section of 'East Coker' I shall read later on.

But the point I want to make at the moment is a criticism of Eliot. While I said just now 'This truth pressed urgently on him', I don't think that in his own implicit account of cultural continuity, 'creative' carries the full value it ought to have. The point is an important one in its bearing on my theme. Eliot was incomparably more subtle, more intelligent and better educated than Pound – the Pound who wrote to a correspondent: 'The Greek populace was PAID to attend the great Greek Tragedies, and darn well wouldn't have gone otherwise, or if there had been a cinema'; but Eliot too was an American. Whatever he might assent to formally, in a notional way, he couldn't in his imaginative, his vital, thinking conceive of a sophisticated art that grows out of a total organic culture. I have remarked somewhere that in what I think of as his bad criticism (that which has earned for him the name of a distinguished theoretical critic) he is, in the pejorative sense of the word, too much an intellectual. It seems to me that we have the limitation (I note it here, manifested in this mode, only as a significant characteristic and not as a disabling vice to be dismissed with critical animus) in this passage from 'East Coker', the Quartet in which he evokes the traditional rustic life – as he imagines it – of the ancestral Eliot countryside:

> In that open field
> If you do not come too close, if you do not come too close,
> On a summer midnight, you can hear the music
> Of the weak pipe and the little drum
> And see them dancing around the bonfire
> The association of man and woman
> In daunsinge, signifying matrimonie –
> A dignified and commodious sacrament.
> Two and two, necessarye coniunction,
> Holding eche other by the hand or the arm
> Whiche betokeneth concorde. Round and round the fire
> Leaping through the flames, or joined in circles,
> Rustically solemn or in rustic laughter
> Lifting heavy feet in clumsy shoes,
> Earth feet, loam feet, lifted in country mirth
> Mirth of those long since under earth
> Nourishing the corn. Keeping time,
> Keeping the rhythm in their dancing,
> As in their living in the living seasons
> The time of the seasons and the constellations
> The time of milking and the time of harvest
> The time of the coupling of man and woman
> And that of beasts. Feet rising and falling.
> Eating and drinking. Dung and death.

The country folk of pre-industrial England, imagined in terms of what we are to take as their representative cultural ethos, are for Eliot yokels –

> Rustically solemn or in rustic laughter
> Lifting heavy feet in clumsy shoes,

And then, the significance only emphasized, it seems to me, by the interposed piece of Tudor prose about the 'dignified and commodious sacrament' that Eliot has arranged as a half-dozen lines of verse and dissociated from himself by retaining the antique spelling – only emphasized by that, we have

> The time of milking and the time of harvest
> The time of the coupling of man and woman
> And that of beasts.

The reductive effect, being so matter-of-course and so clearly without animus, is the more significant. Yet the country folk whom Eliot reduces to this created the English language that made Shakespeare possible. Their speech answered to the brief account I quoted from myself a short while ago. It developed as the articulate utterance of a total organic culture, one that comprehended craft-skills of many kinds, arts of living formed in response to practical exigencies and material necessity through generations of settled habitation, knowledge of life that transcended the experiences of any one lifespan, subtly responsive awareness of the natural environment. Of course, it had always been vitally affected by higher cultural influences of the kind that commended themselves to Eliot's recognition. But the native language – it was the language of the native priesthood – wasn't weakened by such influences, but strengthened; it responded livingly, and didn't become less English. By the time Shakespeare was discovering his genius there was ready to his hand a vernacular that was marvellously receptive, adventurous and flexible, yet robustly itself; capable, that is, of accommodating and making its own all the influxes of the Renaissance.

Shakespeare himself, of course, was a decisive historical fact. I said just now that the language was ready for him, but *his* use of it was preeminently the great creative writer's. It illustrates supremely the importance of the creative writer – more generally, the importance of a really and potently living literature – for the life of a language; an importance that doesn't the less urgently demand recognition from us in our present cultural plight because there's certainly no chance of another Shakespeare.

Shakespeare told decisively in history; he ensured that, in our language and our literature, we should have and retain an immense advantage over France. He realized irresistibly the distinctive potentialities of English and made an immeasurable difference for its future use and development. Eliot somewhere, exalting a superiority he attributes to French civilization, remarks that the important fact is that France had a mature prose before we did. I don't think this one of Eliot's profounder observations, and I doubt whether it rests on any very much more substantial ground than ignorance and inert convention. In any case, the important fact, surely, is that we had our Shakespeare a good half-dozen decades before France had her Racine. By then the great change had taken place in both countries – it had been unmistakenly and irreversibly precipitated; the change that means that, looking back, we see the triumphant accelerating progress of modern civilization as being, in the latter part of the seventeenth century, already well started, and going strong, with a clear course in front of it – towards the consummation we know. The difference between the two languages and literatures in this matter was certainly to England's advantage – an advantage that Eliot, judged by his weaker criticism, would have to be pronounced unaware of, though his poetry testifies to it.

By the close of the seventeenth century the conditions of Shakespeare's kind of greatness had vanished for good. Shakespeare could be at one and the same time the supreme Renaissance poet and draw as no one else has ever done on the resources of human experience, the diverse continuities, behind and implicit in a rich and robustly creative vernacular. By 1700 a transformation as momentous as any associated with the development of modern civilization had taken place, never to be reversed. The new Augustan culture, represented by the poetry of Pope and the prose of the *Tatler* and the *Spectator*, entailed an unprecedented insulation of the sophisticated or 'polite' from the popular. There *could* be no reversal: the industrial revolution, which by the end of the eighteenth century was well advanced, worked and went on working inevitable destruction upon the inherited civilization of the people. Dickens was the last great writer to enjoy anything of the Shakespearean advantage.

What has been achieved in our time is the complete destruction of that general diffused creativity which maintains the life and continuity of a culture. For the industrial masses their work has no human meaning in itself and offers no satisfying interest; they save their living for their leisure, of which they have very much more than their predecessors of the Dickensian world had, but don't know how to use it, except inertly – before the telly, in the car, in the bingo hall, filling Pools forms, spending money, eating fish and chips in Spain. The civilization that has disinherited them culturally and incapacitated them humanly does nothing to give significance, or any glimpse of it, to their lives or to any lives. Significance is a profound human need, like creativity, its associate. The thwarting of the need, or hunger, has consequences not the less catastrophic because of the general blankness in face of the cause. The complacent 'understanding' with which the enlightened contemplate these things is not understanding or enlightenment, but merely a manifestation of the disease from which our civilization is perishing. When the new maturity claimed by Youth Club leaders for today's young has established its right to act out an intuitive new wisdom independent of any derived from past human experience, the achievement of happiness won't have been advanced, however confident the expectation.

I have no doubt that my account of the drive of technologico-Benthamite civilization has sounded the reverse of exalted or hopeful. But if pessimism means inert acquiescence I am certainly not a pessimist. If I was a pessimist I shouldn't be addressing a festival of literature, in England, as if I thought it might listen seriously to a discussion of English literature as a reality, a possible living power in our world. Actually I am convinced that there is something to be done, that there is a sustained effort to be made that those capable of thought and responsibility must promote in every way open to them. If the creative human response that maintains cultural continuity is not to die away altogether, then there must be a new kind of conscious effort to revive and strengthen it. Of what that must be, its nature and working, there can't be a satisfactory simple account. But, addressing a festival of literature, I count on its not dismissing offhand with incredulous surprise the suggestion that, in relation to such provision, literature in the sense defined by reference to value judgment, English literature in that sense, would have an essential part to play. And, with an abrupt, but not unprepared, transition, I will now raise again, and answer, the question: 'How does English literature have its life – how at any time is it "there"?'. – It is 'there' in an educated, cultivated and intelligent public, or not at all.

Again with an abrupt transition, for an hour is short and I haven't forgotten my formulated subject, I turn now to T. S. Eliot. As a poet, a consummate and major poet, he lends himself to my purpose in that to adduce a poem by him is to make present the idea of creative literature in its most sharply definitive value. There it is, the poem, utterly and finally 'right', perfectly itself, and unequivocally 'there'. And the appreciative pondering of the poem – the body of the poems – is very soon found to involve the contemplation of an organic English literature to which it belongs. Of course, Eliot's classical status was recognized in his own lifetime, long before his death, but nevertheless I think his genius has not had due recognition – in that sense has been neglected, and for two main reasons. First, there is the obstinately inert misapprehension that makes *The Waste Land* his supreme thing, tending so to reduce him to the modish poet of the 1920s. And then there is the other major misapprehension, which – for approval or disapproval – identifies his religious poetry with his personal Anglo-Catholicism, and expounds it theologically.

The established unintelligence about his criticism makes matters worse. The indefensible and wholly deplorable emphasis on the 'theoretic' critic goes with a failure to appreciate the very rare distinction of the essays on the seventeenth century – a distinction which is inseparable from the intimate way in which they relate to his aims and achievement as a poet. It is they, and not 'Tradition and the Individual Talent' or the sentences he quotes from himself in the opening of the piece entitled 'The Function of Criticism', that advance thought about the relation between the present and the past.

I have discussed the essays at some length elsewhere, and must confine myself now to making a few points that are indispensable for my immediate argument. The adverse criticism they have received is full of useful provocation, and I take J. B. Leishman, the Oxford scholar, as representative. In his book, *The Monarch of Wit*, after suggesting that Eliot's knowledge of the Metaphysicals is incomplete and unscholarly, and pointing darkly to the fact that he bases his appreciative commentary on the good poems whereas there are many that are not good, he goes on: 'In the second place, both in these essays and elsewhere, Mr Eliot was writing not merely in a spirit of disinterested curiosity but (though he never explicitly admits it) with something of an axe to grind. He was writing, not merely as a critic, but as a poet, or as what he himself calls a "poetic practitioner", and a question always at the back of his mind was this: "From what earlier poets can a modern English poet most profitably learn?" His preoccupation with this question largely explains both his exaltation of the Metaphysicals and that denigration of Milton which he continued intermittently for the next twenty years.'

What Leishman adduces as Eliot's disqualification is his strength and the manifestation of his importance to us. The 'spirit of disinterested curiosity' he invokes against Eliot is the academic spirit, the 'disinterestedness' of which reduces English literature to a mere phrase – a phrase that portends nothing better than the vague idea of an aggregation or of a series in time. Anyone who contends, as I do, that the only possible organ of the creative effort society has to make is the university, conceived as a centre of civilization, which it can't be without having its own centre – a liaison-centre – in a vital English School, is committed, as I am now, not just to denouncing the academic spirit, but to defining, or throwing some illumination on, the nature of its positive antithesis. The best way I know of attempting to do that is to say about Eliot what I should say to any audience genuinely interested in literature, and troubled, therefore, about the state and the drive of our civilization.

Eliot's poetry and his best criticism together lend themselves incomparably to the illuminating of that process of constantly re-created continuity which makes 'English literature' more than a phrase – makes it (in so far as it *is* that) a living reality in the present, where alone there can *be* life. His best criticism is essentially, and not accidentally or marginally, that of a major poet, the great poet of his time. A real critic's disinterestedness is not neutrality, as Leishman seems to imply; it is a living responsiveness, and therefore discriminating, and creative in regard to the sensibility of his time. Eliot's discrimination is that of a major poet who, having a major poet's 'axe to grind', asks: 'Where in the poetry of the past is the life that matters most to me, who aspire to being a poet now and demonstrating that Swinburne wasn't a final dead-end?' The question is prompted by the strong need in him, and the search guided by that. The definition of major quality in a creative writer entails a reference to his being peculiarly alive to his own time – to his having, that is, the profoundest kind of representativeness. The changed sense of the living whole of English poetry – of the relation of the present to the past and of the past in relation to the present – that Eliot achieved for himself proved, in spite of angry resistance, very soon irresistible. It was impossible to recognize his achievement as a major modern poet without having a profound sense of the change – without a recognition that 'English poetry' now differed from what it had been for the cultivated of (say) 1900 by something more than mere accretion.

Nevertheless, though Eliot brought Donne and the Metaphysicals in, I doubt whether there has been much clear understanding of the nature of his interest in them. At any rate, discussion of his criticism has run too much to talk about the metaphysical conceit and Donne's intellectuality. The corrective is to disengage and ponder two sentences. The first (actually, in his essay it comes after the other) gives you the directing preoccupation of the innovating major poet: 'The possible interests of a poet are unlimited; the more intelligent he is the more likely that he will have interests: our only condition is that he turn them into poetry, and not merely meditate on them poetically.' The second tells you what his preoccupation found peculiarly congenial to it in the seventeenth century: 'The poets of the seventeenth century, the successors of the dramatists of the sixteenth, possessed a mechanism of sensibility that could devour any kind of experience'. The phrase to emphasize in this sentence (thus rendering 'mechanism of sensibility' innocuous) is 'the successors of the dramatists': it comes from that rare thing (which the academic detests), an original critic, and it makes quite plain what it was that Eliot valued in Donne. I think that he lent himself far too much to the conventional overvaluation of the minor Jacobeans, but what he was really interested in was dramatic blank verse. It is true that when we look up the plays from which he takes his passages we don't find much more of *that* quality. But we make the important point when we tell ourselves that we shouldn't

have had the verse that makes the Jacobeans interesting and valuable
to Eliot but for Shakespeare. We come again here to the theme I
touched on earlier this evening: though Eliot doesn't specify Shakespeare in relation to his own poetic innovation, Shakespeare is the
great relevant fact in the background.

Donne brought into non-dramatic poetry the Shakespearean use of
English – the living spoken language, the speaking voice, and the
attendant sensitive command of rhythm, tone and inflexion:

> Are not heavens joyes as valiant to assuage
> Lusts, as earths honour was to them? Alas,
> As wee do them in meanes, shall they surpasse
> Us in the end, and shall thy fathers spirit
> Meete blinde Philosophers in heaven, whose merit
> Of strict life may be imputed faith, and heare
> Thee, whom he taught so easie wayes and neare
> To follow, damnn'd?

That is from a satire, but, as you know, we have the same spirit of
versification and diction in the lyrics:

> I wonder by my troth, what thou, and I
> Did, till we lov'd?

Let me read immediately after that this from Eliot; it comes from the
second poem in *Ash-Wednesday*:

> Under a juniper-tree the bones sang, scattered and shining
> We are glad to be scattered, we did little good to each other,
> Under a tree in the cool of the day, with the blessing of sand,
> Forgetting themselves and each other, united
> In the quiet of the desert. This is the land which ye
> Shall divide by lot. And neither division nor unity
> Matters. This is the land. We have our inheritance.

To have read that out saves me from being supposed even for a
moment, I hope, to be committing myself to an absurdly simple
proposition. It is plain at once that the diction there transcends what
is suggested by 'living spoken English' and 'the speaking voice'. But
then so does Shakespeare in his mature dramatic poetry very freely
transcend the spoken English of his time. He draws on *all* the available
resources of the language, yet – this 'yet' registering the fact that he
creates availability – the essential spirit of his use, that which controls
rhythm and tone, is that of living spoken English. So with Eliot in the
passage I read, and in *Ash-Wednesday* as a whole. For all the liturgical
suggestion and the strong presence of the biblical, the appeal to the
reader's sense of how things go naturally in speech is always there –
can at any moment be made overtly and unmistakably:

> This is the land which ye
> Shall divide by lot. And neither division nor unity
> Matters.
>
> I wonder by my troth, what thou, and I
> Did, till we lov'd?

This is a most important point, essential for the enforcing of my observation about *Ash-Wednesday* and Eliot's religious poetry in general: that it is religious in a radically different way from that which seems currently assumed – certainly from that assumed by many Anglo-Catholic admirers. To explain what I mean I must hark back a dozen years and quote from a poem that appeared in 1917 in Eliot's first volume – or the earliest that is explicitly drawn on in the *Collected Poems*:

> Now that lilacs are in bloom
> She has a bowl of lilacs in her room
> And twists one in her fingers while she talks.
> 'Ah, my friend, you do not know, you do not know
> What life is, you who hold it in your hands';
> (Slowly twisting the lilac stalks)
> 'You let it flow from you, you let it flow,
> And youth is cruel, and has no remorse
> And smiles at situations which it cannot see.'
> I smile, of course,
> And go on drinking tea.
>
> 'Yet with these April sunsets, that somehow recall
> My buried life, and Paris in the Spring,
> I feel immeasurably at peace, and find the world
> To be wonderful and youthful after all.'
> The voice returns like the insistent out-of-tune
> Of a broken violin on an August afternoon . . .

'Portrait of a Lady', from which that comes, is a remarkable poem, and it was a remarkable genius that had written it by 1917. The versification and the language – portentous fact – are wholly of the twentieth century, and yet the rhythms and the metric are such that no one brought up on Victorian poetry could have had any difficulty in recognizing them as proper to verse. The significant and profound originality, the pregnant innovation, is to be recognized in the living play of tone and inflexion, a kind of life that depends on the poet's use – which in its precision is unmistakably a poetic use, of the spoken language and the speaking voice.

> A Greek was murdered at a Polish dance,
> Another bank defaulter has confessed.
> I keep my countenance,

> I remain self-possessed
> Except when a street-piano, mechanical and tired
> Reiterates some worn-out common song
> With the smell of hyacinths across the garden
> Recalling things that other people have desired.
> Are these ideas right or wrong?

This doesn't suggest Donne or any other seventeenth-century poet or any intense intellectuality. But actually the command of shifting tone and living inflexion means the possibility of the strong and subtle presence of thought, the never drugged or dulled nerve of intelligence that characterizes Eliot's finest poetry. Looking back we can see that there is no paradox about the development that led from 'Portrait of a Lady' to *Four Quartets*.

'The possible interests of a poet are unlimited' – you recall that phrase of Eliot's. The poetic he achieved excluded nothing that mattered to him (that is what 'interest' means) from his poetry. On the contrary, its creation and development were determined by his need to focus, define and register in words and rhythms his sharpest sense of life and his profoundest searching of experience (which is another way of saying his 'thought'). Whatever his limitations – and our immense indebtedness to his poetry includes its forcing us to recognize and ponder them – he was a distinguished spirit, deeply engaged in *our* world. I've said that to stress in the accepted way *The Waste Land* doesn't suggest fairly how much and in what ways he matters – should be recognized to matter – to us, now, who are troubled about civilization and the prospects for humanity. For a corrective I will read two passages, one from the unfinished *Coriolan* sequence and one from 'East Coker', the second Quartet:

> Cry what shall I cry?
> All flesh is grass: comprehending
> The Companions of the Bath, the Knights of the
>   British Empire, the Cavaliers,
> O Cavaliers! of the Legion of Honour,
> The Order of the Black Eagle (1st and 2nd class),
> And the Order of the Rising Sun.
> Cry cry what shall I cry?
> The first thing to do is to form the committees:
> The consultative councils, the standing committees,
>   select committees and sub-committees.
> One secretary will do for several committees.
> What shall I cry?

That is the opening half of *Difficulties of a Statesman*. The following opens section 3 of 'East Coker':

O dark dark dark. They all go into the dark,
The vacant interstellar spaces, the vacant into the vacant,
The captains, merchant bankers, eminent men of letters,
The generous patrons of art, the statesmen and the rulers,
Distinguished civil servants, chairman of many committees,
Industrial lords and petty contractors, all go into the dark,
And dark the Sun and Moon, and the Almanach de Gotha
And the Stock Exchange Gazette, the Directory of Directors,
And cold the sense and lost the motive of action.
And we all go with them, into the silent funeral,
Nobody's funeral, for there is no one to bury.
I said to my soul, be still, and let the dark come upon you
Which shall be the darkness of God. As, in a theatre,
The lights are extinguished, for the scene to be changed
With a hollow rumble of wings, with a movement of darkness
    on darkness . . .

These passages differ in an essential way from each other, but they
have a preoccupation in common. The first – and earlier – passage is
comparatively simple. It evokes with intensity the world in which ends
are lost and forgotten in the complication of the machinery – adminis-
trative, political, economic, social and so on – and the intensity is protest and despair. Ends are lost and forgotten: look at the leaders,
letters and poised commentaries in the *Times*, the *Guardian*, the *New
Statesman*, the *Spectator*, and you will have to conclude that the public
of the educated and the enlightened that represents the wisdom of our
politicians and statesmen and chairmen of commissions and committees on Higher Education knows of no higher end to be considered
than a rising material 'standard of living'. As J. K. Galbraith, the
American rogue economist, says in *The New Industrial State*: 'St Peter
is assumed to ask applicants only what they have done to increase
G.N.P.' We in this country, of course, believe in fair distribution and
equality of opportunity, and in order to equalize opportunities are
committed to letting standards in education look after themselves –
which in *our* world, make no mistake, means lowering them for good
(and certainly for ill).

In the second passage the poet is engaged more completely – i.e.
with more of himself. The tone is no longer that of protest or satire, but
of one who searches into his own inner plight and responsibility.
Further, the passage belongs to a closely organized context, the
totality of *Four Quartets*, the organization of which is determined by a
marvellously sustained constructive preoccupation. 'The preoccupation' – I quote a sentence from a careful account I wrote a good many
years ago – 'is with establishing from among the illusions and
unrealities of life in time an apprehension of an assured reality – a

reality that, though necessarily apprehended in time, is not of it.' The word I underline in that sentence is 'reality'. You'll have noted how essential to the effect of *Difficulties of a Statesman* the evocation of *un*reality is:

A commission is appointed
To confer with a Volscian commission
About perpetual peace: the fletchers and javelin-makers and smiths
Have appointed a joint committee to protest against the reduction of orders.
Meanwhile the guards shake dice on the marshes
And the frogs (O Mantuan) croak in the marshes.
Fireflies flare against the faint sheet lightning
What shall I cry?

I spoke earlier of the collaborative interplay that sustains cultural continuity as creating the human world; for 'the human world' I might have said 'reality'. By 'spiritual Philistinism' I mean the implicit belief that the only reality we need take account of in ordering human affairs is what can be measured, aggregated and averaged. With this Philistinism goes the elimination of the day-by-day creativity of human response that manifests itself in the significances and values without which there is no reality – nothing but emptiness that has to be filled with drink, sex, eating, background music and what the papers and the telly supply.

Eliot's personal case, of course, was determined by circumstance and idiosyncrasy; nevertheless, in the form it takes it belongs essentially to our phase of human history, and his creative battle has the most intimate bearing on the general plight – for those, that is, who are conscious enough (Eliot's word) to see the plight as a problem. The poetry is not, as I've said, what conventionally Christian appreciation makes it; but genuine preoccupation with the problem (the genuineness entailing the knowledge that 'we do not belong to ourselves' – I adapt what Lawrence says of Tom Brangwen in the opening of *The Rainbow*) is inevitably religious. The point to be insisted on is that Eliot, so far from affirming doctrine or belief, employs all the resources of his poetic mastery of English to explore and test experience non-affirmatively in the hope that the major affirmations will at the close stand there self-affirmed. Hope – he doesn't deny his inner positive bent; that is, his Christian sensibility: it is a basic datum, a given, among those he starts with. But the poem shows no tendency to force anything. A reader who recognizes that it clearly establishes in its marvellous creative way some most important validities may, when, near the end of the third *Quartet*, he arrives at the word Incarnation, comment (as *I* do) that it doesn't for all admiring readers carry from what goes before the full irresistible charge the poet hoped – doesn't, that is, come with the clinching inevitability the poet intended. But I don't think that on any defensible judgment it can be denied to be an astonishing creative achievement with, for all who know that there is a battle for life to be waged against the spiritual Philistinism I've defined, the kind of importance I've intimated – too vaguely, I'm afraid.

To remedy the vagueness by examining *Four Quartets* in detail is out of the question in this evening's conditions. The work is undeniably difficult. *Ash-Wednesday* is not undeniably that. Yet in fact it is major poetry that in preoccupation and technique leads straight on to the later work, though there is nothing intimidating about the subtlety, which therefore tends not to get the attention it needs: the obvious beauty, thus simplified, satisfies the reader. There is then good reason for clinching before I end my discourse the observations I made about the mode of *Ash-Wednesday* earlier this evening.

I illustrated with the close of the second poem –

> And neither division nor unity
> Matters.

– how the spirit of the spoken language is there, ready to take command unmistakably, even where the diction is so strongly biblical, and I remarked that the definition of attitude, the significance, depended on the actual living control of tone and inflexion. That is, in spite of the apparently incantatory rhythm, this poetry demands the full attention of the waking mind; there is no hypnoidal effect. It registers a recoil from the world of *Difficulties of a Statesman*, but the recoil isn't into anything of the nature of the Victorian poetic other world or dream-world (Eliot's terms), but towards the positive constructive effort of *Four Quartets*.

The pervasive tone of the first poem answers to a sentence in the passage I read from 'East Coker' –

> I said to my soul, be still, and wait without hope
> For hope would be hope for the wrong thing

– but, with no violence to the essential logic, the note of effort is there in

Consequently I rejoice, having to construct something upon which to rejoice

And you'll notice when in a moment I read the poem the logical *in*consequences of the 'Consequently'. Though the poem is composed of statements that have to be read as such, the relation between them isn't that of prose at all. The poet's meaning requires both 'is' and 'is not', and in the totality of the poem they don't cancel out. For Eliot's thought here is not something got clear beforehand and apart and then put into words; it is created in each poem, being something that couldn't be grasped and conveyed by words used in any paraphrasable way. Here in *Ash-Wednesday* we have, impressively manifested, that intense interest in the relation of words and linguistic usage to experience which has its supreme creative expression in *Four Quartets*, which (it is very much worth emphasizing in an age characterized by the menaces of linguistic science) is an incomparably profound inquiry into the nature of language. The only further comment I will make before reading the poem is a reminder about the shifts of tone and the essential part they play in the meaning. Note, for instance, that line 4, the slightly altered Shakespearean line, has its own pointed felicity of tone (placing – you speak it in inverted commas) and that the parenthesis about the 'agèd eagle' is an irony directed against self-dramatizing pride (for there may be a pride of humility), and note the factual flatness of the third stanza ('Because I know that time is always time'):

ASH-WEDNESDAY

I

Because I do not hope to turn again
Because I do not hope
Because I do not hope to turn
Desiring this man's gift and that man's scope
I no longer strive to strive towards such things
(Why should the agèd eagle stretch its wings?)
Why should I mourn
The vanished power of the usual reign?

Because I do not hope to know again
The infirm glory of the positive hour
Because I do not think
Because I know I shall not know
The one veritable transitory power
Because I cannot drink
There, where trees flower, and springs flow, for there is nothing again

Because I know that time is always time
And place is always and only place
And what is actual is actual only for one time
And only for one place
I rejoice that things are as they are and
I renounce the blessèd face
And renounce the voice
Because I cannot hope to turn again
Consequently I rejoice, having to construct something
Upon which to rejoice

And pray to God to have mercy upon us
And I pray that I may forget
These matters that with myself I too much discuss
Too much explain
Because I do not hope to turn again
Let these words answer
For what is done, not to be done again
May the judgement not be too heavy upon us

Because these wings are no longer wings to fly
But merely vans to beat the air
The air which is now thoroughly small and dry
Smaller and dryer than the will
Teach us to care and not to care
Teach us to sit still.

Pray for us sinners now and at the hour of our death
Pray for us now and at the hour of our death.

Well, I've of course attempted too much in the hour. When one chooses a theme that one thinks of great present moment – and for this occasion I naturally did that one always has to attempt too much. But I hope I've made plain why I chose to centre it in T. S. Eliot. Against all probability, the major creativity of the English language having since Dickens been going into prose, we had, contemporary with Lawrence, a major poet. There is, as I've said, an obvious sense in which major creativity is more producible, lends itself more to being adduced and made present with effect, in poetry than in prose. And Eliot is unmistakably major, and he is more profoundly of our time – that is my contention – than has been currently recognized. Close acquaintance with his work (and it invites close acquaintance), while sharpening our awareness of the present, sharpens at the same time our insight into the seventeenth century and into that Victorian age in which such indisputably major poetry – poetry as vitally of *its* time – was impossible. That is, it can bring home to us with incomparable force the nature of cultural continuity and its necessity. At the same time it demonstrates in the most cogent way what the creative writer – the kind of writer who truly belongs to English literature, as so many acclaimed writers don't – can do for the English language. Eliot says somewhere that we think of the poets as the maintainers of the language. I should say that all distinguished writers deserve to be called that. But Eliot's remark has point, in that poetry – and notably his – works by concentration. You can produce a page and say with coercive effect: 'There you have it; there's the real thing; there's the clear operative virtue.'

It will be decent to close – if, that is, I don't read too badly – with poetry of Eliot's, and not with words of mine. There are two poems I should like to have read before I conclude, leaving them between you and the discursive discourser.

The first, though also from *Ash-Wednesday*, is strikingly different from the last I read. The thing to note about it is the intensity with which, while appealing to a Christian tradition, it evokes death as extinction. The second, 'Marina', neither comes from *Ash-Wednesday* nor could have belonged there, though it's so impressively an offer 'to construct something upon which to rejoice'. Eliot, though always Eliotic, is wonderfully diverse – more diverse than Donne, Milton, Wordsworth, Keats or Shelley.

II

Lady, three white leopards sat under a juniper tree
In the cool of the day, having fed to satiety
On my legs my heart my liver and that which had been contained
In the hollow round of my skull. And God said
Shall these bones live? shall these
Bones live? And that which had been contained
In the bones (which were already dry) said chirping:
Because of the goodness of this Lady
And because of her loveliness, and because
She honours the Virgin in meditation,
We shine with brightness. And I who am here dissembled
Proffer my deeds to oblivion, and my love
To the posterity of the desert and the fruit of the gourd.
It is this which recovers
My guts the strings of my eyes and the indigestible portions
Which the leopards reject. The Lady is withdrawn
In a white gown, to contemplation, in a white gown.
Let the whiteness of bones atone to forgetfulness.
There is no life in them. As I am forgotten
And would be forgotten, so I would forget
Thus devoted, concentrated in purpose. And God said
Prophesy to the wind, to the wind only for only
The wind will listen. And the bones sang chirping
With the burden of the grasshopper, saying

Lady of silences
Calm and distressed
Torn and most whole
Rose of memory
Rose of forgetfulness
Exhausted and life-giving
Worried reposeful
The single Rose
Is now the Garden
Where all loves end

Terminate torment
Of love unsatisfied
The greater torment
Of love satisfied
End of the endless
Journey to no end
Conclusion of all that
Is inconclusible
Speech without word and
Word of no speech
Grace to the Mother
For the Garden
Where all love ends.

Under a juniper-tree the bones sang, scattered and shining
We are glad to be scattered, we did little good to each other,
Under a tree in the cool of the day, with the blessing of sand,
Forgetting themselves and each other, united
In the quiet of the desert. This is the land which ye
Shall divide by lot. And neither division nor unity
Matters. This is the land. We have our inheritance.

To end with 'Marina' leaves the stress in the right place. There is no
hint of Anglo-Catholicism here or of theology, but there is the characteristic creative quest of the real. You have, in simpler form, the same
constructive method – the co-operative action of different orders of
suggestions. The distinctive note is given by the title, Marina being the
daughter in *Pericles* who was lost and is found, a promise of life for the
father. Working together there is that, the landfall in a new world, and
('I made this' – representing the constructive effort) the ship.

MARINA

Quis hic locus, quæ regio, quæ mundi plaga?

What seas what shores what grey rocks and what islands
What water lapping the bow
And scent of pine and the woodthrush singing through the fog
What images return
O my daughter.

Those who sharpen the tooth of the dog, meaning
Death
Those who glitter with the glory of the hummingbird, meaning
Death
Those who sit in the sty of contentment, meaning
Death
Those who suffer the ecstasy of the animals, meaning
Death

Are become unsubstantial, reduced by a wind,
A breath of pine, and the woodsong fog
By this grace dissolved in place

What is this face, less clear and clearer
The pulse in the arm, less strong and stronger –
Given or lent? more distant than stars and nearer than the eye

Whispers and small laughter between leaves and hurrying feet
Under sleep, where all the waters meet.
Bowsprit cracked with ice and paint cracked with heat.
I made this, I have forgotten
And remember.
The rigging weak and the canvas rotten
Between one June and another September.
Made this unknowing, half conscious, unknown, my own.
The garboard strake leaks, the seams need caulking.
This form, this face, this life
Living to live in a world of time beyond me; let me
Resign my life for this life, my speech for that unspoken,
The awakened, lips parted, the hope, the new ships.

What seas what shores what granite islands towards my timbers
And woodthrush calling through the fog
My daughter.

IV

Dr Richards, Bentham and Coleridge

I admire and revere Coleridge and I am in favour of thinking about poetry – in favour, more generally, of applying intelligence to literature. I should like to have said that in these respects at least I was at one with Dr Richards. But even if I had started reading without premonitions I should very early in this book[1] have conceived a doubt whether Dr Richards's Coleridge would turn out to be mine, or whether the relation between thinking and poetry promoted by Dr Richards would be one I could be happy about. To be fair, I had better say at once that we differ, I think, less essentially about the nature of Coleridge's greatness than about the ways of applying intelligence to poetry: Dr Richards's admiration for Coleridge and his use of him seem to me to be quite unrelated – or to have, merely, a relation such that, contemplating it, we (to borrow a characteristic phrase of Dr Richards's) inevitably adopt a diagnostic attitude.

The doubts I should, even as a reader innocent of earlier acquaintance with Dr Richards's work, have conceived would have taken disturbing forms and proportions by the time I had read the reference to Mr Eliot. If anyone may be said to have been for our time what Coleridge was for his, then it is Mr Eliot. Mr Eliot, like Coleridge, combined a creative gift with rare critical intelligence at one of those moments in poetic history when (if we can think of it as being sometimes otherwise), except in conjunction with rare critical intelligence, there could hardly be a prosperous creative gift – certainly not one capable of important achievement. To have improved the situation for other poets is an achievement of decided importance, and, by his poetry and his criticism together, it is Mr Eliot's: if, as Dr Richards thinks, we are living in, or on the point of living in, a Poetic Renaissance, that is to Mr Eliot's credit in ways for which students of the Romantic movement will provide the parallels.

Though observant already of a tendency in Dr Richards to be less generous towards Mr Eliot than Mr Eliot is habitually towards him,[2] I was nevertheless surprised when I read this:

But I must delay first for a few pages to complain of the very common and rather lazy assumption that intellectual labour will not help the critic. I will quote from Mr Eliot an example of what has become a general custom among literary men in discussing Coleridge. 'Nor am I sure,' he says, 'that Coleridge learnt so much from German philosophers, or earlier from Hartley, as he thought he did; what is best in his criticism seems to come from his own delicacy and subtlety of insight as he reflected upon his own experience of writing and poetry' (*The Use of Poetry*). Yes. But is it an accident that this very peculiar kind of insight is found in Coleridge? His philosophic preoccupations cannot be separated from it. The speculations and the insight incessantly prompt one another.

This already, I am afraid, will be judged to be subtle in an uncomplimentary sense of the term: the sentence quoted from Mr Eliot does not justify – and does not any the more because of the ensuing reasonable commentary – the imputing to him of the 'lazy assumption that intellectual labour will not help the critic'. But when the commentary, having discoursed through a couple of paragraphs on the relation between Coleridge's philosophic preoccupations and his criticism, concludes: 'Is there not something a little ridiculous in saying, "What a fine critic! What a pity he thought so hard about Poetry!"?' – well, one can only hope that Dr Richards hadn't noticed what kind of cue this would inevitably appear to the reader (who may take it, or not). In any case, one reminds oneself that, though there are no doubt different ways of thinking profitably about poetry, Mr Eliot's best criticism stands as an exemplar and a criterion of rigour, relevance and purity of interest – a criterion that very little writing about poetry can afford to challenge.

Actually, the effect of Dr Richards's book (in my opinion) is to justify Mr Eliot's judgment. Indeed, even in conscious intention, Dr Richards might seem again and again to corroborate – or, at any rate, to be insisting on – a not obviously inconsonant distinction. For instance, he says:

But the critical theories can be obtained from the psychology without complication with the philosophical matter. They can be given all the powers Coleridge found for them, without the use either literally, or symbolically, of the other doctrines. The psychology and the metaphysics (and theology) are independent. For Coleridge's own thought, they were not; they probably could not be . . .

Dr Richards's rejoinder lies, of course, in that last sentence – along with his case for giving a great part of his book to the metaphysics. He shows himself, as a matter of fact – and here is the return comment of the reviewer – to be much more interested in the 'philosophical matter' than in the 'critical theories'.

If in his attitude towards the 'philosophical matter' he seems (as in other respects in this book) to be having it so elusively 'both ways', that is because his interest in it is essentially equivocal. The philosopher is no more likely to thank him for his defence of philosophy than Sir Arthur Quiller-Couch to be converted by it. His interest in Coleridge's philosophical explorations is, it may fairly be said, in the interests of Bentham's Theory of Fictions, the aim of the book being to show how out of that theory may be developed a science 'to take' (as Mr C. K. Ogden puts it in his introduction to Bentham's treatise) 'the place of philosophy'. Dr Richards, of course, makes the claim formally for Coleridge and the study of Poetry: Coleridge (as interpreted by an avowed Benthamite) 'succeeded in bringing his suggestions to a point from which, with a little care and pertinacity, they can be taken on to become a new science'.

More than a little pertinacity is demanded by Dr Richards's more abstruse and ambitious chapters (notably 7 and 8) – chapters that justify or otherwise the ambition of the book. An adequate criticism of them would have to come from a critic with a philosophical equipment that I can lay no claim to. (One wonders in what state the matter of them, in the original discussions and lectures, must have left literary students,[3] many of whom would never even have heard of, say, the term 'nominalism' before being, no doubt, introduced to it by Dr Richards.) But even readers without technical qualifications will more than suspect that the ambition is extravagantly disproportionate to the justifying argument: it is one thing to observe that 'to inquire about words is to inquire about everything' and that 'knowledge in all its varieties – scientific, moral, religious – has come to seem a vast mythology with its sub-orders divided according to their different pragmatic sanctions', and much more another thing than Dr Richards seems to recognize to give such observations the rigour and precision of development and statement that are necessary if any problem is to be left where it wasn't before. If one gets the impression that Dr Richards, in these brief chapters, is offering to settle all problems – at any rate, to show us the way to settle them, one is left also with the impression of having been reminded of a number of commonplace philosophic considerations from which strict thinking might start.

Certainly the pretensions are inordinate, and it needs no philosopher (or psychologist or semasiologist) to detect unacceptable compressions and ellipses in key places – failures to make, or to make clearly and hold to, essential distinctions (a debility sorting oddly with the show of analytic rigour, and, it seems, escaping the author's notice by reason of this semasiological zeal itself). For instance, we are given four Natures, IV being the scientist's, and we are told:

Nature, then, even in Senses III and IV, even when all the reflections from our perceiving activity that can be eliminated have been eliminated, remains radically a production of our perceptions.

Again we read:

> We live, today, half in and half out of two projected Natures. One is a Nature
> in Sense III, confused, through lack of reflection, with the unprojected
> ingressive Nature of Sense I. The other is a Nature in Sense II – shot through
> and through with our feelings and thus a mythology for them. These two
> Natures are at war. The enormous development in our conception of Nature
> in Senses III and IV, by seeming to threaten the sanctions of these projected
> feelings, is making them sickly, exaggerated and hysterical.[4]

'Nature' and 'conception (or view) of Nature', Dr Richards thus
reminds us, are interchangeable; where he says 'Nature', we may, if
we like, as here – 'The two conceptions or views of Nature are at war'
– expand it into the longer expression.

Then we remind ourselves that we have just read, on the preceding
page, that 'the perceptions sought by the man of science'

> result in a Nature over which our power of control is increasing with embar-
> rassing leaps and bounds. And through this Nature (the world of natural
> science) it will soon be *possible* for us to remove most of the physical ills that
> oppress humanity.

Is it over a conception (or view) of Nature that our power is increasing
so embarrassingly? Surely it is by means of, with the aid of, our conception that our power is increasing? If so, over what? Over, Dr
Richards answers (I suppose) Nature in Sense I – 'The influences, of
whatever kind, to which the mind is subject from whatever is without
and independent of itself', a Nature that is 'outside our knowledge',
but 'in response to' which we 'take', 'through the perceptive and
imaginative activities of the mind', certain 'images', 'figments',
'things', 'existences' or 'realities' 'to be the world we live in'. And by
the time we come to the passage about 'control' we have been
thoroughly warned against naïve assumptions:

> But *figment* and *real* and *substantial* are themselves words with no meaning that
> is not derived from our experience. To say of anything that it is a figment
> seems to presuppose things more real than itself; but there is nothing within
> our knowledge more real than these images.

Here, clearly, we are in regions where only the technically qualified
should venture comment, and I refrain without difficulty from
suggesting the points in Dr Richards's epistemology at which such a
critic would press his questions and his analysis. I return to the laxity
of expression I seem to myself to have detected in that passage about
our embarrassing power of control (not itself a figment, I assume): – a
mere laxity of expression? I do not think so. If in itself minor, then it
is (to adopt a phrase of Dr Richards's) 'a model for enormous evils'. It

is in any case a laxity without which the subtlety of the following, a subtlety that belongs to the essential purpose of Dr Richards's book, would have been impossible:

> But dissent is not merely probable but certain if this account is applied to all myths, or – to put it the other way – if *all* views of Nature are taken to be projections of the mind, and the religions as well as sciences are included among myths.

This is indeed disarming, the religious reader must feel – very different from the crude attitude of *Science and Poetry* (in reviewing which Mr Douglas Garman,[5] not criticizing from a religious point of view, rudely spoke of the author's 'lick-spittle attitude' to science); if dissent is probable, the dissenter has the emollient assurance that at any rate science and religion are placed on a level and treated with equal respect. The equality, of course, is in courtesy merely. Science is a 'special kind of myth' – 'Other myths do not derive from knowledge in the sense in which science is knowledge' – and the 'fundamentally important difference between the myths of natural science and the myths of poetry in the unrestricted claim upon our overt action of the former (getting out of the way of motor-cars, for example)' is so fundamentally important that, as we see, all other kinds of myth, contrasted with science, fall together under 'poetry'.

I write, not as an indignant religionist who has seen through Dr Richards's blarney, but as a person of literary interests who is nevertheless concerned for rigorous thinking. I have my eye on that term 'myth', which is so generously inclusive, and which does so much of Dr Richards's work for him. Science and 'poetry' are two fundamentally different kinds of thing; science and 'poetry' are the same kind of thing (for some purposes) – anyway, they are both myths, or mythologies. Obviously, the possibilities here of confusion and unconscious sleight are considerable if (as Dr Richards, for his own purposes, does) one insists on using 'myth' as a key term. Naturally, keeping a sharp watch upon the purpose (Tone and Intention, as one registers them locally, are not such as to reassure the suspicious) one looks to the argument for a vigilance and a scrupulousness corresponding to the dangers and temptations. One decidedly does not find what one has a right to expect: it is, indeed, difficult not to conclude, unkindly, that one advantage of a training in the Multiple Definition technique is a certain freedom from inhibition in 'getting it both ways'.

In any case, the conviction remains that the problems Dr Richards offers to deal with lie among the distinctions and differences covered by that embracing concept 'myth' (and its associates), and that he shows nothing approaching an adequate concern for those distinctions and differences. The one difference that is firmly grasped has, as he proffers it, the effect of making science the one kind of myth to be taken seriously ('one gets out of the way of motor-cars'). This may seem unfair, and I am sure that Dr Richards will think so, for, as we shall see, he takes an unusually exalted view of poetry. But 'poetry' – here is another of his embracing terms: it is his lack of interest in the differences he covers with it that produces the effect just noted. I cannot believe that, if you were taking adequate account of the other things besides what I should call 'poetry' that Dr Richards includes under that head, you could be content to leave them there with as little attention to the differences as Dr Richards shows (any more than I can believe that, if you take no more account of the differences, you are, whatever your theories, really a friend to poetry).

Such attention as he does pay to the differences seems merely to emphasize his lack of interest. For instance, we read:

For the claim to be knowledge, in this sense, is the claim to unrestricted control over the anticipation of events . . . We step out of the way of the oncoming motor-bus. But our response to any myth is restricted and conditional. What has gone into it determines what we may properly and wisely take from it. 'We receive but what we give.' If we try to take more from the myth than has gone into it we violate the order of our lives.

If we recognize no more in the way of difficulty here than Dr Richards shows any sign of recognizing, then 'order' (I will risk saying, without indicating where in 'the paradigm of the fluctuations of the word *word*' this use comes) remains, it seems to me, a mere word. Just what has gone into the various necessary myths, how it went, how it determines what we may 'properly and rightly' take, and how we may keep sufficiently supplied with 'myths' into which the appropriate something has somehow 'gone' – these are obviously the important problems, and Dr Richards hardly gives a sign of having noticed them (I will risk, again, adding that he seems to me curiously prone to an uncritical satisfaction with words). He does indeed, extending – in spite of the lapse by which, in the passage just quoted, science, or the motor-bus, becomes contra-distinguished from myth – the term 'Action' to the non-scientific 'mythologies', recognize in a general way that there are various modes of 'Accordant Action' (Belief): 'It includes intellectual assent, feeling, submission in desire, attitude and will – all modes of response to the myth from mere contemplation to overt behaviour'. But here, in what it includes, and remains including – 'intellectual assent, feeling, submission in desire, attitude and will' – are the problems; problems to which successions of distinguished spirits have devoted themselves and concerning which there are important traditions ('wisdom', as Dr Richards uses it, seems to me another mere word).

When he says, 'I have been taking the largest and the smallest myths together,' one can only exclaim: 'You have indeed!' He continues, a sentence or two further on, characteristically: 'Probably the application of my remarks to the larger myths will have most occupied the reader. But an account of the origin and function of myths is more conveniently tested on lesser examples.' 'Conveniently' certainly seems the right word here. But the instances of 'testing' that he adduces – his dealings (to be referred to later) with Landor and the 'Immortality Ode' – make the coolness (for I don't know how else to describe it) of the procedure something for gaping admiration. And actually, whatever might be established or not about the 'larger myths' by analysing bits of poems, nowhere in his book, it must be said, does Dr Richards seriously attempt even such analysis.

To say this, of course, is, by the terms of his own challenge, to dismiss the pretension of the book. But even if, groping one's way through the largenesses of the philosophic argument, one had slipped by the small testings and failed to keep the challenge in mind, and, in philosophic modesty, had concluded that there was a swarm of doubts of which Dr Richards ought to have the benefit, one would, even in one's worst state of dazed fatigue, have been quite sure by the last chapter that something had gone badly wrong – sure, because of where Dr Richards exhibits himself as left by the argument:

To put the burden of constituting an order for our minds on the poet may seem unfair. It is not the philosopher, however, or the moralist who puts it on him, but birth.

The intended force of this claim for 'the poet', so stated apart from the context, would be uncertain, and, indeed, remains so; but that we are to take the claim at the extreme of romantic inflation the context leaves us no room for doubt. Dr Richards has asserted, basing himself mainly on a suggested comparison between Defoe's description of Crusoe's sea-shore and Mr Joyce's of Stephen Dedalus's, that there has been a 'dissolution of consciousness' such that 'the whole machinery through which self-examination with a view to increased order could be conducted by Defoe has lapsed'. It is, as a rule, impossible to pin Dr Richards down locally to any precise meaning; here, for instance, 'machinery' appears to be grammatically in apposition with 'the nomenclature of the faculties, of the virtues and the vices, of the passions, of the moods . . . ' and while, on the one hand, 'nomenclature' when used by Dr Richards is a term to watch very warily, 'increased order', on the other hand, is moderate in suggestion. But a reading of the sequence of pages makes it plain that we are to take 'dissolution' as meaning (for some purposes, at any rate) the effective disappearance of the very principles of order – of the main lines of organization once represented by the old nomenclature and the current 'vocabulary' – and the absence of anything in the nature of appropriate 'mythology'. 'Without his mythologies man is only a cruel animal without a soul'; and it is in any case plain that birth will have to have bestowed on the poet something very considerable indeed besides a burden.

The dissolution of consciousness exhibited in such prose [as that of *Jacob's Room* or *Ulysses* – odd collocation] . . . forces the task of reconstituting a less relaxed, a less adventitious order for the mind upon contemporary poetry.

I still don't understand just how prose is related to poetry in this argument, and the expectation entertained of 'the poet' seems to me preposterously extravagant, but it is nevertheless pleasant to be able to agree that contemporary poetry is, or ought to be, important. Further agreement would seem to follow: agreement, let us say, in the aims represented by *Scrutiny*. It follows, for instance, that it is important to get poetry read – to work towards providing for it, what does not exist at present, an informed, intelligent and influential public. And having made this very obvious point, we find ourselves contemplating the problems presented by the state of current criticism – we find ourselves committed to desiderating (shall we say?) and supporting, when they appear, some serious critical journals; we find ourselves, moreover, committed to hoping (at any rate) that something may come of a determined, concerted and sustained effort in the educational field. And if we take these commitments seriously we shall before long find ourselves contemplating economic and political problems. In any case we shall not be light-hearted.

And here, in this last sentence, I have come to a reason for not being confident that any such measure of agreement as should, I have suggested, follow a common recognition of the importance of poetry does really exist between Dr Richards and myself. He is decidedly light-hearted. He writes, for instance:

Eras that produced no poetry that is remembered have been as disordered as ours. There are better reasons, in the work of modern poets, to hope that a creative movement is beginning and that poetry, freed from a mistaken conception of its limitations, and read more discerningly than heretofore, will remake our minds and with them our world.

Clearly there would be no point in asking for – what would nevertheless be very interesting – a little specificity here; there may be three times as many modern poets, and poets three times as promising, as any I know of, but that would not make Dr Richards's optimism regarding their influence critically respectable. In fact, Poetry in general for Dr Richards – and for him it is always in general – is, it becomes impossible in these places to doubt, a myth that has very little to do with any particular actualities of poetry, or with the actualities of the world in which poets have to produce their work. It is a large private myth into which, seeing what he gets from it, one concludes a great deal must have gone: with the aid of it he evades the motor-buses and other difficulties and dangers in his theoretical path, slipping into the empyrean by something very like the Indian rope-trick.

His view of poetry indeed is unrealistic to a degree almost incredible. Having, for instance, laid the burden upon 'the poet', he says:

There is a figure of speech here, of course, for the burden is not on individual poets, but upon the poetic function. With Homer, Dante and Shakespeare in mind, however, the importance of the single poet is not to be underestimated.

Dr Richards would seem to favour an idealist individualism that amounts to a naïve Marxism inverted. In any case, to suggest that we may reasonably look for anything approaching a modern Homer, Dante or Shakespeare is to endorse the crudest romantic notion of inspired genius: does Dr Richards know nothing about the general cultural conditions represented by the achievements of those poets (if we are to call Homer a poet in the same sense as Dante or Shakespeare) – conditions, in each case, essential to the achievement, and beyond the capacity of the greatest individual genius to provide? If the nature and significance of such conditions had been present to him he could hardly have been so light-hearted about the 'dissolution of consciousness' that he envisages – he could hardly, even if there had been a wide public for poetry in our time and no Book Societies, Hollywoods and Northcliffes, have talked of the necessary new myths as something that a few individual poets, or a Poetic Renaissance, could improvise. It is, as a matter of fact, the very absence of such conditions in our time that he is asking the poet – or the poetic function – to remedy.

These problems raised by the mention of Homer, Dante and Shakespeare get no hint of recognition. Instead we find:

Such an estimate of the power of poetry may seem extravagant; but it was Milton's no less than Shelley's, Blake's or Wordsworth's. It has been the opinion of many with whom we need not be ashamed to agree . . . [Quotation from Ben Jonson follows.]

We haven't yet decided whether this is a careless insult to our intelligence, or merely an incredibly innocent peroration, when we discover that it is modesty. These exalted and reverberant generalities, it turns out, express merely a certain embarrassment at the approach of the real claim – at the shift from oblique statement to the direct. The real claim is not for the poet, but for the semasiologist:

With Coleridge we step across the threshold of a general theoretical study of language capable of opening to us new powers over our minds comparable to those which systematic physical inquiries are giving us over our environment. The step across was of the same type as that which took Galileo into the modern world. It requires the shift from a preoccupation with the What and Why to the How of language.

The step, it appears, has already been taken; something has been established in this book:

And it has this consequence, that critics in the future must have a theoretical equipment of a kind which has not been felt to be necessary in the past. (So physicists may sigh for the days in which less mathematics was required by them.) But the critical equipment will not be *primarily* philosophical. It will be rather a command of the methods of comparing our meanings. As the theory of Poetry develops, what is needed will be disengaged from philosophy much as the methodology of physics has been disengaged.

Dr Richards's book, we are to understand, has both demonstrated the possibility and nature of the new science and provided a start towards the necessary 'mathematics'.

What is there in the book to justify these pretensions? Bluntly, nothing. There are recurrent hints at the revolutionary new technique and its epoch-making potentialities, but, for demonstration, not even a beginning in the serious critical analysis of poetry.

The most determined show of demonstrating the technique and inaugurating the science is chapter 4, 'Imagination and Fancy', in which Dr Richards tries to turn Coleridge's distinction into a precise (or, to be fair, useful) laboratory instrument. Taking Coleridge's own example from 'Venus and Adonis', he notices that in the Fancy passage

> Full gently now she takes him by the hand,
> A lily prison'd in a gaol of snow [etc.]

there is no 'relevant interaction, no interinanimation', between the 'units of meaning'. Shakespeare, he says justly, is not attempting to realize in words the contact of hands, either as felt by the actors or seen by us. 'He is making pleasing collocations that are *almost* wholly unconnected with what he is writing about.' The commentary continues, characteristically:

Why he is doing this (and what this is) are large questions. The answer would
be partly historical . . . It would be partly psychological . . .

But why not, one asks, make the obvious and essential point that
Shakespeare with his 'lily', 'snow', 'ivory' and 'alabaster' is being conventional – conventional in a mode readily illustrated from any
anthology of Elizabethan verse (or from *The Oxford Book*)?

Those 'large questions' are merely a nuisance: they distract Dr
Richards from noticing that the decorative-conventional element, pervasive in the poem, conditions such passages as that which he takes, in
isolation, as imaginative. At any rate, if he notices, he says nothing
about it, but gives a very misleading account of:

> Look! how a bright star shooteth from the sky
> So glides he in the night from Venus' eye.

He does not point out how, when we come to these lines in their place
in the poem, 'realization' is limited and conditioned, the situation
'distanced', so that we suffer no such profound imaginative stir as his
analysis suggests.

He will no doubt reply that he is deliberately restricting his commentary, for the moment, to the enforcement of a given point. To this
one has to rejoin that he nowhere in the book goes any further or
deeper, or suggests the limitations and dangers of this superficial
inspection of odds and ends, or incites to the discipline required for
the serious analysis of poetry. He encourages instead the wholly mis-
directed kind of ingenuity represented by the footnote on p. 80. The
triviality of the demonstration – and, I repeat, we get nothing more
serious – offers an odd contrast with the portentous prelude, 'The
Coalescence of Subject and Object', which we are invited to wrestle
with as essential to the understanding of Fancy and Imagination (the
book in general is characterized by such a contrast – the contrast,
sometimes amusing, between the difficulty of the philosophic argument and the critical greenness presumed in the reader).

This triviality is inherent in the ambition of the undertaking. The
explanation lies in the following sentence:

This, then, is an *observable* difference from which we set out, though it is
unhappily not true that all can observe it equally or equally clearly.

That '*observable*' explains why, after the setting out, there is no
advance. Why is it italicized? Clearly, in order to suggest – the claim
is implicit – that here we have the beginnings of a laboratory
technique. This is the point at which, in unavoidable nakedness, the
nature of the process of 'reinterpreting' Coleridge in Benthamite terms

(or of uniting the realms of Coleridge and Bentham) lies exposed, clear for a moment of metaphysics and semasiology. What do we propose to bring for treatment into the laboratory? Poetry, or bits of poetry. But the data can be possessed only by a delicate inner discipline, and in such possession as is incompatible with producing them in any laboratory, or in any way that the analogy of 'laboratory' does not completely misrepresent. Dr Richards himself (who does not use the word 'laboratory', but merely italicizes 'observable') has said as much again and again, sometimes in quite admirable formulations; for example (*Practical Criticism*):

It might be said, indeed, with some justice, that the value of poetry lies in the difficult exercise in sincerity it can impose upon its readers even more than upon the poet.

But the new science has somehow to be got started. So we find Dr Richards trying to explain how 'something rather like a refreshed atomism – a counting of relations – appears again as we develop and apply Coleridge's doctrine'. This counting must not be crudely confused with valuation – the valuation that involves exercises in sincerity, and so confronts laboratory technique with extremely delicate problems. These problems may be postponed, and dealt with later. Coleridge, of course, used the terms, Imagination and Fancy, as implying different values. 'The conception [Imagination] was devised as a means of describing the wider and deeper powers of some poetry'. Nevertheless, we can, if we wish,

make the terms purely descriptive. We shall then have instances of Imagination which are valuable and instances which are not, and we must then go on to contrive a further theory, a theory of values which will explain (so far as we are able to do so at present) these differences of value. [This is the procedure I attempted to follow in *Principles of Literary Criticism*.]

There is, perhaps, something admirable in the candour of that square-bracketed parenthesis: Dr Richards will hardly contend at this date that the theory of values expounded in *Principles of Literary Criticism* is of any use for any respectable purpose whatever, or that it does anything but discredit the ambition to make criticism a science. In any case, the confusion obscuring the scientific project remains, and it is not lessened by Dr Richards's appearing to put the case against himself in the latter part of the chapter. (He has an odd way of suggesting that by being on both sides at once – or by slipping unobtrusively from one to the other – one reconciles them.)

Coleridge's critical doctrine, of course, cannot be 'developed and applied' into a science; to attempt such development and application is to abandon him for (shall we say?) Bentham. Dr Richards, in his account of the bent of interest and the training that produced the doctrine, curiously slights one important head. Metaphysics and psychology get full insistence:

It is to be expected then that what he found to say after his inquiries will not be understood by those without a similar training. This is true of all special studies. Psychology, however, is peculiar in that those who are not students in it feel ready so often to correct those who were.

Against this it seems to me important to set – we have Coleridge's own words[6] – another aspect of his training:

O! when I think of the inexhaustible mine of virgin treasure in our Shakespeare, that I have been almost daily reading him since I was ten years old – that the thirty intervening years have been unintermittingly and not fruitlessly employed in the study of the Greek, Latin, English, Italian, Spanish and German *belle-lettrists* . . .

With these intense literary interests and this training, Coleridge (he was indeed a 'subtle-souled psychologist') was equipped to think rigorously about poetry and to understand the nature and conditions of the process of analysing it. Even if the theoretical knowledge 'available' in his time had equalled the modern psychologist's, he could hardly have asked (at any rate, with Dr Richards's intention): 'Do we yet know enough about what we are doing when we try to analyse a passage of poetry to settle its merits or demerits by *argument?*'[7] I say 'with Dr Richards's intention' because the question is not unambiguous. But (though – or is it 'though'? – Dr Richards says that, with our present knowledge, 'the answer must be a firm "No" ') the dealings with the 'Immortality Ode' that follow compel us to interpret 'settle by argument' in the way the pervasive laboratory pretension suggests.

Dr Richards undertakes to dispose of Coleridge's strictures on the 'Mighty Prophet! Seer blest!' passage. Some of the replies admit of very damaging rejoinders, but few readers interested in poetry will bother to argue with Dr Richards: it is so plain that the piece of arguing he offers (though it is a large proportion of the illustrative practice on which he bases his science) neither illustrates, nor furthers, the analysis of poetry. It will perhaps be enough (space being limited) to quote his conclusion:

My comments on Coleridge's misunderstandings do not aver that the Ode is a piece of scientific psychology. Nor would I say that – apart from some twenty lines, five or six of which are 'truths that wake, to perish never' – it is at Wordsworth's highest level. But its weakest lines deserve respect as the frame of what they support.

No critic who had gone through the Ode in (to use Dr Richards's own admirable phrase) 'experimental submission' could have committed himself to this summing-up, or have supposed that the argument leading to it was doing anything but distract from the relevant analysis. (Of course, an account of the Ode is assumed here that I am, naturally, ready to supply.)

Coleridge's interest in developing his theories was of a kind that did not tempt him to forget the nature of 'experimental submission' (without which, whatever it is that is analysed, it is not poetry). And the central passage on the Imagination, we do well to remind ourselves, begins with the sentence about the poet's bringing 'the whole soul of man into activity, with the subordination of its faculties to each other according to their relative worth and dignity'. It is one thing for Coleridge to point, by means of examples, to the kind of way in which Imagination manifests itself locally. It is very much another thing to suppose that one is developing his theory into precision when, by much argument about isolated odds and ends of verse, one arrives at this:

> But Imagination, as I have described it, can be shown in trivial examples. And Fancy can be shown in important matters . . . In Imagination, as I have taken it, the joint effect (worthless or not) . . .

Coleridge's theory can be developed only in an arduous and scrupulous exploration of the organic complexities of poetry by a developing analysis – by an analysis going deeper and deeper and taking wider and wider relations into account; that is, becoming less and less disguisable as laboratory technique. Dr Richards's procedure, heading away from the concrete, leaves him (it is an ironical fate for one who warns us so much against this sort of thing) the happy servant of a set of abstract terms. It is comment enough on the new science that it should enable him, in the effort to explain how 'the sense of musical delight', which is a 'gift of the imagination', can be given by 'The Faerie Queene', which is 'chiefly a work of Fancy', to discover in that poem

> an architectural, which is here an imaginative, unity. And it may be this other unity which produces 'the sense of musical delight'. It is thus that Spenser 'has an imaginative fancy'.

The ingenious undergraduate will certainly find that the new apparatus has its uses.

It is plain that, when Dr Richards remarks that 'persons with literary interests today frequently suffer from lack of exercise in careful and sometimes arduous thinking', he lays himself open to the retort that, if one is going to think with effect about literature, there must be no lack of intensity in one's literary interests. They must be intense enough to ensure disinterestedness. It is here that Dr Richards, in certain very obvious ways, fails. That his literary interests derive from an interest in theory rather than his theory from his literary interests has never been a secret. The fact is apparent (Dr Richards insists upon one's coming out with this delicate kind of judgment) in his prose. Mr Eliot made a radical criticism when he corrected that 'enormity' in the Ritual for Sincerity. The insensitiveness is pervasive. (Even in descending to slang one should respect the peculiar force of the given expression, and I take the occasion here to protest against the jocular reference to Coleridge as the 'Highgate spell-binder': 'spell-binding' surely implies a combination of contempt for one's audience with desire to impress it, and Coleridge, I imagine, was at no period guilty of that sort of thing.)

But the disability that beyond any question matters is that apparent both in the infrequency, in Dr Richards's theorizing, of any approach to the concrete and in the quality of such approach as he ventures on. *Practical Criticism*, for instance, is valuable in spite of the title's being a misnomer; and the theoretical considerations – the hints thrown out, the questions asked – would have been more valuable if they had derived from a more adequate interest in particulars. That book, too, offers depressing instances of the relation between insufficiency of interest and lack of disinterestedness, the most remarkable of them being Dr Richards's 'case' about the Longfellow poem. No one concerned merely to see what was there in front of him could have found that poem 'extremely urbane' and 'rather witty' (references to 'Dryden, Pope and Cowper'); or have supposed that the case made out, with 'suppleness (not subtlety)', was even faintly plausible.

The offence (there are others of the kind in *Practical Criticism*) is a very serious one in a champion of the serious study of poetry. It is shocking to find Dr Richards, in the present book, impenitent about another offence of the same kind. He refers back to his *Fifteen Lines of Landor* as a serious experiment. But I have not been able to discover that he has replied anywhere to the letter from Mr Bonamy Dobree printed in *The Criterion* for October, 1933. Mr Dobree there points out that 'Dr Richards deliberately made a puzzle for his students by omitting to inform them what Landor was talking about' (the information being necessary because of the wresting of the passage from its context). 'It is one thing,' comments Mr Dobree, 'to conduct scientific experiments on the reactions of people to certain collections of words, another to discover, by a little calm thought, what a poet was talking about.' Mr Dobree, moreover, in his closing sentence, puts his finger on the irrelevant 'idea', the imported interest, that led Dr Richards to set his students at exercises so much the reverse of conducive, in nature and spirit, to the sensitive reading of poetry.

The last chapter of the present book is called 'The Bridle of Pegasus' and it is especially full of irresponsible generalities, bright ideas and uncritical tips. Who, for instance, are these 'new-fanglers' who are unable to construe the 'meaning structures' of 'Shelley, Keats or Wordsworth' (and what have the 'meaning structures' of these three poets in common)? Is it, again, a critical, or scientific, proceeding to base any conclusion about the development of consciousness on a comparison between Daniel Defoe and James Joyce? Ought Dr Richards to throw out such large generalizations about the history of reading capacity so lightly, and so lightly to 'decline the invidious task of demonstration'? Is it helpful to point out that the 'agèd eagle' passage in *Ash-Wednesday* is 'dramatic', without noting too that it falls (its significance being that it does so) within a poem an essential characteristic of which is to be much less 'dramatic' than most of Mr Eliot's work? Has Dr Richards not read the 'Mad Prince's Song' since he wrote *Science and Poetry* that he should still think that poem (in which Mr de la Mare makes a characteristic use of Ophelia) a 'quintessence' of *Hamlet*? Does he still think that Mr Yeats in 'The Wind Among the Reeds' was writing 'an unusually simple and direct kind of love poetry' (*Science and Poetry*)?

But I must leave the rest of my notes unused. It is depressing to realize, in any case, that this commentary has been so completely adverse. But Dr Richards does seem to me to be heading completely away from any useful path – and to be heading others: his past work has won him prestige enough to make this explicitness unavoidable. It is a great pity, when one thinks of what, had he limited himself to any given discipline, he might have accomplished. As it is, one can only turn against him the terms of his own challenge:

But the study of poetry, for those born in this age, is more arduous than we suppose. It is therefore rare. Many other things pass by its name and are encouraged to its detriment.

The literary discipline and liberal education

To think, at all seriously and insistently, about the teaching of literature is to tackle the problem of liberal education – that problem which,
as it confronts us in the world we live in, is so desperately urgent and
so desperately difficult. This proposition will not, perhaps, strike the
reader as anything more than a truism. I must confess, however, that
I myself didn't realize its full meaning (or the meaning it has for me
today) until, as a university teacher, I had for some years been preoccupied with the means of making the study of literature a discipline
of intelligence – a specific discipline, with a field of its own, and pre-
rogative rights within that field; preoccupied, that is, with critical
method, and with the 'literary' in a decidedly limiting sense. I was
bent on insisting that the study of literature should have as its informing principle an idea of criticism.

I later came to recognize the need for a complementary insistence,
and, after having been accused of a 'narrow' preoccupation with the
'words on the page', I now drew the comment that I appeared, in my
'Sketch for an English School'[1] to give more attention to non-literary
studies than to literature. And I had here better say at once that my
sense of the inevitableness with which serious literary studies lead outside themselves, and of the cogency with which they ask to be
associated with studies outside the strictly literary-critical field, is such
that I must necessarily, in this symposium, give myself the freedom of
the whole field of interest represented for me by the 'teaching of literature'. If I am to discuss the 'teaching of literature' seriously I must be
discussing liberal education and the Idea of a University.

This may seem not to have needed saying. That I should have felt
called on to say it goes with the particular history and the particular
situation out of which I write. I am explicitly making my approach in
terms of that history and that situation, and I offer no apology for
doing so. It is a kind of particularity that seems to me to have a necessary place in the discussion. It is not only that generalities need to be
weighted and edged as much as possible with the concrete; the complex problem of liberal education (while general principles are, of
course, involved) doesn't admit of one complete general answer. The
answer we have to hope for will be a matter of bringing together dif-

ferent partial solutions that have been worked out in different terms at different places. We need a multiplicity of experiments – experiments that will give one another mutual stimulus, correction, and (the academic world being what it is) support.

I myself write as an Englishman, whose work has been in England and at Cambridge. This means, of course, that the terms in which the problem has presented itself to me differ in various ways from those in which it is likely to be seen by any American. But, having 'placed' myself as an English academic, I must hasten to disclaim any representative status. For, to be more specific, I write from my own college, and anyone who goes to any British university with the idea that what goes on at Downing in the way of English Studies is representative of 'Cambridge English' will be very soon corrected. And what 'goes on' at Downing, what I have learnt from the opportunities given me there, and what might, I am convinced, go on, some not unimaginable new conditions favouring – here, essentially, is what I am reporting as my contribution to the symposium.

If I stress the intransigence associated by common repute with Downing, that is not merely by way of enforcing my disclaimer; it is not for any reason that can be made to look like modesty, but because I draw a general conclusion from my experience. The conclusion is this: it is in the interstices of the official system, in holes and corners and chance islands, that, in respect of this problem of liberal education, the real work will be done, the life fostered, the energy generated, the possibility proved. This, I am profoundly convinced, should be our expectation. No one, I think, who both grasps the nature of the problem and has had experience of the institutional mind on the 'humane' side of universities can suppose that anywhere, in any major instance, the official system will for long tend to promote any serious attempt at an answer – or to foster life.

I don't say this as an expression of pessimism, but as a reminder of conditions that it can never be salutary to forget: we have to be vigilant against the temptations of use and fatigue – inert acquiescences, concessions to social amenity, tacit agreements to take the form for the reality and the running of the machine for the movement of life. Something worth doing can, I am sure, be done. But, if it is to count for much in the sum of things, there must be the utmost collaboration among those who, in different places, really care – and collaboration includes the play of challenge, criticism and mutual recall to standards.

I am conscious that my own situation has afforded certain marked advantages. Cambridge is not yet 'the University for East Anglia' (as the late Miss Ellen Wilkinson, Minister of Education in the Labour government, thought it ought to be, even as Manchester is the University for Lancashire): with Oxford, it creams the country. This means that one hasn't to try and do at the university what ought to have been done at school: one's students are ready for work at the fully adult level – this is the assumption on which one forms one's expectations of them. Further my own college has for a decade and a half run an independent yearly examination for scholarships in English – an examination designed (and it has justified itself) to discover not the 'good student', but the live intelligence potentially capable of creative thought. This means (I ought to say that it isn't merely a matter of awards actually given – there is a wide effect of attraction) that one can count on an accession every year from the schools of (say) half-a-dozen really distinguished men – men who have a good background of reading, who are far from novices in the critical discussion of literature, and with whom one can talk, without cramping allowances, at the top level from the start.

I stress this advantage, since it has an essential bearing on the high expectation I may be judged to entertain of the student. I do consciously entertain a high expectation: I am avowedly concerned with the training of an élite, and my discussion postulates the appropriate material. Everyone concerned with liberal education at the university should be able to say the same. I think it worth making so obvious a point since in England too we have now, and shall have more and more, to fight against that interpretation of democracy which amounts to the law that no one may have anything everyone can't have. Situations and opportunities vary, but it can hardly anywhere or at any time be unnecessary to insist that, when standards are let down, everyone suffers and the whole community pays the penalty. And the reasonable maintenance of standards everywhere depends on their uncompromising assertion at the highest possible level somewhere. We have our duties as we are confronted with them by our opportunities.

The situation I have described offers, then, very high opportunities. Of course, the bringing together of a society of intelligent young men in such a milieu as Cambridge conduces, of itself, to the ends of liberal education, whatever the deficiencies of syllabuses and teachers – conduces the more the more satisfactory is the formal academic scheme of requirement, guidance and stimulus. It is a good test of any scheme, actual or proposed, to ask whether it promotes to the utmost this informal life of mind and spirit (by the quality of which it is to be judged whether a university is really a university).

Of the English Tripos at Cambridge an impressive report might be made. It certainly presents opportunities and advantages. A major

advantage, which gives reality to the opportunities, can be put nega-
tively: there are no philological or (in the narrow sense) linguistic compulsions. A man needn't spend his time on Anglo-Saxon and the
related things; he can devote his two or his three years (according as he
chooses to take one or both parts of the Tripos) to literature and to
liberal studies, unhampered by mere academic grinds or by wasteful
and distracting irrelevancies. Positively, the syllabus offers a rich field
of opportunity – as rich, it might appear, as an intelligent student or
his director could reasonably ask for. But, of course, no one seriously
concerned with discussing liberal education draws his conclusions
from syllabuses, or builds his hopes merely on changes in them. What
a syllabus means depends, we all know, on the system of examining or
testing the student with which it is associated, and also on the arrange-
ments for his instruction and guidance. The English Tripos, as a
matter of fact, is officially and formally an examination, the scope of
which is defined in terms of 'papers' to be taken. 'Nothing,' says Dr
Alexander Meiklejohn in *The Experimental College* 'is more revealing
of the purpose underlying a course of study than the nature of the
examination given at the close.' I have caused some offence, I gather,
by saying, in my *Education and the University*, that, judged in this
light, the underlying purpose of the Cambridge English School is to
produce journalists. This conclusion still seems to me an unanswerable one. The man reading English knows that his placing, the credit
he gets for his two years' work (and again, if he takes Part II, his subsequent one year's), will be determined by his performance in an end-
of-course race, or series of races, against the clock: he will have to
prove his quality and exhibit the quality of his studies by scribbling,
if he can, from three to five essay answers in each of half-a-dozen three-
hour periods in the examination room. He knows, on the other hand,
that there will be a wide choice of questions, and that, if a paper on a
given stretch (say) of English Literature offers, according to
precedent, twenty or thirty or more questions to choose from, it
should be possible, with the help of back papers (the series is available), and in the interests of economy, to do some intelligent
anticipating.

The worst thing about this system, it will be seen, isn't the unsatis-
factoriness (striking as that is) of the test of quality it applies, but that
the test becomes an end, determining the use to which a man puts his
time, and the way in which he works. Knowing on what kind of
exhibition and what kind of athleticism his class will depend, he is a
very remarkable man indeed if his studies don't tend to be a matter of
acquiring in any field, with a canny economy, what can be unloaded
with effect in the scribbled half-hour answers to three or four

judiciously anticipated questions. Worse, the kind of readiness in delivery, the lack of inhibition, he knows he must cultivate, is inimical to the development that any real education would be fostering. It is impossible not to judge that those who contentedly accept and operate such a system take for first-class the mind that moves happily among clichés, and exhibits a glib accomplishment in handling them because it hasn't begun to know what real thinking is like.

Of course, real thinking, with the kind of effort and stamina even a little of it requires, isn't common, but it should be one of the first concerns of a liberal course to insure that the student at least knows, as the result of painful as well as exhilarating experience, the difference between it and the usual business of a more or less adroit arranging of the counters to form a neat surface. By this criterion there can be no favourable judgment on the English Tripos. Not that there aren't worse systems. Far worse is that by which, in a close correlation of lecture room and examination room, the student is made to vomit up, from stage to stage in his course, the regulation intake for that stage. The candidate for the English Tripos has at least his full year in which to take his risks of disinterested study, and no one supposes that lectures need be taken seriously (the intelligent men – women tend to be more faithful – go to very few after their first term). The syllabus being reasonable, a few of the best-equipped and most self-reliant, especially if they are lucky enough to find the right friends, do get something of a real education during their time at Cambridge. But this is no sufficient defence of the system. And to the question, so often asked, 'What better can be devised?', the answer, it seems to me, is: 'Read Meiklejohn's *Experimental College*, paying special attention to pages 93–6.' I differ profoundly from Dr Meiklejohn about various things, and I have radical criticism to offer of the lines on which the experiment at Madison was conducted. But Dr Meiklejohn's report of it is a classic for those of us who are preoccupied with the problem; it conveys the stimulus of a real, disinterested and intelligent experiment, and in certain essential matters, it seems to me, the experimenters were unanswerably right. Among these is the insistence that the student must be judged by 'pieces of work' done under proper working conditions during the course, and not by examination-room tests. This method of judging is seen, as Dr Meiklejohn reports its operation, to go with a régime of relations between students and their guides involving, as its distinguishing characteristic, a free and flexible use of the methods of discussion group and seminar. And here again, it is plain to me, the Experimental College was right.

An intransigent working in the situation I have described as my own, working therefore with students who, whatever else they may do, have in any case to take, and be placed by, the end-of-course examination, can only make the most of grievously limited and compromised opportunities. Nor is he one of a team of duly assorted and enthusiastic collaborators. So it will be gathered that what I am offering to report is not anything fully and properly *done* at Downing but what I can nevertheless affirm to have been sufficiently shown, in practice, to be practical possibilities, and well calculated in view of the desired ends.

One thing can, I report, be effectively and without compromise done even in so limiting a situation: that is to vindicate and establish in practice the idea of literary study as a discipline of intelligence. I have spoken above of the need, if a liberal education is to amount to anything, to bring home to the student the nature of real thinking. It is in the field of *literary* study, in the strictest sense, that we have to do that. What I have to say seems to me so obvious that I am always embarrassed about insisting on it. Yet, judging by what I observe, hear, and read, the insistence is necessary.

The specific discipline in the field of literary study is the literary-critical. This should surely be a commonplace and a truism. Yet, contemplating the English Tripos, I have been moved to write:

It must be said bluntly that as things are, even where enlightenment most prevails and literature is emancipated from linguistics, a bad economy is positively prescribed, and the student wastes his labour not only through lack of guidance, but in compliance with authoritative misdirection. Are the principles that should govern a School of English so hard to grasp? Here, to begin with, is a negative formulation: there is no more futile study than that which ends with mere knowledge *about* literature. If literature is worth study, then the test of its having been so will be the ability to read literature intelligently, and apart from this ability an accumulation of knowledge is so much lumber. The study of a literary text about which the student cannot say, or isn't concerned to be able to say, as a matter of first-hand perception and judgment – of intelligent realization – why it should be worth study is a self-stultifying occupation . . . Literary history, as a matter of 'facts about' and accepted critical (or quasi-critical) description and commentary, is a worthless acquisition; worthless for the student who cannot as a critic – that is, as an intelligent and discerning reader – make a personal approach to the essential data of the literary historian, the works of literature (an approach is personal or it is nothing: you cannot take over the appreciation of a poem, and unappreciated, the poem isn't 'there'). The only acquisition of literary history having any educational value is that made in the exercise of critical intelligence to the ends of the literary critic.

It is not enough to permit a vaguely 'appreciative' study of literature, uncontrolled by the relevant specific discipline. The best result of such a study will be to further the contemptible kind of literary 'culture' in which literary fashions are the social currency, and a glib superficiality – quickness in the uptake, an impressive range of reference, and knowingness about the latest market-quotations – usurps the place of intelligence, disinterestedness and real interest. And where you don't entertain and enforce a strict idea of the relevant specific discipline you will find yourself looking for your discipline in irrelevancies – in restored linguistic compulsions, in philosophy, in semantics (a present American tendency, I have been led to suspect), or in the bogus science of semasiology.

What I take to be the relevant and essential discipline, it will have been gathered from the self-quotation I permitted myself above, is a training of perception and critical judgment. I have chosen to describe it as a discipline of intelligence, the means of starting the student towards real and creative thinking, because that, it seems to me, is where the stress peculiarly needs to be laid. The study of literature has its key place in liberal education because, properly pursued, it involves a discipline of intelligence that is at the same time a training of sensibility – of perception, qualitative response and judgment. This discipline is that which begins with the 'practical criticism' analysis of passages and short poems. This matter is so crucial that, in my *Education and the University*, in order to guard against misapprehensions as to what I meant, I not only thought fit to give some account of the nature of critical analysis, but went on further to offer some illustration. I will here, by way of suggesting what insistence on elementary things my experience of the academic (and the literary) world in my own country has shown to be necessary, quote part of the account I gave.

That the problem of demonstration should arise as such brings home how little, in the way of performance of their function, is commonly expected, or to be expected, either of literary critics or of English Schools. For surely, as one might say to one's beginning students, it should be possible, by cultivating attentive reading, to acquire a higher skill than the untrained reader has: a skill that will enable the trained reader to do more with a poem than ejaculate approval or disapproval, or dismiss it with vaguely reported general impressions, qualified with modest recognition that (in Arnold Bennett's words) 'taste after all is relative'. Analysis, one would go on, is the process by which we seek to attain a complete reading of the poem – a reading that approaches as nearly as possible to the perfect reading. There is about it nothing in the nature of 'murdering to dissect', and suggestions that it can be anything in the nature of laboratory method misrepresent it entirely. We can have the poem only by an inner kind of possession; it is 'there' for analysis only in so far as we are responding appropriately to the words on the page. In pointing to them (and there is nothing else to point to) what we are doing is to bring into sharp focus, in turn, this, that and the other detail, juncture or relation in our total response; or (since 'sharp focus' may be a misleading account of the kind of attention sometimes required), what we are doing is to dwell with a deliberate, considering responsiveness on this, that or the other node or focal point in the complete organization that the poem is, in so far as we have it. Analysis is not a dissection of something that is already and passively there. What we call analysis is, of course, a constructive or creative process. It is a more deliberate following through of that process of creation in response to the poet's words which reading is. It is a re-creation in which, by a considering attentiveness, we ensure a more than ordinary faithfulness and completeness.

As addressed to other readers it is an appeal for corroboration; 'the poem builds up in this way, doesn't it? this bears such-and-such a relation to that, don't you agree?' In the work of an English School this aspect of mutual check – positively, of collaboration 'in the common pursuit of true judgment' – would assert itself as a matter of course.

To insist on this critical work as discipline is not to contemplate the elaboration of technical apparatus and drill. The training is to be one in the sensitive and scrupulous use of intelligence; to that end, such help as can be given the student will not be in the nature of initiations into technical procedures, and there is no apparatus to be handed over – a show of such in analytic work will most likely turn out to be a substitute for the use of intelligence upon the text. Where help can and should be got, of course, is in examples of good practice, wherever these can be found. 'Instruction' will take the form of varied and developing demonstration, offered to the actively critical student (i.e. in discussion-work conditions) as exemplifying a suitable use of intelligence.

And it is not only good examples that have an educational function. A useful exercise for the moderately seasoned student would be to go through W. Empson's *Seven Types of Ambiguity*, or parts of it, discriminating between the profitable and the unprofitable, the valid and the vicious. Empson's extremely mixed and uneven book, offering as it does a good deal of valuable stimulus, serves the better as a warning – a warning against temptations that the analyst whose practice is to be a discipline must resist. It abounds in instances of ingenuity that has taken the bit between its teeth. Valid analytic practice is a strengthening of the sense of relevance: scrutiny of the parts must be at the same time an effort towards fuller realization of the whole, and all appropriate play of intelligence, being also an exercise of the sense of value, is controlled by an implicit concern for a total value judgment.

This kind of work, it will be plain, is far from being concerned merely with the training of a narrowly 'literary' faculty – some specialized 'taste' or sensibility. The preoccupation with words in their subtlest organizations is a preoccupation with the nature of thought and expression, and the training seems to me to have the most essential bearings on any kind of thinking that uses language. It is sensitizing, and it promotes an otherwise unattainable awareness; and for lack of it thinkers in various special fields are, to the detriment of their work, apt to be unnecessarily naïve about the processes of conceptual thought they are employing. The force of this point about the general intellectual value of the literary-critical discipline can be made plain in a series of analyses that starting (say) with Blake's 'Sick Rose' is designed to culminate in 'Burnt Norton' – which was one of my reasons for including a discussion of Eliot's later poetry as an appendix to *Education and the University*.

Where the student's training within the literary field is concerned, the aim must be to bring home to him how, in spite of the growing difficulty of control by reference to the words on the page, the analysis of short things can be developed, without change of essential method or kind, into more extended and comprehensive criticism. But he will not need to have gone far in order to realize that what he has to do with is no special realm of 'aesthetic values' or 'poetry for poetry's sake', and that the judgments he has to make may very well have obvious moral bearings.[2] And by the time he comes to (say) *Macbeth* and *Nostromo* he knows that to insist on literary criticism as a specific discipline is not to imply any definition in terms of a boundary round a given class of interests; it is to be defined, rather, in terms of a cultivated ability and concern to be relevant, in attending to interests and making judgments, where a given kind of relevance is seen to be required.

He will also have been led, inevitably, and by the most effective way, to an intimate realization of the truth that works of literature are not isolated, but have their relation with other works, both of the past and of the writer's own time. Literary study, properly pursued, gives an incomparable initiation into the idea of tradition. And the perception of relations with other works goes, of course, with a perception of relations with things and conditions outside the literary order. It is the business of instructors to make the most of these potentialities of literary study and to devise plans for exploiting them. The American teacher, intent on developing literary studies into a study of civilization in America, has to hand an ideal opportunity – one that I intend to use for my own purposes, hampered as I am on this side of the Atlantic by the difficulty of getting American books. The hint is sufficiently conveyed in 'Maule's Curse', that admirable essay by Mr Yvor Winters in defining a specifically American tradition in literature, and relating it to American history. The opportunity, I say, is an ideal one; the tradition is really there, the group of writers is small, the essential material compact and the central field of attention limited, but the wealth of interest is very great, and the significance wide in scope. If my views counted for anything the study would be one of the special ones from which the student may choose for Part II of the English Tripos.

My own approach was by way of the criticism of fiction. How did Henry James escape from the tradition of 'the English novel' – the

novel of Thackeray and Trollope and the 'novel of manners'? George
Eliot counted for a great deal. But one no sooner, taking the hint from
James himself, looks at Hawthorne than one has no doubts about the
indebtedness to him. And then Melville – is it another odd chance that
Melville can be so clear of the tradition that spoiled Fenimore Cooper?
His association with Hawthorne is plainly significant, and the three
together, Hawthorne, Melville, and James, provide an opening into a
rich but controlled study of a background of civilization and cultural
tradition. Anyone who had pursued this study intelligently would not
only have a better understanding of America; he would be a better
critic of 'the novel'.

A conception of literary criticism as a real discipline, then, carries
with it the complementary realization that a serious interest in literature leads inevitably outwards into other than literary-critical
interests. But it is not enough to say that the planner of the liberal
course, while insuring that the student shouldn't forget the literary
discipline, must make the most of that leading. This would be to
suggest too simple an approach to so formidable and complex a problem. The problem – of working out and putting into effect a modern
humane education – was brilliantly discussed a decade and a half ago
by Mr Brooks Otis, Mr Reuben A. Brower, and others in the short-
lived *New Frontier*, and I remember that Mr Otis described it as one
of restoring the idea (and the reality) of the Educated Man. What is so
desperately needed is the trained non-specialist mind that, while
qualified by its training to represent humane tradition as a living force,
has at the same time enough understanding of the modern world and
the complexities of its civilization to act as a kind of co-ordinating consciousness. When we contemplate the complexities, and the correlated
predominance of the specialist and other varieties of the uneducated,
the problem, so formulated, does indeed look desperate. I have
suggested in *Education and the University* that it may be formulated so
as to look just a little less daunting. I mustn't, however, try and
recapitulate my argument here. I will merely make the obvious point
that if we believe anything worth doing we must believe there is an
effort to be made in liberal education.

And if we grapple with the problem there we shall see it as one of
bringing together different special studies without promoting dissipation, smattering and superficiality. Dr Meiklejohn reports how this
problem was tackled at Madison. My own grateful tribute to the
experiment he describes is to say that we all ought to have studied it
and to be able to give our criticism of the lines on which it was conducted. I say this in unaffected humility, knowing that what I myself
have to suggest can't be offered as the report of an equivalent experi-

ment. The conditions of work I have described are clearly very far from amounting to another Experimental College. What, nevertheless, I do offer by way of constructive suggestion I offer as sufficiently based in experience to be offered with complete conviction. And I offer it as a kind of paradigm of a possible partial solution of the problem. To put it a little less modestly, I am sure the problems must be tackled on these lines, though there may – and must – be great variety in the particular exemplifying practice and in the total context, the inclusive liberal scheme.

Obviously, I must confine myself to the briefest suggestive sketch. My cue, both for my inevitably compromising practice, and for framing my plans of what might, more ambitiously, be done, has been to seize on the hints and sanctions provided by the English Tripos as it is. I find what I want in the *Literature, Life and Thought* formula with which, under Part I, certain periods are prescribed for study, and in the setting, under Part II, of a period which varies from time to time for special (i.e. relatively intensive) study. My proposal is that all students, as a major part of their course, shall make a study of the seventeenth century – the seventeenth century not merely in literature, but as a whole; the seventeenth century as a key phase, or passage, in the history of civilization. These last few phrases are quoted from my book, and I had better now give the paragraphs in which I explain to my hypothetical committee on the reform of the English Tripos the reasons for the choice of period.

The reasons for choosing the given period are contained in that phrase thrown out above, 'key passage in the history of civilization'. The seventeenth century is pre-eminently that; and (with, of course, some reference outside) it lends itself admirably to study – integrating study – in terms of England. It is at one end in direct and substantial continuity with the world of Dante, and it shows us at the other a world that has broken irretrievably with the medieval order and committed itself completely to the process leading directly and rapidly to what we live in now. In the course of it capitalism 'arrives', finally overcoming the traditional resistances, so that its ethos becomes accepted as law, morality and controlling spirit in the economic realm; the age of parliamentary rule begins, as does that of economic nationalism; crucial issues in the relations between Church and State, the spiritual and the secular, religion and the individual, are decided in a spirit going against the tradition of centuries – the principle of toleration is established along with that of 'business is business'; the notion of society as an organism gives way to that of society as a joint-stock company; science launches decisively on its triumphant accelerating advance.

The mention of these main heads is enough to enforce the point that the study of the seventeenth century is a study of the modern world; that it involves an approach to the characteristic problems of the modern world that answers admirably to our requirements. For the seventeenth century is not the modern world, and the study of it lends itself to the attainment of those ends

which, in the Experimental College as described by Dr Meiklejohn, were
sought through comparative studies of Athenian civilization and modern
America. Such a study would have the necessary comprehensiveness, complexity and unity: it would be a study in concrete terms of the relations
between the economic, the political, the moral, the spiritual, religion, art and
literature, and would involve a critical pondering of standards and key concepts – order, community, culture, civilization and so on.

This study would be carried out by the methods and under the conditions of the discussion group and 'pieces of work'. Discussion,
co-ordinated with reading and writing, would be planned to explore
key aspects of the century and cover the main heads of interest. Each
student, in consultation with authority, would choose his three or four
themes for his 'pieces of work' (the written papers on which mainly he
is to be judged) so as to ensure his approaching the century from different angles. By the selection of the themes it could be ensured that,
though he wouldn't have distributed his attention equally over the
whole century, he would nevertheless have gained a more than superficial acquaintance with the whole. 'An apparently very limited
theme,' I tell my committee, 'may, in the treatment, become a
perspective of a wide and varied range from a particular point of view.
For instance, attempting to explain the decisive appearance of modern
prose in the first decade of the Restoration, a student would find himself invoking something like the whole history of the century, political,
economic, social and intellectual. And the student who, in addition to
such a piece of work or prose, should have done one on the relation
between sophisticated and popular culture in the period, one on the
causes of the Civil War and one on the new science would have done
more than write four essays on circumscribed subjects. He would have
acquired a better knowledge of the period than a man, preparing
under the present system the sufficient number of likely "questions"
with an eye to what can be unloaded in a half- or three-quarter hour's
race against the clock, is likely to acquire of any field of study.'
    Here is the list of heads and topics I jotted down by way of suggest-
ing what a group of planners might have before it when organizing
work for the year – planning discussions, arranging for specialist help,
and considering what combinations of theme students might be
allowed to choose for their special enterprises:
    The background in religious history.
    Calvinism to Puritan individualism.
    Puritan to Nonconformist.
    Church and State.
    Tolerance.

'The England of Shakespeare and Bacon was still largely medieval.'

The rise of capitalism.

Economic individualism.

Its alleged relation with Protestantism.

The causes of the Civil War: the relation between the religious, the political and the economic.

The reaction against Whig history.

The Restoration ethos: social, literary and cultural changes.

The development of Augustanism.

The new science. Philosophical developments.

Political thought: 'The great and chief end of men uniting into Commonwealths and putting themselves under government is the preservation of their property.'

The Revolution of 1688 and its significance.

The social-economic correlations of literary history.

The changing relations between sophisticated and popular culture.

The evidence regarding popular culture.

The significance of the history of the theatre.

The rise of the press.

General comparison with French development. Some particular comparisons.

These rough jottings (which don't, of course, represent anything like an organization of work on the century – the actual scheme of discussions and seminars could only be determined in immediate touch with practice) are enough to give point to the possible comment that what I am supposed to be discussing is the teaching of literature. (It was said by a critic that in my 'Sketch for an English School' I appeared to be more preoccupied with history than with 'English'.) My reply is that the advanced literary teaching that doesn't undertake the kinds of responsibility I have tried to illustrate has defaulted – it has failed of its function. The point is not merely that literary studies seriously and intelligently pursued lead outside themselves in the ways suggested; it is that until the mind properly trained in literature is brought, with its training, into the other fields of study, the attack on the problem of liberal education hasn't really begun. The process of bringing the different fields into relation must be promoted positively and intensively, with considered strategy as well as tact; that *is* the business of liberal education. And unless it is undertaken by the 'teacher of literature' it will be undertaken by no one; the responsibility lies with him (though in discharging it he needs the collaboration of others).

It is of the essence of my scheme that the work of all kinds should be approached and carried through by an intelligence with the sensitiveness, the flexibility and the mature preoccupation with value (and the relation between the present and the past), that should be the product of a literary training. It is an intelligence so trained that it is best fitted to develop into the central kind of mind, that co-ordinating consciousness, so much needed by our specialist-run world, which it is the function of liberal education to produce.

The way in which my scheme proposes to encourage such development will be plainer, perhaps, if I now specify a further 'piece of work' that, lying before the student from the outset as something that must ultimately be done, would represent a major guiding and sensitizing interest. This 'piece of work' would be a summing up of the changes taking place in England in the special period – an evaluating survey of the changes as they affect one's sense of England as a civilization, a civilized community, a better or worse place to have been born into and to have lived in. In this way the end would be attained that I had first thought of seeking through a comparison between seventeenth-century England and the England of today (moving by way of Macaulay's third chapter, which would very usefully introduce a third comparative term). The student, in pondering his criteria, would have to do a great deal of thinking and stocktaking of peculiarly valuable kinds, and there would obviously be an implicit bearing on the present. And in this evaluative 'piece of work' we have, pre-eminently, that complete activity represented towards which the literary discipline tends and which the habit fostered by it implies. It is the business of the 'teacher of literature' to initiate into this completer activity; no one else will or can.

The seventeenth century, of course, is especially rich in literature, and this literature bears illuminating relations to the changing social and cultural background.[3] It can serve as evidence in the ways illustrated by L. C. Knights in *Drama and Society in the Age of Jonson* and it can serve as an index in the ways suggested by T. S. Eliot's observation: 'The age of Dryden was still a great age, though beginning to suffer a certain death of the spirit, as the coarsening of its verse-rhythms shows.' The student would make the most of these uses. But they are far from representing to the full the part that his literary training would have in his work. It would be present generally in a tact and delicacy of interpretation, a mature evaluative habit, a perception of complexities, and an awareness of the subtle ways in which, in a concrete cultural situation, the spiritual and the material are inter-involved.

It would be carried, then, into the work he did outside the seventeenth century – for I hope it hasn't been supposed that he wouldn't be doing a great deal besides that major special study. That study itself would take him outside England (I expect my people to read French fluently). And within the English field he certainly wouldn't be confined to studying the seventeenth century as an island – a phase with no before and after. But I must refrain from going into further detail, though I am uneasily conscious of the drastic simplifying involved in any brief account. The principle, however, and the pattern – these I can hope to have made sufficiently plain. And what I want to insist on now is the responsibility of the 'teacher of literature' towards other studies: he must lead his students outside literature for the sake of those other studies, as well as for the sake of giving the literary training its proper development. Can we hope for satisfactory general histories if we do not produce educated historians – historians with the kind of literary training I have described, for which there is no substitute? Can we expect Faculties of Modern Languages to do much to further the business of liberal education without some stimulus not yet, apparently, provided? Is it not highly desirable to produce some educated psychologists and sociologists – psychologists and sociologists who can read creative literature intelligently (Shakespeare, Blake, James, Conrad, and D. H. Lawrence), with the powers of perception and judgment of an educated man? Wouldn't it be better that philosophers (and even Classical humanists) should be above supposing that the *Shropshire Lad* is supreme lyric poetry, that (I write with my eye on the English scene) Miss Dorothy L. Sayers writes fine prose and that Mr Charles Morgan (or the equivalent) is contemporary literature?

In the situation that conditions my own work there are certain opportunities for bringing different studies together such as I should wish to have in any situation. For an Honours Degree a student must take two parts of a Tripos, but they may be parts of different Triposes. Accordingly, when a man has a special bent I like him to go over to the corresponding other Tripos when he has done his Part I English. Or he may take his other Tripos first, doing, during these two years, a certain amount of English work in consultation with me. A variety of combinations are possible, involving, not mixed courses such as promote dissipation and distraction, but sustained intensive study in different fields. Some day, perhaps, I shall permit myself to brag of the psychologist, the medievalist, the anthropologist, the critic of French literature, and so on, distinguished in their respective lines, who once 'read English' with me.

Actually, to revert to my own situation, it is not, where so important a subject as History is concerned, a matter of merely telling a man, now that he has his English behind him, to go and do what he can in this new foreign field, achieving such liaison between the new and the old as he can unaided. My college is fortunate in the accession of a historian who is keenly interested in the idea of liberal education and strongly convinced of the need to relate historical with literary studies. Mr R. J. White and myself, in ways I have suggested, have to work within the limiting conditions that are 'given'; we are not free experimenters, and the official schemes were not devised to further our collaboration. Nevertheless, we are finding that a good deal of collaboration will be possible. We may, perhaps, have something to report in a few years' time.

The profit of such a *rapprochement* between subjects is not to be estimated merely in terms of better essays and more intelligent reading by the student; it is to be looked for in the direction of the Idea of a University. This is an obvious point, but one that tends not to get the notice it ought to have in any radical discussion of the teaching of literature. For, as I have said, any such discussion must be a discussion of the problem of liberal education. And to discuss that problem merely in terms of syllabuses, teaching and examining method, and an end-product graduate-type to be turned out, is to court pessimism, if one faces the problem squarely, with a full realization of what it is. The way to see it as not utterly desperate of solution is to see it as at the same time the problem of contriving that universities shall be universities; that is, in themselves living centres of humane consciousness, capable of a real influence in the community.

At Cambridge I have been forced to the conclusion that with the sciences and the laboratories encroaching year by year, and the specialist mind more and more predominant and more and more unaware of any idea of the Educated Man, it is only in the constituent college that one can hope to save the Idea of a University. To foster the intellectual–social life of one's college, to make the college a real humane community and focus of spirit – my interest in the teaching of literature and in liberal education is inseparable from that aim, and I no longer dream of getting endowments for another experiment of the order of that reported by Dr Meiklejohn; my thoughts, immediately practical, turn on the means of setting up in the college a stir of life that will act as a kind of vortex, drawing from the surrounding university what the college needs in order to be truly a centre of liberal education.

In bringing my contribution to a close I can't help wondering whether what I intended for modesty hasn't appeared as something quite other. Perhaps, indeed, it wasn't in any case anything properly to be called modesty. For though I didn't claim to be reporting the full operation of the scheme I describe, I do claim the right to assert from experience that this scheme can be made to work, and work well; it is sufficiently based in practice. This is the witness that, as one who has the cause enough at heart to have devoted a life to it, I am bound to bear. By way of support and encouragement to experimenters else-where (and heaven knows we need mutual support and encourage-ment) I say: 'I can testify, from experience, that even without an *ad hoc* team of collaborators a great deal can, with luck and some favouring circumstances, be done.' *With* the team – but, in a country where we are every day being made to feel the marginal status of the higher cul-tural values, this is an unwholesome day-dream. Yet, knowing well that, whatever funds may go to universities for this and that modern purpose, nothing, on the humane side, will be found for the financing of irregularities, I still can't help pondering, wistfully, how much difference *one* chosen collaborator would make (I can tell you who he is and why I choose him).

I end on the note of this parenthesis by way of emphasizing the practical spirit in which I write.

The responsible critic:
or the function of criticism at any time

Essays in Criticism, one gathered at the outset, was to be, in a positive way, a criticism of *Scrutiny*. *Scrutiny* was lacking in scholarship: the new quarterly from Oxford would show us how a critical vigour not inferior to *Scrutiny*'s might, as it should, be combined with true scholarly precision. How many of the readers of *Essays in Criticism* – or of the Editorial Board – judge that intention to have been realized I do not know, and I shall not, perhaps, be taken for an impartial observer; but I can only, with a whole and very regretful sincerity, report that we have not as a matter of fact felt ourselves challenged or rivalled by *Essays in Criticism*; that we have not at any time found its pages characterized by such notable examples of scholarly or critical or scholarly-critical practice as might call forth the blush of shame and stimulate us to higher endeavours; and that we should have supposed the formulators of the initial pretension themselves not unready to wonder whether *Essays in Criticism* has yet begun to teach the lessons, and provide the high pattern, aimed at.

And here perhaps I point to the significance of the long statement of position and elaboration of programme contributed to the issue for January this year by the editor, Mr F. W. Bateson, under the heading, *The Function of Criticism at the Present Time*. Mr Bateson surveys the varieties, as he sees them, of contemporary critical practice, tells us what is wrong with each, and at the same time gives us his account of the right performance of the function of criticism – the ideal to which we are to regard *Essays in Criticism* as henceforward dedicated. This account, in its confused and confusing largenesses, might not have been altogether easy to comment on if Mr Bateson had not done some demonstrating. The demonstrating shows us – it shows us decisively – what that 'discipline of contextual meaning', which as expounded strikes us so disconcertingly as both the progeny and the destined progenitor of confusion and misconception, in effect means; there is no reason for not pronouncing bluntly on it.

The observations from which Mr Bateson starts are that we may be too precipitate in supposing ourselves in a position to judge a poem, and that sometimes some scholarly knowledge may be necessary. The first (its truth is signally exemplified in Mr Bateson's own practice) may be freely granted, and the second, stated with that generality, will not be disputed. I am thus guarded in respect of the second because experience has taught me that, when it is invoked, one needs to inquire into the intention. This may very well be of the kind represented by Miss Rosemond Tuve, whose books were discussed by R. G. Cox in the last issue of *Scrutiny*. Those books illustrate the spirit of a scholarship that, whatever it professes (and even believes), is inimical to criticism, that is, to intelligence.

I do not like, let me say at this point (it seems a fitting one), the way in which scholarship is commonly set over against criticism, as a thing separate and distinct from this, its distinctive nature being to cultivate the virtue of accuracy – it is a way I had occasion to object to in an exchange with Mr Bateson some eighteen years ago. Accuracy is a matter of relevance, and how in the literary field, in any delicate issue, can one hope to be duly relevant – can one hope to achieve the due pointedness and precision of relevance – without being intelligent about literature? Again, how does one acquire the necessary scholarly knowledge? Some of the most essential can be got only through much intelligent reading of the literary-critical kind, the kind trained in 'practical criticism': in the interpretation and judgment, that is, of poems (say) where it can be assumed that the text, duly pondered, will yield its meaning and value to an adequate intelligence and sensibility. Such intelligent reading, directed upon the poetry of the seventeenth century, cannot fail to be aware of the period peculiarities of idiom, linguistic usage, convention, and so on, and of the need, here, there and elsewhere, for special knowledge.

The most important kind of knowledge will be acquired in the cultivation of the poetry of the period, and of other periods, with the literary critic's intelligence. Miss Tuve's insistence on an immense apparatus of scholarship before one can read intelligently or judge is characteristic of the academic overemphasis on scholarly knowledge; it accompanies a clear lack of acquaintance with intelligent critical reading. And of so extravagant an elaboration of 'contextual' procedures as Mr Bateson commits himself to one would even without the conclusive exemplifying he does for us, have ventured, with some confidence, that the 'contextual' critic would not only intrude a vast deal of critical irrelevance on his poem; he would show a marked lack of concern for the most essential kinds of knowledge.

The astonishing manifestations of irresponsibility (to take over the offered word from Mr Bateson) that he actually achieves, however, could hardly have been divined. I will deal with the instances in which he undertakes to correct myself. And I start by noting what I had to note when I had my first exchange with him all those years ago, and

have had to note again in the interval: in framing his charges of default
of the scholar's trained and delicate scruple he displays something
strikingly other than scrupulousness in presenting the alleged
defaulter.

The implications and ramifications of context can be best demonstrated by a
concrete example. A good one can be found in *Revaluation*, where Leavis has
printed side by side four lines of Marvell (from 'A Dialogue between the Soul
and Body'):

> A Soul hung up, as 'twere, in Chains
> Of Nerves, and Arteries, and Veins.
> Tortur'd, besides each other part,
> In a vain Head, and double Heart

and four lines by Pope (*Dunciad* IV, 501–4):

> First slave to Words, then vassal to a Name,
> Then dupe to Party; child and man the same;
> Bounded by Nature, narrow'd still by Art,
> A trifling head, and a contracted heart.

Leavis's point is the 'affinities' between the two passages. It is part of his
case that Pope's 'wit' represents a continuation of the Metaphysical tradition.
Whatever the merits of the general thesis, it receives no support from these
lines, since the 'affinities' only exist within a verbal context of meaning. The
verbal similarity between the last line of each passage is, of course, striking
and obvious. But Leavis makes the collocation in order to establish a
resemblance between Marvell's and Pope's poetic styles, and once the matter
is raised to a stylistic context the 'affinities' disappear.

It turns out that once a matter is raised to a stylistic context by Mr
Bateson most of the things that concern a literary critic are likely to disappear; but perhaps it is worth my pointing out that the 'resemblance'
discussed in those pages of *Revaluation* is a very different matter from
what Mr Bateson suggests: I take some trouble to make plain that it is
a matter neither of the Metaphysical tradition nor of the verbal
similarity between the last lines of the passages from Marvell and
Pope. The reader of *Revaluation* will find, immediately after the piece
of Pope reproduced by Mr Bateson, this:

But such particularity of resemblance may hinder as much as help; it may be
better to adduce something as insistently unlike anything Pope could have
written as King's

> 'Tis true, with shame and grief I yield,
> Thou like the *Vann* first took'st the field
> And gotten hast the victory
> In thus adventuring to dy
> Before me, whose more years might crave
> A just precedence in the grave.

A certain crisp precision of statement, a poised urbanity of movement and tone, that relates this passage to the other two becomes very apparent in the last line. The effect is as of an implicit reference, even here in King where personal feeling is so indubitably strong, of the immediate feeling and emotion to a considered scale of values – a kind of critical 'placing', as it were.

That last sentence, with its carefully related words and phrases, associating mode of 'statement' with 'movement' and 'tone', defines well enough, I think, in relation to the *three* quoted passages, the qualities upon which I wanted to focus attention. What, in fact, I am doing is to develop the proposition that immediately precedes, in *Revaluation*, the passage quoted from Marvell: 'It is, then, plain enough that Pope's reconciliation of Metaphysical wit with the Polite has antecedents'.

I am indicating the way back from Pope to Ben Jonson, and if Mr Bateson had thought the whole presented case worth attending to he might have been led to observe in Marvell some marked antecedents of the Augustan to which 'the implications and ramifications of context' leave him blind.

It is depressing when one's immense pains to be precise in observation and delicately firm in thought go so unrewarded, but in justice to Mr Bateson I have to admit that what I complain of is as nothing, measured by the treatment he accords Marvell and Pope. It is at their expense that he confounds me. This is the way in which he demonstrates how completely wrong I am:

In terms of literary tradition the meanings of 'head' and 'heart' are demonstrably quite different in the two passages. In Marvell's lines the vivid images of the first couplet almost compel the reader to visualize the torture-chambers of the 'vain Head, and double Heart'. It is the kind of allegory that was popularized in the early seventeenth century by the Emblem Books, in which a more or less conventional concept is dressed up in some striking new clothes, the new clothes being the real *raison d'être*. In Pope's last line, however, the abstract or quasi-abstract words which lead up to it make it almost impossible to *see* either the 'trifling head' or the 'contracted heart'. Obviously Pope's 'head' and 'heart' belong to the same order of reality as his 'Nature' and 'Art'. They are simply items in his psychological terminology, one the antithetical opposite of the other, and their modern equivalents would, I suppose, be the intellect and the emotions. Nothing could be further removed than these grey abstractions from Marvell's picture-language.

So far the analysis of the two passages has been verbal and stylistic. The apparent verbal identity is, as I have shown, contradicted by the very different figures of speech and stylistic conventions employed by the two poets.

But Mr Bateson has shown nothing at all. What he has asserted about the 'very different figures of speech and stylistic conventions employed by the two poets' he has merely asserted; and it can, by any-

one who *reads* Marvell's poem (to take that first), immediately be seen
to be in great part false. Here is the whole first speech of 'A Dialogue
between the Soul and Body':

> O who shall, from this Dungeon, raise
> A Soul inslav'd so many wayes?
> With bolts of Bones, that fetter'd stands
> In Feet, and manacled in Hands.
> Here blinded with an Eye; and there
> Deaf with the drumming of an Ear.
> A Soul hung up, as 'twere, in Chains
> Of Nerves, and Arteries, and Veins.
> Tortur'd, besides each other part,
> In a vain Head, and double Heart.

There is undoubtedly some 'vivid', that is (to avoid the visual
suggestion) potent, imagery here; but can Mr Bateson describe what
he *sees* in response to Marvell's 'picture-language'? Can he, in fact,
give any account of the poem that will begin to make the expression,
'picture-language', anything but disconcertingly inappropriate? Can
he suggest what picture *could* be drawn of the Soul 'inslav'd' in the
dungeon of the body in *any* of the 'many ways' against which it
protests?

None *could* be that bore any relation to Marvell's poem, which is an
utterly different thing from what Mr Bateson says it is. Of its very
nature it eludes, defies and transcends visualization. So one is surprised to be told, by a scholar (who should know these things), that it
is 'the kind of allegory that was popularized in the early seventeenth
century by the Emblem Books'. To call it an allegory at all can only
mislead, and to say, as Mr Bateson does, that it 'dresses up' a 'more or
less conventional concept' in some 'new clothes' (these being the 'real
raison d'être') is to convey the opposite of the truth about it. For it is a
profoundly critical and inquiring poem, devoted to some subtle
exploratory thinking, and to the *questioning* of 'conventional concepts'
and current habits of mind.

The paradoxes with which it opens may not be unrelated to convention, but that undoubted force which so strikes Mr Bateson
(though he hasn't bothered with significance) is not in the least a
matter of their compelling us to *visualize* anything; it is that they are
paradoxes the essence of which is to elude or defy visualization.

> With bolts of Bones, that fetter'd stands
> In Feet, and manacled in Hands.

– How do we see the Soul? What visual images correspond to 'fetter'd'
and 'manacled'? We certainly don't see manacles on the Soul's hands

and fetters on its feet: the Soul's hands and feet are the Body's, and it is the fact that they *are* the Body's that makes them 'manacles' and 'fetters'. No doubt there is in every reader's response to those words some kind of visual element; but the reader for whom the response is in any major way a matter of *seeing* manacles and fetters has not adjusted himself to the poem. Reading this rightly, we feel, as something more than stated, the Soul's protest (paradoxically in part physical – this is where 'imagery' comes in) against the so intimately and inescapably associated matter: the introductory 'with bolts of Bones' makes the antithesis, Soul and Body, seem clear and sharp.

In the next couplet Mr Bateson himself can hardly have explained the effect as a matter of our being made to visualize:

> Here blinded with an Eye; and there
> Deaf with the drumming of an Ear.

The Soul is protesting against the conditions and limitations of life in a world of sense-experience. And the eye is a physical organism – it can be pulled out; and a diagram can be drawn of the ear. But the antithesis, Soul and Body, has lost some of the sharpness it had when the Body was represented by 'bolts of Bones'. This development is confirmed by what follows. The comment on

> O Soul hung up, as 'twere, in Chains
> Of Nerves, and Arteries, and Veins

is made by the Body when it, in turn, speaks. The effect of these lines is immediate, and it is one concerning which we can say that we certainly do not *see* the Soul hanging in its 'Chains'. And when we come to the 'vain Head' and 'double Heart' it takes the wit of 'double' to remind us that the heart (and the head too) can be thought of as a mere physical part of the material body. We don't, with that reminder, see them, or think of them, as 'torture-chambers'; it is not in them as 'torture-chambers' that the Soul is tortured, and Mr Bateson's criticism derives from a striking failure of attention: 'In Marvell's lines the image has run away with the antithesis (it doesn't really matter whether the torture-chamber is the head or the heart or some other part of the body) . . . '

The poem offers no such simple scheme as he supposes. It is devoted to exploring a sense of the relation between 'soul' and 'body' that couldn't have been expressed in any simple scheme – emblematic, allegorical, diagrammatic, or what. The 'vain Head' and the 'double Heart', though they stand here for the Body, are clearly not just the physical part and the muscular organ. And this is not inadvertence, or slackness of grasp, in Marvell, whatever Mr Bateson may be inclined to suggest (he writes of a 'half-realization [in Marvell's 'Dialogue'] that his medium was on its last legs and could no longer be taken with complete seriousness'). When the Body speaks we have this:

> O who shall me deliver whole
> From bonds of this Tyrannic Soul?
> Which, stretcht upright, impales me so,
> That mine own Precipice I go . . .

Will Mr Bateson say that he finds himself compelled to visualize the Soul 'stretcht upright' and 'impaling' the Body? Hardly. What is conveyed with such power here is the Body's sense of the perilous game that, in its erect posture, it plays with gravity.[1] The passage answers (concave to convex, as it were) to that in which the Soul speaks of being hung up in chains – a passage that expresses a sense of the inseparable, indistinguishable, implication of life in 'nerves and arteries and veins'. It wouldn't, the comment came as one read, have been 'hung up' if life had not informed the nerves and arteries and veins, and made them more than a material network. And now, as one reads, the comment comes that the conditions against which the Body protests are those which make it a body. It is a comment that is insisted on by what follows:

> And warms and moves this needless Frame:
> (A Fever could but do the same).

A Frame that has lost its warmth, its power of motion and its needs is on the way to becoming a 'kneaded clod'.

> And, wanting where its spight to try,
> Has made me live to let me dye.

The Body (as Claudio testifies), having acquired its needs and become a body, cannot want to become 'needless'.

> A Body that could never rest,
> Since this ill Spirit it possest.

To 'rest' would be to die, which the Body, of its very nature, cannot wish to do. What it rebels against is the state, entailed in its state of being a body, of needing to fear death: 'mine own Precipice I go' – the point is now made with fuller significance.

A body that fears to die, and has to fear to die because it has been made to live by the Soul, is not so readily to be set over against the soul, as something clearly distinguished, as the title of the poem seems to imply. And that is the point of the poem. The succeeding speech of the Soul develops it:

What Magick could me thus confine
Within another's Grief to pine?
Where whatsover it complain,
I feel, that cannot feel, the pain.
And all my Care its self employes,
That to preserve, which me destroys:
Constrain'd not only to indure
Diseases, but, what's worse, the Cure:
And ready oft the Port to gain,
Am Shipwrackt into Health again.

The Body's ills may be the Body's, but 'I feel, that cannot feel, the pain': the other's 'Grief' is equally the Soul's, for all the distinction that has been stated as an antithesis. I need not comment on the rest of the speech – except, perhaps, to ask how much picture-language Mr Bateson finds even in the closing couplet of it. The Body's counterpart in this speech concludes the poem:

But Physick yet could never reach
The Maladies Thou me dost teach;
Whom first the Cramp of Hope does Tear:
And then the Palsie Shakes of Fear.
The Pestilence of Love does heat:
Or Hatred's hidden Ulcer eat.
Joy's chearful Madness does perplex:
Or Sorrow's other Madness vex.
Which Knowledge forces me to know;
And Memory will not forego.
What but a Soul could have the wit
To build me up for Sin so fit?
So Architects do square and hew,
Green Trees that in the Forest grew.

The maladies of the Soul – described as that because they are of the kind that Physick cannot reach – are equally the Body's. The Body is exposed, it says, to suffering them by Knowledge and Memory, which it speaks of as belonging to the Soul, but which are nevertheless sufficiently of the Body to involve the Body in maladies.

I am not suggesting that Marvell rejected the distinction between the soul and the body. But, plainly, this poem has for theme the *difficulty* of the distinction – its elusiveness; it explores with remarkable originality and power the perplexities and problems that, for one bent on distinguishing, must, in concrete experience, be found to lie behind the distinction as conventionally assumed – as assumed, for instance, by an allegorical or emblematic writer. I will not here go into the significance of the closing couplet (I confess, indeed, that I have not wholly convinced myself with any account of the development that, with its curiously satisfying effect as of a resolution, it gives to the theme). The poem is among Marvell's supreme things, profoundly original and a proof of genius; and my notes on its not unobvious (I should have thought) characteristics are enough to bring out the remarkable nature of Mr Bateson's feat. Of this poem he can say: 'It is the kind of allegory that was popularized in the early seventeenth century by the Emblem Books, in which a more or less conventional concept is dressed up in some striking new clothes, the new clothes being the real *raison d'être*.' With his eyes (presumably) on it he can tell us:

There is an obvious connection between Marvell's metaphors and the analogical thinking of the Tudor and Stuart divines. (Hooker, for example, uses the regularity of the motions of the heavenly bodies as an argument for imposing ecclesiastical law upon the Puritans.)

How can we explain such a performance? Can it be said that the critic who can tell us, with this serene assurance, these things about such a poem has, in any serious sense of the verb, *read* it? And Mr Bateson tells us them in a considered pronunciatory essay in which he offers to expose the irresponsibility of other critics, and to show us how we may achieve precision, and a certitude of correctness, in analysis, interpretation and judgment. What makes the performance the more astonishing is that he circulated the essay, he tells us, among his editorial colleagues (the note on the Editorial Board in front of *Essays in Criticism* lists eight) before publishing it. Is it possible that none of them made any remark on the extraordinary aberrations I have adduced?

But the essay contains much more, of various kinds, that is equally matter for wonder, and seems equally to have escaped remark from Mr Bateson's colleagues. He treats Pope, for instance, with as confident and dumbfounding an arbitrariness as that which Marvell suffers:

In Marvell's lines the image has run away with the antithesis (it doesn't really matter whether the torture-chamber is in the head or the heart or some other part of the body), whereas in Pope's lines the concept has almost killed the imagery, the progress being towards a mathematical purity with the sensuous elements segregated into a separate compartment of their own. And there is a still further contradiction. The most interesting feature in the lines is that the Metaphysical style in which he was writing has *forced* Marvell to say what he cannot have wanted to say. And Pope's Augustan style has forced his hand in the same way.

Marvell's poem is a thoroughly serious affair, but the vividness of the imagery has resulted in a blurring of the argument by making it impossible for the reader not to equate – or, indeed, in terms of the poetic impact, *subordinate* – the immoral head and heart with such relatively innocent and secondary members as the nerves, arteries and veins. So gross a breach of the poem's logic cannot possibly have been intended by Marvell. The passage from the *Dunciad* raises a similar problem. How is it Pope, a master of language if ever there was one, has used his concrete terms with so little precision? In these lines 'slave', 'vassal' and 'dupe' are virtually interchangeable. And so are 'Bounded', 'narrow'd' and 'contracted'. These tautologies can't have been *meant* by Pope.

Mr Bateson's ability to believe, and judicially to pronounce, that Marvell has been guilty of a 'breach of the poem's logic' such as 'cannot possibly have been intended' goes, we have seen, with his decision that Marvell shall have intended what, on the unequivocal and final evidence of the poem itself, he clearly didn't – the poem offers not the faintest ghost of a ground for the belief, which wholly denatures it. Mr Bateson's confidence that Pope can't have meant what *he* wrote exposes itself immediately, in what stands there on Mr Bateson's page, for the purely gratuitous achievement it is – exposes itself at the first cursory reading, one would have thought, by what within the compass of a single glance it commits Mr Bateson to (and again one can't help wondering that none, apparently, of his editorial colleagues should have brought so disastrous and undeniable a fact to his notice). What he brands 'tautologies' are obviously not tautologies, and it is not Pope ('a master of language if ever there was one') who has shown himself, in respect of precision in the use of words, astonishingly indifferent. Here again are the four lines of Pope:

> First slave to Words, then vassal to a Name,
> Then dupe to Party; child and man the same;
> Bounded by Nature, narrow'd still by Art,
> A trifling head, and a contracted heart.

How can Mr Bateson so have anaesthetized himself as to be able to pronounce 'slave', 'vassal' and 'dupe' 'virtually interchangeable'? That the forces of these words should have something in common is essential to the intention: 'child and man the same'. But that the forces are different, and that each word has a felicity in its place, is surely apparent at once, without analysis. What analysis yields I need only briefly indicate.

Words should be servants – the servants of thought and of the thinker; the badly educated child is made a 'slave to words' (the cliché has point, as clichés usually have). Such a child, grown to political years, naturally becomes 'vassal to a Name'. The felicity of this expression takes us beyond cliché (the 'mastery of language' shown here is characteristic of Pope): the relation of personal subservience to a great patrician name (and a 'mere name', it is suggested) – a relation substituting for service of Principle[2] – is with special point described contemptuously by the feudal term in an age in which feudalism is Gothick. And such an initiate into politics, expecting his reward for faithful service of Party, finds himself a 'dupe': he has been used, but can command no substantial recognition from 'Int'rest that waves on parti-colour'd wings'. 'Vassal' and 'dupe' express quite different relations, and a moment's thought will show that they couldn't be interchanged. And neither noun could go with 'words': 'vassal' expresses a relation between persons, and 'dupe' implies an exploiting agent. There is hardly any need to argue that 'slave' could not, without loss of point, as these words stand, be substituted for 'vassal' or 'dupe'. And since 'slave to words' is something of a cliché, the progression 'slave', 'vassal', 'dupe', gives us a climax.

As for Mr Bateson's assertion that 'bounded', 'narrow'd', and 'contracted' are tautologies, that need not take us long. 'Bounded by Nature' – this refers to the limitations imposed by innate constitution. The person thus limited is made 'by Art' – i.e. by education – even more limited than he need have been: anyone who *reads* the passage can see that 'bounded' and 'narrow'd' are *not* interchangeable (and that 'virtually' doesn't help Mr Bateson's case). And if Pope had described the heart as 'bounded' or 'narrow'd' – but clearly he couldn't have done that. If, then, he had *not* described it as 'contracted' he would have forgone a marked felicity. 'Contracted' – which picks up 'trifling' alliteratively, with a gain of expressive value for both terms – has something like the effect of 'double' in Marvell's 'vain Head and double Heart': it keeps us in touch with the heart as a physical organ. It suggests the muscular contraction, though *this* contractedness is permanent, and not part of the vital rhythm; and the presence of the muscular effect gives to the evoking of life meanly constricted a force that it wouldn't otherwise have had.

There are wider and more varied possibilities of imagery than Mr Bateson would have seemed to have supposed. And he clearly assumes a naïve account of the pair, concrete–abstract, as a simple antithesis. I cannot help thinking that if he had concentrated his attention on reading Pope's poetry he would have got a better understanding of those changes in the English language which marked the later part of the seventeenth century than he has derived from all his exercises in 'the discipline of contextual reading'. He might certainly have learnt something about the possibilities of 'abstract' diction in poetry, and, going on to Johnson, might have discovered that there may be concreteness and imagery in verse that is wholly Augustan in idiom, convention and way of using language. As it is he can tell us, with that impressive poise of the contextually responsible critic, such absurdities as this: 'by his infusion of the Picturesque (the object of his thefts from the Metaphysical poets) Pope was able to mitigate to some extent the abstractness of his medium'. The changes in civilization that can be studied in the poetry of Dryden, Pope and Johnson are indeed of great interest. But Mr Bateson tells us little about them when he tells us – as any first-term undergraduate can be relied on to – that 'the abstract character of Pope's diction can be related without difficulty to the philosophies of Hobbes, Locke, Berkeley and Hume'.

Mr Bateson, however, goes on:

> But this intellectual context, important though it certainly is for understanding Marvell and Pope, does not seem to provide the ultimate framework of reference within which their poems need to be read. Behind the intellectual context lies a complex of religious, political and economic factors that can be called the social context. As this level of meaning seems to be the final context of which the critical reader of literature must retain an awareness, it will be worth while trying to summarize, however baldly, the social context implicit in these two passages.

In spite of the defensive 'however baldly', it is impossible not to comment severely on the gratuitousness, the flimsy and fanciful arbitrariness, of what Mr Bateson then offers us as summaries of the implicit 'social contexts' (and his 'social' is a term we need to note). I don't know whether he has read the parts of Harold Smith's work that have appeared in *Scrutiny* over the past eighteen months – parts of an inquiry into the cultural changes manifested in the language and conventions of poetry during the period in question, but if he wants to expound the 'intellectual context' and the 'complex of religious, political and economic factors' that lie behind it, he can't do better than go to Smith for light. Smith has a full sense of the complexities, is delicate and precise in formulation, and never loses his grasp of the fact that the poetry is both the focus of his inquiry and of unique value as evidence.

And here we come to the sad truth about Mr Bateson's discipline of contextual reading. 'What general conclusions', he pleasantly asks, 'can be drawn from this analysis of the two passages quoted by Leavis?' Mr Bateson draws conclusions of decided largeness; but, of course, none that are valid *can* be drawn, since the 'analysis' ignores the passages. And – what we have now to note – the consequences of this last fact is that his discipline is not merely irrelevant; it isn't, and can't be, a discipline at all; it has no determinate enough field or aim. That he shouldn't notice, or be embarrassed by, this disability is characteristic of his whole project; the indeterminateness makes possible (for Mr Bateson – and, apparently, his colleagues, or most of them) the confident ambition of the project, and the remarkable pretension that (as we shall see) crowns it.

He starts from the commonplace observation that a poem is in some way related to the world in which it was written. He arrives by a jump (at least, his arrival there is not by any steps of sober reasoning) at the assumption that the way to achieve the correct reading of a poem – of say, Marvell's or Pope's – is to put it back in its 'total context' in that world. No idea of such an undertaking troubles the reader whose attention is really and intelligently focused upon the poem, and if the undertaking were proposed to him he would see its absurdity at once. He would see that it was gratuitous, and worse; and at the same time he would see that any achievement corresponding to it is impossible – that the aim, in fact, is illusory. What *is* this 'complex of religious, political and economic factors that can be called the social context', and the reconstruction of which enables us (according to Mr Bateson) to achieve the 'correct reading', 'the object as in itself it really is', since it is the product of progressive corrections at each stage of the con-textual series'? How does one set to work to arrive at this final inclusive context, the establishment of which puts the poem back in 'its original historical setting', so that 'the human experience in it begins to be realized and re-enacted by the reader'? Mr Bateson doesn't tell us, and doesn't begin to consider the problem. He merely follows up those plainly false assertions about the passage of Marvell and Pope with some random notes from his historical reading.

That is all he *could* do. And all he could do more would be to go on doing that more voluminously and industriously. For the total 'social context' that he postulates is an illusion. And so it would have been, even if he had started by reading the poem. But he would then – at least, if he had really *read* the poem, and kept himself focused upon that – have seen that in the poem, whatever minor difficulties of con-vention and language it might present, he had something determinate – something indubitably *there*. But 'context', as something deter-minate, is, and can be, nothing but his postulate; the wider he goes in his ambition to construct it from his reading in the period, the more is it *his* construction (in so far as he produces anything more than a mass of heterogeneous information alleged to be relevant).

It will not, I think, be supposed that I should like to insulate litera-ture for study, in some pure realm of 'literary values' (whatever *they* might be). But on the one hand it is plain to me that no poem we have any chance of being able to read as a poem requires anything approaching the inordinate apparatus of 'contextual' aids to interpretation that Mr Bateson sees himself deploying. On the other hand it is equally plain to me that it is to creative literature, read *as* creative literature, that we must look for our main insights into those characteristics of the 'social context' (to adopt for a moment Mr

Bateson's insidious adjective) that matter most to the critic – to the reader of poetry.

I do indeed (as I have explained in some detail elsewhere) think that the study of literature should be associated with extra-literary studies. But to make literary criticism *dependent* on the extra-literary studies (or to aim at doing so, for it can't be done) in the way Mr Bateson proposes is to stultify the former and deprive the latter of the special profit they might have for the literary student. To suggest that their *purpose* should be to reconstruct a postulated 'social context' that once enclosed the poem and gave it its meaning is to set the student after something that no study of history, social, economic, political, intellectual, religious, can yield. The poem, as I've said, is a determinate thing; it is *there*; but there is nothing to correspond – nothing answering Mr Bateson's 'social context' that can be set over against the poem, or induced to re-establish itself round it as a kind of framework or completion, and there never *was* anything. The student who sets out in quest of such a 'context' may read historical works of various kinds and he may assemble a number of general considerations such as Mr Bateson offers us as explaining why Marvell has been 'forced to say what he cannot have wanted to say', but he will find that the kind of 'context' that expands indeterminately as he gets from his authorities what *can* be got contains curiously little significance – if significance is what, for a critic, illuminates a poem. And he may go on and on – indeterminately.

It may be said that in these comments I do not sufficiently recognize that a preoccupation with 'context' would involve a continual reference back to the poem. To this I can only reply that (firstly) Mr Bateson himself doesn't pay any attention to the poem; and that this is not, so to speak, an accident, because (secondly) no one who was actually concerned with the problem of arriving at the correct reading of a poem could have conceived Mr Bateson's phantom scheme of 'contextual checks' – and called it a discipline.

The seriousness with which he takes his 'social context' as a fact, determinate and determining, is complete. 'It is to be noted', he tells us, 'that the culminating desideratum, the final criterion of correctness, is the awareness of the appropriate social context.' He goes on:

The discipline of contextual reading, as defined and illustrated in the preceding paragraphs, should result in the reconstruction of a human situation that is demonstrably implicit in the particular literary work under discussion. Within the limits of human fallibility, the interpretation will be *right*. But the process provides no guarantee, of course, that the reader's response to the essential drama, however correctly that is reconstructed, will be equally correct.

I confess that I don't know what this means; but Mr Bateson would seem to be suggesting that one may reconstruct the 'essential drama' of a poem correctly without responding to it correctly; that the taking possession of it is independent of valuing. That is an error of Mr Bateson's which I remember to have corrected some eighteen years ago.[3] He insists, however, that 'the question of values must not be excluded'. But I find what he says about the nature and process of judgment so wholly unintelligible that I will quote the crucial passage:

the reservation must be immediately made that the judgment is not separable in criticism – as distinct from ethics and aesthetics – from the particular structure of meanings that is being judged. A poem, for example, is not good or bad in itself but only in terms of the contexts in which it originated. For us to be able to use it, to live ourselves into it, the essential requirement is simply an understanding of those original contexts, and especially the original social context. A social order, as such, is necessarily the affirmation of certain values. In the social context, therefore, the values implied in the poem become explicit, and its relative goodness or badness declares itself. Because of its final dependence on the setting of the poem within its social context the mere process of responsible reading *includes* the necessary value judgments.

I can, I say, extract no meaning from this. It cannot, I suspect, be explained, because the author's conviction (it seems to me) that he had coherent thought to express was an illusion. It would be interesting to be told what sense was made of it by the editorial colleagues ('most of them') who gave the article their 'general approval'. One thing I am certain of: whatever sense can be given it, the passage is incompatible with any true account of value judgment. One judges a poem by Marvell not by persuading a hypothetical seventeenth-century 'context', or any 'social context', to take the responsibility, but, as one alone can, out of one's personal living (which inevitably is in the twentieth century). The 'mere process of responsible reading', if we take 'responsible', not in Mr Bateson's inverted sense, but in the ordinary sense, '*includes* the necessary value judgments' (and 'valuation' is not a simple idea in analogy with 'putting a price on', and not a mere matter of 'relative goodness or badness') because, if the poem is an important challenge, it engages, in the response that 'reconstructs' it, and as an inseparable part of the response, the profoundest and completest sense of relative value that one brings from one's experience. No one realizing the nature of such responding could lay Mr Bateson's stress upon the 'original social context', whatever precisely such a context may be, and whatever precisely may be the evaluative efficacy that Mr Bateson ascribes to it.

I have observed earlier that 'social' is an insidious word. The nature of the attraction it has for Mr Bateson reveals itself to us when he comes to the importance he claims for the responsible critic:

> The more closely you read a work of literature – the more, that is, you learn to respond correctly at all the levels of context – the more you will profit by it. But 'profit' is an inadequate word to describe the contribution to the community – with the status such a contribution inevitably confers – that the trained reader brings to a muddled mass society. If it is true that a work of literature cannot be properly understood or appreciated except in terms of the social context in which it originated, the skilled reader of literature will tend, by the nature of his skill, to understand and appreciate contemporary social processes better than his neighbours.

What in particular actuality the 'contribution' of the 'trained reader' to his muddled 'context' could be we are left to divine from these large intimations – and *their* context. But the nature of the ambition, or hankering, they express is made clear enough. Of the essay of Arnold's that remains for him 'the supreme model' Mr Bateson says:

> There are two phrases in that essay, each only four words long, that everyone who has read the first series of *Essays in Criticism* cannot help remembering. They are the four words in which Arnold summed up the case against the English Romantic poets (they 'did not know enough') and the four words he quoted from a newspaper report of a particularly sordid child-murder ('Wragg is in custody'). No two phrases could well be more unconnected and apparently irrelevant to each other. Arnold's essay derives its peculiar distinction from its success in persuading us that the two worlds of reference which the phrases symbolize, the literary world and the social world, are in reality closely interrelated. Yes, in the last analysis Wragg was in custody *because* the Romantic poets did not know enough.

Did Mr Bateson explain to his colleagues what he meant by that last sentence? Did any one of them ask him to explain it? And if he *had* been asked, what would he have said? Anyone not predisposed by the desire to be told something of the kind can see at once that it is one of those impressive utterances the impressiveness of which depends upon one's not asking what they mean. The conviction with which Mr Bateson brings it out depends upon the confusion he has engendered with the word 'social'. When he tells us that the 'infusion of social issues, in the widest sense of the term, into purely literary criticism is probably the most crying need of all', we divine the general nature of the intention. We know that this 'widest sense of the term' hasn't the wideness that seemed to excuse the initial use of 'social' in the phrase, 'social context', and we suspect that the intention is closely related to Mr Bateson's 'impenitence' about Auden.[4] Not that we know in any strict sense what he means; it is impossible to believe that he himself knows. How do you 'infuse social issues' into 'purely literary criticism'? What *is* purely literary criticism? Mr Bateson clearly feels that he has disposed of this last question, and justified the dismissing and placing work to which he puts the phrase, in his remarks about Mr Cleanth Brooks, designed as these are to give force to his statement that 'the exclusion of historical and social factors by some modern critics begins to assume a more sinister aspect'. That he should feel so only exemplifies the extravagant irresponsibility that characterizes his whole essay.

A suspicion of the irresponsibility of criticism as known to him in his most intimate acquaintance with it might be diagnosed as the real significance of the portent. Let us prove that 'scholarly criticism' isn't a mere club-game for academics! But the way to vindicate criticism as a serious function is not to claim for the critic a kind of responsibility or competence that doesn't belong to him as such, but to assert and vindicate its true responsibilities. Intent on these, one will see little need to talk about 'literary values' (and I don't know what 'purely literary criticism' would be – unless strictly relevant criticism). The critic, by way of his discipline for relevance in dealing with created works, is concerned with life. But Mr Bateson's posited relation between poem and 'social context' is a matter of vain and muddled verbiage; the student who supposes that there is, or was, or can be, any reality answering to those impressive formulations will at the best be able to say that he has had the pleasure and the profit of disabusing himself.

The business of the literary critic as such is with literary criticism. It is pleasant to hope that, when he writes or talks about political or 'social' matters, insight and understanding acquired in literary studies will be engaged – even if not demonstrably (and even if we think it a misleading stress to speak of his special understanding of 'contemporary social processes'). But his special responsibility as critic (and, say, as the editor of a critical review) is to serve the function of criticism to the best of his powers. He will serve it ill unless he has a clear conception of what a proper working of the function in contemporary England would be like, and unless he can tell himself why the function matters. If he tells himself (and others) that it matters 'because a skilled reader of literature will tend, by the nature of his skill to understand and appreciate contemporary social processes better than his neighbours', he misrepresents it and promotes confusion and bad performance.

'It is important', he says, 'to emphasize the *utile* as well as the *dulce* of criticism.' The confusion, pregnant with ill consequences, is *there*, in that distinction of his which he offers with such confident matter-of-factness. The *utile* of criticism is to see that the created work fulfils its *raison d'être*; that is, that it is read, understood and duly valued, and has the influence it should have in the contemporary sensibility. The

critic who relates his business to a full conception of criticism conceives of himself as helping, in a collaborative process, to define – that
is, to form – the contemporary sensibility. What it should be possible
to say of 'the skilled reader of literature' is that he 'will tend, by the
nature of his skill', to understand and appreciate contemporary *literature* better than his neighbours. The serious critic's concern with the
literature of the past is with its life in the present; it will be informed
by the kind of perception that can distinguish intelligently and sensitively the significant new life in contemporary literature.

These reminders of the conception of the critical function that the
editor of a literary review ought to have are enough to enforce my
point. If literature, as the critic is committed to supposing it does,
matters, then what in relation to it matters above all is that it should be
what it ought to be in contemporary life; that is, that there should be
such a public as the conception I have pointed to implies: a public
intelligently responsive and decisively influential. It is through such a
public, and through the conditions of general education implied in the
existence of such a public, that literature, as the critic is concerned
with it, can reasonably be thought of as influencing contemporary
affairs and telling in realms in which literary critics are not commonly
supposed to count for much.

That is the faith of the critic. Where contemporary cultural conditions give no ground for such a faith – where there is no such public,
and literature, in the critic's sense, is not a power in contemporary life
– then for a critic to encourage himself with talk of the important role
that the 'skilled reader' plays in a 'muddled mass society' by reason of
his superior understanding of 'contemporary social processes' is
irresponsible trifling or solemn self-deception. What does Mr Bateson
mean when, appealing for support to poor Arnold, he says, 'The
values of the modern world would seem to the layman to be embodied
in literature to a far greater degree than they are in modern religion or
philosophy'? Does he suppose that there is any close relation (or, as
things are, any but a discouraging one) between the conception to
which, with the help of the reference to Arnold, we can see him to be
pointing (in spite of his unhappy phraseology), and the kind of importance he offers the 'skilled reader'?

There *is*, however, a special understanding of 'contemporary social
processes', and a special preoccupation with them, that a critic as
such, and above all the editor of a critical review, ought to show. I am
thinking of those 'social processes' for my preoccupation with which
I was rebuked, in the October issue of *Essays in Criticism*, by Fr Martin
Jarrett-Kerr – the social processes that have virtually brought the function of criticism in this country into abeyance. I say, I was rebuked for

that, though actually the nature of the preoccupation got no recognition in the course of some strictures on the persistence in *Scrutiny* of the evidence of it. Why, my critic wondered, should I have thought it worth devoting several precious pages of *Scrutiny* to 'a series of derogatory comments on an unimportant autobiography by Mr Stephen Spender'? The reference was to an article (vol. XVIII, no. 1), 'Keynes, Spender and Currency Values', in which I related Mr Roy Harrod's *Life of Keynes* to Mr Spender's book in an account of the processes that have, as I say, virtually extinguished the critical function. Again, a discussion of the significance of one of those British Council 'Surveys' becomes an attack on Mr John Hayward and the Warden of Wadham.

I look with some anxiety for evidence that Fr Jarrett-Kerr was not expressing a sense of these matters that he shares with Mr Bateson and the Editorial Board of *Essays in Criticism*. I know of none – which is a surprising thing, in view of the daily battle that has to be fought (if one takes either education or the function of criticism seriously) against the processes of civilization that have been documented in *Scrutiny* (with *Fiction and the Reading Public* in the background) during the past twenty years. Does Mr Bateson share Fr Jarrett-Kerr's view that it doesn't matter what the reviewing in the weeklies or the Sunday papers is like; or how the B.B.C. uses its immense resources, and its formidable powers of literary influence; or what the British Council does with its prestige, its authority and the public funds; and that it doesn't matter if all these are shown (by a redundance of such evidence as may be represented by Mr John Hayward's *Survey*) to work together in a system that brings in also the universities, and if the system imposes the valuations and the ethos of the Sunday reviewing?

Will he deny the evidence, or dismiss it without consideration? Or, does he think that, if at Oxford *Essays in Criticism* (strengthened by 'going to school with both Mr Empson and Mr Trilling') opens its 'Critical Forum' quarterly, and at Cambridge *Scrutiny* (in its less scholarly way)[5] still continue to carry on, the function of criticism in this country is being pretty well provided for? If so, I cannot take seriously his idea of the function of criticism, or his interest in literature, or his conception of its importance – and a peculiarly ironical light is thrown on his own view that the 'skilled reader' may be counted on to contribute to the community (winning thus 'the status such a contribution inevitably confers') a superior insight into 'contemporary social processes'.

If you propose to place the importance of literary criticism in some non-literary-critical function, you betray your unbelief that literary criticism really matters. And, if you don't believe in literary criticism then your belief that literature itself matters will have the support of an honoured convention, but must be suspect of resting very much on that. And if you don't see that literature matters for what really gives it importance, then no account you offer of the intellectual superiority that may be expected to bring the 'skilled reader' of literature 'status' in the community can be anything but muddle and self-delusion. On the other hand, as I insisted with close argument and particularity of illustration in *Education and the University*, to be seriously interested in literary criticism as a discipline of intelligence is inevitably to be led into other fields of interest. I have remarked on the irresponsibility with which Mr Bateson assimilates me with Mr Cleanth Brooks, under the head of that 'purely literary criticism' which ignores its 'social duty'. For that is what he does, with his not uncalculating, but characteristically irresponsible procedure (he doesn't, I think, *mean* any harm). No one would gather from his essay that (so far as producible evidence is concerned) I have paid considerably more attention to relating literary criticism with other studies and disciplines, and to defining its importance for anyone seriously concerned with the problems of contemporary civilization, than he has done.

The substance of *Education and the University* (as also the closely related essay printed later as an introduction to *Mill on Bentham and Coleridge*) appeared in *Scrutiny*, the spirit of which has been in keeping. But what matters most about a mainly literary review is its performance in actual literary criticism. It is impossible to gather from Mr Bateson's so promisingly styled essay that he has any notion of what a justifying, or a creditable, performance of the function discussed by him would be. You cannot adequately discuss the 'Function of Criticism at the Present Time' in terms of critical method – even in terms of critical method as variously exemplified by the string of names that for Mr Bateson constitute the 'new critical movement' to the 'splendid qualities of which' we have 'gradually got used'.

To make my point effectively it is necessary to have recourse to the concrete: you cannot cogently present the idea of criticism as a matter of generalities. In so far then, as the function of criticism (which, for a full performance, demands interplay between different centres) *can* be performed in one organ, *Scrutiny* represents a sustained attempt, over the past twenty years, to perform it in relation to contemporary England. And for the performance, in spite of all deficiencies (of which the editors would perhaps give a severer *just* account than anyone else), this sober claim can be made: the volumes offer an incomparable literary history of the period, and, at the same time, in such consonance as to be an organic part of the whole coherent critical achievement, what will be recognized to amount to a major revaluation of the past of English literature. That is because *Scrutiny* was concerned to determine the significant points in the contemporary field and to make, with due analysis, the necessary judgments, and because its judgments have invariably turned out to be right. 'While literary people in general,' testified Mr Eric Bentley,[6] 'waited till recently to discover that Lawrence was great and that Aldous Huxley is not great, *Scrutiny* made the correct appraisals from the start.' Mr Bentley here is offering an illustration of a general truth. I say that the judgments have turned out to be right: after what was often the most indignant resistance in the world of literary fashions, they have been accepted, and now pass current as what has been always known.

It may be said that Mr Bateson disagrees about Auden. But Mr Bateson's disagreement, by the signs, is a very half-hearted last-ditch affair. 'On the status of Auden,' he says (*Essays in Criticism*, April 1953), 'I am impenitently on Fr Jarrett-Kerr's side.' Apart from the fact that Fr Jarrett-Kerr's grounds are Anglo-Catholic, stressing Auden's later development, while Mr Bateson's, I suspect, are wholly different, Fr Jarrett-Kerr has explicitly abandoned the claim of major status for Auden. But it was the belief that Auden *was* a major poet, a luminary comparable in magnitude with Yeats and Eliot – superseding Eliot, in fact – that gave him his immense influence. *Scrutiny* challenged the estimate from the start with steady criticism, and challenged the whole Poetical Renascence – Auden, Spender, the present Professor of Poetry at Oxford, and the rest – at a time (let it be once again recorded) when the Royalist, Anglo-Catholic and Classicist *Criterion* gave the movement, a 'gang-movement' if ever there was one, the freedom of its review pages.

To place Auden and that Public School Leftism; to stand by Eliot (who in the early thirties needed it), while making duly the limiting, qualifying and adverse judgments; to insist on Eliot's immense superiority as a creative force to Pound, while at the same time insisting on Lawrence's immense superiority to Eliot; to justify a lack of sustained interest in Joyce – I need not enumerate the other and related judgments in the contemporary field that *Scrutiny* established critically: my point is that *here*, in such work, we have the *utile* of criticism (and it is *creative* work). In the creating, with reference to the appropriate criteria – the creating in an intelligent public – of a valid sense of the contemporary chart (as it were), or sense of the distribution of value and significance as a mind truly alive in the age would perceive them, the 'function of criticism at the present time' has its fulfilment. It is to such a fulfilment that a critic must look when he inquires into the nature of his special responsibility. And if, really believing that

literature matters, he ponders the importance of such a fulfilment, he
will hardly feel the need to prove his seriousness by claiming, as a
critic, any more direct efficacy of engagement upon the 'social' and
political world.

But Mr Bateson shows something like an unawareness of the function of criticism so conceived. In relation to the contemporary writers,
the critics, it falls within his purpose to discuss he betrays what I can
only call an inertia of judgment. His uncritical largeness of respect for
the 'splendid qualities' of what he styles the 'new critical movement'
might be taken for tact. But why should he 'respect and admire' the
criticism of Wyndham Lewis? That reputation was never grounded in
anything but fashion, and fashion of the frothiest kind. To commend
Christopher Caudwell is perhaps less of an offence, since the inertness
of the acclaiming judgment that perpetuates his book as a classic is in
general tacitly recognized; few besides the critic who reviewed it for
Scrutiny have really read it through, and no one, at this date, is likely
to be persuaded that he ought to try and read it. But what excuse can
Mr Bateson allege for saying that he 'respects and admires' the
dialectic of Kenneth Burke, which some earnest souls may very well
suppose that they ought to devote themselves to mastering? Itself it
represents astonishing energy and devotion, but how utterly unrelated
its rigours are to any problem that may concern an intelligent student
of literature Marius Bewley has, in a very thorough examination,
shown in *Scrutiny*. And why does Mr Bateson speak of the 'thorough-
ness, the usefulness' and the 'general good sense' of Wellek and
Warren's *Theory of Literature*? To have suggested that the student may
go hopefully to it for help or enlightenment is an irresponsibility that
ought to trouble Mr Bateson's conscience. There are too many of these
conventional values which, once established, are perpetuated by inertia, and it is *not* the function of criticism to countenance them.

I am provoked, then, by Mr Bateson to point out that, in the field
in which he has offered himself as the astringent and pioneering representative of discrimination, it is *Scrutiny* that has done the work. The
history is a long one. *Scrutiny*, twenty years ago, provided the radical
criticism of the 'psychological', pseudo-scientific, and, generally,
Neo-Benthamite enterprises of I. A. Richards – who, oddly enough,
owed his prestige and his then virtually unchallenged institutional
status in so large a part to the support of T. S. Eliot. In the matter of
Eliot's own criticism, it was in *Scrutiny* that the discriminations were
established.

As for the function of criticism in regard to the life in the present of
the literature of the past, that, I may fairly say, has not been neglected
in *Scrutiny*. To take the novel: not only have the main particular

Scrutiny revaluations become generally current, but the associated idea of the significant tradition from Jane Austen to Lawrence (as well as a totally new conception of Jane Austen's importance and of the nature of her achievement) has become a fact of general acceptance at the same time, with the implication that it has always been so. About this, and all the other work of major revaluation, affecting radically the prevailing sense of the past, that has been achieved in *Scrutiny*, I will say no more than this: if Mr Bateson would like evidence of what has been done, and evidence that it has *told*, he will find it on an impressive scale if he looks through the files of *Essays in Criticism*, starting backwards from the present issue, and engages in some genuine comparative scholarship.

I have not ended on this note in any spirit of vainglorious pleasure. But there are occasions when the idea of modesty is out of place, and to be intimidated by it is to neglect (in Mr Bateson's phrase) one's 'social duty'. This seems to be decidedly one. One cannot, as I have said, effectively present the idea of the critical function – the Function of Criticism at the Present Time – in generalities: one must show it in the concrete, in action. To present it as effectively as possible seems to me, in the circumstances, what is called for. And the way I have taken is the best I know – I know of no other, in fact – of enforcing what I have said, making plain what I mean by it, and vindicating my right to say it, with some astringency, to Mr Bateson.

Literary studies: a reply

I have hesitated a great deal before deciding to comment on the essay by Mr W. W. Robson that appeared in *Universities Quarterly* for February. I have hesitated because of the severity of what I should be bound to say. However, Mr Robson will perhaps reflect that to ignore his essay would have been to dismiss it as negligible. For not only does it bring my name in controversially; I don't think I am being egotistical when I say that it has the appearance of being as much as anything a challenge to me. And the reader who was not in a position to supply his own corrective commentary will have been left by it with a very false notion of what I stand for and (I am convinced) with deplorably confused and mistaken ideas in relation to the matters discussed – which we both think important.

At any rate, the argument in which he offers to define a sound conception of literary education has an insistent effect of being directed *against* something, and that something, whatever it may be, is certainly not anything that one associates with Oxford – which is *not* what one would say of the something of his own that his argument leaves us with. He speaks in his article of 'The New Criticism' (once with capitals and inverted commas and once without), and he mentions I. A. Richards. But when, after those oddly inconsequent (but not, it turns out, functionless) first two pages, he settles down to business in the more serious sense of the word, it is mainly by adducing me and *Education and the University* that he gets his effect of having sufficiently defined the position he wishes to oppose. And he can hardly (I think) have been unconscious, in insisting on the separableness of criticism and literary history, that he was offering to confute the argument that I addressed a good many years ago to Mr F. W. Bateson ['Criticism and Literary History', *Scrutiny*, vol. IV, 1935].

The argument by which Mr Robson reaches his own conclusion in the matter is impressively difficult to follow, and I won't pretend (I have had no philosophical training) that I understand it. But it seems to me that one needn't worry too much about one's inability to follow the logic confidently through; all one need do is to consider, in relation to parts or aspects of the argument, the formulation in which it emerges by way of justifying the ostensibly plain and unequivocal

207

proposition: History and criticism *are* separable. Mr Robson's offer to justify the proposition is an argument about the distinction between the 'descriptive' and the 'evaluative'. He concedes that 'what are sometimes called "evaluations" occur' in the process of that 'description' which is the business of the 'historian'. But these, he says,

> are of a kind that can quite properly be made by a historian wholly unconcerned with the general or comparative valuation of the work he is studying; as, indeed, they commonly are by those who have not *yet* made the general or comparative valuation that is their final purpose. They are, indeed, simply part of those descriptive features of a work which constitute the subject matter equally of history and criticism. The point is, then, that the critic differs from the historian, not in being concerned with valuations, but in being concerned with *general* and *comparative* valuation; it is this that is the peculiar, though of course not the only, province of the critic. The end of literary education is to enable the student to make it for himself. But this end will be defeated if any one general and comparative valuation is supposed to be *entailed* by the intelligent reading of a work studied.

I find it odd that Mr Robson should get any satisfaction out of this kind of dialectic, or suppose himself, when he produces that *ad hoc* definition of 'criticism' (depending on those italicized vaguenesses for its efficacy), to have done anything towards establishing the 'separation' he needs. Taking an adjective from the last sentence of his quoted above, I am moved to offer him *ad hoc*, as another implicit definition of criticism, a proposition of my own (and I think that *my* italicized adjective bears the italicizing better than *his* couple): only in so far as he is a critic can a historian – or an undergraduate – achieve the *intelligent* reading of a creative work. The intelligent reader, faced with describing a piece of creative literature, knows that, unless he had entered into it and attained to a kind of re-creative possession, he cannot give an intelligent description of it, and that the testing and verifying of the necessary possession is a work of critical intelligence. The 'mere knowledge about' literature of which, as Mr Robson remarks, I 'speak disparagingly' is knowledge that can be displayed by persons – literary historians, authorities, examinees – who give us no grounds for supposing that they can read creative literature intelligently. It is the kind of knowledge fostered by English Schools where the study is not focally centred in literature – literature *as* literature; where the possibility of the study of literature as a discipline of intelligence is not really believed in.

Though, in the last sentence of his quoted, Mr Robson speaks of the 'intelligent reading of a work studied', 'intelligent' is not a word that gets any major stress in his article. The word he favours is given in his next sentence: 'Hence the essential requirement of a literary School is an intellectual discipline.' The precise force of the logic here is not obvious to me, and Mr Robson himself goes on to say: 'This, of course, may mean anything or nothing.' But, whatever it means, one thing at least is plain to me: Mr Robson has something very different in mind from what I have when (as in *Education and the University*) I describe the distinctive discipline of an English School as a *discipline of intelligence*. To this considered and essential emphasis of mine Mr Robson pays no heed. Instead, he makes his own distinction between 'intelligence' and 'sensibility', the point of which is the point that emerges when, by implication, he leaves *me* with 'sensibility' as *my* distinctive concern:

But to aim *directly* at training and modifying sensibility is dangerous. The more gifted and persuasive the teacher, the harder is it for the student to separate what is a matter of individual independent decision from the facts upon which that decision is based.

Would Mr Robson say that to aim directly at training *intelligence* is dangerous? I have not, it will be seen, repeated his 'modifying'; it clearly doesn't apply to *this* noun, and, as he uses it, it is an insidious word, and a betraying one: it shows how decidedly the 'sensibility' he presents me with is *not* intelligence, but something quite other (as what he says a little later about 'judgment' confirms). But *my* emphasis, let me repeat, has been on intelligence. And I have been at pains to make plain what I mean by saying that the essential discipline of literary studies is a discipline of intelligence, and that the training of intelligence in question (Mr Robson, I take it, doesn't object to the training of *intelligence*) cannot but be at the same time a training of sensibility. The alleged practice against which Mr Robson directs his criticism and his advocacy is a mere figment, an empty postulate, which derives what plausibility it has from the current prejudice that Mr Robson implicitly invokes ('The more gifted and persuasive the teacher' etc. – the more he may be counted on to have that sinister kind of Influence of which we hear so much and to foster that 'discipleship' for the castigation of which the columns of *The Times Literary Supplement* are happily open).

But what teacher, gifted or otherwise, devotes his and his pupils' time to anything remotely answering to the kind of 'Practical Criticism' addiction – the turning of 'sensibility' on 'aesthetic' aspects and the slighting of 'facts' and of the need for serious mental effort – that Mr Robson suggests? 'Aesthetic', I regret to say, is a word that he uses in crucial places to cover the absence of clear thought; and that this should be so is in keeping with the immense amount of work he leaves to the word 'facts'. Immediately after the last-quoted sentence of his he says: 'That these *can* be separated it is essential to hold, if we are to keep the notion of criticism at all'. This proposition remains unelucidated. What are these 'facts' upon which the 'decision' is based? Mr Robson makes no attempt to examine, distinguish or explain; he merely assumes that the word, for his purpose, explains itself. Facts are facts; concentration on facts constitutes the proper discipline of an English School, leaving us for sole alternative (he implies) something that amounts to specialization on 'aesthetic' aspects. This something he now associates with 'judgment', a term that for him, it seems, is linked with 'sensibility'. And he comes out with these astonishing and revealing propositions:

Over-concentration on 'judgment' leads to over-concentration on 'style' and 'form'; Sir Thomas Browne becomes a major hero of an English School; Locke or Bolingbroke, William Law or Burke, writers to 'judge' whom you must *know* what they were talking about, are neglected. One reason for the soft-option flavour of English Schools is the evasion of works with interesting *content*; a terror of the cognitive.

From what experience, what actual observation, does Mr Robson derive his notion about Sir Thomas Browne? The exaltation of Browne and the interest in 'style' and 'form' that *that* kind of callowness offers to our view go, surely, with the kind of academic régime advocated by Mr Robson. No moderately intelligent student whose intelligence has been directed upon literature as the centre of his studies suffers any distress (so long as he hasn't to listen) at the thought of handing over 'Urn Burial' to the golden-voiced elocutionist – any more than he has any difficulty in seeing that the gravediggers' scene in *Hamlet* (which has to be saved from the comic actor – and the academic view that it is 'comic relief' – rather than from the narcissistic mouther, whom it doesn't attract) is a truly profound and moving treatment of the theme of death, and great poetry (though it is in prose, and not prose of the 'poetic' order).

How little Mr Robson's student is to have his intelligence directed on literature as such those two sentences last quoted bring home to us with embarrassing force. In order to save him from the ignorance and unintelligence about literature that make Sir Thomas Browne a 'major hero' he is to be sent to Locke, Bolingbroke, Law and Burke: *these* are writers who will make him use his mind; *their* works have 'interesting *content*'. What, then, would Mr Robson say about *Mansfield Park*, 'Dialogue between the Soul and Body', *Measure for Measure*, Book IV of *The Dunciad*? Would he say that these works are *not*, in their various ways, characterized by interesting 'content', or that they don't demand, if one is to take what is *given*, a sustained and difficult effort of thought, entailing a delicately exacting discipline for relevance? What does Mr Robson mean by his 'cognitive' if it doesn't apply here at least as much as to the texts he himself favours? The answer, I'm afraid, is that 'cognitive' works along with the emphasis on 'facts' to suggest that the propositions about 'an intellectualist doctrine' and an 'intellectualist conception of literary education' on which he closes have been given a respectably clear meaning and resume a coherent argument, while actually such an impression, in any reader who gets it, must be an effect of mere suggestion.

'Many well-meaning people,' says Mr Robson, 'cavil at an intellectual conception of literary education.' A well-meaning person myself, I have to comment that, even if what Mr Robson offers can properly be called a 'conception', a conception of *literary* education is what it certainly isn't. Inconsequence, I am obliged to judge, is the note of his essay, which however is consistent in putting the centre or focus (if these words are not too flattering in suggestion) outside literature as such. Think of the programme of work that faces his students – and he specifies that he has especially in view the weaker ones; it is these who would determine his policy for a university English School. Explaining the force of the principle that the ' "selection" of the subject-matter' should be as 'historical' as possible, he says, with significant grimness: 'True, the result may be that the teacher may find himself giving more time to work that is difficult than to work that is intrinsically valuable; for, generally speaking, the further back you go, the more difficult literature is.' Mr Robson doesn't mean, primarily, difficult as literary art; he is explicitly intent on stressing the difficulties that have to be overcome before the student can *begin* to consider these works as that. Reinforcing the effect of stern 'intellectualist' rigour, he tells us that the 'standing of many great writers is simply a historical fact, worth study like any other'. I am curious to know who these many great writers are who exhibit (Mr Robson intimates) the given kind of difficulty – a kind of difficulty that, more than some people suppose, is to be found (he hints) even in most post-Renaissance writers. Literary study, in any case, is to be for Mr Robson's student, a matter, primarily, of 'intellectualist' discipline, the profit of which is that, while it doesn't encourage any literary-critical exaltations or excitements, it 'sets free the judgment'.

I am reminded of a conversation I had many years ago with the Professor of English from a very provincial American university. 'But when', I was finally moved to ask, 'do they read Shakespeare as *literature*?' 'We hold', he replied, 'that the men have no right to have an opinion about Shakespeare till they can explain every word in every single line; they can go on then to read him as literature.' 'And when

do they do that?' 'When they go down.' Mr Robson's men, before
their judgment is to be deemed 'set free' to deal with literature as such,
are to be thoroughly exercised in the further 'intellectualist' discipline
intimated by the references to Locke, Bolingbroke, Law and Burke –
writers who, various as they are, have this in common: proficiency in
summarizing and discussing 'what they are talking about' can be
impressively demonstrated by a student (or a teacher) who displays a
confident unintelligence in the face of works of creative literature.

Inconsequence, I have said, is the note of Mr Robson's essay.
Towards the end of it he produces some propositions in which I
strongly concur – or should, if I didn't wonder whether one ought to
take them as meaning what they ought to mean: 'No literary education
is worth having that doesn't emancipate the student from the tyranny
of the present.' And I can imagine myself saying too that the 'best corrective to academic orthodoxies and literary fashions is the historical
sense' – though I should make it quite plain that the 'historical sense'
in question will be a real and lively intelligence about literature. Mr
Robson, however, goes on: 'And to stress literature as history is,
paradoxically, a way of escaping from history into literature.' But he
has not, in his essay, stressed literature at all – he has done the
opposite; and, on the other hand, though the words 'history' and 'historical' play so large a part in his argument, they remain, as he uses
them, mere words, unsupported by any evidence that he has even
thought of the problem of giving them a meaning – of forming
coherent and sufficiently definite conceptions such as might make an
argument relying so heavily on the words intellectually respectable.
The 'historical sense'! – a 'historical sense' that shall do for the student
what Mr Robson postulates ('No literary education is worth having
that does not emancipate the student from the tyranny of the present')!
The inconsequence must surely be embarrassingly apparent to Mr
Robson himself when, in cold blood, he contemplates the clear
suggestion of his essay that such a 'historical sense' is likely to supervene in his student as a sequela of the educational régime he has
sketched. And that student is explicitly offered to us as one of the
weaker!

Why, it is now time to ask, should Mr Robson set his eye-line by the
weaker man? Can he imagine a mathematician doing so? or a scientist?
or a historian? or a musicologist? or a philosopher? I mean, when
determining or proposing schemes of study for an Honours School at
one of the ancient universities? That Mr Robson should treat his own
subject in a spirit so different from theirs causes me as much dismay
as any aspect of his essay. And perhaps I can without offending say
that, in the reason he gives for the 'soft-option flavour of English

Schools' ('the evasion of works with interesting *content*; a terror of the cognitive'), we have another instance of the inconsequence of which I have spoken. A more obvious reason, surely, for the 'soft-option' flavour is, I will not say a 'terror' of the first-class man, but a failure to arrive at an intelligent enough idea of what a first-class man should be; and the spirit advocated by Mr Robson would clearly be indistinguishable in tendency. The given failure is hardly distinguishable from the failure on the part both of Mr Robson and the ordinary 'English' don to believe that their subject presents its own serious discipline of intelligence. It is surely a pathetic futility to try and escape the reproach of 'soft option' by bringing in rigours from outside – and rigours conceived as especially suitable for the 'weaker man'.

And let me, with simple and suitable brevity, enunciate at this point what seems to me a self-evident truth, and a truth of the first importance: whatever may or may not hold elsewhere, it is the business of Oxford and Cambridge to make the top-level man their eye-line – even in English. Where will it be done, if not at Oxford and Cambridge? If it is not done – done seriously and influentially, where it *could* be – there will, in this central realm of intellectual life which (Mr Robson agrees) matters so much for the present and future of our civilization, be no mature notion of possibilities, no currency of intelligent ideas, no trained intelligences, no standards, no morality and no maps: in short, none of the conditions that make good work generally possible at lower levels.

Mr Robson is right, then, in suggesting that I 'think in terms of the very best students', and, so far as my own responsibility is concerned, plan and guide work accordingly. But I am sure that he is very wrong if he believes that such a policy and practice are not the best for the 'weaker students' – such weaker students as an ancient university may properly admit. The 'weaker students' we ought to have at Oxford and Cambridge (it is a relatively numerous class) would profit by our making the first-class man our eye-line. It is their desire and ability to enjoy that advantage that justifies their presence. This, it seems to me, is peculiarly a time when we should be clear and uncompromising about the principle reaffirmed here.

To revert now to 'history', the word that plays so large a part in Mr Robson's argument. It seems to me that, on the evidence of his essay, he is very far from having the right to suggest that *I*, in my conception of literary education as set forth in the book he refers to and as manifested in practice, show a less real and substantial concern for history, or assign the historical a less *real* and important place, than he does. It is true that I don't use the *words* with the loose freedom that I find so astonishing in him. But, surely, no one preoccupied with the study of literature and having the ends in view shared by Mr Robson and myself can *not* have given much thought to the concept of 'history'. At any rate, from the first week of the first term, in many different ways and by various approaches, taking every occasion and opportunity to enforce the injunction and bring its meaning out in terms of the work they may have in hand, I tell my men that they should be all the while asking themselves: 'What *is* literary history?' (for literary history as we find it in Elton and Saintsbury is hardly what Mr Robson can be appealing to when he attributes such virtue to the 'historical sense'). The question becomes: 'What *ought* literary history to be?' And very early the recognition imposes itself that every man reading English who is capable of an intelligent response to the opportunity and the challenge will be working towards his own answer – an answer that will not be a matter of generalities, but his own grasped 'history' of English literature; such a history as is implicitly postulated in the 'historical sense' that Mr Robson rightly values so highly. When I frankly avow that I wrote my *Revaluation* in an effort to 'define' or present, in this spirit, the idea of 'literary history', I make it quite plain that my view of the relation between 'history' and 'criticism' *is* very different from Mr Robson's.

That is, I think that the intelligent study of literature is advanced only in so far as literature is approached *as* literature. In the study of English literature in an Honours School I think that the focus should be on *English literature* – on English literature as apprehended and defined by the intelligence that deals (to invoke the Arnoldian distinction) in *real* estimates. The selection of focal points for study will be determined accordingly, and determined in recognition of the truth that there is a literature (necessary concept) as well as individual works and authors. It follows, too, from this idea of literary education that the student will *not* be made to give the major portion of his time and energy to periods in which the offered 'literature' is most difficult to approach as such, and where academic study, for the most part, takes no cognizance of the distinction between the '*real* and the *historic* estimate'. Intelligence about literature can be acquired only in the frequentation of works that are pretty directly accessible – that are not formidably 'difficult' in Mr Robson's sense. Only when acquired in this way can it be taken into the 'difficult' periods (and until this truth wins general acceptance, serious attempts to win intelligent and real interest for the creative achievements of the 'difficult' periods will be met in the academic world with animus and derision).

It isn't that, as Mr F. W. Bateson has persisted in suggesting, I would have the student believe he can read works of three centuries back – read and re-create – with no more knowledge and experience than he brings from works written yesterday. But the question begged, or naïvely disposed of, by both him and Mr Robson is that of how one acquires the necessary knowledge and experience. It is characteristic of Mr Robson that he should enforce his insistence on the priority of 'scholarship' by adducing I. A. Richards's ignorance about the meaning of 'housel' ('*fact*') while ignoring the far more difficult and important kind of 'difficulty' represented by the failure of intelligence – of *literary* intelligence – in the same book (*The Philosophy of Rhetoric*) exposed in the ingenious sophistry about a metaphorical passage from *Othello*. The essential and most valuable challenges to the intelligence of the student presented by great literature – these seem to play no part in the literary discipline as conceived by Mr Robson. Challenges of so many kinds: consider, for instance, *Measure for Measure*, and ask how many of the difficulties that hinder the recognition of the greatness of that work come under any head of 'scholarship'.

'Historical' knowledge *is*, of course, required for the understanding of (say) seventeenth-century poetry; but how can Mr Robson assume so naïvely that the way to acquire what is most essential is to postpone or play down the intelligent, that is the literary-critical, frequentation of the poetry itself? Has he forgotten (what I am sure he must have read) Mr Bateson's offer to prove to the world, with all the resources of specialist seventeenth-century scholarship, that Marvell's 'Dialogue between the Soul and Body' is an unconvinced exercise in an outworn and dull convention? Or is it possible that he agrees with Mr Bateson? – agrees that what Marvell wrote is a poor thing, and that I, by the advantage of sheer ignorance, have been enabled to enjoy, when confronted with the text, a better poem than Marvell himself wrote or than a duly equipped scholar can admit to be *legitimately* there? It is plain that the creative literature itself, read with the perception and sensitiveness that it demands, gives an incomparable access to the past – an access that it is one of the worst offences of Mr Robson's play with the word 'aesthetic' to obscure.

The literary-critical study of Marvell, for instance, yields other interests besides that I have just alluded to (the fascinating subtlety of a great poem taken by itself). What intelligent student of the seventeenth century, duly focused on the poetry of the age, will not find himself taking up the challenge represented (say) by Marvell's *œuvre* as a whole, and asking in what sense *this* is a great poet – the writer of this very small body of classical work which is yet so curiously varied in its characteristic distinction? Inquiry will turn on his representativeness, which in the first place demands analysis in terms of convention, idiom and versification, an analysis that leads one to consider

Marvell's relations with Ben Jonson, Donne, the Courtly poets, and Herbert, and his relation also to Dryden, to Cowley and to the Restoration. And this endlessly rewarding inquiry into convention and style is no merely literary inquiry, it cannot be intelligently pursued except as an inquiry into the civilization of that crucial century – civilization in its larger and its finer complexities and changes. In what sense is the 'Horatian Ode' (so convincing in its 'contemporary' seventeenth-century quality) Christian – that poem which was written in honour of a great Puritan? And how profoundly Christian is that very different poem, the 'Dialogue between the Resolved Soul and Created Pleasure' – a poem that, while it sends us back to the Courtly poets rather than to Ben Jonson, is at the same time explicitly 'puritan' in theme?

There is something more than stylistically interesting in so surprising a blend of elements or poise of attitudes. It registers something in life – something in the contemporary civilization; for it is more than merely personal or merely literary; and there is a significance to be taken, a cue to be pondered, in the operatic flourish of the Choruses, with their suggestion of a development towards the Restoration.

I am merely, with these illustrative hints, trying to convey to Mr Robson that the alternative to his intellectualist and factual rigours is not the exercise of a limited responsiveness called 'judgment' (or 'sensibility') to some alleged 'aesthetic' aspect of literary art, tending towards the exaltation of Sir Thomas Browne. Positively, I am trying to convey to him what I mean when I say that the literary-critical study of poetry is the way to an essential knowledge – an essential understanding – of the past that cannot be got in any other way. And I might have illustrated from Pope, to whom the study of Marvell leads on. What substitute is there for the insight into Augustan civilization afforded by the art of that great poet – an insight asking to be developed *intellectually*? And who, seeing what Pope offers, would suggest that the student, in his all-too-limited time, should go on to focus on Bolingbroke or Law or Burke, rather than on Johnson, who is a great prose-writer with interesting 'content' (surely); who is a poet too, with an art that bears the most intimate relation to his profound intellectual and moral ethos; and the study of whose work in relation (say) to Pope and Addison can be a study of the development of Augustanism and of eighteenth-century civilization generally. I myself suggest, on the other hand, that Mr Robson might see illustrated in the resolute contentions of his editorial colleague, Mr Bateson, about the fourth book of *The Dunciad*, the dangers of the 'intellectualist' training, and of the attendant assumption that extraneous scholarly information can determine what a poem means and is.

Of course the intelligent reader of poetry has sometimes to learn or verify the meanings of words and phrases by referring to sources outside the poem and to bring up knowledge of other kinds; there are such things as necessary notes and commentaries. And, as I have implicitly recognized, creative literature leads outside itself to the study by other ways of the civilization that produced it. My notion of the extent to which the student in an English School should pursue that study led a friendly critic to remark that I seemed, in *Education and the University*, to be more concerned with history than with literature. Further, blank ignorance of Locke (I assure Mr Robson) would shock me in any pupil, and I expect a first-class man to be able to give a decidedly intelligent account of him. I expect everyone, too, to know what Burke stands for, and to be able to recognize his prose – though I shouldn't, I confess, incite anyone to spend long on his works: looking at the stretch of them on my shelves, and remembering the boredom I suffered from them as a young historian, I make no effort to resist the conviction that the man reading English has more important ways of using his time.

In any case, wide as must be the range of reading and thought, literature will always provide the focus. The kind of intelligence that *can* be trained only in the study of literature as such; the strong beginnings (at any rate) of a real inward grasp of English literature – a good acquaintance, that is, with the classics and a sense of the whole in its development and its inner and external relations; a correspondingly informed interest in the development of civilization and culture – these represent the aim. Mr Robson may summarize them, if he likes, as a historical sense and (I must insist on his adding) a vigorous intelligence informed by it. I cannot see how else than in the kind of way I describe the 'historical sense' answering to the function he assigns it can be produced.

Scrutiny: a retrospect

That it should be the Cambridge University Press that undertakes this reprint of *Scrutiny* seems to me altogether right, for *Scrutiny* was essentially Cambridge's achievement. To convey in saying this the implication that it was an historic one is to make the claim, or state the assumption, in what, I hope, is a sufficiently modest way, the occasion and the circumstances being what they are. One does not in any case give oneself to such an enterprise (I mean *Scrutiny*) and maintain it, in the face of every discouragement, for twenty years, without a clear conception of its nature and a strong conviction that the causes served are of great moment, so that to achieve any marked success might be to make a difference in history. But the emphasis I lay on Cambridge is inevitable and unaffected.

Only at Cambridge could the idea of *Scrutiny* have taken shape, become a formidable life, and maintained the continuous living force that made it hated and effective. It was (to deepen the emphasis) a product, the triumphant justifying achievement, of the English Tripos. I express, and intend to encourage, no simple parochial enthusiasm or loyalty in dwelling on these truths. I had better, in fact, add at once the further testimony that *Scrutiny* started, established itself and survived in spite of Cambridge. And it will be my duty to insist on this ungracious note. If you are intent on vindicating the Idea of a University (an inseparable undertaking, we felt – we who founded *Scrutiny* – from that of vindicating the Idea of Criticism), and on the peculiar need, at this moment of history, to have the Idea realized in a potent living actuality, you will have no difficulty in understanding how the word 'academic' acquired its pejorative force, and you will know that, even at the cost of indecorum, you must do all that can be done to discourage illusions. You will know that the academic spirit may smile upon and offer to take up the causes of your advocacy, but that it will none the less remain what it is and be, in the academic world, always a present enemy.

We who founded *Scrutiny* could have no illusions. It was an outlaws' enterprise, and we were kept very much aware of that from the outset to the close. The research students and undergraduates who used, in the early 'thirties, to meet at my house, which was very much a centre, did not suppose that they were meeting at an official centre of 'Cambridge English', or one that was favoured by the official powers. They gravitated there because it had become known as a place where the essential nature, the importance and the possibilities of the English Tripos were peculiarly matters of preoccupation – where in such preoccupation the 'Cambridge' ethos that had made Cambridge the university to come to had an intensified conscious life. We had most of us taken the English Tripos; a couple of us – I should have said *'our house'* in the sentence before the last – were (without salaries – an important point) teaching for it; the research students aspired to prove that they had subjects in dealing with which they could vindicate conceptions of 'research' answering to the spirit of the English Tripos. *Fiction and the Reading Public*, the appearance of which was a contemporary event, worked in the intellectual climate as a pervasive and potent influence – the more potent because everyone knew that the book had been written as a dissertation in the English School.

Such a milieu favoured discussion of the state of criticism – discussion urgent and unacademic. I mean, we had no tendency to confine ourselves to questions of method or theory, and the 'practicality' of the 'practical criticism' we were indeed (taking 'practical' as the antithesis of 'theoretical') concerned to promote was not just a matter of analytic technique and brilliant exercises. What governed our thinking and engaged our sense of urgency was the inclusive, the underlying and overriding, preoccupation: the preoccupation with the critical function as it was performed, or not performed, for our civilization, our time, and us. The discussion was probably a little naïve, as intelligently concerned with fundamentals, and as truly practical and realistic in spirit as any that could have been reported from an English-speaking milieu at that time. To say this is not, I think, to be wantonly or indecently assertive, or at all extravagant: it is to insist on the essential significance of Cambridge in the way that belongs to my theme.

In the immediate background, then, was *Fiction and the Reading Public*, with its documentation and analysis of the developments that had left our culture in the plight that disquieted and challenged us. The reflections incited by that work were reinforced by the reviewing it suffered in the organs addressed to the educated public – *The New Statesman* ('Best-sellers Massacred'), the Sunday papers, and so on. Our observations and conclusions in regard to the contemporary performance of the critical function at the level of the higher reviewing were those presented in my article, 'What's Wrong With Criticism?', which appeared in the second number of *Scrutiny* (September 1932). That article, there is point in recording, was drawn from a pamphlet I wrote at the invitation of the editor of *The Criterion* (who liked, he wrote to tell me, my recent 'Minority Pamphlet', *Mass Civilization and Minority Culture*) for the 'Criterion Miscellany'. When he had my typescript he let me finally understand (much time having passed) that he preferred not to publish it. I will not modestly say that no doubt it was the inadequacy of my work that made him regret his commission and decide to go back on it. The truth is that I found reason, and found steadily more as perception became sharper and the evidence multiplied, for the conclusion I at first resisted but have long had to rest in as clear and significant fact: what he objected to was the pamphleteering strength. Perhaps (though editor of *The Criterion*) he had not realized what his commission taken seriously would mean. But, in any case, reading what I had written and the illustrative matter I had assembled (see 'What's Wrong With Criticism?'), he knew that such a pamphlet would arouse unforgiving hostility in the dominant literary world, and knew too that it was not at all his vocation to incur such hostility for himself.

An advanced Cambridge intellectual, who had the art of being advanced without offending anyone, and of being anti-academic while remaining academically acceptable, said to me, I remember, at about the same time, with quiet admonitory irony: '*I* am not a moral hero.' Whether the editor of *The Criterion* would ever have liked to be one I have found it impossible to tell, but the effects in *The Criterion*, of the editorial determination to maintain a solidarity with that world to which any real offer at asserting the function of criticism must give mortal offence were plain to see, once one's eye had lost its respectful innocence. And they were becoming rapidly plainer.

My point in recalling these things is that when we discussed the state of criticism, and reflected that the whole of the English-speaking world could not – or would not – support one serious critical review, the existence of *The Criterion* did not seem to us a reason for qualifying.

Of what a serious critical review might be we had an example before us in *The Calendar of Modern Letters*, which belonged to the recent past, having died in 1927 after two and a half years of life (1925–7). *The Calendar* did most unquestionably represent a real offer (it was a very impressive one) to establish a strong and lively contemporary criticism. Its reviewing had the weight, responsibility and edge given by disinterested intelligence that perceives and judges out of a background of wide cultivation and of acquaintance with relevant disciplines. At the core of its contributing connection was a group of half-a-dozen intelligent critics who really were, it was plain, a group. Discussion playing over a body of common interests could be felt behind their writing. And a quick perceptive responsiveness to the new creative life of the time had determined the interests, the idiom and the approach. In the middle 'twenties, for instance, *The Calendar* recognized unequivocally that a basic change had occurred in poetry – and not merely that the Eliot of *The Waste Land* had talent and would repay more attention than, for instance, *The London Mercury* contrived to suggest. The recognition was apparent in the reviewing, as in the verse *The Calendar* itself printed, but I will refer in particular to Edgell Rickword's essay, 'The Re-creation of Poetry: Art and the Negative Emotions' which I included in the selection of *Calendar* work, *Towards Standards of Criticism*, that, as a calculated demonstration, I brought out in 1933, when *Scrutiny* had started.

The name of our new quarterly was itself thought of as a salute and a gesture of acknowledgement – an assertion of a kind of continuity of life with *The Calendar*, whose 'Scrutinies', set critiques of the Old Guard, the modern 'classics', it overtly recalled (for there was a very current volume, *Scrutinies*, reprinting those of Barrie, Bennett, Chesterton, De La Mare, Kipling, Masefield, George Moore, Shaw, Wells and Galsworthy – the last being D. H. Lawrence's).

We did not, however, suppose that we were repeating *The Calendar*, or attempting to do so. We saw a finality in the brief episode of its life: if an organ at once so intelligent and so lively could not find and hold a public large enough to support it, then no serious literary review, it was plain, could hope in our time to maintain itself on business lines – meeting costs and paying contributors, that is, out of the revenue from sales and advertisements. The processes of civilization that were associated with the symbolic name of Northcliffe had brought us here. But it did not, we thought, follow that, because the potential public for a critical review was not large enough to make it, in the ordinary sense, pay, there could not be one. There *must* be one – that was our assumption; and the problem was that of finding some other than the old business way of keeping it going. We were not thinking of possible subsidies, and that was not merely because we did not think of the talent for attracting them as one of the qualifications we could muster, but because we were intent on a solution of a more significant kind.

We were of course empirical and opportunist in spirit: we were very conscious of being in a particular place at a particular time, and the cue, we should have said, was to make the most of the advantages the accidents of the place and the time offered. But we were very conscious too of what was more than accidental in and behind the accidents, and of what the advantages were. This was the heyday of the Marxizing literary intellectual. We were anti-Marxist – necessarily so (we thought); an intelligent, that is a real, interest in literature implied a conception of it very different from any that a Marxist could expound and explain. Literature – what we knew as literature and had studied for the English Tripos – mattered; it mattered crucially to civilization – of that we were sure. It mattered because it represented a human reality, an autonomy of the human spirit, for which economic determinism and reductive interpretation in terms of the Class War left no room. Marxist fashion gave us the doctrinal challenge. But Marxism was a characteristic product of our 'capitalist' civilization, and the economic determinism we were committed to refuting practically was that which might seem to have been demonstrated by the movement and process of this. The dialectic against which we had to vindicate literature and humane culture was that of the external or material civilization we lived in. 'External' and 'material' here need not be defined: they convey well enough the insistence that our total civilization is a very complex thing, with a kind of complexity to which Marxist categories were not adequate.

Cambridge, then, figured for us civilization's anti-Marxist recognition of its own nature and needs – recognition of that, the essential, which Marxian wisdom discredited, and the external and material drive of civilization threatened, undoctrinally, to eliminate. It was our strength to be, in our consciousness of our effort, and actually, in the paradoxical and ironical way I have to record, representatives of that Cambridge. We *were*, in fact, that Cambridge; we felt it, and had more and more reason to feel it, and our confidence and courage came from that. In the strength of the essential Cambridge which it consciously and explicitly represented, *Scrutiny* not only survived the hostility of the institutional academic powers; it became – who now questions it? – the clear triumphant justification to the world of Cambridge as a humane centre. In Cambridge it was the vitalizing force that gave the English School its reputation and influence, and its readers in the world at large, small as the subscribing public was, formed an incomparable influential community. A large proportion of them were concerned with education in schools and universities. The achievement of our quixotic anti-academic design, the demonstration of the power of essential Cambridge to defeat the academic ethos from within in the most positive and creative way, could not have been more complete and significant.

For there was nothing academic about *Scrutiny*'s performance. Through two decades it discharged the responsibilities of criticism with decisive force. It had no equivalent of the Marxist or the *Criterion* philosophy and no critical orthodoxy, but its large connection of very varied critics, serving an ideal of living perception and real judgment, came to form, in respect of sensibility and criteria, a community, out of whose essentially collaborative work a consistency emerged, so that *Scrutiny* established, for those concerned, in the face of the contemporary confusion, with value and significance and the movement of life, something like an authoritative chart. Its main valuations *were* authoritative; that is, they imposed themselves, and, however derided or resented at first, have become accepted currency. It established a new critical idiom and a new conception of the nature of critical thought. Its critical attention to the present of English literature was accompanied by an intimately related revaluation of the past – for the attention paid to the past in a sustained series of critiques and essays amounted to that.

It is plain that while it was proper to say, as I did a few lines back, that *Scrutiny* had no philosophy (none, at any rate, answering to the current polemical requirements) and no orthodoxy, it had behind it in respect of idea and conviction something very far from negative: there was a strongly positive conception of what a real offer to perform the critical function would be – a conception of the state and drive of civilization in this country, the cultural need, and the way of meeting this. That is, we who collaborated in *Scrutiny* recognized, for all our diversities of creed and 'philosophy', that we belonged to a common civilization and a positive culture. That culture was for us pre-eminently represented by English literature. We believed there *was* an English literature – that one had, if intelligently interested in it, to conceive English literature as something more than an aggregate of individual works. We recognized, then, that like the culture it represented it must, in so far as living and real, have its life in the present – and that life is growth. That is, we were concerned for conservation and continuity, but were radically anti-academic. We were concerned to promote that which the academic mind, in the 'humanities', hates: the creative interplay of real judgments – genuine personal judgments, that is, of engaged minds fully alive in the present.

Where the Idea of a University was in question, we were concerned to demonstrate that Cambridge need not be academic – that the essential Cambridge *was* not. Our special business was literary criticism but we saw nothing arbitrary in our taking the creative processes of criticism – that interplay of personal judgments in which values are established and a world created that is neither public in a sense congenial to science nor merely private – as representative and type of the process in which the human world is created and renewed and kept living; the human world without which the 'scientific edifice of the physical world . . . in its intellectual depth, complexity and articulation' (pronounced in Sir Charles Snow's Rede Lecture not long ago to be the 'most beautiful and wonderful collective work of the mind of man') would have had no meaning or use – would not have been possible. We knew, as I have put it in commenting on that lecture, that this prior human achievement, the creation of the human world, is not one we can rest on as on something done in the past, but lives in the living creative response to change in the present. We saw it as the function both of criticism and of the English School at our ancient university to be the focused effort of the larger cultural community at making that response.

That *Scrutiny*, then, was a very different kind of enterprise from those subsequent American quarterlies which have long represented the main possibility of one's finding, now and then, an intelligent critique or an informed, thorough and responsible review, should be plain. The difference lay in the charged positiveness of conception and intention with which we were engaged in something more specific, ambitious and (to the academic mind) offensive than, merely and generally, running an intellectual literary organ. It lay in the strong positive conception of function and means in relation to time and place and opportunity, contemporary civilization (of which we had a pondered relevant view) being what we saw it to be. It lay in the fact that *Scrutiny*, unlike the American quarterlies (and *The Criterion*) had no subsidy (and none in prospect). Indeed, *not* to be subsidized was a part of the conception. We were out to prove that, with such a *pied-à-terre* as we, the ringleaders, were somehow contriving to keep, the enterprise we conceived could be made to maintain itself – to the extent, that is, of paying the printing costs.

It was essential to the conception of *Scrutiny* to demonstrate that, the total function having been challengingly presented and the challenge enforced in strong, convinced and intelligent performance, a public could be rallied, a key community of the élite (one therefore disproportionately influential) formed and held. *Scrutiny* made its own reputation and made it, in spite of the fierce (and unscrupulous) hostility of the literary and academic worlds, very rapidly. Our contributors wrote, if anything more than devotion to the common idea were required, for the honour: there was advantage as well as satisfaction in being printed in a place that conferred distinction. Instead of paying them (we couldn't – or pay ourselves, the 'staff') we maintained a notoriously exacting standard. In this way we attracted talent from outside Cambridge, as well as known and established names we didn't want (a burden and an embarrassment – and however tactful the rejecting note, animus was incurred). But the core of the contributing connection, at any rate in the earlier years, were young graduates, products of 'Cambridge English', at the research stage and frequenters of the house at which the idea of *Scrutiny* was conceived.

The relation with 'Cambridge English' was close and essential, though institutionally uncountenanced, and known not to enjoy official favour. It represented a realized part of our conception of *Scrutiny*; here we had the active association of the concern for the critical function with the concern for the university as a humane centre. For the nucleus actually at Cambridge, work for *Scrutiny* was inseparable from their studies and teaching in (however unofficially) the English School and from their research. *Scrutiny* would not have been possible if there had not been the English Tripos and the established actuality of 'Cambridge English', and 'Cambridge English' without *Scrutiny* would, these thirty years, have been without the vitalizing force that has made it a decisive influence in education (and more than education).

And lest in these observations I should be taken to be in any way confirming the idea that *Scrutiny* was the organ of a small and narrow group, or cultivated ethos of coterie, I will add that before it stopped it had printed well over a hundred and fifty contributors. These were of diverse creeds and outlooks, and their range of subject corresponded to our contention that the English School should be a liaison centre. Of the attention given to foreign literatures it is proper that the French should have had the greatest proportion, the long relation between English and French having its unique importance and its key significance. Some of the work on the *Grand Siècle* done in *Scrutiny* is very well known, though – long current in book form and much favoured in the metropolitan literary world – it tends not to be credited to *Scrutiny*, which, indeed, has not altogether escaped the smear of 'Francophobia' with which a representative editor, the one now writing, has been, oddly enough, distinguished. But there is a great deal else on French, and if it was characteristic of *Scrutiny* to print reappraisals of Corneille and Racine, it was equally characteristic that it should, after the war, have been first in the field with its reports on Sartre and Camus. And if, with one of the essential aspects of *Scrutiny*'s achievement in view, I may point to a distinguished and highly individual product of not very commonly co-present qualifications as representative, in its way, of *Scrutiny*'s differentia, I will point to the essay that James Smith wrote on Mallarmé (vol. VII, p. 466) as a review of a book on that poet by a German – a book of which I think it likely that it received no other serious review in any journal in the English language. If we aimed to be free from academicism, it was not by being unqualified academically.

James (now Professor) Smith's essay is a searching piece of critical thought; it could have been written only by a critic capable of intelligent original judgment in the poetry of his own language who was also wholly inward with both German and French. It is, in fact, with its combination of sensitive perception and intellectual sinewiness the work of the author of that essay on 'Metaphysical Poetry' which we printed in our second year (vol. II, p. 222), and which became (with the blessing of Professor Grierson) a recognized critical classic almost at once. The fact that James Smith was for us one of the most highly valued of the inner group of collaborators (he contributed besides a long critique on Chapman and essays on 'The Tragedy of Blood' and Marlowe's 'Dr Faustus', examinations of Croce and of Alfred North Whitehead) may be seen as giving the positive correlative of our dead set against sciolism and bogus intellectuality – a divined dead set and hatred that earned us much hatred in response.

It is true in general of our criticism of foreign work, French, German and Italian, that it comes from writers who not only have an intimate knowledge of the given language, but are also critically alive in the way that is tested by a man's performance in relation to the literature of his own speech. And it goes with this that, though we started fashions, our critics were not any more given to modishness in dealing with foreign literatures than in dealing with our own. It may fairly be seen as characteristic of the ethos we cultivated that one of the most influential of D. A. Traversi's essays printed in *Scrutiny* was his critique of *I Promessi Sposi* (vol. IX, p. 131). On the other hand, where German literature, to which we gave much more space than to Italian but – and properly – less than to French, was concerned, though we took prompt note of Kafka (who had the attention of more than one critic), and were far from neglectful in respect of Rilke and Stefan George, we printed during the war D. J. Enright's[1] sustained examination of Goethe – to give to whom, at that time, so much space was in a sense our 'politics'.

The explorer of those volumes will see that we did not fail to find, the qualifications being of the kind indicated, admirably qualified American representatives;[2] they, indeed, will be judged to have constituted one of our distinctive strengths. But, with a view to recalling the current talk about 'the two cultures', I will, instead of dwelling on the extent and variety of *Scrutiny*'s achievement on the American side, pass with a jump to the remote other end of the range of interests from literature, and make the immediately relevant point that J. L. Russell, whose essay, 'The Scientific Best Seller', dealing with Jeans and Eddington, will be found on page 348 of volume II,[3] was a research scientist who belonged to what I may call our early *Scrutiny* group and was a familiar of the discussions at the hearth that was our centre. Jeans and Eddington have not now the representative or symbolic value they had then, but I can testify that the essay made a great impression ('The purpose of the present article', the first sentence runs, 'is to discuss the causes of the popularity of the books listed above, and their value from a general cultural and philosophical point of view'), had much influence, and earned a world-wide reputation, as I knew from the comments of visitors to Cambridge (and visitors from abroad, I will take the opportunity to put on record, had commonly formed flattering notions of *Scrutiny*'s status – flattering to Cambridge, at any rate).

J. L. Russell was not our only scientist contributor. But what I oughtn't longer to leave unreferred to, for it was a major manifestation of the Idea of *Scrutiny* as we conceived and realized it, is the way in which we endeavoured to illustrate and enforce the conviction (expressed, I may properly say, since the book came out first in *Scrutiny*, in my *Education and the University: a Sketch for an English School*) that literary studies should be developed outward from the centre and, by way of 'background' (that accepted and honoured category), take the intelligence trained in 'English' into quite other-than-literary fields. The work initiated and given so powerful an impulsion by *Fiction and the Reading Public* (with its derivative, *Culture and Environment*) went on in *Scrutiny* – it was one of our staple preoccupations. And, if one is to speak of 'sociology', what has been so much heard of in the last few years as a new 'sociological' approach to literature, entertainment and culture and is supposed (it seems) to have been invented by writers enjoying in *The Guardian*, the weeklies and the Sunday papers a favour that *Fiction and the Reading Public* and *Scrutiny* most certainly did not, may fairly be said, in so far as disciplined studies requiring the literary–critical intelligence are in question, to have been demonstrated and established by *Scrutiny* and the research work, with the documented thesis, out of which *Scrutiny* very largely took its start.

Further, in order to insist properly that when we spoke and thought of *disciplines* of intelligence that derive, so far as the subtlety of control and evaluation they cultivate is concerned, from the training got in intelligent 'English' studies we were not using the word 'discipline' lightly or irresponsibly. I must put on record that at least five of the familiars of the *Scrutiny* milieu, students of 'English', became anthropologists. Certain of them are now well known and of recognized distinction in their field, and a group of them have made *Scrutiny* a not unknown name in their School at an ancient university. I have in front of me as I write a letter (written somewhere in Africa) from one of them, in which he speaks of the experience of 'English' acquired in the *Scrutiny* milieu as having told decisively in his development as an anthropologist.

One of our editorial team, D. W. Harding, now holds a Chair of Social Psychology in London. Professor Harding read English in the first place, and went over from the English Tripos to Psychology. He, then, might reasonably have been said (more reasonably than I. A. Richards, with whom in those days the formula was associated) to be 'the point at which psychology and literary criticism meet'. It is a familiar kind of irony that *The Times Literary Supplement* should have found it possible a long quarter of a century after Harding's critique of I. A. Richards (vol. I, p. 327) to go on telling its readers, as if referring to known and indisputable fact, that *Scrutiny* aimed at making criticism a science.

The ambition, of course, was associated with Cambridge, and the Cambridge was that of I. A. Richards, C. K. Ogden, Basic English and Neo-Benthamism. It is, I think, fair to say that the only effective criticism that Richards, who represented the influence of that Cambridge on critical thought (or quasi-intellectual fashion), ever received was in *Scrutiny*, and it was decisive – a good instance of what can be done against the ostensible odds if the clear and unanswerable truth can be put trenchantly and be both heard and known to have been heard. Harding's critique appeared in 1933, and I reprinted it in *Determinations* (1934). No attempt that I am aware of was made to answer Harding's drastic analysis, and Richards moved on to 'semasiology', the book in which he offered to found that science being *Coleridge on Imagination*, where he proposes to 're-state Coleridge in terms of Bentham'. That book, under the heading 'Dr Richards, Bentham and Coleridge', *Scrutiny* dealt with in a long review which appeared in 1935 (vol. III, p. 382 [see above, p. 151]. *Scrutiny*'s criticism of the Neo-Benthamite drive was, as I have said, decisive – decisive in that curious and characteristic way we came to know so well. The academic Establishment in 'English', which had shown itself decidedly hospitable to Richards (*Coleridge on Imagination* was accepted – and prescribed – as an authoritative work on Coleridge), did not give a sign of recognition that anything had occurred that might be supposed to be within its proper intellectual purview; nor did the modish literary world, that reflected in *The New Statesman and Nation*, *The Times Literary Supplement* and *The Criterion*. A student of those organs will find that the habit of knowing reference and assumption (and 'Cambridge criticism' – meaning, without any recognition of it as such, the Neo-Benthamism – had become one of those familiar 'placed' features of the literary intellectual's pocket-map which make confident critical mastery of the scene possible) continued as before. But actually the chapter of Cambridge Neo-Benthamism – and it was by way of the English School that Neo-Benthamism implicated

Cambridge – was finished; Basic English superseded semasiology as overtly Richards's major interest, and Neo-Benthamism was, in this form, associated thereafter, if with any university, with Harvard.

Another of the editorial team who combined academic qualifications in two different fields was W. H. Mellers (now Andrew Mellon Professor of Music at Pittsburgh). Mellers, an Exhibitioner in English at Downing College, took both parts of the English Tripos and then (having always been a vital dynamism in the musical life of the College, which became in his time a well-known musical centre) proceeded to his Mus.Bac. His very frequent contributions earned him a great reputation, and were for some years a major feature of *Scrutiny*. As a critic, he rapidly earned a name for his exploring intelligence and pioneering judgment. He wrote as musician and musicologist, but his criticism offers yet another illustration of the way in which the discipline and the education we, in the *Scrutiny* group, held to be central and basic can tell in the field of a non-literary discipline. The characteristics by which his approach in general belonged to the *Scrutiny* ethos are seen plainly in his first book, *Music and Society* (1946), a large proportion of which had been written for *Scrutiny*. Here, among other things, it will be noted, we have the line that runs from *Fiction and the Reading Public*.

We had a distinguished music critic before Wilfred Mellers began to write for us. Bruce Pattison (now Professor of Education in London) as a research student was a member of the early group. His contributions will be found in the first half-dozen volumes. The ways in which his approach is characteristically '*Scrutiny*' come out especially well in his article 'Musical History' (vol. III, p. 369) and the review of Westrup's *Purcell* headed 'Orpheus Britannicus' (vol. VI, p. 106), which has been gratefully conned by innumerable literary students of the seventeenth century.

Scrutiny, then, enforced and justified the conception of 'English' as a liaison field of study.[4] The centre for us was beyond question in literary criticism, and it really was vitally a centre. And *Scrutiny*'s basic achievement was in literary criticism. It will be proper for me, then, to say a little more about what that achievement was. *Scrutiny*, I said, effected something like a revaluation of English literature, and I said it when emphasizing the nature of our concern with the present. *Scrutiny*'s treatment of the past was scholarly. It was resented by the scholars (those commonly meant by the description) because the scholarliness was that of the critic who knows what literature is, can recognize it for himself when he finds it, and can discuss it intelligently. I can best bring the point home by referring to John Speirs's studies of medieval literature. One is always hearing of contemptuous

discrimination on the part of academic 'authorities' against his body of
work on Chaucer and his essay on *Sir Gawayne and the Grene Knight*:
students are told not to read it, just as they were once told not to read
Scrutiny work on Shakespeare. Yet reasons for the attitude that will
bear considering are never given: they cannot be. Speirs's offence is,
by being an intelligent and vitally interested scholar, to have brought
an implicit criticism against what ordinarily passes for specialist
scholarship, to have questioned (that is) its authority; and the offence
is not forgiven even when the 'scholars' (the common practice) take
over so far as they are able the fruits of the offending work. They make
no acknowledgement for what they take, and when some ambitious
academic intellectual serves up as proof of his own pioneering originality Speirs on *Sir Gawayne and the Grene Knight* (say) his proof is
acclaimed as sound and brilliant and his career is advanced. This is the
pattern of what has happened again and again to *Scrutiny* writers.

Speirs's work on 'The Scots Literary Tradition' (the book under
that title, bringing together the work published in *Scrutiny*, came out
in 1940) was truly original. And that constitutes with the accompanying work on medieval English literature a major achievement, shaping
and creative in its unifying intelligence and vitality and in its critical
justice. Where medieval literature is in question, what Speirs did was
to perform the characteristic *Scrutiny* office of taking it out of the hands
of the specialists and professionals and laying it open to the cultivated
reader as living literature. This is the offence which the specialists and
professionals call lack of scholarship.

There was a respect in which the hostility touched off by *Scrutiny*'s
work on medieval literature closely resembled that which met its
Shakespeare criticism. And this indignation on behalf of the sound
approach to Shakespeare has not yet been altogether forgotten:
academic reviewers commonly remark how much better Professor
L. C. Knights is now as a critic of Shakespeare than he was in his
Scrutiny days, when he was associated with the campaign against
Bradley. Of course the guilt, if guilt is to be attributed, was not solely
or even especially L. C. Knights's. *Scrutiny*'s Shakespeare criticism,
contributed to by a good many different hands, shared the ethos and
the impulsion of its criticism in general. It did indeed effect the
relegation of Bradley, and did it by bringing home to the academic
world, in the course of exemplifying positively a number of more
subtle and intelligent approaches to Shakespeare, how inadequate and
wrong the Bradley approach was. Eight or nine different critics,
writing critiques of particular plays or reviewing books on Shakespeare, demonstrated, implicitly or explicitly, that it would not do to
discuss a Shakespeare play as if it were a character-novel answering to

the established Victorian (and post-Victorian) convention. The unsettling suggestion was an offence resented in the same way as the suggestion that, for an intelligent appreciation of Chaucer and Langland and *Sir Gawayne and the Grene Knight*, a subtler equipment of critical ideas was required than a scholar would bring with him in a Victorian habit of approach to poetry.

The relegation of Bradley has been so complete that the intensity of resentment aroused by *Scrutiny*'s work needs some insisting on. A rising young Cambridge Shakespearean, I remember, one who was both a Charles Oldham prizewinner and an amateur of modern poetry (he backed Auden and Spender), took the opportunity, when doing a review for *The New Statesman and Nation*, to make his soundness superabundantly plain with a fervent 'Thank God for Bradley!'

Scrutiny stood for one method or approach. Its reviewers in the early thirties, while urging some astringent criticism and caveats, insisted – and this was far from being the general thing in those days – that Wilson Knight deserved serious attention. It introduced the critic whose Shakespearean criticism has been immensely influential, and in a less qualified way salutary than Wilson Knight's has been – D. A. Traversi. Its concern was to prevent the hardening into accepted 'rightness' of any supposed new method or approach or set of critical conceptions. Its habit and the nature of its influence are fairly given by the exchanges that will be found in volume X between Fr A. J. Stephenson (who is criticizing F. C. Tinkler's earlier essay – see vol. VII, p. 5) and F. R. Leavis, and between L. C. Knights and the last-named. And not the less for having been emancipating as well as impelling and fertilizing, *Scrutiny* will be credited in literary history with having effected a reorientation in Shakespeare criticism.[5]

The main creative force of modern literature, we all know, has gone into the novel. And *Scrutiny*, it may fairly be claimed, established a new sense of the kinds of critical approach called for by significant fiction – fiction that is serious art – and a new idea of the history and tradition of the novel in English. Its influence on the criticism of the novel has been immense. It is seen representatively in the decisive change that has been brought about in the conception of Jane Austen's art and achievement. The revolution was effected (for it amounted to that in respect of Jane Austen's accepted standing – and the change in general in critical approach to the novel can be seen to be entailed) by essays that appeared in *Scrutiny* during the war; by this, and developments of the same scholarship (scholarship that functions as criticism) in Q. D. Leavis's introductions to *Sense and Sensibility* and *Mansfield Park* in the Macdonald edition – but in essentials the work had been done in the *Scrutiny* essays. It too has been taken over, and those who have used it, including the supremely scrupulous specialist scholar, have shown the characteristic absence, or antithesis, of honesty and generosity. In general, the attitude is that this account of Jane Austen has always been commonplace. Yet how recent and revolutionary the change in conception has been may be established by a study of back Tripos papers and the type of question they asked.[6] And the nature of this change is registered in the cautious ironies of the consciously stranded belletrist who, defiant champion of the receding Oxford civilization[7] that conferred an honorary doctorate on P. G. Wodehouse, protests that Cambridge undergraduates, being trained into a priggish scorn of the view that literature exists to be *enjoyed*, take Jane Austen with a ridiculous kind of seriousness and stare at the suggestion that she is amusing. At Oxford, one hears, it is a different suggestion that gets stared at. 'What, *Mansfield Park* as reasonably to be called "tragedy" as "comedy"? You *do* take life seriously.'

The contemporary quickening of critical interest in Dickens, the readiness to consider him as a great artist – one of the greatest of novelists (that is), was initiated in its pages. R. C. Churchill's 'Dickens, Drama and Tradition', which appeared in 1942 (vol. X, p. 358) was both original and seminally suggestive in its approach, and the present writer's essay on *Hard Times* (vol. XIV, p. 185), while first received with ridicule, has now been taken over (for the shows of corrective re-formulation have been mere shows). The essay was the first of a long series printed under the general head, 'The Novel as Dramatic Poem', a formula that, at first much derided, has been in effect taken up: the critical implications regarding profitable approaches to the novel, enforced (as they were in *Scrutiny*) by abundant and diverse illustrative criticism, have told very generally. G. D. Klingopulos's study of *Wuthering Heights* (vol. XIV, p. 269) came under the same head, and will be seen by those who consider relative dates (for *Wuthering Heights* has received much subsequent attention) to have been wholly original and decidedly influential.

Scrutiny printed an immense body of pioneering criticism of the novel. The work restoring George Eliot to her position among the greatest novelists (for Elton's view, odd as it seems now, that her genius had properly been found less compelling than those of both Meredith and Hardy, her successors, was in keeping with the general acceptance) was done in *Scrutiny*, and has been very much drawn on. So has the work, equally to be claimed as *Scrutiny*'s, that established Conrad in his now recognized place among the great, and *Nostromo* as his greatest novel.

Many further claims might justly be made, but I will confine myself to two points more. The modern cult of Henry James is not altogether a thing that admirers of his genius can contemplate with satisfaction – that is, if one judges it by what is written on him and written up in the journals that make the reputations of critics. What, however, I have to record (the investigator will be able without difficulty to verify what I say) is that *Scrutiny* started it. There was no cult in the 1930s when the considerable body of James criticism we produced began to appear. Those of us who took a hand in it didn't find our start in the work of earlier critics. We were the originators, and from our work was derived the incitement – and often a great deal more. Some of the most pregnant criticism and the most useful to later offenders is to be found in reviews that have never (until the present historic occasion) been reprinted; as, for instance, Q. D. Leavis's discussion of *The Lesson of the Master*, along with other tales, in 'Henry James: the stories' (vol. XIV, p. 223).

The other point is that the work that established D. H. Lawrence as a great novelist and critic was done in *Scrutiny*. This is so simply and indisputably true that the brief statement need not be added to, and so important in relation to any account of what *Scrutiny* achieved and signifies that it must be said. This work too has been, without acknowledgment, much used by writers. I will put on record that I brought out my own book on Lawrence when I did because it had become plain to me (matter appearing in another journal had made it so) that if I did not, but completed first the book I was working on, my book on Lawrence, when it appeared, would be convicted by the reviewers (the confraternity of whom were most certainly not *my* friends) of dependence on my exploiter. There could be disadvantages in lying open for long in *Scrutiny* (and work was in danger before it reached that stage: it sometimes got into print from lecture-room notes, leaving the real author to follow).

The vast amount of book-making that has been done (and is still being done) out of *Scrutiny* is a tribute to the level of quality maintained in its contents – the vitality and originality for which it was known in the literary and academic worlds where it was rarely mentioned unless for a sneer. I am thinking in the first place, in this observation, of the great volume of parasitic indebtedness, but the characteristics making that possible were those manifest also in the fact that a remarkable number of books – I can count off-hand at least fifteen – were written, so to speak, in the pages of *Scrutiny*. Our contributors had, each of them, his developed and developing special interests and themes, and his fund of thought and knowledge. His contributions were, to use Dr Johnson's word on Dryden, 'occasional' in the right way: the occasion offered or endorsed editorially by *Scrutiny* was for him an opportunity and a stimulus. Another aspect of the same fact is the way (and I have left behind now my reference to the gross and contemptible kind of parasitism – though there are of course various degrees to be noted between that and the derivativeness that can be judged unexceptionable) in which *Scrutiny* has been an inexhaustible source of ideas and themes for books and studies throughout the English-speaking world.

In spite of the denial of the ordinary publicities, it very early won a reputation that got it the kind of expectant attention implied in what I have just said. It was again and again remarked to us that each number of *Scrutiny* was read as a book, and kept as a book for indefinite reading. I have explained the conditions that made this quality possible. There was the nuclear group with its variety of developed interests and its special equipments of knowledge; there was the background of discussion, resumed, renewed and continued, out of which each number emerged. And so much of each number was written as part of a book, the author writing it as such even when he didn't positively envisage later separate publication in hard covers. Indeed, a good deal that was printed in *Scrutiny* has not been published since in book form but deserves to be and ought to have been. I would mention particularly R. G. Cox's work on 'The Great Reviews' (vol. VI, pp. 2 and 155). This work represents a most thorough research, conducted with the eye for significance belonging to the critic who did for us an immense amount of varied reviewing of a high order, and whose essay, 'The Critical Reviews of Today: Prolegomena to a Historical Enquiry', expresses directly the living contemporary interest that supplies the life and meaning of his scholarship. And his research, with which we were familiar, illustrates the way in which our enterprise in *Scrutiny* was accompanied by an unusual and immediately relevant historical awareness.

I will not close this brief sketch of *Scrutiny*'s creative critical achievement, the comprehensive revaluation of English literature, shaping and reordering, that went with its performance of the critical function in relation to the present, without reverting to the insistence that there can be no real – no truly creative – performance that doesn't entail much offending 'negative' criticism. The major and most notorious 'negative' service called for and performed, one the justice and necessity of which are now generally recognized (though it has never been forgiven), was to deal firmly with the 'Poetical Renascence', the coterie movement that opened triumphantly in the early thirties. It would be hardly credible now that (for young schoolmasters and their pupils) Auden, Spender and Day Lewis rapidly became contemporary glories of English poetry along with Yeats and Eliot, if the movement had not been so successful that the linked names were retained, with the conventional values inertly adhering to them, by generation after generation of schoolboys and undergraduates, and are still being immortalized by historians of Modern Poetry.

Scrutiny pointed out that talent and promise might plausibly be found in only one of the famed cluster – Auden, and that Auden, with his modish, glib and sophisticated immaturity couldn't go on being credited with promise if, gainsaying the ominous characteristics, he didn't soon begin to prove himself capable of developing. Critic after critic in *Scrutiny* (we took care to give him a number of different and clearly independent reviewers), dealing with his books as they came out, did the appropriate variant of the diagnosis, which became depressingly familiar. For Auden did not develop – or what development he showed was not into maturity. That *Scrutiny*, affirming and enforcing it again and again, should have come to the adverse judgment in the heyday of the Public School Communists and Fellow-travellers, when Keynes himself – a power in the world of cultural fashions[8] – acclaimed with high enthusiasm Auden's poem on Spain with its proud challenge ('And then the battle!'), was held confidently and venomously against us.

Thirty years after we put the case against Auden it passes as a commonplace. True, there is a suggestion that he has 'gone off', and that it is the late Auden who compels the current adverse criticism. But if the criticism is admitted, then the Auden of no phase can be saved. And in fact that has been implicitly granted. Quietly, by tacit consent, his spell of glory has lapsed – though in the tough sophistication that enables young poets to offer their immaturity as a mature aplomb the influence persists.

It was in *Scrutiny*, too, that Eliot, invested and confirmed as we were entering on our long battle in his now time-worn institutional status, received the limiting and qualifying criticism that tells, or at any rate is justified, in the sense of him and of his oddly disappointing distinction so generally expressed today. *The Criterion*, one remembers, was (in its review pages) as much the organ of the triumphant coterie as *The New Statesman* was. Yet the intransigent and acclaimed young poets were Marxist or Marxizing. We in *Scrutiny* were continually being challenged to 'show our colours', the implication – or the overt taunt – being that since we rejected Marxism (or Fellow-travelling), nothing remained for us, if we wished to be taken seriously, but to make without evasion the *other* choice, identified for purposes of literary polemic with T. S. Eliot, the Rightist man of principle, who, Anglo-Catholic himself and admirer of Charles Maurras, handed over to the Leftist poets to use for their ends the review pages of his quarterly. We, of course, while appreciating the ironies of this particular comedy, repudiated altogether the suggestion that, for responsible minds, it could be a matter of 'showing colours', or that there were any relevant 'colours' to be shown. We did indeed reject Marxism and we had no use for any proposed antithesis, Fascist, Poundian, Wyndham-Lewisite or Criterionic.

It is necessary, in an attempt to constate the nature of *Scrutiny*'s achievement, that this history shall have been recalled. Few people today, I think, will hold it against us that we refused to take the fashionable way of showing that we were 'responsible' (to show one's colours *was*, in the Auden–Spender heyday, to show one's responsibility). And I hope that what I have said in this introduction makes it difficult for anyone to suggest that *Scrutiny* turns out, in fact, to have been less responsible in regard to the problems of contemporary civilization than the promoters of the Auden–Spender enlightenment or the editor of *The Criterion* (which had – its acclaimed distinction – a philosophy). I will record here, as a relevant and representative datum, this: we had a great influence – and not the less because *Scrutiny* was known to be an outlaw enterprise – on generations of Cambridge students from the Indian subcontinent who now form key élites in India and Pakistan. How measure the effect of such influence? And who will pronounce it negligible?

Scrutiny had, I have pointed out with some specificity, a positive attitude, entailing beliefs and affirmations that enabled us, the permanent direction at the centre, to face ostracism and the long penalty-rewarded effort (it indeed brought no worldly advantages). It was an attitude thought out, pondered and reconsidered in all its aspects and implications, and, while 'philosophy' was not a word we were fond of, capable of being set forth and developed with precision and delicacy (as well as the force of the exemplifying concrete) in what might after all, in a common respectable usage, have been properly called our philosophy. So far as a representative presentation of it can be given in a discussion that centres in the Idea of a University (and that centring entails no wrench or paradox), one may be pointed to in my *Education and the University: a Sketch for an English School* (1943), which was thought out in close connection with the running of *Scrutiny* and largely written in its pages. And the little book, it seems very relevant to say, contains the answer that I should give to the Neo-Wellsianism of C. P. Snow – that representative phenomenon of our own day.

Though a review that doesn't pay its contributors and staff falls short of performing the full function, *Scrutiny* may be said, then, to have made its inability to pay a reinforcement of its strength. And though I could say much about the greater effectiveness *Scrutiny* might have had if the hostility of the academic and literary worlds had been less complete and intense, nevertheless our position as outlaws was certainly an advantage in the matter of maintaining standards; we were less troubled by the anti-critical pressures incidental to 'belonging' (though the self-esteem of aspiring or well-known intellectuals cannot be expected to take kindly in any case to the probability that its type-scripts, if submitted, would be judged not good enough to print). And here, in my intentness on the significance of our experience for later attempts to serve the critical function, I think it perhaps worth saying in so many words that no such attempt, if it is serious, will fail to generate resentment and hostility in the literary and academic worlds. The truth is a truism; but, *Scrutiny* having become a fact of accepted literary history, one has heard of offers from academic milieux to profit by the example, and show how the virtues of *Scrutiny* (for *Scrutiny* is granted some virtues – unavoidably, one might say, seeing how immense is the clear book-making indebtedness to it that couldn't plausibly be determined) can in fact be reproduced without the vices – the vices being the 'narrowness', the proneness to 'negative' criti-cism, the offensiveness: in short, all the qualities that made it 'alarm-ing' (the word actually used by a great Establishment potentate at Cambridge[9] – and his name now serves the offerers as a test for broad-ness and non-negativity) to intellectuals, distinctions and authorities whose recognized status as such depended on an institutionally secured value-convention, feared sanctions and a safe currency.

But even 'positive' criticism, when it presents new valuations challengingly and unanswerably, gives offence, and is greeted with animus; the negative implications (there cannot be criticism of any moment without them) will be taken, with resentment, by the conven-tional reader: in questioning his judgment they give a jolt to his edu-cated superiority and may seem to leave his personality damagingly criticized. And, inevitably, a genuine offer to perform the critical function in a periodical must maintain a play of criticism that is in large measure 'negative' in more than implication. But who today, looking through the score of volumes with the sustained integrative collabor-ation they represent, and pondering the originality of the criticism, its nature and influence, and the significance of the large body of unpaid collaborators and of the larger body of attached and critical readers, will contend that the work and achievement of *Scrutiny* were not creative?

As for the hostility that met them, that belongs to the essential sig-nificance it is my business to convey. In the milieux where hostility is the natural reaction to such challenges there has been a habit, now that the *Scrutiny* judgments have been on the whole taken over as right and *Scrutiny* itself accepted as a fact of history, of making the history pleasanter, and discounting any suggestion of subversive lessons to be learnt from it, by dismissing any reference to the hostility as evidence of persecution mania.

So far as the academic world is in question I will only comment that anyone who cares to know the truth can, without arduous research, very soon assemble real evidence, unequivocal in force, and sufficient to expose the tactic for the significant and mean dishonesty it is. And there is immensely more than those categories of overt official fact that could be drawn on – as no doubt it will, some time, be.

On the attitude of the literary world a modest piece of research might very profitably be done; it would yield an illuminating and suggestive 'contribution to knowledge', of a kind that ought to be judged important by the criteria favoured in an English School. The researcher, to specify one place out of many in *Scrutiny*, will find clues and hints that will start him off well in the comment that begins on page 224 of volume XVIII: 'Mr Pryce-Jones, The British Council and British Culture.' So launched on his investigations into the literature of the British Council, he will discover things that, whatever his predisposition, he is likely to find surprising – startling, even (if in such places and under such an aegis he expects a moderately cautious concern for decency or discretion), in that the light they throw is the reverse of blinding. They entail a consistent and undeniable *parti pris* against *Scrutiny* – against giving it any publicity that can be withheld, or representing it, when mention can't be avoided, as concerned for anything but 'cold' analysis and the 'methodical and uncompromising destruction of reputations' by a 'hypercritical minority group'. The significance in general can be sufficiently intimated by quoting from the comment referred to above:

Three years ago another British Council publication, *Prose Literature since 1939* (by Mr John Hayward), evoked this comment in *Scrutiny*:

It would of course be 'hypercritical' to suggest (though Americans and foreigners in the present writer's hearing have said it) that nothing could be worse for the prestige and influence of British Letters abroad than Mr Hayward's presentment of Metropolitan literary society and the associated University *milieux* as the distinctions and achievements of contemporary England.

Who can doubt that this suggests fairly enough the way in which the promotion of cultural ends by instruction and guidance 'published for the British Council' must, in sum, inevitably work? A perusal of the booklet in which Mr Pryce-Jones's article appears will hardly tend towards any other conclusion. The valuations, the ethos and the criteria promulgated through the weeklies, the Sunday papers and the B.B.C. are provided by the British Council (financed out of public funds) with further means of imposing themselves and with a kind of institutional authority.

This authority, with the comprehensive system it served, we had steadily against us. It is relevant to put on record here that, as the investigator will have learnt from the Comment in volume XVIII referred to earlier, the Mr Pryce-Jones who contributed to the British Council booklet, *The Year's Work in Literature 1950*, was also the editor of *The Times Literary Supplement*. And I can tell the investigator that, on the 'notorious occasion' referred to in that Comment (page 228, first paragraph) I had had a prolonged correspondence with the editor of *The Times Literary Supplement*, which journal, in the issue for 25 August 1950, had published a 44-page 'Critical and Descriptive Survey of British Writing for Readers Overseas'. The otherwise very comprehensive account of 'Literary Periodicals' in that survey contains no mention of *Scrutiny*. My first letter to the editor began: 'Seeing, I confess, in the exclusion of *Scrutiny* from among the Literary Periodicals in your Survey of Contemporary British Writing for Overseas Readers a familiar kind of discrimination against which, as a rule, there is no point in protesting (though third-party testimony is another matter), I had intended to let it pass.' I was writing, I said, because of the justification offered by the editor in replying to a third-party protest, a letter that had in fact been printed. The unsatisfactory and provocative nature of the editor's reply to my own letter (which wasn't printed) compelled me to write back, a process that was repeated again and again. The correspondence, though it will not be found in the files of *The Times Literary Supplement*, can be consulted (the investigator should note) in the London Library, where (headed 'Virtue in Our Time', the title of some broadcast talks by my correspondent) copies are preserved.

In this way inquiry will have been set going into the files of *The Times Literary Supplement* – and will have continued, perhaps, not the less expectantly because no letter of mine is to be found in the numbers succeeding the 'notorious occasion'. Such a habit of discrimination against *Scrutiny* on the part of *The Times Literary Supplement*, with its air of institutional disinterestedness, may perhaps strike the researcher as more significant and disturbing than twenty years of hostility less directly expressed in *The New Statesman and Nation*, which may be regarded as, over the given period, pre-eminently representative of the modish London literary world. Yet, if he takes account of the literary editor's policy in general, the particular abstentions from notice where books notably associated with *Scrutiny* were concerned, the suppressions (let him for instance consider those selected lists of the coming season's publishing), the convention of sneering reference in the review pages, and the related convention of wit on the competitions page, he will certainly conclude that the habit of *The New*

Statesman and Nation too (as Mr R. H. S. Crossman, never a member of the *Scrutiny* connection, has recently testified in *The Guardian*) is significant. As for *The Criterion*, the researcher must also go through that: I don't know that he will find a single reference to *Scrutiny* there – which is not to say that he won't come away with a great deal of relevant illumination.

I have been concerned to bring out the full significance of *Scrutiny*'s having survived for twenty years. It did indeed meet with hostility in the places that, together, might have been thought decisive: that I hope I have put beyond question, and I know that inquiry can only multiply corroborative evidence. But the significance in sum (perhaps I have the right to insist) is positive. Our success in keeping *Scrutiny* going demonstrated the sense of need, the life, in our culture that will not acquiesce in the developments of our civilization I have been pointing to. I say this with my mind on the prospect of further demonstrations, and on the chances they may have (for there would be little point in this reprint if it were not an incitement). I ought here, then, to answer the question (how often has it been put to me!): Why did *Scrutiny* stop?

It was not because we failed to hold our public and were not selling enough copies to pay the printer's bill. We sold out, and could certainly have sold at least twice as many as we printed. In the 1930s we printed 750, a large proportion of which went to subscribers, the rest selling out in due course. This figure tells nothing about the size of the actual public, for very many copies – including many of those subscribed for – went to key places and had, each of them, a great many readers in sixth forms and universities all over the world. It was with the war that the demand began to grow pressingly, and the irony we had to stomach was that the very strict rationing of paper vetoed any increase in the printing: we had a battle, in fact, to maintain the established printing without an insufferable reduction in the number of pages and a cramped make-up. The paper restriction, of course, outlasted the war, but by 1950 we had been able to raise the printing to 1,500. It was a quite different consequence of the war that brought *Scrutiny* to a stop.

As soon as mobilization started, which was well before the declaration of war, our contributing connection registered the consequences. As the war went on the problem became with each number more difficult, so that, looking ahead to the next, one wondered desperately how it was to be brought out, so impossible did the mustering of a sufficient team appear. Still, number after number, *Scrutiny* did come out, at what cost in strain to the permanent nucleus of the connection those who examine the volumes for those years will perhaps guess. The difficulty continued for long after the end of the war. For all that time we had not been enlisting and training up recruits in the way peacetime Cambridge had made possible. And now men came back very conscious of the lost years, pressed by the urgency of catching up and becoming qualified, often married, and, in general, without the margin in life for gratuitous concentration on work for *Scrutiny*. The struggle to keep going was desperate, bearing more heavily even than before on the editorial protagonist (who, well on into his fifties, achieved at last in these postwar years a full University Lectureship), and the decision to stop was sudden. It was precipitated by a quick succession of disappointments: contributor after contributor of those counted on wrote regretting the impossibility of keeping his promise. It became plain that if we went on after the completion of the volume we should be courting the embarrassment of never being able to come out on time or to prevent the lag continually growing. So we stopped. The editor now writing was for months afterwards snowed under with letters of protest and inquiry – tributes, and avowals of indebtedness, from readers all over the world in key positions in higher education and literary and cultural study and from writers and critics. But no one who could be thought of as a voice of the 'English' Establishment – at Cambridge, or in the country – was heard from on this occasion. And *The Times* refused to print a letter of testimony to the work of *Scrutiny* from Professor Henri Fluchère, Director of the Maison Française at Oxford. The distinguished military figure at the head of the British Council, however, sent us a few proper lines of official condolence, hoping we should believe that the Council had always done its best for *Scrutiny*, and ending: 'I hope you will soon start another magazine.'

In the subsequent decade the situation for those who might contemplate an enterprise dedicated, in our spirit, to the same ends has changed. If the initiator were (as he will not be) myself, I should be able to say that I knew of a score or more potential contributors who had been produced since the death of *Scrutiny*. If, however, I leave this parochial (though not irrelevant) note and give my impression of the scene in general, I can't pretend to see anything more encouraging than before in the contemporary performance, if that is the word, of what must pass for the critical function. The reviewing, in fact (and the system controlling it is much strengthened by command of the air and the television screen), is more clique- and mode- and time-serving than ever, and less inhibited, in its pursuit of its non-critical ends, by knowledge and education, or any sense of a critical public that might listen or read. A comparison between the Sunday papers of today and those of ten years ago would bring out the significant development by which, catering now with immensely more lavish expenditures for the 'educated classes' (circulations have soared), they have virtually abandoned, though they still print some reviews, all pretence of expecting what can plausibly be called educated attention. Attention is not what they expect or claim anywhere from any section of their public. They see as their freely avowable function today that of being agreeably distracting and time-passing, and they have the effect of offering the customer his main reading matter for the week.

It might be commented that journals that must sell a million copies in order to live are inevitably like that. But the point I have to make is that what one finds in the review pages of the intellectual weeklies is essentially the culture of the Sunday papers. And the culture of the Sunday papers is what tends more and more to prevail at the senior levels in universities – as has been astonishingly demonstrated of late at Cambridge. The assimilation is of the essence of that modern process which made Sir Charles Snow a voice of wisdom about our culture, and his Rede Lecture a classic in our schools. One aspect of the menace is that the world of large circulations and expanding and multiplying universities is in important ways a very small one – small, though in effect comprehensive. Well-known dons, thought of widely as distinguished intellectuals, are assiduous journalists, establish themselves as names and authorities by frequent performance on radio and television, and form what Sir Charles Snow calls a 'culture' with the other practitioners of their kind, whether or not these claim academic standing, and the standards they favour will naturally be those by which they feel themselves safe as distinguished intellectuals. It has become very difficult to make an effective appeal against this 'culture': to what outside it or transcending it can the appeal be made, and how? The puritan or intransigent who questions its standards finds that he has incurred the enmity, immensely resourceful and quite unscrupulous, of a comprehensive system, one that commands, for the control of the currency, all the organs and channels of suggestion, inculcation and influence – supplies, that is, the 'education' that determines the knowledgeableness, the value sense and the critical assumptions of the greater number of dons. (I had almost inserted here a qualifying 'outside their own disciplines', and of course it will have been understood; but I recollect the Cambridge historian who wrote to *The Spectator* affirming that Snow's history of the Industrial Revolution was sound.)

Yet, on the other hand, *Scrutiny* has effected something, and, what is more, is known to have done so – known and felt in the world of the weeklies and the Sunday papers. That is the significance of the multiplying signs of insecurity, the gratuitous jibes, the obsessed references to 'proliferating disciples'. 'They feel themselves hemmed in', an acute observer of that world – the metropolitan literary world – said to me recently. 'They' are aware at any rate that their status as intellectuals is ironically questioned; that a key public, one that exercises a frightening influence through the universities and the schools and seems to determine in the long run the opinion that matters, finds their pretensions ridiculous. At present it is rather a menacing potentiality that makes itself strongly felt than fully what 'a public', in this context, should suggest; for without a critical organ it cannot have that assured sense of itself as positively and effectively a public, forming a community of consciousness and responsibility, which would make it one, and it is not 'there' for the critic to appeal to even if he had the means of appealing. To summon it into full life – that would have an effect out of all proportion to the numbers.

It could most certainly be done – I say it with the authority given by the long experience of *Scrutiny*. I am not suggesting that *Scrutiny* is to be repeated; it couldn't be. Conditions change – for one thing, as I have recalled, those who founded *Scrutiny* were freelances, without salaried posts of any kind; it is hardly conceivable that a successful enterprise in the spirit of *Scrutiny* could today come from, and continue to depend on, outlaws in that position. But I have already dwelt on the way in which we conceived our enterprise in terms of the time, the place and the circumstances. A renewed enterprise conceived and conducted in the same spirit would inevitably be in important ways different. But *Scrutiny* nevertheless is the sustained and strong demonstration of the thing done, and the proof of possible success – success attained by consistent severity of standard and an uncompromising service of the function. I have suggested that *Scrutiny* – the fact and the notoriety of the achievement – leaves the situation in some ways more favourable for our successors. A new critical challenge, unmistakably real and courageous, would draw together a comparatively large public, one that might even make payment of contributors possible. But the emphasis to close on is this: even a very small public may, the matters at issue being such as I have discussed in this introduction, be disproportionately influential. *Scrutiny* proved that.

Standards of criticism

It's characteristic of our field of thought that we have to use terms we can't strictly or neatly define. Of the term 'standards' worse can be said: it invites the user to endorse and adopt false suggestions that make intelligent thought about the nature of criticism impossible. The standards of criticism are not at all of the order of the standards in the Weights and Measures Office. They are not producible, they are not precise, and they are not fixed. But if they are not effectively 'there' for the critic to appeal to, the function of criticism is badly disabled. In fact, it is always a part of the function of criticism to assert and maintain them; that is, to modify them, for to maintain is to vitalize, and to vitalize is almost inevitably to modify.

Of the criteria by which we judge I might have said that, if the work in front of us is a great one, they will be affected by it – that is, altered. A major experience of creative literature being in question, say the impact of Tolstoy or D. H. Lawrence, the alteration, we all know, may be a very significant one. So as the influence of great writers achieves its work through the educated public, standards undergo change. And in a less traceable way there is change – the life, the living continuity that a culture is, being a response to changing conditions.

A reference to 'standards' involves reference to an educated public that we implicitly postulate: standards are 'there' for the critic to appeal to only in so far as there *is* such a public; one capable of responding when appealed to, and of making its response felt. Where there *is* such a public certain judgments, or kinds of judgment, can be dismissed with some equivalent of the word or gesture that Matthew Arnold borrowed from the French, *saugrenu*; dismissed as obviously (to an educated mind), and ridiculously absurd. It is in this negative kind of way, though they're very much a positive affair, that we can best describe standards. Indeed, it's when they've become difficult to appeal to with effect that we – I mean, we who know what their nature is and feel their necessity – tend most to talk about them. I'm both invoking standards, *and* suggesting that they haven't been effectively 'there', when I say that it's absurd and deplorable that Auden should have been for years a classic in the schools, having been accepted by the dominant literary world as a major poet, to be bracketed with Yeats and Eliot.

Standards, I said, are 'there' – *can* be there – for the critic to appeal to only in the existence of an educated public: such a public as can be brought, by the critic, to see (before the real artist, the real creative force, fades out in discouragement) that the Lytton Strachey, the Aldous Huxley, the Auden of the age is not what the journalist intellectual takes him to be – not the writer who is, as we say, at the 'conscious point', or the point of growth; not the real thing. Let me, by way of proceeding to clear (if possible) any haze from that distinction, remind you of Lawrence's way of receiving some critical advice offered him by Arnold Bennett:

Tell Arnold Bennett that all rules of construction hold good only for novels that are copies of other novels . . . What he calls faults, he being an old imitator, I call characteristics.

Bennett, I can testify, was not at that time – and later – clearly recognized by the cultivated public for the not very important kind of writer he was, but we have no difficulty now in recognizing the essential justice, given the provocation, of Lawrence's description of him. Few even of the respectable admired writers of a given time are original in the important sense. No one at any time who was capable of distinguishing the signs of genuine new life could have been taken in by J. B. Priestley's calculating manufactures (he's in 'Everyman' though). But writers found impressive in their effect of technical modernness and significant originality, writers such as Huxley and Auden, in their time, may be really *no more* original – no more so in any essential way. They may be significant only at the level of the journalistic intellectual who acclaims them, and thinks them original – profound interpreters of the modern human situation – because he can respond to them and feel advanced without having been called to make any effort of readjustment. Writers of this class can be, like those I've named, intelligent, even talented, and yet they are not the kind of writer because of whom literature matters. And there can be subtler challenges to the critic than Huxley and Auden. So that the real original critic is very necessary: he has an important function. And for what is meant by the real original critic I'll resort again to Lawrence:

Literary criticism can be no more than a reasoned account of the feeling produced upon the critic by the book he is criticizing. Criticism can never be a science: it is, in the first place, much too personal, and in the second, it is concerned with values that science ignores. The touchstone is emotion, not reason. We judge a work of art by its effect on our sincere and vital emotions and nothing else. All the critical twiddle-twaddle about style and form, all this pseudo-scientific classifying and analysing of books in an imitation-botanical fashion is merely impertinence and mostly dull jargon.

A critic must be able to *feel* the impact of a work of art in all its complexity and its force. To do so, he must be a man of force and complexity himself, which few critics are. A man with a paltry, impudent nature will never write anything but paltry, impudent criticism. And a man who is *emotionally* educated is rare as a phoenix. The more scholastically educated a man is generally, the more is he an emotional boor.

More than this, even an artistically and emotionally educated man must be a man of good faith. He must have the courage to admit what he feels, as well as the flexibility to *know* what he feels. So Sainte-Beuve remains, to me, a great critic. And a man like Macaulay, brilliant as he is, is unsatisfactory, because he is not honest. He is emotionally very alive, but he juggles his feelings. He prefers a fine effect to the sincere statement of the aesthetic and emotional reaction. He is quite intellectually capable of giving us a true account of what he feels. But not morally. A critic must be emotionally alive in every fibre, intellectually capable and skilful in essential logic, and then morally very honest.

The representative quality of the genuinely and significantly original writer – the writer who is 'at the conscious point' of his age – is what doesn't get readily recognized; in fact, it tends, in so far as it makes itself felt, to be ignored – resistantly ignored; or it even generates overt animus. It's the critic who distinguishes, and makes the due claim for, the creatively original writer, and wins for him what recognition he gets.

To do this is to exercise a function that has in a clear way, as Matthew Arnold noted, a creative aspect. For a significant work that is not recognized and appreciated is not an effective and operative value or power: it's not fulfilling its destiny, its *raison d'être*; it's not playing its part in life. What its part potentially is can only be determined experimentally, by its getting due attention. How, as we come to appreciate it and to realize its significance, does it affect our sense of the things that have determining significance for us? How does it affect our total sense of relative value, our sense of direction, our sense of life?

I am invoking the truism that a work of art hasn't, unrelated, standing by itself, its full significance. Appreciation entails relating, implicit and explicit. And here we have the critic's function. He is performing that function not only when he wins recognition for contemporary works, but also when he helps to determine what works of the past shall be actively alive in the contemporary mind – when he alters accepted valuations; as Eliot altered, in the existing sense of the relation of the past to the present, the place of the seventeenth century as it bore on poetic practice and taste (and so on more); or as I should like to alter the accepted valuation of Dickens.

I am implicitly saying in this what I said before: the critic helps to form the contemporary sensibility. And the contemporary sensibility is 'there' in a responsive educated public, which is the presence in the total community, in our civilization, of literature as a power – if it *is* one. If we are required to give some account of what the phrase portends, and I think that there's no need to be at any pains to elaborate one, we can say that it is a practised readiness of response over a certain selective range, a habit of implicit preference and expectation. The word 'expectation', of course, points to the problem; without some appropriate setting of the receptive apparatus, without some relevant predisposition, we can't really perceive, and perception in respect of a complex work of art is a decidedly sophisticated achievement. But if a new work of art deserves to be acclaimed as both new and notably significant, its significance will be in some measure a matter of its defeating and correcting habit, for the readiness to respond carries with it a correlated blankness, or resistance – even animus, in the face of what is not attuned to it, but asks to be taken seriously.

There is no easy reassurance to be given; life is what it is. We can only, besides training ourselves to keep this truth about its nature as manifested in the critic's province livingly present to ourselves, hope that the critic in Lawrence's sense, the critic *par excellence*, won't be lacking. Or rather, we can hope too (and in a university English School hoping should be a positively active business) that the critic will have the ear of a responsive élite influential enough to make a speedy educating of the larger 'educated public' not out of the question. It is this larger educated public one is thinking of when one talks about standards. I almost put educated public here in inverted commas, thinking of the state of affairs we are confronted with today; but the public of *The Times Literary Supplement* – can't that be properly and unhesitatingly referred to as just *an* educated public, representative of *the* educated public? That's a rhetorical question, preparatory to making an illustrative point. Few people, I suppose, who pick up *The Times Literary Supplement* read a large proportion of it, but all of them must have noticed the phenomenon of its review headings – the new style that greets us brightly, untiringly and shamelessly on every page, above every review. Last week my eye was caught by 'Down With Alice'. When I looked below the heading I found that the book was one on the disaster to the ship *Alice*, which, as the reviewer told us, cost more lives than any other such disaster in home waters on record except that of the *Royal George*, which capsized and went down with 'eight hundred of the brave'.

This, one may comment, is not precisely a collapse, or abeyance, of standards in literary criticism. No; but it's something immediately and intimately related. The vulgar, brassy, fatuous and insulting demonstration of brightness is kept up with mechanical pertinacity.

The fact is that standards as the literary critic invokes them are not a matter of some sealed-off literary province. When they decay, when they are no longer 'there' for the critic to appeal to with effect, there are general consequences. They are 'there', if at all, as I have said, in an educated public that can respond and is in a position to make its response felt. Where there is no such public – and it must be *a* public, integrated, and conscious of its existence as a public, which if it hasn't influential organs of expression, it can't be – standards have ceased to be 'there' to appeal to, and the critic who challenges the accepted currency of valuations, and what I may call the social corruptions and betrayals of criticism is guilty of anti-social ill-will, dogmatic assertion and bad manners.

I have described the present state of affairs. I hope I shan't be summarized as having asserted that there is today *no* educated public. There are, of course, many cultivated, intelligent and responsible persons for the critic to appeal to, and there are centres of enlightenment and intelligent judgment. But there is no public large, integrated, conscious and influential enough to insist on the maintenance of the critical function in any reviews or journals run on business lines – paying staff and contributors, that is, and paying its way. The simple, stark and indisputable fact is that the whole of the English-speaking world can't, or won't, support a single periodical seriously devoted to asserting and serving the function of criticism, and the existence or otherwise of critical reviews in our civilization is not a matter of indifference.

As for the processes of civilization by which the present state of affairs has come about, everyone is aware of their general nature. I needn't do much more than refer to the Education Act of 1870, and the name of Lord Northcliffe, symbolic and representative; representative of the discovery of new fields where profit would follow the application of the principles and methods of mass-production. Mass-production entails standardization and levelling down, the standards of mass-production being quite other in nature from those I have been discussing. The process was immensely accelerated by the 1914 war, which brought a rapid rise in costs with consequences that I myself witnessed in the 1920s, when there was a heavy mortality among the weeklies in which the performance of the critical function was then centred. It seems to have been supposed at the beginning of the decade that an intellectual journal could be run on a sale of a few thousands. It very rapidly became plain that it was not so. The truth was demonstrated that if you are to pay your way you must have an impressive advertisement revenue, and that you have no chance of that unless you have an impressive circulation. The workings of this logic as they affected the standards that concern *us* could be illustrated with convincing, and depressing, particularity and redundance, but I won't go in for that. I won't even expatiate on the history of *The New Statesman* under Mr Kingsley Martin, who became editor in 1930 (the year when Lawrence died); *The New Statesman* having amalgamated with, or swallowed the *Nation* (which had long ago absorbed *The Athenaeum*, once under Middleton Murry's editorship), *The Saturday Review* and *The Weekend Review*. Under Kingsley Martin the sales of *The New Statesman* reached 90,000. About the price in quality or standard paid for that success I'll say no more than I've implicitly said already.

As for quarterlies or monthlies that could be seen as making a discussable offer to assert and maintain the critical function in the face of the 'literary intellectual's journalism' (Snow's term) that was supposed to do the work in the flimsier prints, there was *The Criterion*, which was subsidized, and regarding which my report is that its review pages, where the contemporary literary scene was concerned, were hardly distinguishable from those of *The New Statesman*. That was the situation which, in 1930, we young and youngish irregulars, out of whose informal frequentations of a congenial milieu *Scrutiny* issued, found ourselves contemplating. We saw the failure of the *Calendar of Modern Letters* (1925–7) to establish itself as a final episode. The *Calendar* was an attempt to prove that a serious critical review could both pay contributors adequately and pay its way, and the *Calendar* was lively as well as very good. Our conclusion was that if there was to *be* a critical review – and we didn't question that there *must* be – it would have to be run on other than commercial lines. And here came in the Idea of the University and the Idea of an English School as they must be conceived and, more than that, realized, in the technological age, if humanity is not to suffer disastrous impoverishment.

A hope for the function of criticism that looks to the university will not be an easy or trustful hope. Anyone aware of the conditions who is able to entertain it will have at the same time a strong sense of the insidiousness of the academic spirit – a spirit that can academicize the very recognition that the academic won't do, and prevail in its ostensible self-repudiation. And, actually (I speak with my own university in mind), the worst enemy, at the university, of the cause we are concerned for is today something very different from what 'academic' in its pejorative sense ordinarily suggests; though, being as it is so representative and formidable, it may properly be called the new academic spirit. We have it in recent appointments to prestige Lectureships and Chairs; we have it in the election of Mr Kingsley Amis as Fellow of a distinguished and very selective college; we have it in the preponderance of demonstrated support and sympathy that Snow got at Cambridge after the notorious violence committed on him; we have it in the Head of a House (now along with his ally Snow in the House of Lords) of whom, when I said to a member of his college, 'Can't he see he is selling the pass?' (a politico-demagogic public utterance being in question), replied 'He doesn't know there's a pass to sell'; we shall soon have it, I'm afraid, in the form of an accepted research project on the time-patterns in Iris Murdoch's novels, or the philosophy of Angus Wilson. It is the presence of the enemy, at ease and at home, within the citadel; a state of affairs eloquent of that lapse of standards which, having made it possible, prevents its being recognized for what it is.

You gather that I not only don't acquiesce in this state of affairs, but think that no one sincerely and intelligently committed to literary studies – to the study of English literature – can. To acquiesce is impossible, for, as I've tried to bring home, the idea of Criticism isn't – can't be – a matter of mere theory. I have no excuse for entertaining easy illusions, but I believe that there is, in the face of our rapidly developing civilization, a deep human need to appeal to, a human instinct of self-preservation, and that, whatever else is done, something must be done at the university. And, at a time when so much emphasis is laid on the need for multiplication of universities, perhaps it won't everywhere be dismissed as an obvious and idle paradox when we insist that, properly conceived, the university has a function the realization and adequate performance of which matters as it has never done before. The creative and recreative maintaining of the full human heritage, the vital and unimpoverished cultural heritage, the human world, can't be left to the old traditional processes. The 'educated class' most certainly – whatever it is – isn't adequate to performing the function in the old ways. As I've observed, it won't, in the whole of the English-speaking world, support one organ seriously, responsibly and intelligently devoted to maintaining the Function of Criticism at the Present Time. And for a classical reminder that more is involved than something to be referred to with limiting intention as 'literary taste', one can point to Arnold's essay.

But, of course, it's an essential characteristic of the state of affairs that has to be dealt with that it should seem almost impossible to get recognition for what it is: the facts, the conditions are ignored, and, if one insists, pooh-poohed. Aren't there the immense sales of the Penguin and Pelican books to point to? Wasn't Wordsworth in his time treated with derision? Haven't the critics always been inadequate to their responsibilities, and the public always stupid? That is the attitude, and a convention prevails of seeing no need to answer any presentment of the facts that expose its absurdity.

People whose experience doesn't go back beyond the past quarter of a century don't easily believe that things have ever been essentially different from what they themselves have always known; and no one will look to esteemed and established writers and intellectuals for a quickness to acclaim, or even to see, the truth about the condition on which their status as writers and intellectuals depends. Yet that the unprecedented and accelerating developments of material civilization over the past century have had, in the field of our special interest, the kinds of consequence that an intelligent and well-informed observer in the mid-Victorian age, say a Tocqueville, would have forecast isn't difficult to show. The ways in which the truth of the far from paradoxical contention manifests itself, and the lines on which one would proceed, if necessary, to elucidate and enforce that truth, have been repeatedly and challengingly indicated. There has never been any attempt to refute the case that has been argued and documented (in *Fiction and the Reading Public*, for instance), and again and again insisted on, with appropriate publicity, as contemporary illustration offered itself. To rehearse it, or to summarize more fully than I have done the processes of civilization that have produced the present state of things, is out of place here. I will confine myself to recalling some representative history that falls within the immediate field of interest of students reading English.

When Leslie Stephen, for reasons of conscience, threw up his Fellowship at Trinity Hall, Cambridge, he went into the literary world and committed himself to earning his living by his pen. He complained from time to time of poverty, but, actually, we know, he made in every sense a marked success of the literary life; he wrote a good body of solid work, some of which remains classical, and he was able to maintain his family at the level of well-being, amenity and cultivation required by the standards of a Victorian gentleman. In education he was an admirable product of his university, his equipment was formidable, and of his work in general, the work by which he earned the necessary income, it can be said that it demanded the powers and resources that he brought to it. It was very varied work, and not all work of authority. Its significance in relation to the present discussion asks to be recorded in this: from 1871 to 1882 Leslie Stephen edited *The Cornhill Magazine*. *The Cornhill* published most of 'Culture and Anarchy', part of 'Friendship's Garland', three instalments of the scandalously unorthodox 'Unto this Last' (a destructive analysis of the most potent and confident Victorian orthodoxy, the politico-economic), and, of Stephen's own work, several of the essays collected in 'Hours in a Library'. Others of those essays, scholarly and critical, that we know in the collections appeared in *The National Review*, *The Fortnightly Review* and *Fraser's Magazine*.

That is, *The Cornhill* was very far from being the only periodical that printed articles and critiques addressed to an unequivocally 'highbrow' public, and long enough to be properly argued and documented. It would be gathered (rightly) from this fact alone that the play of criticism on intellectual life in the critical field and on the contemporary scene in general, was favoured by corresponding conditions of advantage. The point I have to emphasize at the moment is that the existence of so generous a provision of established reviews, magazines and journals (among newspapers, for instance, *The Pall Mall Gazette* included among its contributors Arnold, George Henry Lewes, Fitzjames and Leslie Stephen, R. H. Hutton, Ruskin and John Morley – who became editor) – the existence of so generous a provision of organs addressing a cultivated, informed and morally responsible public is proof of existence of such a public on a large scale.

At the centre of this public was the correspondingly large body of writers it supported: writers conscious of the dignity of their profession, qualified for it by knowledge and intelligence, and able to live by the serious exercise of their qualifications. Here we have the conditions in which standards are 'there' for the critic to appeal to and in which he can appeal to them with effect. I'm not making any naïve assertion. I don't mean that such conditions guarantee the timely appearance of the real and authoritative critic. I don't mean that they guarantee the immediate or swift recognition of the Wordsworth, the Hopkins, or the Lawrence, or exclude the possibility that the Thackeray, the Tennyson or the Meredith may be widely and for long overvalued. But they make it impossible for a Snow to be accepted even for six months as a profound mind, or for a Kingsley Amis to be defended by a Cambridge custodian of the humanities as engaged in serious studies of amorality. And they are the conditions a critic must wish for; they are those which favour most his endeavour to get for the significant new life, the 'alteration of expression', the neglected or misvalued writer of the past, the due recognition and appreciation. Where they obtain there can be no such record as our ancient universities have to show in the matter of honorary degrees conferred for distinction in literature; no illusion such as Peterhouse suffered from when it accepted Kingsley Amis as a distinguished creative writer, no tolerance for brassy editorial fatuity in *The Times Literary Supplement*; and no imposing of the dogma that there are two Cultures – and we know the practical accompaniments in education – on the Sixth Forms.

Reading out poetry

I am a little uneasy, or more than a little, about the present undertaking. When having said 'yes' to the invitation to visit Belfast, I was in due course asked what my subject would be, I answered, when slightly fatigued, as one whose habit was to talk to literary students of English literature and whose invitations came more often than not from English societies. I hadn't at that time anticipated the honour of having you,[1] Sir, in the Chair, and a large comprehensive assembly as audience. Not that there isn't at the centre of my own grave preoccupations extra-departmental concerns, but simply I can't help wondering how far in an hour's discourse it's possible really to bring that home to a general university audience composed, at any rate in large measure, of students (I assume we are all students) whose serious thinking is not centred in creative literature or based on it. I'd almost said not centred in the literary field, but recalling how the late Aldous Huxley accused me of standing for literarism, as opposed to Snow's distinctive deviation of scientism, I flinched away from the word 'literary'. Long before that – Huxley brought the charge in, I think, his last book – I had done my best to get known as protesting that literary values were not a concern I stood for. I didn't know what the phrase meant. Critical judgments, this seems to me the indisputable truth, should be thought of as judgments about life, and literary criticism should be thought of as a discipline for relevance in judging and commenting. It goes with this position, as I hold it, to insist that the distinctive discipline of a university English School is a discipline of intelligence *sui generis*. Of course that is irreplaceable; of course a conception and definition of intelligence are involved, and that conception is for me associated with an Idea of the University, with an insistence on the way in which we conceive the complicated function of the university at the present critical moment of human history.

I want the English School to *deserve* to be thought of as representing a distinctive discipline of intelligence, so that it can be seriously thought of as one of the special disciplines, the living interactive co-presence of which makes a university really a university. I remember once having said that I have the same conception of the university in mind when I say that what a society desperately needs is what it now

253

lacks, a real and influential educated public, and that the university is
society's organ for re-creating and maintaining such a public. Of
course I am not going to develop these observations now. The pre-
tention implicit in them couldn't be substantiated in a brief hour's discourse on my stated theme, but perhaps I shall have evoked the context of preoccupations that conditions my interest in the reading out of
poetry sufficiently to make it plain, in spite of the restriction and
paucity entailed by the time-limit, that I am concerned with matters
that seem to me of the utmost importance. What's involved is not the
comparative triviality suggested, for me at any rate, by the phrase
'aesthetic propriety' or 'aesthetic felicity', but the very nature of
creative literature, of language, of thought – creative literature,
language of thought.

Since the word linguistic is used a great deal in the exposition and
discussion of Wittgenstein, I am prompted to come to my formulated
subject in an immediately relevant recollection of him. Now and
then, at his request, I found myself forty years ago reading out parts,
indicated, prescribed, of Dickens's *The Uncommercial Traveller* to
him. I remember an occasion when he exclaimed with his characteristic curt finality: 'Don't interpret.' Of course he knew that one can't
read things out neutrally. Wittgenstein was not only a subtle man but
he was cultivated, he had a cultivated background, so he knew that.
What he meant was that he didn't like my interpretation.

Actually I wasn't much interested in those pages of Dickens, I
hadn't chosen them and I simply couldn't guess what it was in them
that had taken possession of Wittgenstein. But when one tentatively,
experimentally, feels one's way to the reading out of a poem, one has
implicitly judged that for one reason or another it is worth the trouble,
and I'll avow that where poems that I care about are concerned I
myself, as a rule, don't like other people's interpretations. I'm very
intolerant – I don't think that is mere egotistic intolerance on my part.
For it's my considered judgment that very little intelligence has been
devoted to what should be the recognized necessity of reading poetry
out. Years ago I had for review the records of T. S. Eliot's reading of
Four Quartets. It was embarrassingly bad, suggesting that shame-faced
helplessness of a British public schoolboy of say 40 years, 50 years
back. Since Eliot, to use his own word, was the practitioner who
imagined and composed his poetry, one can hardly suggest that *he*
couldn't in his mind hear it with sensitive precision as something fully
and livingly there; but the mere reader of poetry who doesn't do a
great deal of full reading out won't be able to read out in imagination.
That is my central insistence, my implicit insistence, all the way
through. How disastrous critically (that is, for perception, under-

standing and appreciation) the incapacity may be, I can hope to demonstrate briefly and decisively by considering some of the most approachable of Eliot's own major work.

I repeat the statement I made a short while ago; what's involved is not the comparative triviality suggested by the phrase 'aesthetic propriety', but the nature of creative literature, language and thought; if language, then of thought, because even mathematical thought would have no meaning if there weren't language behind it – implicitly, tacitly referred to. I take that point from Michael Polanyi. The point to be made in relation to the word 'thought' is that Eliot demands not only what the full attention of the waking mind suggests; he demands a sustained and alert delicacy of attention, a quick and delicate responsiveness of full apprehension. I can illustrate this, in a way peculiarly germane to my present purpose, from poetry of his that with its plangent canorousness might be taken for hypnoidal, but is de-natured if it is read in that way, since actually it demands all the attention that the alert, waking mind can command.

I am thinking of the poetry of *Ash-Wednesday*. That work is one in which the poet devotes the subtleties of his art to *not* affirming, to not even appearing, though on the very edge of affirmation, to affirm unequivocally. To explain what I mean I must refer back briefly to *The Hollow Men*, the poem that stands between *Ash-Wednesday* and *The Waste Land* printed just before it in the collected volume. In its evocation of emptiness and impotence and unbearable nostalgic hunger it's a significantly new thing in the Eliotic canon. There is in it no irony and no protest, the voice is the voice of despair, or rather of desperation.

> Shape without form, shade without colour,
> Paralysed force, gesture without motion;
>
> Those who have crossed
> With direct eyes, to death's other Kingdom
> Remember us – if at all – not as lost
> Violent souls, but only
> As the hollow men
> The stuffed men.

Now Eliot couldn't rest there, no man could rest there – and it's the religious poetry that in his case follows. But this poetry is not religious in the way the Anglo-Catholicizing commentators seem to believe. Eliot's extreme need, his desperate need, makes him desperately sincere and his need is to achieve a state in which he can assure himself that he has a firm grasp of some supreme and unquestionable reality, a firm apprehension of the really real. He can't satisfy that need, in the

Ash-Wednesday stage, with determinate affirmations. The approach, the quest, is exploratory–creative, tentative. What he has, beside hunger in the emptiness, is the Christian nisus, for after all he was brought up in what was in some sense a Christian culture, and from the recognition of that nisus in himself he starts.

It doesn't in the six poems or movements of *Ash-Wednesday* attain to unequivocal affirmation. The nisus manifests itself there as strong and pertinacious, but the inclusive poem in its totality, I think, has no more affirmed at the end than it does at the beginning. I'll read the first poem, the one that begins 'Because I do not hope to turn again', having made a few comments first by way of illuminating and justifying my point – which I hope I shall proceed to illustrate – that this poetry demands the full attention of the waking and thinking mind – waking *and* thinking. You see I insist on that word 'thinking'. I'm thinking of the way I insisted on that word 'thought' earlier – the nature of creative literature, of language, of thought. For all the strong biblical and liturgical characteristics, there is something else not suggested by those adjectives and it manifests itself in the subtle shifts of tone, inflection and attack: shifts that one misses and eliminates if, tranced by the melodiousness and simplifying the rhythmic flow, one reads the verse as hypnoidal – as it is commonly read.

Note then the fourth line of the first paragraph, 'Desiring this man's gift and that man's scope'. That of course is a slightly altered quotation from one of the best known of Shakespeare's sonnets 'desiring this man's art and that man's scope'. You might note that in that sonnet 'scope' rhymes with 'hope'; it brings the word up at once, which is very relevant, of course, to 'Because I do not hope to turn again'. You have, in reading out the poem, to read Eliot's line, the fourth line, in inverted commas as it were. I don't find that so easy to do, but one must tell oneself that is what one must do – and one can't do that sort of thing without practice. The shift of tone establishes a certain distance, it conveys an attitude of detachment from the envy and ambition while intimating their normality. The next line but one is the parenthesis, 'Why should the agèd eagle stretch its wings?'. It has to be read out with a delicate but unmistakable ironic inflection. The irony is plainly there in 'the agèd eagle'. So far as striving involves a will, and willing involves self-assertion and the desire to exalt the self, there is to be no more striving – that's Eliot's resolution. The irony of the parenthesis is directed against the self. Even in self-abnegation there may be the taint of self-exaltation or self-approval. Lastly, note the flatness of factual statement that marks the third paragraph and the paradoxical nature of 'Consequently' in 'Consequently I rejoice, having to construct something / Upon which to rejoice'.

Whether I should be able to render those effects reasonably well is, of course, a question. I'm not at all events likely to render them to my own complete satisfaction. I hope at least to leave you convinced that the meaning, the force, the distinction, in short the *raison d'être* of Eliot's poetry depends on them. I don't overemphasize when I say 'depends on them'. For if you register *them* with any sensitiveness that means that you know you are reading the whole poem *as* a whole with a delicately perceptive responsiveness that registers many other subtleties or precisions. It's only in sensitive relation to context – and the context is the whole poem – that you can render such effects as I have pointed to. It isn't merely those particular local challenges that I'm considering; but if you master them I think you may feel that you have been adequate to the others. I will now read a poem which I read by itself first more than 40 years ago in a French organ, with the French translation *en regard*:

Because I do not hope to turn again
Because I do not hope
Because I do not hope to turn
Desiring this man's gift and that man's scope
I no longer strive to strive towards such things
(Why should the agèd eagle stretch its wings?)
Why should I mourn
The vanished power of the usual reign?

Because I do not hope to know again
The infirm glory of the positive hour
Because I do not think
Because I know I shall not know
The one veritable transitory power
Because I cannot drink
There, where trees flower, and springs flow, for there is nothing again

Because I know that time is always time
And place is always and only place
And what is actual is actual only for one time
And only for one place
I rejoice that things are as they are and
I renounce the blessèd face
And renounce the voice
Because I cannot hope to turn again
Consequently I rejoice, having to construct something
Upon which to rejoice

And pray to God to have mercy upon us
And I pray that I may forget
These matters that with myself I too much discuss
Too much explain
Because I do not hope to turn again

Let these words answer
For what is done, not to be done again
May the judgement not be too heavy upon us

Because these wings are no longer wings to fly
But merely vans to beat the air
The air which is now thoroughly small and dry
Smaller and dryer than the will
Teach us to care and not to care
Teach us to sit still.

Pray for us sinners now and at the hour of our death
Pray for us now and at the hour of our death.

I spoke in my prefatory remarks of the 'consequently' in 'Consequently I rejoice' as paradoxical. To emphasize the point of saying *that*
I'll read the paragraph again in order that you may take full note of the
*in*consequences whereby the phrase introduced by 'Consequently'
clinches the effect of the immediate following phrase:

Because I know that time is always time
And place is always and only place
And what is actual is actual only for one time
And only for one place
I rejoice that things are as they are and
I renounce the blessèd face
And renounce the voice
Because I cannot hope to turn again
Consequently I rejoice, having to construct something
Upon which to rejoice

The 'having to construct something / Upon which to rejoice' corresponds to the 'Thus devoted, concentrated in purpose' of the next
poem, which I shall read. The 'purpose' here being something set over
against personal will, the propositional form and effect of what we are
offered as propositions is essential to the 'logic' of the poetry – is essential to the constructive organization. But as the absence of punctuation
intimates, the consequence with which they follow one another isn't
logical with the logic of the commonsense world or of prose discourse.

And this is the moment to emphasize my point in insisting on the
way in which Eliot's poetry, even at its most canorous, challenges the
full attention of the thinking mind. I'm insisting that I really meant it
when I said that to think, with intentness on practice, about the problem and the critical necessity of learning what the reading out of poetry
involves, is to reflect in an intimate way on both the nature of thought
and the nature of language. By thought here I will, for convenience, let
myself say – reverting to the antithesis by way of making my point
clear – I mean the anti-mathematical kind of thought. I have to add at

once that though my using the word antithesis in this way seems to me reasonable, it's necessary to insist that there is no disjunction. Michael Polanyi makes this plain, emphasizing that any thinking must be done by an individual mind – there's no such thing as just 'mind', you know – mind is represented always in the concrete by a particular mind. Emphasizing that any thinking must be done by an individual mind, and a person – it is necessarily, in the various senses of that adverb, associated with a body and a personal history – Polanyi says: 'deprived of their tacit coefficients, all spoken words, all formulae, all maps and graphs are strictly meaningless; an exact mathematical theory means nothing unless we recognize an inexact, non-mathematical knowledge on which it bears, and a person whose judgment upholds this bearing'.

This is not a theme I'm offering to develop; I'm merely concerned to bring home to you that when in my own context I say thought, I'm not using the word gratuitously or irresponsibly. I'm calling attention to what should be the obvious fact that Eliot by means of his own technique, which is a delicate and disciplined use of language, achieves his own kind of precision and so lays an exacting responsibility on the reader – the reader who judges this and that poem to be a work of creative genius. *Ash-Wednesday* is overtly heuristic; one couldn't from it have foreseen the later culminating work *Four Quartets*, about which no one will think it paradoxical to say that it is concerned with thought. But looking back from it to *Ash-Wednesday* we can see no paradox in the poet's having gone on to the later work.

In registering, as I read the first poem, the effects I had commented on beforehand, I was, to use Polanyi's phrase, implicitly recognizing 'the tacit coefficients' on which the total, precise, unparaphrasable meaning of the integrated poem depends. For the limited conscious recognition I was explicit about carries with it the delicate pervasive responsiveness without which there is no genuine poetic life in the reading – responsiveness that is far wider than what the word 'recognition' suggests. For if something that might be called recognition is involved, it's tacit, fluent, or current and unanalytic. You will notice that I have defined the term 'thought', that I have shifted from the term 'thought' to the term 'meaning'. That is an implicit recognition on my part that in relation to many poems, with the clear undeniable claim on one's highest responsibility, one would hardly find oneself coming out immediately with the term 'thought', but in the passage from thought to the other word – to meaning – there is again no disjunction. I shall not, let me reassure you, continue in this vein; I needed to guard myself and my theme from the word 'aesthetic', which tends in this matter, as in so many others, to beg the important questions and trivialize the issues. And by way of transition back to the actual reading of the poetry, I'll pick up again from Wittgenstein's word 'interpret'. It's, of course, the usual word; the trouble is its ambiguity; no clear distinction being made, it means so often what the great Shakespearean actor, say Sir Laurence Olivier, does to Shakespeare. I myself avoid the word for the reason I've tactfully intimated. I think rather in terms of the ideal executant musician, the one who, knowing it rests with him to re-create in obedience to what lies in black print on the white sheet in front of him, devotes all his trained intelligence, sensitiveness, intuition and skill to re-creating, reproducing faithfully what he divines his composer essentially conceived.

Faithfully reading out a poem, a poem that one admires, one should think of oneself as both the violinist and the violin, and not as an impressively personal elocutionary voice blessed with an opportunity. (That's the usual attitude, as a matter of fact.) This is to challenge a test from which one can hardly hope to emerge wholly self-satisfied. With this self-admonition to myself I'll now make an attempt to read the second poem in *Ash-Wednesday*. What I call your attention to is the way in which, while being so insistently liturgical and biblical, so strongly evocative of a given Christian tradition, it evokes death as extinction. In doing so I point to the way in which the poem defies all show of paraphrase. Its precise thisness of meaning entails – *is* – a creative precision in the evoked concrete of what we may properly call the complete process of thought – a complexity poignantly significant because unresolved.

> Lady, three white leopards sat under a juniper-tree
> In the cool of the day, having fed to satiety
> On my legs my heart my liver and that which had been contained
> In the hollow round of my skull. And God said
> Shall these bones live? shall these
> Bones live? And that which had been contained
> In the bones (which were already dry) said chirping:
> Because of the goodness of this Lady
> And because of her loveliness, and because
> She honours the Virgin in meditation,
> We shine with brightness. And I who am here dissembled
> Proffer my deeds to oblivion, and my love
> To the posterity of the desert and the fruit of the gourd.
> It is this which recovers
> My guts the strings of my eyes and the indigestible portions
> Which the leopards reject. The Lady is withdrawn
> In a white gown, to contemplation, in a white gown.
> Let the whiteness of bones atone to forgetfulness.
> There is no life in them. As I am forgotten
> And would be forgotten, so I would forget
> Thus devoted, concentrated in purpose. And God said

Prophesy to the wind, to the wind only for only
The wind will listen. And the bones sang chirping
With the burden of the grasshopper, saying

Lady of silences
Calm and distressed
Torn and most whole
Rose of memory
Rose of forgetfulness
Exhausted and life-giving
Worried reposeful
The single Rose
Is now the Garden
Where all loves end
Terminate torment
Of love unsatisfied
The greater torment
Of love satisfied
End of the endless
Journey to no end
Conclusion of all that
Is inconclusible
Speech without word and
Word of no speech
Grace to the Mother
For the Garden
Where all love ends.

Under a juniper-tree the bones sang, scattered and shining
We are glad to be scattered, we did little good to each other,
Under a tree in the cool of the day, with the blessing of sand,
Forgetting themselves and each other, united
In the quiet of the desert. This is the land which ye
Shall divide by lot. And neither division nor unity
Matters. This is the land. We have our inheritance.

Whenever I come to 'This is the land which ye / Shall divide by lot.
And neither division nor unity / Matters', I recall John Donne's 'I
wonder by my troth what thou and I / Did till we loved'. 'Did' is the
first word of the second line. You see the point of my mentioning that
Eliot's interest in Donne, which was given distinguished but misleading critical expression in the essay – really a review – called 'The
Metaphysical Poets', was essentially a matter of Donne's having
brought into non-dramatic poetry the Shakespearean use of the
English language. In saying that I'm thinking of the way in which the
speaking voice and the spirit of the spoken language prevail in Shakespeare's mature blank verse. It's only by appealing to the reader's
sense of the way things go naturally that a poet *can* command subtle

shifts of tone, inflection and attack as Eliot does. And I have to make in relation to him the point I found myself making in relation to the very different Wordsworth. I found myself saying in a seminar apropos of 'The Ruined Cottage' – that early poem in which Wordsworth's genius first is compellingly present and which, though a neglected poem, is surely a classical success – that it was absurd to speak of his blank verse as Miltonic and that in that poem he showed he had the power of bringing in, with poignant effect and without any touch of incongruity, the natural speaking voice quite freely and naturally. As a matter of fact you have the influence of Shakespeare there. That is, though he habitually drew in various ways on the literary resources and formalities of the language, the spirit of his use of them was such that even at his most Miltonic or least un-Miltonic – that's the way of putting it, the right way – the movement and inflection of the current spoken language and the suggestion of the idiomatically speaking voice could be recognizably and congenially introduced.

So in Eliot, in his much more various way, 'Lady, three white leopards', the poem I have just read, has the strong effect of liturgical stylization. But when prompted by the closing, 'And neither division nor unity / Matters. This is the land. We have our inheritance', we look back to the poem, we see that the actual unliturgical suppleness of the voice, the living diversity of tone, movement, tempo and distance depends upon Eliot's power to invoke effectively the way things go in natural speech. What Eliot did, as a matter of fact – he would have been very embarrassed if I had put it to him in this way in his lifetime, it didn't occur to me to do that in the proper aggressive way – what he did was to replace Milton, as the prepotent influence on poetic practice and the conventionally cultivated ear, by Shakespeare. He nowhere says that it was by the study of Shakespeare's verse that he above all learnt to use the English language for his own poetic purposes, but that it was so is plain, and his tacit recognition of the fact is to be found, constructively, in the essay on the Metaphysical poets, as I could show you if there were time.

Instead I'll proceed at once to Shakespeare himself. You may think that in the circumstances that is worse than reckless, but I am safeguarded against desperate entanglements by the limitations I've established in my insistence on the importance of shifting tone, inflection, distance and attack in Eliot's poetry. It will bring home to you how important they are dramatically – dramatically, this being my point at the moment; in Shakespeare it's poetically. This is very important to remember; it's obvious, it's axiomatic. But it's ignored in what we suffer or what we countenance in the theatre in the performance of Shakespeare. To bring home to you how important they are dramatically I need consider only two well-known passages, both of them in *Othello*, Act V, scene II, the last scene. The first is the opening speech in the scene, Othello's, as he steels himself to the murder, the homicide, the justifiable homicide – the speech beginning 'It is the cause, it is the cause, my soul'. The nature and significance of the changes in rendering imposed on any moderately perceptive reader are plain. The reason for my loathing of the actor is that even if one can imagine him intelligent, he will, in his accomplished and trained conceit, ignore the poetry, having decided on his own interpretation. He will see only opportunities for elocutionary impressiveness.

Yet the nature of Othello, the man, the hero, the way in which he is tragic and the theme or essential situation that makes the play a tragedy are given here, locally in this part of the play, locally in the poetry, which the actor ignores. I ought to add the critic usually does too. I'll first distinguish the constituent phases of the speech, making some preliminary observations and I will then try to read the speech whole as the Shakespearean poetico-dramatic felicity it is – wonderful in its felicity and like the play very painful in a very distinctive way. 'It is the cause, it is the cause, my soul; / Let me not name it to you, you chaste stars! / It is the cause.' The tone here is one of holy horror at the unspeakable obscenity of Desdemona's offence. The overwhelming cause – that's the word that Othello uses – the overwhelming cause of her imminent expiatory death – death by murder. You get the sudden change, 'Yet I'll not shed her blood', as a recoil. The recoil that we find there after a bit is at the thought of the irrevocableness of homicide. But there's a further change of tone at the next line. No longer recoil where poor Desdemona is in question; the tone becomes one of caressing appreciation: 'Nor scar that whiter skin of hers than snow, / And smooth as monumental alabaster'. Well, now, that of course is sensuality; this is an essential psychological observation. I'm not being moral, no, not in the least, at the moment. As a person with feelings and rights to be respected, Desdemona simply doesn't exist for Othello. He knows that she is worthless – this is the final *donnée* for him at the moment – he knows that she is worthless and we discover in a moment that he is going to smother her to death, without pretending to himself that that would be a kinder way than shedding blood. He is not thinking about her as a person at all, he doesn't in this speech, in this final scene of the play. It's his own feelings about her person that are in question; these he with noble resolution replaces: 'Yet she must die, else she'll betray more men'. And before the end of the speech he reinforces this good reason with another – justice. Immediately he dwells on the irrevocableness of what's coming and he moves into an indulgent self-pity. Well, that's enough for pre-analysis. I'll read the speech, the whole speech:

> It is the cause, it is the cause, my soul;
> Let me not name it to you, you chaste stars!
> It is the cause. Yet I'll not shed her blood,
> Nor scar that whiter skin of hers than snow,
> And smooth as monumental alabaster.
> Yet she must die, else she'll betray more men.
> Put out the light, and then put out the light:
> If I quench thee, thou flaming minister,
> I can again thy former light restore,
> Should I repent me; but once put out thy light,
> Thou cunning'st pattern of excelling nature,
> I know not where is that Promethean heat
> That can thy light relume. When I have pluck'd the rose,
> I cannot give it vital growth again,
> It needs must wither: I'll smell it on the tree.
> [Kisses her]
> O balmy breath, that almost dost persuade
> Justice to break her sword! One more, one more.
> Be thus when thou art dead, and I will kill thee,
> And love thee after. One more, and this the last:
> So sweet was ne'er so fatal. I must weep,
> But they are cruel tears; this sorrow's heavenly,
> It strikes where it doth love. She wakes.

Well, it's plain enough what the nature of the inner conflict is, but Othello, the man of action, is, for all his self-ignorance and, worse, self-deception, impressive, so we can feel the conflict to be in its way tragic. But – well, the 'but' points to what makes our response almost untragically painful – we feel exasperation surely; I think that's the right word. I myself want to kick Othello and he – at the end of the play, I mean – wants to kick himself. But that doesn't, I think, improve one's valuation of him. I'll now read the last speech – his last speech. He starts, and starts convincingly, as the stern man of action, the man of few words. He's beautifully realized and presented as that by Shakespeare. 'Keep up your bright swords, for the dew will rust them', and they do; and he knows they will, and of course that implies that he is conscious of the impression he makes, as he has to be. But then of course one moves next to the recognition that he has the habit of self-dramatization, which is dangerous, and this prevails of course at the close here.

He enjoys a magnificent death in his own private theatre, which is also for the actor the only theatre. He starts as a stern man of action, the man of few words, but equally convincingly in a few lines he is revealed as bathing in a flood of self-pity and revealed too as blind to his own nature and his tragic situation. He is not a tragic hero who has learnt from suffering to know himself – that's the peculiar painfulness for us about the tragedy of *Othello*. It's the very antithesis of *Lear* in that matter. 'Then, must you speak / Of one that lov'd not wisely but too well; / Of one not easily jealous.' What! it took about three lines: 'But being wrought, perplexed in the extreme'. The only kind of perplexity and complexity he manifests is the conflict enacted in the first speech, and the mistake he tells himself and the world he made is the base Indian's who 'threw a pearl away / Richer than all his tribe'. And the contrite reaction is, in all the nobility of the grand style, 'I could kick myself' – it is nothing more than that, it is just that. Desdemona is only an adjunct, she is not a realized person.

Of course, if you had pointed it out to A. C. Bradley, he would have replied (he does say this): 'But of course they didn't know one another, they didn't really know one another, they had no opportunity, but they were in *love*, you see, they didn't know one another.' I hadn't read Bradley's critique of *Othello* for many years when I found myself having to lecture on *Othello* and I thought I'd better read Bradley again. Though I don't usually laugh out loud reading, I found myself guffawing about half a dozen times; I just couldn't contain myself. I remember Chesterfield's remark – a gentleman is sometimes seen to smile, but is never heard to laugh – but I did laugh. Well, I'll read the passage.

> Soft you; a word or two before you go.
> I have done the state some service, and they know't;
> No more of that. I pray you, in your letters,
> When you shall these unlucky deeds relate,
> Speak of me as I am; nothing extenuate,
> Nor set down aught in malice: then, must you speak
> Of one that lov'd not wisely but too well;
> Of one not easily jealous, but, being wrought,
> Perplex'd in the extreme; of one whose hand,
> Like the base Indian, threw a pearl away
> Richer than all his tribe; of one whose subdu'd eyes
> Albeit unused to the melting mood,
> Drop tears as fast as the Arabian trees
> Their med'cinable gum. Set you down this;
> And say besides, that in Aleppo once,
> Where a malignant and a turban'd Turk
> Beat a Venetian and traduc'd the state,
> I took by the throat the circumcized dog,
> And smote him thus.

Well, I mean, who could wish for a better death? Now that has been the general reaction. It's a magnificent *coup de théâtre* in a double

sense. It takes place in Othello's private theatre, but – Shakespeare
didn't intend this – it's accepted and enacted by the actor with all the
satisfaction endorsed that Othello feels. In doing this I have merely
been calling attention to one kind of manifestation, itself complex, of
Shakespeare's mastery of the English language, or rather his creative
inwardness with it. Obviously shifting tone, inflection, movement and
attack can't be separated from meaning in the ordinary, taken for
granted, not very determinate sense of that word. What I have been
illustrating in terms of Eliot's poems and Shakespeare's dramatic
poetry is the essential part played by changing tone – and the rest – in
meaning, in the full communication made by language as used by
creative writers. And great creative writers are always engaged in
thought – in thought that matters.

   This is a very necessary emphasis, judging by the usual habit, and
if philosophers realized this more fully I think their philosophy would
be more satisfactory. They have always been interested in language,
they are certainly concerned with language, but they generally show
such an imperfect realization of what the full concept imports. Endless
as the scholarly and critical comment on Shakespeare's art has been,
the characteristic I have pointed to – essentially this – doesn't I think
get nearly enough attention. Where the emphasis usually falls, when
his concreteness and compelling thisness of meaning are in question,
is on his 'imagery'. I put that word in inverted commas, meaning I
shouldn't like to have to define it or define 'image', though one has to
use the words. I know where the centre of the field they portend is, but
I don't know where to draw any bounding line round it. I confine
myself to saying that if you are capable of using the words defensively
you'll know that you can't pull an image out of the poetic texture; you
can't defensively do what a minor Shakespearean, out of date now,
Caroline Spurgeon, did in *Shakespeare's Imagery*. You can't pull out
the dogs and put them in that box, and the fruit in the next box and
flowers in another. The context makes all the difference to the
presence or otherwise of the image.

   I'm not going to develop these remarks except implicitly in the consideration of Gerard Manley Hopkins. I offer them as a way of now
moving on to him, but I want to have read out representative things of
his, having convictions as to his essential success – and I suspect that
many people who speak respectfully of him haven't such convictions,
in any strong form at least. The point of my relating him to Shakespeare should be plain. I remember this in *Macbeth* – 'If it were done
when 'tis done, then 'twere well / It were done quickly: if the assassin-
ation / Could trammel up the consequence, and catch / With his
surcease success . . . ' You see that as we pass with Macbeth from the

one word to the other, 'surcease' becomes 'success', turns into success and that kind of effect – the analogical enacting, instead of the mere saying – falls for me within the field the centre of which is the metaphorical image: say, 'trammel' in that passage. For you know – in any case it's easy to establish – that imagery is not merely visual, although the word seems to suggest it, and the notes in most of my copies of the *Arden* editions of Shakespeare plays seem to suggest that the editor fosters the implicit conviction that the images must be visual – it's a matter of seeing pictures. But there can be, of course, images corresponding to all the senses that can be involved; but, more than that, there can be images of different kinds of effort, of which there may be very many kinds. You can see how the field extends, so you can't really comfortably cover it with one definition. But the phrase is 'as if', react 'as if'. I don't know any other way of putting it. Of course there are qualifications, but analogically the successful creative writer does it; so he is no longer saying, he is *doing*; the thing is done in the creative writer's way, because it is already inevitably distanced. I am now pointing of course to the impossibility of filming a literary work; it can't be done. You can *use* a literary work, which is something quite different, but the image you know on the screen is there; it's life, it's life immediately, and you never forget, while you are reading Shakespeare, or you shouldn't – and you shouldn't be able to forget, when you are seeing a Shakespeare production – that this is *art*, not life. So you are not inclined, when the villain creeps up behind the hero with a dagger in his hand, to shout out 'Look behind you'; you are not in danger of having your active responsibility, your responsibility for action, triggered off. This is a necessary condition of the nature of art – and of thought too.

Well, it's the effect I've pointed to, represented by Shakespeare's 'surcease success'; it's the kind of effect that Hopkins develops and exploits. There go with it in his verse-habit many other characteristics of spoken English that make for concreteness, precision and strength in that poetic which some cultivated people, since Robert Bridges, have found rebarbative. Frequentation of Shakespeare, we divine, stimulated Hopkins to go for the same source from which Shakespeare got his poetic strength – the spoken, living English language. It has changed since Shakespeare's time, but we can tell from Dickens it was still essentially the same, and speech was still an art, as it has ceased to be virtually. It was still an art fifty years ago during the 1914 war. There was always some village wit, or virtuoso, who could talk for hours with strong poetic vividness.

But I will not lecture you about Hopkins, I will merely add these two observations before reading some pieces of his. During Hopkins's life Tennyson *was* English poetry and that explains the extremeness of Hopkins's experimentation. You know, of course, that Tennyson's ambition was to bring English as near the Italian as possible: 'The long day wanes: the slow moon climbs: the deep / Moans round with many voices, Come my friends'. Well, it is, of course, wonderful, it lends itself very much to the purposes and accomplishments of, let's say, Italian elocutionists. The English language is at the other extreme from Italian, in its very nature it depends upon those collocations of consonants and even the sibilants that Tennyson eliminated – it became second nature. He had a genius right enough; it's a question of how he used his genius.

My second point is: Hopkins in the nature of his temperament and his poetic drives had no need in his own work for the subtleties of shifting tone and inflection that prompted me to move from *Ash-Wednesday* to *Othello*. I'll read four stanzas from the first elaborate exercise that Hopkins wrote, of which I seem to remember Bridges, in his introduction to the first edition which came out long after Hopkins's death – in fact I was in time to buy it when I got back in 1919 – said: 'It stands like a dragon in the very front of Hopkins's work.' And Hopkins protested: 'But I need to be read by the *ear*, not by the *eye*, if only you would *try*'. And Bridges was his friend. It was a terrible situation; because poor Hopkins was divorced from the world where poetry mattered as important. I'll just read these four stanzas, the first four of the second part of 'The Wreck of the Deutschland' and I hope that my confidence that you will find nothing odd about them or baffling will be justified because *I* am reading as one who reads not only by the ear but by the body. I mean with the ear and the body, as one reads or should read Shakespeare, and not only Shakespeare and Hopkins, but other poets, all poets that matter except perhaps Tennyson and Swinburne:

'Some find me a sword; some
    The flange and the rail; flame,
Fang, or flood' goes Death on drum,
    And storms bugle his fame.
    But we dream we are rooted in earth – Dust!
Flesh falls within sight of us, we, though our flower the same,
    Wave with the meadow, forget that there must
The sour scythe cringe, and the blear share come.

On Saturday sailed from Bremen,
    American-outward-bound,
Take settler and seamen, tell men with women,
    Two hundred souls in the round –
O Father, not under thy feathers nor ever as guessing
The goal was a shoal, of a fourth the doom to be drowned;

Yet did the dark side of the bay of thy blessing
Not vault them, the million of rounds of thy mercy not reeve even them in?

　　　Into the snows she sweeps,
　　　Hurling the haven behind,
　　The Deutschland, on Sunday; and so the sky keeps,
　　　For the infinite air is unkind,
　　And the sea flint-flake, black-backed in the regular blow,
　　Sitting Eastnortheast, in cursed quarter, the wind;
　　　Wiry and white-fiery and whirlwind-swivellèd snow
Spins to the widow-making unchilding unfathering deeps.

　　　She drove in the dark to leeward,
　　　She struck – not a reef or a rock
　　But the combs of a smother of sand: night drew her
　　　Dead to the Kentish Knock;
　　And she beat the bank down with her bows and the ride of her keel:
　　The breakers rolled on her beam with ruinous shock;
　　　And canvas and compass, the whorl and the wheel
Idle for ever to waft her or wind her with, these she endured.

There you see Hopkins's un-Tennysonian – anti-Tennysonian – art is
devoted to conveying the harsh enmity, the violence of the storm. But
now I'll turn to more inward work. I'll read two sonnets and then I
shall have done with Hopkins. There's the one he hopefully dedicated
to R. B. (Robert Bridges).

　　　The fine delight that fathers thought; the strong
　　　Spur, live and lancing like the blowpipe flame,
　　　Breathes once and, quenchèd faster than it came,
　　　Leaves yet the mind a mother of immortal song.
　　　Nine months she then, nay years, nine years she long
　　　Within her wears, bears, cares and combs the same:
　　　The widow of an insight lost she lives, with aim
　　　Now known and hand at work now never wrong.
　　　　　Sweet fire the sire of muse, my soul needs this;
　　　I want the one rapture of an inspiration.
　　　O then if in my lagging lines you miss
　　　The roll, the rise, the carol, the creation,
　　　My winter world, that scarcely breathes that bliss
　　　Now, yields you, with some sighs, our explanation.

Well, that seems to me utterly un-Miltonic – that's one importance –
but obviously successful, and a moving poem. Now I'll read one of the
terrible sonnets. The complexity in Hopkins's religious life as a Jesuit
wasn't of Eliot's kind at all. He's not afraid to affirm. I think it was a
kind of complexity that in his type is very common. I'll read this one:

I wake and feel the fell of dark, not day.
What hours, O what black hours have we spent
This night! what sights you, heart, saw; ways you went!
And more must, in yet longer light's delay.

With witness I speak this. But where I say
Hours I mean years, mean life. And my lament
Is cries countless, cries like dead letters sent
To dearest him that lives alas! away.

I am gall, I am heartburn. God's most deep decree
Bitter would have me taste: my taste was me;
Bones built in me, flesh filled, blood brimmed the curse.

Selfyeast of spirit a dull dough sours. I see
The lost are like this, and their scourge to be
As I am mine, their sweating selves; but worse.

That is one of the 'terrible' sonnets, that is the accepted phrase for it; it comes I think from Hopkins himself. His letters are very remarkable and it's from them that one gets the strong sense of his personality. Though I cannot see myself developing in his way, I have not only respect for him but affection; I think everyone feels that. And I may have a given kind of respect for Eliot, but I have no affection. The terrible sonnets are very personal, rendering a kind of inner conflict, but not a kind that calls for Eliot's complexities and subtleties of shifting tone and equivocation. Hopkins knows where he stands, his conflicts are those of a relatively simple man. I don't mean simple in any pejorative sense, but he was simple, he didn't suffer from Eliot's self-contradiction. There was a complexity; you see that in the developing poetry, quite apart from what you know about the man's life. He might have been – had he not had that strain in him which led him to be converted at the tail-end of the Oxford Movement and become a Jesuit – the Victorian poet most like Keats. Tennyson is not like Keats at all, but Hopkins was really sensuous. But, on the other hand, he was a natural ascetic and I suppose that's related to his inner conflict. He had the creative drive in him, but for him – and he was the judge necessarily – the other vocation, the religious vocation, was the important one. His conflicts were those of a simple man and one of complete integrity. What I want to emphasize is that the licences entailed for compression's sake – and compression is essential for his purpose – become perfectly natural when heard, when he is taken through the ear and not through the eye, when he is read with voice and body.

Now, I'll turn again to a very different kind of art, to poetry that equally needs to be read out but takes the executant's powers of perception and response in a very different way. I'll first read out the eight lines that form the opening paragraph of what seems to me the most undervalued major poetic work in the language.

> Yet, yet a moment, one dim ray, of light
> Indulge, dread chaos, and eternal night!
> Of darkness visible so much be lent,
> As half to show, half veil, the deep intent,
> Ye powers! whose mysteries restored I sing,
> To whom time bears me on his rapid wing,
> Suspend a while your force inertly strong,
> Then take at once the poet and the song.

Now that, of course, you'll recognize as Pope. Actually it's profoundly characteristic of Pope, no one else could have written it, but how unlike it is the kind of thing that Pope's name usually suggests. The fourth book of *The Dunciad*, of which that is the opening, is the great celebrant poem of Augustan civilization; it is a great poem – that is my profound conviction. Pope himself has an immense variety of manners and this is made plain in the 600 lines between the opening and the close of the fourth book. But for all its diversity it is a poem, a great one. The conditions of the impressive solemnity, the sublimity of what I have read out, are there all the way through. 'Order and light', which I shall very soon read out, are not mere words for Pope; they stand for a marvellous human achievement, threatened. You'll note the astonishing way in which that opening paragraph I read out is Milton and not Milton. It isn't merely the couplet versification that makes it not Milton, but the wit, the wit that goes with the Augustan couplet and goes with the Augustan use of the English language and makes this paragraph surprisingly but felicitously the opening to a satire. I'll now read the first two paragraphs together, which complete that first extract from the fourth book. There is nowhere but in Pope anything like this poetry. To call it satire tells us nothing. Unlike as it is to both Eliot and Hopkins, it's profoundly and intensely possessed by a positive concern for the real, as all serious human action and endeavour is, I believe.

> Yet, yet a moment, one dim ray of light
> Indulge, dread chaos, and eternal night!
> Of darkness visible so much be lent,
> As half to show, half veil, the deep intent.
> Ye powers! whose mysteries restored I sing,
> To whom time bears me on his rapid wing,
> Suspend a while your force inertly strong,
> Then take at once the poet and the song.
>   Now flamed the dog-star's unpropitious ray,

Smote every brain, and withered every bay;
Sick was the sun, the owl forsook his bower,
The moon-struck prophet felt the madding hour:
Then rose the seed of chaos, and of night,
To blot out order, and extinguish light,
Of dull and venal a new world to mould,
And bring Saturnian days of lead and gold.

Well, I apologize for my stumbling, but it's inevitable at the
moment, I can't avoid it. I really read that, striking as I found it, as a
way – this is my apology – as a way of giving myself a better chance of
not failing or faltering too obviously with the close of Book IV, which
seems to me even more remarkable. It's a thing that I'm very intent on
having read out not too badly. The contrast – you see why I put something between me and Hopkins – the contrast, which is extreme, will
be less dangerously disconcerting. What I think you might bear in
mind, as I have to, is the suggestion that the perfection of Pope's
couplets entails monotony of movement. The life here is unmistakably
diversity, the diversity of movement involves constantly varying
inflections, these made possible by the perfect Augustan versification.
In reading, one registers the subtleties of movement and inflection by
paying the most delicate attention to the prose sense, which is
seasoned with wit. Yet the vision is transcendently imaginative and, I
should say, with my thoughts on Eliot and *Four Quartets*, essentially
spiritual too, with a spirituality different from Hopkins's. Pope – his
poetry is a witness to that – believes in civilization, celebrates creativity
that works through human agency. Well, I'll read now the close of the
fourth book of *The Dunciad* and the whole poem. And you can imagine
if you like, lying down sometimes, reading with a pencil in your hand
and marking the kind of curve in a line, above each line. You'll find,
when you've done that – of course, you won't have done anything that
is of permanent value, but you will then realize – the astonishing
diversity, the essential diversity of movement (which, of course, is a
very complex concept) from line to line.

In vain, in vain – the all-composing hour
Resistless falls: the muse obeys the power.
She comes! she comes! the sable throne behold
Of night primeval and of chaos old!
Before her, fancy's gilded clouds decay,
And all its varying rainbows die away.
Wit shoots in vain its momentary fires,
The meteor drops, and in a flash expires.
As one by one, at dread Medea's strain,
The sickening stars fade off the ethereal plain;

As Argus' eyes by Hermes' wand opprest,
Closed one by one to everlasting rest;
Thus at her felt approach, and secret might,
Art after art goes out, and all is night.
See skulking truth to her old cavern fled,
Mountains of casuistry heaped o'er her head!
Philosophy, that leaned on heaven before,
Shrinks to her second cause, and is no more.
Physic of metaphysic begs defence,
And metaphysic calls for aid on sense!
See mystery to mathematics fly!
In vain! they gaze, turn giddy, rave, and die.
Religion blushing veils her sacred fires,
And unawares morality expires.
Nor public flame, nor private, dares to shine;
Nor human spark is left, nor glimpse divine!
Lo! thy dread empire, chaos! is restored;
Light dies before thy uncreating word;
Thy hand, great anarch! lets the curtain fall,
And a universal darkness buries all.

I'll read one more poem and then stop. It is Hardy's best poem. Hardy is a major poet in some eight or nine or possibly ten poems and this is the supreme one. Most of them come under the epigraph which I use as a title 'Veteris vestigia flammae' ('The Traces of the Ancient Flame'). They are all memories of some particular occasion 40 years back, which is the ideal situation for Hardy's genius to function. They are memories of a particular episode with a given woman, 'Forty years back when much had place that since has vanished out of mind'. Hardy – as I have remarked recently, Montale the great Italian poet hasn't – had to struggle with Victorian poetic diction. He couldn't – it would have been natural to him in another age – write directly out of the living language. He does very odd things with poetic diction, introduces many elements of his own and very often produces effects of incongruity. You'll find dialect words, pseudo-dialect words invented by Hardy himself, technical words, 'a lone cave stillicide' – you look up in the dictionary to see what's the relation to suicide and homicide and you find there's none at all – architectural terms (he was professionally an ecclesiastical architect). But here, in this poem, as in all the best poems, these characteristics are present, but they are no longer faults. So here, for instance in 'The unseen waters' ejaculations awe me', what 'ejaculations' does is to give you the slappings of water against the walls of the cave down below where they are standing. Well, I'll read this and not strain my voice by talking more, unnecessarily. I simply just hope I shan't stumble, though the omens are bad.

Hereto I come to view a voiceless ghost;
    Whither, O whither will its whim now draw me?
Up the cliff, down, till I'm lonely, lost,
    And the unseen waters' ejaculations awe me.
Where you will next be there's no knowing,
    Facing round about me everywhere,
        With your nut-coloured hair,
And gray eyes, and rose-flush coming and going.

Yes: I have re-entered your olden haunts at last;
    Through the years, through the dead scenes I have tracked you;
What have you now found to say of our past –
    Scanned across the dark space wherein I have lacked you?
Summer gave us sweets, but autumn wrought division?
    Things were not lastly as firstly well
        With us twain, you tell?
But all's closed now, despite Time's derision.

I see what you are doing: you are leading me on
    To the spots we knew when we haunted here together,
The waterfall, above which the mist-bow shone
    At the then fair hour in the then fair weather,
And the cave just under, with a voice still so hollow
    That it seems to call out to me from forty years ago,
        When you were all aglow,
And not the thin ghost that I now frailly follow!

Ignorant of what there is flitting here to see,
    The waked birds preen and the seals flop lazily;
Soon you will have, Dear, to vanish from me,
    For the stars close their shutters and the dawn whitens hazily.
Trust me, I mind not, though Life lours,
    The bringing me here; nay, bring me here again!
        I am just the same as when
Our days were a joy, and our paths through flowers.

That is one of the most moving poems that was ever written and I
think it is Hardy's supreme success. It's technically a masterpiece
because he has done this with the resources that he is so familiar with,
but which elsewhere, and usually, obviously involve disadvantages,
difficulties and flaws and failures. You notice here, I mean, his originality, the creative kind of originality 'Where you will next be there's
no knowing, / Facing round about me everywhere'. Well, 'Facing', of
course, hasn't, I think, the ordinary sense. The ordinary sense carries
you by the new sense, which I hope you recognize; you don't feel
there's any wrenching at all. 'Facing' means producing face to my
imagination, wherever I look I see your face – that's what 'facing'
means there. 'Facing round about me everywhere, / With your nut-
coloured hair, / And gray eyes, and rose-flush coming and going.' And

you notice in the third stanza, second line, 'when we haunted here together'. This is a kind of haunting of course now, and the word carries its weight – it's not just a holiday word – because the theme of haunting is so implicit in the whole poem, it's the theme itself.

Valuation in criticism

You can't discuss 'valuation' intelligently except in a general account of the nature of criticism. You can't profitably discuss the 'standards' of criticism apart from the purposes and the methods, or apart from the actual functioning of criticism in the contemporary world. And apart from the ability to arrive at intelligent and sensitive judgments in the concrete – except, that is, as informed by real critical experience – understanding of the nature of critical judgment in the abstract can amount to little. To consider the nature of 'standards' involves considering the function of criticism in the full sense of that phrase, and apart from intelligence about the actual functioning in the world as we know it (where, that is, we have the closest access to the concrete) that consideration will hardly achieve a living strength, the living strength of real understanding. Real understanding, in fact, can't be a mere theoretical matter; it will entail real critical engagement in relation to the contemporary scene.

I have intimated, then, that I am not proposing to attempt a philosophical discussion. I am not much interested in establishing in any thorough-going theoretical way that the phrase 'the standards of literary criticism' means something; that their basis must be this, their nature that. On the other hand, I *am* very much preoccupied with vindicating literary criticism as a specific discipline, a discipline of intelligence, with its own field and its own approaches within that field. And in particular I am preoccupied with insisting that there is an approach to the problem of valuation, 'standards' and criteria that is proper to the literary critic as such – that you don't need to be a philosopher to make it.

It seems therefore appropriate to take for my opening a representative challenge from *The Times Literary Supplement*. The editor (since superseded by the present incumbent of the office, who is without any doubt less likely than his predecessor to be thought of as an educated man rather than a journalist), dismissing, with his eye avowedly on me, what he judged to be an unnecessary fuss about the critical function as it is performed – or not performed – in our time, wrote: 'There is, in other words, no desirable life of which literary reviews are an essential component, and in which fixed standards of criticism get a kind of legal backing.'

Coming from so well-known and institutional a source, this fortifies me in my sense that there may be some excuse for saying elementary things about the nature of literary criticism. If the attitude about literary reviews seems a remarkable one in the editor of *The Times Literary Supplement*, the conception (if that is the word) of 'standards' is decidedly not less remarkable: there is at least that congruity, and it could be said that no more intelligent attitude could well accompany such a conception. To emphasize the force of 'fixed standards' as he conceives them, Mr Pryce-Jones speaks also of 'imposing accepted values' – and speaks as if that were something I myself notoriously advocated. I am obliged to comment that no one who knows what 'standards' are and what is the nature of critical authority *could* talk about 'fixed standards' or 'providing them with a legal backing', and that no one who understood the nature of judgment could talk about 'imposing accepted values'.

A judgment is a real judgment, or it is nothing. A real judgment is a judgment that has been really judged. I cannot take a judgment over; that is, I cannot have my judging done for me by someone else. Either I judge for myself, or there is no judging. And the judgment I arrive at *is* what it is, and not something other.

A judgment, then, to be more than a mere external or conventional gesture, must be personal and sincere. But it is never content to be merely that, whatever the 'modesty' enjoined by the academic admonisher: a real critical judgment, of its very nature, always means to be more than merely personal. This is not to say that it is in spirit 'dogmatic', an adjective I put in inverted commas because I am familiar with it in enemy use as a weapon of offence – as anyone must expect to be who energizes for a serious conception of criticism and thinks that the function should be served in a real discipline of intelligence. To say that of its very nature a critical judgment means to be more than personal is not to say that it seeks to impose itself. Essentially, a critical judgment has the form, 'This is so, isn't it?' And the agreement appealed for, the confirmation, must be real, or it serves no critical purpose and can bring no satisfaction to the critic – to the critic as critic.

What, of its nature, the critical activity aims at, in fact, is an exchange, a collaborative exchange, a corrective and creative interplay of judgments. For though my judgment asks to be confirmed and appeals for concurrence in a recognition that the thing is *so*, the response I expect at best will be of the form, 'Yes, but – ', the 'but'

standing for qualifications, corrections, shifts of emphasis, refinements, additions. The process of personal judgment from its very outset, of course, is in subtle ways essentially collaborative, as any thinking is – as any use of the language in which one thinks and expresses
one's thoughts *must* be. But the functioning of criticism demands a
fully overt kind of collaboration. Without a many-sided real exchange
– the implicitly and essentially collaborative interplay in which the
object, the poem (for example) in which the individual minds meet,
and, at the same time, the judgments concerning it, are established –
the object, which we think of as 'there' in a public world for common
contemplation, isn't really 'there'.

To make the point quite plain, let me remind you of the nature of the
analysis we do in what is called 'practical criticism'. What we call
analysis is a creative or re-creative process. It is a more deliberate
following-through of that process of creation in response to the poet's
words (a poem being in question) which any serious reading is. It is a
re-creation in which, by a considering attentiveness, we ensure a more
than ordinary faithfulness and fulness. And actually, when one is
engaged in analysis, one is engaged in discussion, even if only
implicitly. That is a point I made earlier in saying that a judgment has
the form, 'This is so, isn't it?' One is engaged in discussion; discussion
of? – the poem, which is there *for* discussion only in so far as the
discussers have each for himself recreated it.

The discussion, in fact, is an effort to establish the poem – the
re-created poem, as distinguished from the mere text on the page – as
something standing between the discussers in a common world, and
thus to justify our habitual assumption that it does so stand. The poem
(if I may insist on the truism) is not the text, the black marks on the
paper; it's the effect of the text when this is taken by you and me – by,
that is, separate minds. It's 'there' only when it's realized in separate
minds, and yet it's not merely private. It's something in which minds
can meet, and our business is to establish the poem and meet in it.

Merely private, on the one hand, and, on the other, public in the
sense that it can be pointed to – the poem is neither: the alternatives are
not exhaustive. There is a third realm, and the poem belongs to that.
I don't know that a philosopher would put it in that way, but that is as
far as the literary critic *qua* literary critic need go epistemologically or
metaphysically. It's all very familiar – with the familiarity of things
that are so fundamental, so necessarily taken for granted, that we don't
ordinarily bother to recognize them. If difficulty should seem to be
caused by the demand for full conscious recognition – which is necessary where there is question of justifying the pretensions of criticism,
and the implicit pretensions of all mature interest in literature and art

– if there should seem to be difficulty, the critic can say: 'But consider language'.

A language – apart from the conventional signs and symbols for it – is really *there*, it really exists in full actuality, only in individual users; it is *there* only as its idioms, phrases, words, and so on, with the meaning, intention, force in which their life resides, are uttered and meant by me (for example) and taken by you. Do they then belong to the public world (you can't point to them), or are they merely personal and private? We know that the brisk and businesslike 'either – or' doesn't meet the case. And language, in the full concrete reality that eludes any form of linguistic science, not only gives us an analogy for explaining 'culture' in that sense which eludes Lord Snow and the immense body of important people who share his state, it is very largely the essential life of a culture. And literature, of course, is a mode or manifestation of 'language'.

What, in all this, I have been trying to bring into clear and full recognition is the collaborative-creative nature of criticism. I have my eye now particularly on the word 'standards'. Criticism is concerned with establishing the poem (or the novel) as an object of common access in what is in some sense a public world, so that when we differ about it we are differing about what is sufficiently the same thing to make differing profitable. But analysis – which is a re-creating and a taking possession – entails value judgment. You can't, as some scholars seem to suppose you can, have the poem in a kind of neutral possession, and then proceed to value it or not as you choose – or leave the critic to do the valuing. Any reading of a poem that takes it *as* a poem involves an element of implicit valuation. The process, the kind of activity of inner response and discipline by which we take possession of the created work, is essentially the kind of activity that completes itself in full explicit value judgments. There is no such thing as neutral possession.

Of course, 'valuation' is not a simple idea, and the process of valuation is not in simple analogy with putting a price on. And we don't necessarily carry the process to the completion that the critic aims at when, taking (he feels) all relations into account, he attempts a comprehensive 'placing'. But it is with the major kinds of valuation that I am now concerned. The term 'standards' presents itself when there is question of getting recognition for the justice of large judgments affirming relative value and importance. It's a representative use, for instance, when I say that the acceptance of Auden as a major poet, to be bracketed with Yeats and Eliot, so that for two decades he has been a classic in our schools, and still is (though now with more than incipient hedging) in *The Times Literary Supplement*, would have been possible only in a period marked by a collapse of standards. We talk about 'standards', in fact, at times when it is especially hard to invoke standards with effect.

This point I won't now develop. I wanted to separate off, to disengage, the word 'criteria' as I use it when I ask: what are the *criteria* actually involved when we make our major value judgments – judgments, I might say, in connection with which the word 'moral' tends to come in. For it does. In fact, to inquire into the way the word is used by literary critics as unlike as Arnold and Lawrence is an immediately relevant proceeding.

The critic, when he agrees that a literary-critical judgment of his has a moral significance, doesn't mean that he is subscribing to and applying some specific ethical theory or scheme – something other than his critical sensibility, other and apart from it, that takes over the function of critical judgment. However the force of the term 'moral' is to be defined, what it does in the critical use I am referring to is to insist – that is its essential effect – on the significance and scope of the more important kinds of literary judgment. In using it one implicitly makes the point that Arnold makes when he says that poetry is to be judged as 'criticism of life', a phrase that conveys much the same intention as that which he expresses in this characteristic utterance (it comes from the essay on Wordsworth): 'A poetry of revolt against moral ideas is a poetry of revolt against life; a poetry of indifference towards moral ideas is a poetry of indifference towards life.'

I don't altogether like Arnold's way of putting things, and the way of putting things, I think, carries with it deficiencies and uncertainties of thought. Nevertheless, at the level of his soundest intentions his use of 'moral' for laying a given kind of emphasis seems to me justified, and in the best critical tradition; and it is not fairly treated by making it, as Eliot does, express a belief on Arnold's part that he 'finds morals in poetry'. And the retort that, with such a use of the term, it can't always be easy to say what is, and what is not, a moral judgment doesn't, I think, dispose of it. The conclusion I draw is that the demand for strict limiting definitions is not always in place.

The term 'moral' has what seems to me a wholly justified use as a reminder, in this, that and the other specific context, of the nature, in literary criticism, of the radical criteria. There is no way of defining these with any profit. It is significant how Arnold, in the quoted passage, links 'moral' with the word 'life'; the insistence will have been noted (he has Aestheticism in view): 'A poetry of revolt against moral ideas is a poetry of revolt against life; a poetry of indifference towards moral ideas is a poetry of indifference towards life.' I might myself, referring to Lawrence's advantage as a critic over Eliot (it is a creative

one too), and speaking of his sureness and centrality in value
judgment, say that his genius manifests itself in a sure sense for the difference between what makes *for* life and what makes against it. I do say
it; it is not merely something there seems point in saying, it is something that *has* to be said in any serious attempt to indicate the nature
of Lawrence's distinction. But 'life' is a large word. What *is* life? To try
and define it would be futile. The advantage the critic enjoys when
justifying *his* use of it and of his other indispensable terms is that he has
the work of a creative writer in front of him; he is preoccupied with
referring as sensitively, faithfully and closely to *that* as he is able. The
terms are prompted by the created thing, and he in turn gives them,
for the reader, their charge of special meaning, their due specific force,
by means, essentially, of a tact of particular reference to the given work
as present – that is the aim – in the evoked experience of it (a critical
process that is, in its wholly subservient and instrumental way,
creative).

I am assuming that the work in front of the critic *is* one that challenges the most serious criteria. Speaking of the kind of book that
challenges *his* most serious criteria (and he thinks of the novel as the
supreme human invention in art – supreme in potentiality), Lawrence
describes the nature of the criteria here, in this passage in *Phoenix*:

Supposing a bomb were put under the whole scheme of things, what would we
be after? What feelings do we want to carry through to the next epoch? What
feelings *will* carry us through? What is the underlying impulse that will provide the motive power for a new state of things when this democratic –
industrial – lovey-dovey – take-me-to-mama state of things is bust?

It is when we feel that the radical kind of criteria are notably challenged that the term 'moral' comes up; it comes up *because* they are
challenged. Asked very near the end by a visiting young novelist what
had been the impelling force in his own writing, Lawrence replied:
'One writes out of one's moral sense; for the race, as it were.' Again,
in one of the essays in *Phoenix* ('Art and Morality') he says: 'The true
artist doesn't substitute immorality for morality. On the contrary, he
always substitutes a finer morality for a grosser. And as soon as you see
a finer morality, the grosser becomes relatively immoral.'

That is, significant art challenges us in the most disturbing and
inescapable way to a radical pondering, a new profound realization, of
the grounds of our most important determinations and choices. Which
is what Arnold meant by saying, in terms in which Eliot professed
himself unable to find any respectable meaning, that literature is to be
judged as 'criticism of life'. Another formulation, emphasizing the

creative function, is that in creative literature one finds the challenge to discover what one's real beliefs and values are.

This, then, is my offer to suggest the nature of the criteria a critic invokes in making his judgments of value and significance. I have at the same time been indicating my answer to the question: why does it matter so much that the function of criticism should be really and strongly at work? I have suggested that to be committed to the study of literature is to be committed to the practice of criticism. I have insisted also that all criticism is collaborative, and that serious critical discussion is an obvious illustration of that truth. When we think and talk, in Arnold's felicitous phrase, about the 'function of criticism at the present time', we are thinking of the performance, or the non-performance, of the critical function in relation to the society and the civilization in which we live. The performance or non-performance of the function in that sense certainly affects our own private work, our *implicitly* collaborative work, and our overtly collaborative work in a university English School. If the function of criticism at the present time is being badly served, we all work at a disadvantage; that hardly needs arguing. Standards are 'there' to appeal to only when there is an educated and influential public that is habituated to making its response felt when challenged by intelligent and responsible criticism.

I won't now pursue that theme. Shifting the attack – the attack on my whole complex subject, I will risk the truism that, though we who read creative literature seriously are all critics, the critic in the special sense – the critic whom one refers to as such, and with considered respect, isn't very common. It is important to be able to recognize critical distinction when one comes on it, and it is very much in point in relation to my general theme to be clear what the qualifications are and what the marks portend.

'A critic', says Lawrence, summarizing (in the essay on Galsworthy) a discussion of the necessary qualities, 'must be emotionally alive in every fibre, intellectually capable, skilful in essential logic, and then morally very honest.'

It's an account that comes from that rare thing, a great critic, and it seems to be a good one. 'Emotionally alive in every fibre'; with an obvious propriety, that qualification comes first. To be alive is to be alive here and now. That might seem to be a pointless truism, but to be alive in the sense of Lawrence's intention is not, after all, common, and there is a good deal of reason for saying with some emphasis that the real critic, the critic who matters, will be manifested in the delicacy and sureness of his response to the new life of his own time – in his power of distinguishing between the truly, vitally and profoundly new, and that in which the higher journalist, unaided, sees without difficulty the Zeitgeist.

There is always change, change the inner nature and meaning of which doesn't tend to get ready recognition even from metropolitan intellectuals or distinguished humanists at ancient universities. They resist the Eliot as long as they can, but jump to acclaim the Auden. The great creative writer in whose work the change and its significance are registered (if the age is fortunate enough to have a great creative writer) not only wins no immediate general recognition for what he is; he may seem at first – and sometimes for long as Lawrence did – obscure, perverse, immoral, rebarbative as art and in spirit a portent of discontinuity hostile to civilization. By now it is hardly disputed that Lawrence's genius, his originality, was to be in his time the great servant, the profound spirit, the very effort of continuity, vital and traditional. Judgments of the kind to which Lawrence brings the critic – judgments regarding Lawrence himself and the consequent judgments bearing on the relative placing of his contemporaries – represent the essential business of criticism, which is to establish where, in the age, is the real centre of significance, the centre of vital continuity, the creative centre where we have the growth towards the future of the finest life and consciousness of the past. The qualifications for this work are those needed for the inseparable business of criticism, that concerned with the life in the present of the literature of the past.

Of course, the individual critic answering most formidably to this account can't be by himself all that the 'function of criticism at the present time' requires for its due performance. Yet where there isn't the truly creative critic – the critic who is capable of original creative conviction, and whose work expresses it compellingly, and justifies it – the function is disabled; and, on the other hand, one such, even in unpropitious conditions, may have a decisive effect. I use the word 'creative' after some hesitation: what is ordinarily called 'creative criticism' is neither criticism nor creative. I use the word as I do because the given use seems to be both proper and necessary; I don't know how without it to convey with force and economy what it is that makes the literary critic as I have him in mind so different from the sociologist or the social psychologist. The conviction impelling any effective work for the recognition of a neglected creative writer is the conviction that he matters – matters in specific ways. The *raison d'être* of the work, of the *œuvre*, is to be read, to have its due effect and play its part in life; failing to do which it is frustrate. If it fails to be read, and to tell, it might as well not have been written (except that it remains a potentiality). To get for it the due recognition is to perform a function that is itself creative. And 'the due recognition' – what is that? There can be nothing demonstrable corresponding to that phrase. It represents a conviction in the critic, and a conviction the justice or injustice of which no event can, in any strict sense, prove. (The rightness of one's convinced reading of a poem cannot be proved either; one knows that, and yet doesn't acquiesce in the suggestion that one's poem is an arbitrary and merely personal thing.) When the neglected writer is a great one the conviction informing the critic's effort is a conviction that the due recognition will make a difference – a difference of some moment in the contemporary sensibility.

I use this convenient phrase, 'the contemporary sensibility', without more ado, supposing that its purport is sufficiently defined by the context. That there *is* something corresponding to the phrase is for the critic a necessary assumption. And he may properly think of his effort, especially where valuations of a major significance are in question, as a creative effort (in intention an essentially collaborative one) directed upon the contemporary sensibility; an effort of modification and renewal.

Thought, meaning and sensibility:
the problem of value judgment

The title sums up the preoccupations that have led me in my last two books[1] to present myself as an anti-philosopher.

Language, which is nothing apart from meaning, is the product of human creativity, and therefore *meaning* is equally the product of human creativity. Unless someone means and someone else takes the meaning, there is no meaning. It follows that 'objectivity' in an immediately recognizable sense is a product of human creativity. In creating language human beings create the world they live in. When language is impoverished – and it is being fast impoverished today – *the world* is impoverished.

How hostile modern civilization is to what I am convinced is the plain truth in these matters, and how disastrously for humanity, I realized long ago. There was in the 1930s my exchange with René Wellek. I didn't think Wellek distinguished or particularly intelligent. He may be said to know something about literature but he certainly doesn't know what literature is. With another authority[2] he's author of *Theory of Literature* that's a classic in the U.S. That's the American world, which we're all going to have to live in.

A philosopher,[3] commenting on my reply to Wellek's demand that I should give a more explicit account of the standards I invoke in making my value judgments, writes: 'But it would still, even after reading Leavis's account of the growth of taste, be open to a philosopher to reply: "Yes, that's an excellent account of how tastes are formed, become more or less firm, and so forth, but now I would like a justification of the taste that has *been* formed."' One of my first comments would be that I myself should never have used the word 'taste' with the intention imputed to me; I should have spoken of the eliciting and developing of sensibility. I have remarked somewhere that the most important words don't really admit of being fixed by dictionary definition. 'Taste', of course, has more than one meaning; but, in thinking about critical questions, I haven't thought of it as being among the *most* important words. My objection to it, and to 'training' used along with it, comes out in the reasons I give for using the other word. 'Sensibility' is more complex in its ambiguity than 'taste', and that conditions Eliot's ability to make his meaning plain in this sen-

285

tence: 'Sensibility alters from generation to generation in everybody, whether we will or no, but expression is only altered by a man of genius.'

The sentence comes from one of Eliot's good essays – an introduction to an edition of one of Johnson's satires. If instead of 'sensibility' Eliot had used the word 'taste', that would have implied that the important consequence of the man of genius would have been the establishment of a different taste. 'So positive was the culture of that age that it crushed a number of smaller men who felt differently, but did not dare to face the fact.' Eliot in that sentence has for a moment shifted the focus from the Augustan age to a general proposition which might seem to imply a suppressed alternative taste. But what actually happened as a result of creative genius was an *escape* of creativity – or rather, various types of escape from the 'so positive' Augustan taste, succeeding which there was nothing *as* 'positive'. Eliot *doesn't* discuss the characteristics of the contrasting age of Wordsworth, Shelley and Keats; and there is only, in his criticism, the equivocal essay on Blake to suggest at all relevantly the unconventionalizing drive of genius. Eliot in that generalizing sentence is speaking with the confidence of the 'practitioner' who proved so effectively that something *could* happen in English poetry after Swinburne.

The presence of 'positive' along with 'unconventionalizing' in my last paragraph explains why I, for my purpose, shy off from the word 'taste', which implies convention and positive expectation. I recall how at one time I *was* myself, as the notorious anti-Miltonist, accused of requiring all poets to write like Donne. Actually, of course, without something to be called 'expectation' you can't read anything; but the education of sensibility implied in my phrase, ' "English" as a discipline of thought', aims at fostering the completest receptivity that can be attained – the most unprejudiced and sensitive readiness to perceive, and to respond to, subtle intimations of new 'values', new kinds of significance, that may be communicated. The 'man of genius' is impelled to 'alter expression' by his apprehension, his intuition, of significance or 'value', to which conventional expression isn't adequate. That is, he is possessed of the artist's creativity, which is never wanton – he is the 'growing tip'. His importance is that he enables people who aren't creative in the great artist's way to *endorse* his perceptions by sharing them.

I don't think that my discrimination in favour of 'sensibility' is inessential or arbitrary. I was not concerned in my exchange with Wellek to give an account of the growth of taste, or of the process by which tastes (plural this time) are formed, but to *correct* Wellek's misconception of the nature of value judgment in literary criticism – a misconception that seems to me as disastrous for thought and humanity as any. I am not quite sure what the demand for a 'justification of the taste that has *been* formed' might mean. But in any case the all-important issue regarding the nature of value judgment is involved, and this philosopher assumes that it must inevitably be an issue to be dealt with, if at all, by philosophical analysis.

The consequence, or concomitant, of being a philosopher is manifested in the assumption that closely relevant thought which isn't mathematical or scientific *must* be philosophico-logical. The compound, 'biographical-psychological', seems to me to have no one clear meaning, but I am sure that *my* analytic commentaries on creative writing aren't legitimately called biographical-psychological descriptions. Neither are they substitutes of any kind for philosophical analyses. There is a third thing besides the two philosophically recognized, and that is literary-critical analysis – focused on what, in critical reading, we 'meet' in.

But I concede that my undertaking in *The Living Principle* wasn't simple; my purpose was complex, with a complexity that didn't admit of being intimated in any approach to lucidity in any title, however that might be helped by the three epigraphs. The purpose, on the other hand, in the interests of the unifying totality of the meaning, necessitated spareness in the developing of the complexity. I couldn't, in the given book, devote enough space to clarifying and enforcing my statement about the relation between great creative writers and the thought I credit them with – the most important kind of thought.

I'll repeat the basic propositions. Firstly, there could be no developed thought – thought about life – without a highly developed language. Secondly, the most complete use of the English language, which has an incomparably rich literature, is in the major works of great creative writers. Thirdly, every creative writer of the greatest kind knows that in a major work he is developing thought – thought about life.

These three propositions constitute the basic postulate on which my contention that 'English' should be the liaison centre of a real university is supported. The idea of a university is a major concern of my book, and the idea as I advance it in the face of the modern human crisis entails the position of the university's constitutive function as being to restore and maintain the 'educated public'. Without an influential cultivated and knowledgeable public – and the problem of what 'influential' means and might be is a fertile challenge to any thought – English literature might as well not exist, and in so far as influential existence can hardly continue without a continuing life of new creation, has already ceased to exist. All of these considerations are involved in my handling of the strictly critical issues between me – non-philosopher (or anti-) – and the philosopher as professional habit makes him, or tends (I assume) to make him, in characteristic approach.

The problem of value judgment is more complex – or less limitable as simply and describably *one* problem – than is commonly assumed. 'Value' is, or should be, a notoriously tricky word. To value a thing is to put a price on it. This use of the word is in resonance with the quantitative, or mathematically treatable, meaning it has for scientists. But value judgments in literary criticism are not quantitative, and, if they are capable of 'verification', it is in a sense of the word very different from what it means when it is used by philosophers contemplating the scientific process of establishing the validity of a scientist's constatations.

The literary critic, however, doesn't intend his value judgments to be merely personal; they aspire to a general validity. They are of the order of those we make of actual life and living, but, since the challenge that evokes them is in the most important cases the insight of a rarely gifted being, they deserve to be regarded as very important indeed. Yet philosophy of its very nature, its essential habit, can show no aptitude for explaining how 'general validity' is established – that is, what the equivalent of 'verification' must be recognized to be. This problem must be left for the thought to tackle – thought that is neither philosophical analysis nor biographical-psychological commentary, but based on the literary *criticism* from which it derives.

An evaluative summing-up can never be proved to be right, but in a case in which there would be point, one feels, in 'justification', since dawning perception is to be developed in others, it should be possible to get beyond mere assertion. Some short or not too long poems lend themselves to an ideal demonstration of the process. One moves judiciously, in discussing them, from critical judgment to critical judgment and makes a comment the justice of which no one would think of disputing. When one has arrived at the final comment there is hardly any need for the critical summing-up; the case is made.

It is essentially the process by which we 'meet' in a meaning; the poem stands there between us, and we 'meet' in it. That is the reason for the emphasis represented by *thought* in my argument – thought conceived as profoundly other than philosophical. Its otherness is a matter of the inevitability and inwardness with which it realizes the nature of meaning – its sure, delicate and modest understanding of what my phrase, 'we meet in a meaning', portends. In what sense we 'meet', language – certainly language as used by philosophers – isn't adapted to discussing. We contemplate the fact of 'meeting' when we turn our thought on language as we do in literary criticism. Great creative writers are sharply concentrated in their individuality, but the intensity of this isn't self-insistence on the part of the ego or selfhood; genius is intensity of aliveness. Its creations make it impossible for us not to see that 'life' is a necessary word – and at the same time that life itself is not on all fours with electricity, which doesn't need to be incorporated to be 'there'. One of the ways in which the malady of our technologico-industrial civilization manifests itself is in a tendency to be uncertain about this difference, which is after all immense.

In any case, ever since I (necessarily) paid some attention to the problem of meaning in *The Living Principle*, and coined the phrase, 'we meet in a meaning', I have borne in mind that I *must*, as soon as possible, revert to the misgiving I confessed there, and say more about the reasons for it. The phrase, of course, is metaphorical, and the infelicity of the metaphor – of *any* metaphor – is that it plays down the *sui generis* uniqueness of the relation that individuals achieve when they 'meet' in meaning; plays down, in fact, the primacy of life. 'Meet' suggests that a diagram might be drawn of the relation (if 'relation' *is* the right word), but any suggestion of the spatial misrepresents the nature of the Third Realm – the realm of those realities which make up the world we live in, yet can't be brought into a laboratory, tripped over, or even pointed to. No one can point to the poem that, discussing it with competent readers, you are sufficiently agreed together about the value-reality to feel that it stands there as a poem between you. One can point to the black marks on the printed page, but the poem isn't those. It stands 'there', the object of a common recognition, in a non-spatial world. I am convinced that no one, scientist, philosopher or literary critic, could justify any attempt, however subtle, to go beyond that phrase, 'a common recognition', into a greater, a more explicative, explicitness. The phrase intimates what we start with, and we have to start with something. As individuals, we are life, which transcends us.

Meaning, apart from which a language is nothing, exhibits essentially the same kind of 'being there', and the collaborative creation of a language has played a major part in creating the world we live in – the human world. Without language and the human world there could have been no natural science.

It's not by stressing the words 'simple' and 'simplify' that one would hope to make plain how scientific objectivity comes to be so rigorously opposed to natural human perception – the natural perception that is registered in language. Experiment and genius, given the fact of living communication, achieved the development, and success brought science almost limitless authority. Philosophers are not scientists and don't reckon to apply strict scientific method, but nevertheless the traditional philosophic discipline aims at an intellectual strictness that in ethos is closely related to science. I remarked in a recent book that philosophers in general seem to start at the mathematico-logical end of discourse and never to be able to escape from the implicit criteria. Certainly my philosopher-critic would seem to exemplify the generalization, demanding as he does that one's value judgments shall be 'justified' – that is, justified in philosophic analysis.

He will undoubtedly know of Whitehead, and probably feels some sympathy with him; for Whitehead was not only the collaborator with Russell in *Principia Mathematica*, but, as a man of general cultivation, criticized the reigning intellectual ethos, stigmatizing (as others had done) its gross self-contradiction: a scientific realism, based on mechanism, is conjoined with an unwavering belief in the world of men and of the higher animals as being composed of self-determining organisms.

I recalled that I had at least one volume of Whitehead on my shelves, having bought it when it came out (1925): *Science and the Modern World*. I leafed through it on the chance of lighting on some passage that dealt usefully with the relation between science and philosophy, and I found this, which is worth quoting:

The origin of modern philosophy is analogous to that of science, and is contemporaneous. The general trend of its development was settled in the seventeenth century, partly at the hands of the same men who established the scientific principles . . . There was in fact a general movement of European mentality, which carried along with its stream, religion, science and philosophy.

Whitehead's characterization of philosophy as it should, he contends, conceive itself, justifies – though he would clearly have been surprised to be told so – the conclusion that for such a purpose as mine one must be consciously an anti-philosopher. Indeed, I can't see that my philosopher-critic disagrees fundamentally with Whitehead. This passage from *Science and the Modern World* seems sufficiently to suggest my reasons:

I hold that philosophy is the critic of abstractions. Its function is the double one, first of harmonizing them by assigning to them their right relative status as abstractions, and secondly of completing them by direct comparison with more concrete intuitions of the universe, and thereby promoting the formation of more complete schemes of thought. It is in respect to this comparison that the testimony of great poets is of such importance. Their survival is evidence that they express deep intuitions of mankind penetrating into what is universal in concrete fact. Philosophy is not one among the sciences with its own little scheme of abstractions which it works away at perfecting and improving. It is the survey of sciences, with the special objects of their harmony, and of their completion. It brings to this task, not only the evidence of the separate sciences, but also its own appeal to concrete experience. It confronts the sciences with concrete fact.

The literature of the nineteenth century, especially its English poetic litera-ture, is a witness to the discord between the aesthetic intuitions of mankind and the mechanism of science.

The 'aesthetic' in that last sentence explains my avoidance of that adjective in such a critical use. Its association with 'beauty' makes it a betrayingly infelicitous conventionality for Whitehead's purpose; if an inclusive adjective was needed for the intuitions that science ignores, 'vital' would have been more appropriate. But Whitehead's whole assumption that the philosopher himself will be capable of achieving the more complete kind of thought he postulates is ludicrously uncon-vincing. If chapter 5, 'The Romantic Reaction', was regarded as very impressive in the cultivated world of the 1920s, that only shows how little critically exacting general cultivation always is. It was important as possibly inciting other thinkers to take the prompting decisively further, that an eminent mathematician and philosopher should insist on the corrective importance to scientific thought of Wordsworth and Shelley. But where Wordsworth is concerned there is nothing to suggest a capacity in Whitehead to develop critical thought beyond the appreciative commonplaces, and, on Shelley, originality of perception manifests itself in the assertion that, born a century later, he would have been a great chemist. What confirms the implication that White-head isn't capable of developing original thought out of literary-criti-cal perception, and sees no need for the development, is his failure to realize that regarding the 'meaning'. In fact, the basic attitudes or intuitions *are* the spiritual values.

By way of intimating how the poet of genius capable of creating the reality is qualified I might say to begin with that the Shelley of 'Adonais' most certainly isn't that poet. For, accomplished product of inspiration as 'Adonais' is, it is inspired by self-intoxication, self-pity, and, in general, unconscious egoism. But the poetic genius capable of creating out of his lived experience poems in which gifted individuals 'meet' is *ipso facto* capable of an ego-free disinterestedness that is creatively positive. The tiny élite, by 'meeting' non-spatially 'out there' in a poem, and so participating in the poet's creatively re-lived experience, demonstrates its capacity to achieve ego-free disinterested-ness likewise. I speak in my book (*The Living Principle*) of this élite as being the 'core' of an 'educated public'. But not only does the philosopher as such fail to recognize the poem as anything to do with thought; there is no *proving* that the perciiently responsive 'core' do really 'meet' in it.

These philosophic incapacities and difficulties are reasons for insisting on the supreme necessity of *not* acquiescing in them; positively, for insisting on the considerations that lead us to be sure that thought which has any chance of coming close to life in the living of it must defy and, in authority, be judged to transcend (at whatever expense of ostensible finality and proved rightness) the logic of the philosopher.

He may very well point out that, though 'ego' by itself hasn't the force it necessarily has as a constituent of the nouns 'egoism, egotist and egotism', I haven't the logical right to describe anyone sane as 'ego-free'. Have I not emphasized the difference between life and electricity, and said repetitiously that 'life' is a necessary word, but that life is *there* only in the individual being, and isn't he inescapably 'I' to himself? And have I not described what I call the 'core' of an 'educated public' as an élite, and insisted that only a highly developed individual is capable of belonging to such an élite – capable of the unprompted, or very readily prompted, percipient response that issues in a convinced judgment that *this* is a poem, a significantly new poetic experience? Wordsworth himself, the great master of expression in language, who achieves in his best poems that perfection of 'natural' rightness, is as robustly individualized as a human being can be. Unassertive as his personal idiosyncrasy is, we recognize him in his naturalness as easily as we recognize Swinburne, whom I think of as in obvious ways a foil to him.

In saying these things I state the essential and desperate need for anti-philosophers that afflicts the civilization we live in. What seems impossible must be attempted – there is an unprecedented necessity in our time. It is that, what, since the triumph of *la raison* in the seventeenth century, has assumed with complacent assurance that it has established the exclusive right to be called 'thought', should be consciously and articulately challenged. Once it should have mattered a good deal less: without calling it 'thought', or thinking of it as that, the cultivated were tacitly impelled from within to recognize that there were limits to the authority of thought conventionally conceived, and the cultivated had great influence. But change has accelerated disconcertingly in the advanced technologico-industrial age. I have felt justified in saying that the almost universal habit of treating the sickness of humanity as a purely economic matter means that a crudely philistine commonsense prevails for which the clear distinction between life and electricity no longer holds – it promotes readiness to contend, with implicit contempt for the unnecessary, that a computer can write a poem.

There is now someone in the editorial office of *The Times* who is ready to encourage that belief. This is plain from the second leader of

Wednesday, 10 November 1976. The context of the leader is the dispute about intelligence and education. The leader-writer is clearly under the impression that he is developing a parallel between a computer (which is a 'physical object') and the 'human brain' (which is also a 'physical object'):

Without denying the possibility of the human mind having a spiritual dimension, it is clear that the human brain is a physical object which operates by physical processes. Its function is that of communication and control; in order to operate effectively it has to be able to perform a number of different tasks. As with a computer, those tasks can be simplified into input, or the acceptance of incoming signals, data processing, the storing and retrieval of memory and output.

The essential argument (if we may call it that – actually it seems to be an innocent self-confidence-trick performed by the writer on himself) *doesn't* develop the alleged parallel between the computer and a human being at all. It couldn't, for the parallel doesn't exist. The insistent suggestion that it does merely expresses the crude common-sense *parti-pris* which actually exposes the non-existence of the parallel at every step in the process of exploitation.

'Without denying the possibility of the human mind having a spiritual dimension' is tactful meaninglessness, serving to oil the way for the reduction involved in the leader's calling the human brain a 'physical object' that operates by physical processes, which reduces the human being's brain to the status of a computer. But the brain is alive and the computer isn't. That the leader-writer doesn't think *that* matters he makes plain when he says (as if concessively): 'The brain is much more complicated than any computer yet designed and much less perfectly understood'. Yet the brain, he tells us, has to be 'programmed', which confidently reduces the brain to the computer that hasn't been 'as yet' designed. That smooth piece of reductive heedlessness is alone sufficient to convict the leader of being the vicious nonsense it is.

The play on 'physical' which is offered us in an innocent way as if in good faith focuses the assumption on which the callously vulgar superstition of the whole is based. One remembers the title of Polanyi's *magnum opus*, *Personal Knowledge*: the human body, Polanyi points out, is the body of a human mind, the human mind of a human body, and the whole is inseparable from a human person.

The middle leader in *The Times* of 10 November 1976 is a development, but a logical one. Not that Marxism itself is strictly logical, but in its materialism – its refusal to recognize the difference between life and electricity – it is consistent. Both the capitalist 'democracy' of the West and Marxism are enemies of life. My protests against the steady

endorsement by *The Times* of the shameless commonsense of the age
have insisted that to make restored and rising standards of living,
meaning welfare, conceived materialistically, the ruling intention in a
'culture'*won't* conduce to social stability; it will lead to the breakdown
of civilized order and all the misery brought by that. It's not a mysterious paradox that the bureaucratized humaneness of the nanny-state
should be accompanied by the wholesale savageries of terrorism and
its callous blood-relations. The reductive 'commonsense' which *The
Times* endorses has no living belief in life. The naïvely idealistic
Marxism of the Left is (like idealistic terrorism and nationalism) a
religion-substitute that is obscurely felt, deep-down, by upholders of
'democracy' to be more realistic and logical than their own pseudo-
belief. Who can really believe in the mass-democratic franchise in a
country run by modern politicians and the bureaucrats who pullulate
and look cannily after themselves in the now cliff-hanging welfare-
state?

Those who believe in the importance of art-speech, then, must not
only know what it is, but be articulately intelligent about its nature as
thought. They don't need telling that they are in a tiny minority. The
minority for some time now has been growing, but one can be certain
that it will never be a majority. Its influence, including its action in
politics, doesn't depend on any possibility that change will make it
that. The becoming articulate about the nature of art-speech in
relation to thought is a difficult process, but those of us who think it
our business to spread and strengthen in civilization, as it is, the belief
in life, must tackle the difficulty and go as far as we can.

A reviewer of *Thought, Words and Creativity*, in one of the more
intelligent journals, among some not savagely hostile comments,
brusquely dismissed the notion that, in the creative writer's use of
language, 'one ought to make contact with the "source"'. What we
mean by this word, and by the whole phrase, must emerge in the
thinking out of what 'meeting' in a poem implies and involves.

The poem standing there between us for the verifying and perfecting of the judgment that it is a significant creation we 'meet' in is not
decisively the black marks on the page, but the response to them. The
poet from whose imagination the poem came was an individual, else he
couldn't have created it. In the creating he was intensely an individual;
as such he attains to what in literary criticism we call 'impersonality'.
And we don't call it that wantonly: the impersonality of the process of
'meeting' is what we testify to when we 'meet' in the poem. You can't
justify the word 'precision' without realizing that it concerns the poem
as thought, and is a prompting to felicity in articulate defence of the
emphasis, which is wholly justified, on the word 'thought', though

professional habit fails to *see* the justification and the philistine commonsense of the age we live in doesn't bother to notice.

Wordsworth, for example, in any poem worthy of his genius, gives
us a clear exemplary instance, and is moved by a creative impulsion
that, developed, may become one of the best. The developing is a
matter of intermittent hard work over a long period, the intermittences
playing an active part. The goal to which the poet labours is a rightness
that has a compelling impersonal authority; it is something other than
the poet's self. 'Precision' entails thought. The steps by which the poet
moves towards the final rightness compel him to cultivate a considering, weighing, testing consciousness. The rightness, then, is
precision; it is an achievement of thought: in the achieving of it,
thought of a non-philosophic and non-scientific kind has played an
essential part.

I betray here my sense that 'consciousness' is one of those important
words that are not susceptible of sharp definition. In my brief account
of the poet's laborious movement towards precision I stressed 'consciousness'. But the contents of 'consciousness' are not at all immediately accessible – they may be deeply and shyly, even obstinately,
tacit. The poet himself may become more conscious of what his satisfy-
ingly precise formulation means by thinking about it. But he knows
that consciousness can't eliminate the unconscious.

The precision sought in art-speech bears an ironical relation to the
utterly different precision sought by science. The scientific precision
is associated with an ideal of impersonality too. The scientific impersonality fosters the philistine commonsense of the age of technologico-
industrialism. But that commonsense is devoid of intellectual respectability. I was on the point of saying that the immense army of
scientists, or laboratory professionals, share in the intellectual lack
and the philistine commonsense that goes with it, when I checked
myself in order to make an important distinction. True science is what
is represented by great creative scientists, who are not common; they
exhibit neither the lack nor the humanly reductive commonsense.
Lawrence put it in this way in his *Introduction to These Paintings*:

Any creative act occupies the whole consciousness of a man. This is true of the
great discoveries of science as well as of art. The truly great discoveries of
science and real works of art are made by the whole consciousness of man
working together in unison and oneness: instinct, intuition, mind, intellect all
fused into one complete consciousness, and grasping what we may call a complete truth, or a complete vision, a complete revelation in sound. A discovery,
artistic or otherwise, may be more or less intuitional, more or less mental; but
intuition will have entered into it and mind will have entered too. The whole
consciousness is concerned in every case.

He adds in the next paragraph:

> And the same applies to the genuine *appreciation* of a work of art; or the *grasp*
> of a scientific law, as to the production of the same. The whole consciousness
> is occupied, not merely the mind alone, or merely the body.

Impersonality and precision for the common scientist are linked as
ideals with a superstitious belief in the attainableness of pure objectivity. Of course the human 'common world' has always been, very
humanly, more inclusive than the objective world of science. But
objectivity in the scientific sense is a late and sophisticated derivative
of the creativity that has built up the human world by creating
language. The concept has been arrived at in the pursuit of *demonstrable* precision – arrived at therefore by trying to eliminate every
trace of anthropocentricity. But mankind is incurably – inevitably –
anthropocentric. Pure reality *an sich* – reality not humanly created – is
beyond our experience; great scientists – though they have to be
mathematicians – know that; they haven't Russell's lordly confident
naïvety.

I was considering the paradox of the poet's achieved precision –
which for the critic is the paradox of those who 'meet' in the poem.
They are life of the most living kind and as such they are intensely individuals in 'meeting'. The mark of a human individual is that he is 'I'
to himself, which is 'ego'; but in 'meeting' they attain to a demonstration of the human power to achieve impersonality, which is freedom from egoism and egotism. We recognize 'egoism' and 'egotism' at
once as pejorative terms but the phrase *'le moi haïssable'* intimates that
the state of having an individual identity is a state of balance between
pejorative possibilities. But we don't dispose of the paradox in saying
that by the study of the precisions created by poetic genius we advance
our knowledge of ourselves. The paradox remains – remains a problem that defies the attempt to state it explicitly in direct articulate
speech.

In saying this I am thinking of both the creative writing itself and
intelligent discussion of it, for intelligent discussion is necessary to full
appreciation and to the fullest profit that one is capable of in terms of
the thought stimulated by the work of genius. Lawrence's *Psychoanalysis and the Unconscious* isn't a poem, or what 'creative masterpiece' would be taken to mean, but it is, in its marvellous lucidity
which is irresistibly convincing, a work of genius. The whole short
book of course is relevant, but immediately there is special point in
invoking chapter 2. Against the background of Lawrence's implicit
exposure of the reasons why the philistinism of the industrial age is

blank in face of the most important truths regarding man I can safely practise the economy that suits my present needs.

Art-speech, which conveys its meaning by 'indirections' and suggestive means, may be 'the only speech', but it requires an individual being to 'speak' it, and the endorsing reader doesn't 'speak' back in reply – doesn't exchange utterance with the poet; he merely 'meets' others in the poem. So we rest at the paradox.

Or do we? The inverted commas signify that in 'meeting' we got beyond paradox, which is a word that belongs to the linguistic mode of *la raison* and the testable commonsense for which there are respectable criteria. The relation between life and the living individual (if it is properly called a relation, for it means that only in the individual can life be pointed to) is *sui generis*, and the importance of art-speech is that it establishes a recognized expressive relation – a relation belonging to a mode of articulate thought – between what can't be stated directly and language. The religious significance involved – 'at the maximum of our imagination we are religious' – makes as vivid as possible to us the poignant force of the dying Lawrence's reply to the young novelist: 'For the race, as it were.'

Appendix: Notes on Wordsworth

Of the acclaimed great poets, Wordsworth seems to be the great neglected one; by which I mean that he's a very great poet, who may be judged to speak peculiarly to our present sick civilization. Eliot seems not to be interested in Wordsworth; one certainly wouldn't have guessed from the essay – the Introductory Essay to the edition of Johnson's satires – that Wordsworth was the genius who liberated sensibility, that it was he who did the liberating that Blake didn't achieve, and thereby launched the great poets of the early nineteenth century. Having quoted passages of Mallet and Akenside, Eliot comments:

> But besides this Miltonic stuff, which is respectable only because Cowper, Thomson and Young made this line the vehicle for reflection and observation which prepared the way for Wordsworth, and besides the innumerable Odes, of which none but Gray's and Collins's are remembered, there was a considerable output of five-foot couplets of which one can only say that this form of verse is hardly more unsuitable for what the man had to say than any other would have been.

This is to dismiss Wordsworth under 'nature' in the context of academic 'literary history' in the usual academic way. Eliot would seem not to know, or not to have paid any intelligent attention to, Shelley's significant tributes in *Peter Bell the Third*. It is true that the word 'nature' appears frequently in Wordsworth's poetry and proposes itself still oftener to his reader, but to speak of his interest and achievement as having had the 'way' prepared for them by Akenside, Cowper and the eighteenth-century Miltonizers is to falsify: it eliminates Wordsworth's genius and importance – eliminates not merely the difference in magnitude of gift between him and those versifiers, but also the quite other preoccupation and profoundly directed effort. For it was Wordsworth whose sustained and successful work on the problem of being a poet as he saw it liberated the genius of the two other great poets of the 'Romantic' period, Shelley and Keats – who are very different from one another as both are from Wordsworth.

★　　★　　★

298

Whether Eliot recognized it or not, the equivalent of what he himself achieved in the three or four years before and after the armistice of 1918 was achieved at the turn of the eighteenth century by Wordsworth: he strove for articulate consciousness and, being a genius of a poet, he 'altered expression'. His creative success and his influence were 'conditioned' by the fact that he *thought* intensely about the problems of language and expression, and that his thinking was informed by the creative sensibility of a truly great poet. He couldn't have accomplished the work of liberation if he hadn't been so intensely interested in the language of poetry, or English hadn't been the language of Shakespeare rather than the language of Dryden – or of Milton. 'A good part of the dreariest verse of the time is written under the shadow of Milton.' That is Eliot himself. It is so obvious that the influence of Shakespeare was decisive for Wordsworth that the blank verse of 'The Ruined Cottage', which is not in the least Miltonic, but, rather, in its naturalness and flexibility, Wordsworthian, owes its Wordsworthian quality to the influence of Shakespeare.

*   *   *

Wordsworth's distinctive characteristics bring out effectively the sense in which creative genius pushes forward the frontiers of language and in the perception which is thought achieves the new. He affects us as a creative force of life. We can't but recognize how that enters into our sense of *him* as the 'growing tip' when we consider the rightness of the terms 'purity' and 'precision'; art-speech and purity of being are inseparable for us. And it is by the study of the precisions created by poetic genius that we advance our knowledge of ourselves. But we shouldn't have been impressed by the purity and precision if Wordsworth hadn't written the poems to which the words apply – Wordsworth, whose poetic endeavour was the exploration in the medium of language of human being in the quest for stances from which adequately to admit his own experience to recognizing and judging consciousness that the poem so written is the kind of poem it is: a coherent act of expression capable of carrying the reader into the realm of 'knowledge and being' the poet entered with that act of creation.

*   *   *

The difference between a symbol and one of the best of Wordsworth's poems enables us to recognize the poem as an achievement of thought, and it is as calling attention to that aspect of the poem that we accept the word 'precision'. If one is still troubled by an obstinate sense of the fact that those who 'meet' in the poem are individuals and individuals may still have their differences of response in 'meeting' – or their different ways of describing what the poem communicates – the rightness of the emphasis which the word 'precision' gives is not disposed of. But as a matter of fact I think of what I have said about paradox ceasing to be paradox when we 'meet' in one of the perfect poems of Wordsworth's. We really 'meet' (don't forget the inverted commas), and in 'meeting' we are individuals who have ceased to be individuals. Or (this is another way of aiming at complete felicity of verbal statement – which is unattainable) we are individuals whose individuality is in abeyance, and replaced with something else – unanimity at a high level instead of the oneness of a flock of birds on the wing.

*   *   *

There is reason for saying that the effort to be articulate about Wordsworth's peculiar importance as implicit in his best poems is a good way of compelling oneself to think vitally, that is profitably, that is intelligently, about the *sui generis* nature of life. One invokes that 'compelling' because the nature of articulateness makes such thinking extremely difficult. Yet it is an urgent matter to achieve articulate thought about meaning, value and art-speech in a civilization whose philistine commonsense has lost any sure sense of the difference between life and electricity.

*   *   *

Why is Wordsworth's *Preface* worth attention? How can you say that it gives a poet's intelligence grappling with his own problems? The answer to the questions – this is my self-reassuring thought – is involved when we consider that stretch (Book II) of the *Prelude* and ask: 'Why won't John Beer's statement do to the effect that Wordsworth's blank verse is Miltonic, though of course adapted? Why is that statement utterly misleading?'

Humble and rustic life, the language of real life, language really used by men – phrases of this kind don't, in and by themselves, tell you much about Wordsworth's actual poetic. They get their significance in relation to the negative formulations – among which the only one I can remember, 'Gaudy and inane phraseology', isn't the *most* significant. Wordsworth is reacting against eighteenth-century convention, and the associated expectations in the poetry. 'Don't expect *this* from me,' he insists. 'If you do, you'll be blind and deaf to what I offer.'

★   ★   ★

Wordsworth's individual mind was not a peasant's or a statesman's – his insistence on 'humble and rustic life' is a mode of emphasis. His individual mind is that of an *educated* man, who remains inescapably that when he has escaped from the 'positive culture'. He's very unlike Blake – who reproved him for his interest in nature, non-human nature, 'vegetable nature'. And yet, when you inquire into Wordsworth's greatness, into what it is that makes him so different from Akenside, the answer is of a kind that brackets him with Blake rather than with any eighteenth-century poet. The word 'creative' as Wordsworth keeps bringing it in conveys a Blakean insistence – the Blakean protest or testimony, against the universes of Newton or Locke.

Notes

T. S. Eliot – a reply to the condescending

1 ' . . . a collection of essays on miscellaneous subjects to which the author has not succeeded in giving that coherent force which is the quality of a very determined character – the kind of force, for instance, which Dr Saintsbury, whose predilections are very much what Mr Eliot asserts his own to be, gives to all his writings'.

D. H. Lawrence

1 D. H. Lawrence, *Nettles. Criterion Miscellany* II (Faber & Faber).

Marxism and cultural continuity

1 'Under Which King, Bezonian?'
2 Also in *The Adelphi* for October and November 1933.

'Under which king, Bezonian?'

1 'Industrialisation is desirable not for itself, but because Communism is only possible in an industrial community.' A. L. Morton, *The Criterion*, October 1932. Cf. 'The essential point is that agriculture ought to be saved and revived because agriculture is the foundation for the Good Life in any society; it is, in fact, the normal life . . . And it is hardly too much to say that only in a primarily agricultural society, in which people have local attachments to their small domains and small communities, and remain, generation after generation, in the same place, is genuine patriotism possible . . .' T.S.E., *The Criterion*, October, 1931.
2 See J. and C. Gordon, *Star-Dust in Hollywood* (1930).
3 Prince Mirsky refers to 'la classe où appartenait Donne'; but what has that 'bourgeoisie' in common with that of the Victorian age or that of today?

Restatements for critics

1 Some readers, of course, will demand more at this point, appealing to 'the judgments of the experience of the race'.

Felix Holt, the Radical

1 See his essays on the novel in *Phoenix*.
2 See 'Count Leo Tolstoi' in *Essays in Criticism*, 2nd series.

George Eliot's Zionist novel

1 In *The Great Tradition*.

Genius as critic

1 'Phoenix: the posthumous Papers of D. H. Lawrence' (Heinemann, 1936).

Dr Richards, Bentham and Coleridge

1 *Coleridge on Imagination*, by I. A. Richards (Kegan Paul, 1934).
2 Those who hoped that the Intention conveyed by the bracketing, noted in these pages by D. W. Harding (see *Determinations*, p. 238), of Mr Eliot with Max Eastman and Irving Babbitt was not intended will have been painfully convinced by the time they have read the last chapter of the present book.
3 Of whose reading capacity Dr Richards can, one imagines, have had no high opinion.
4 Dr Richards, by the way – confirming the reviewer – contradicts this last sentence on p. 174: 'But it will not have been our theoretical knowledge of Nature in Sense III that has discredited these myths. It will have been the results of the power given us by that knowledge, our changed situation and the changes in our feelings that ensue.'
5 See *Towards Standards of Criticism*, p. 170.
6 *Coleridge's Shakespearean Criticism*, T. M. Raysor, vol. I, p. 220 (1930).
7 'The "yet" is there to suggest that our present theoretical knowledge is only a beginning' (p. 127).

The literary discipline and liberal education

1 *Education and the University: a Sketch for an 'English School'* (1943).
2 Perhaps I may say that I have tried to illustrate with special rigour in the study of Shelley in my *Revaluation* how 'technical' analysis of imagery, etc. may develop into explicit moral judgment.
3 There is also an exceptional wealth of stimulating and useful critical and scholarly work in the century; e.g. T. S. Eliot's essays; L. C. Knights's *Literature and Society in the Age of Jonson*, and his *Explorations*; H. C. J. Grierson's *Cross-currents in English Literature of the 17th Century*; Mark Van Doren's *John Dryden*; Basil Willey's *Seventeenth Century Background*; R. H. Tawney's *Religion and the Rise of Capitalism*; E. A. Burtt's *The Metaphysical Foundations of Modern Science*.

The responsible critic: or the function of criticism at any time

1 'After he was stretch'd to such an height in his own fancy, that he could not look down from top to toe but his Eyes dazzled at the Precipice of his Stature.' *Rehearsal Transpros'd* i.64 (quoted in the Commentary to the Poems, edited by H. M. Margoliouth).
2 Cf. twenty lines further on:

> A Feather, shooting from another's head,
> Extracts his brain; and Principle is fled;

Lost is his God, his country, everything;
And nothing left but Homage to a King.

3 I am glad to see that Mr Bateson took the point. He sums up a discussion
   thus (*Essays in Criticism*, April 1953, p. 235): 'And the moral? It is, I
   suppose, that a poem cannot in fact be discussed at any level – above the
   bibliographical at any rate – unless it has first been read critically. Other
   people's criticism won't do instead.'
        That is what I told him. I regret to have to say that it is wholly character-
   istic of his work, in relation to what has appeared in *Scrutiny*, that his grasp
   of a point he has in a way taken should be so imperfect.
4 'On the status of Auden at any rate I am impenitently on Father Jarrett-
   Kerr's side.' F. W. Bateson, *Essays in Criticism*, April 1953.
5 A way that, nevertheless, to judge from the pages of *Essays in Criticism*,
   'scholars' find substantially helpful as well as stimulating.
6 In his Introduction to *The Importance of Scrutiny* (George W. Stewart, New
   York), a volume of selections from *Scrutiny*. Mr Bentley conceived and
   carried out this project in America, wholly on his own initiative.

Scrutiny: a retrospect

1 He now holds the Chair of English at Singapore.
2 See especially the work of Henry Bamford Parkes and of Marius Bewley,
   whose *The Complex Fate* was very largely written in *Scrutiny*.
3 I reprinted it with other essays from *Scrutiny* in *Determinations*, which we
   sold outright to the publisher in aid of *Scrutiny* funds.
4 It is relevant to note here that of others of the changing editorial team,
   L. C. Knights and F. R. Leavis were Scholars in History who took English
   as a Second Part, Denys Thompson read Classics before English, and
   H. A. Mason, an Oxford recruit, was qualified academically in Classics and
   Modern Languages, having a scholarly and critical equipment that has produced original work on the Tudor period (see his book, *Humanism and
   Poetry in the Early Tudor Period*).
5 A very producible and cogent relevant document that can be pointed to is
   Professor Henri Fluchère's *Shakespeare: Dramaturge Elizabéthain* (1940).
   Henry Fluchère, from the early days one of the *Scrutiny* connection, was
   pre-eminently our representative in France. His book, translated, is known
   today as one of the most current books on Shakespeare in this country.
6 And see the anthology of quotations from critical comment and appreciation assembled by D. W. Harding in 'Regulated Hatred' (vol. VIII, page
   346).
7 It is very relevant to refer the reader to 'The Discipline of Letters; a
   Sociological Note' by Q. D. Leavis (vol. XII, p. 12). This will introduce
   him to the series of studies and notes in which *Scrutiny* dealt with the
   'sociology' of the academic world. It refers back to an essay on A. C.
   Haddon: 'Academic Case-History' (vol. XI, p. 305). And it is in place to
   mention here, to be set alongside 'The Discipline of Letters' – an astringent
   analysis of the tradition of *belles-lettres* – the positive appreciations of representative figures of what we judged to be the vital Cambridge tradition:
   'Leslie Stephen: Cambridge Critic' (vol. VII, p. 404); 'Professor Chadwick

and English Studies' (vol. XIV, p. 204); and 'Henry Sidgwick's Cambridge' (vol. XV, p. 2) – all these by Q. D. Leavis.
8 See 'Keynes, Spender and Currency-values' (vol. XVIII, p. 45). Reviewing Stephen Spender's autobiographical work, *World within World*, and *The Life of John Maynard Keynes* by R. F. Harrod, I deal in some detail with the crucial chapter of history glanced at in the above paragraphs; in particular, with the part played by Keynes in the development of the old Bloomsbury into the dominant coterie of the thirties, the 'literary world' of which the Auden–Spender group was the centre and Kingsley Martin's *New Statesman* the faithful and very dominant organ.
9 '*Scrutiny* is very alarming.' This was in the middle thirties, when we, the prime movers and indispensable permanencies at Cambridge, without social position, private resources, post or salary, were shut off (it might seem) from all possibility of being dangerous in what looked like hopeless ostracism.

Reading out poetry

1 Sir Arthur Vick, Vice-Chancellor, Queen's University, Belfast, 1966–76.

Thought, meaning and sensibility

1 *The Living Principle* and *Thought, Words and Creativity*. *The Critic as Anti-Philosopher* was published posthumously.
2 Austin Warren.
3 Michael Tanner, Lecturer in Philosophy, University of Cambridge.

Cambridge Paperback Library

CHAUCER AND THE ITALIAN TRECENTO

Edited by Piero Boitani

A thorough assessment of Chaucer's debt to fourteenth-century Italy and its literature. Thirteen essays by different Chaucer experts examine all aspects – political and religious as well as literary – of the poet's contacts with Italian culture.

'The new evidence [these scholars] bring to Chaucer demonstrates . . . that many of the conventional judgments of literary historians, narrower in their approaches, have to be considerably modified.'

The Times Literary Supplement

DANTE PHILOMYTHES AND PHILOSOPHER
MAN IN THE COSMOS

Patrick Boyde

A detailed examination of Dante's ideas and the ways in which they influenced the construction of the *Divine Comedy*.

'The reader of this book will find time and again how difficult passages can be elucidated to reveal both inner unity of science and poetry and their participation in a single conception of the cosmos.'

The Times Higher Education Supplement

COLLECTED ESSAYS
VOLUME 1: THE ENGLISHNESS OF THE ENGLISH NOVEL

Q. D. Leavis
Edited by G. Singh

The first of a three-volume edition of the collected critical writings of Queenie Leavis. This volume contains essays on Jane Austen, the introductions to the Penguin editions of *Sense and Sensibility*, *Mansfield Park*, *Jane Eyre*, *Villette* and *Silas Marner*, a late lecture

'The Englishness of the English Novel' and her own short autobiographical memoir 'A glance backward, 1965'.

'This quiet and careful book truly opens new vistas.'   *The Guardian*

COLLECTED ESSAYS
VOLUME 2: THE AMERICAN NOVEL
AND REFLECTIONS ON THE EUROPEAN NOVEL

Q. D. Leavis
Edited by G. Singh

This second volume collects Queenie Leavis's lecture 'The American
Novel'; her essays and lectures on Henry James, Hawthorne,
Melville, and Edith Wharton; and the lectures 'The French Novel',
'The Russian Novel', and 'The Italian Novel'.

WOMEN WRITERS OF THE MIDDLE AGES
A CRITICAL STUDY OF TEXTS FROM PERPETUA (†1203)
TO MARGUERITE PORETE (†1310)

Peter Dronke

This book provides for the first time a picture of the contributions that
women have made to Western literature from the third to the
thirteenth centuries. With the emphasis on personal testimonies, the
book affords new insights into many comparatively neglected writers
who are exceptional in their gifts and individuality.

'This must be one of the best books on women's writing. Mr Dronke
is like the Chaucer who took such pains, in his *Legend of Good Women*,
to write in the service of women, literature, elegance and wit.'
The Times Literary Supplement

A RHETORIC OF THE UNREAL
STUDIES IN NARRATIVE AND STRUCTURE,
ESPECIALLY OF THE FANTASTIC

Christine Brooke-Rose

This book is a theoretical examination of essential differences between
the various types of narrative to which the rather loose term 'fantastic'
has often been applied: short stories, horror tales, fairytales,
romances, science fiction.

'*A Rhetoric of the Unreal* is . . . a work by a dazzlingly brainy writer who conveys unfamiliar ideas and attitudes in a familiar apprehensible manner.' Bernard Bergonzi, *Encounter*

THRESHOLD OF A NATION
A STUDY IN ENGLISH AND IRISH DRAMA
Philip Edwards

'Professor Edwards's superb new study is divided into two sections: seven chapters are devoted to the Elizabethan, Jacobean and Caroline stage and three to the Irish theatre in this century. Throughout, his focus is on the complex relationship between the author and Authority which he illuminates with an impressive scholarship.'
The Times Higher Education Supplement

THE DARK SIDE OF THE LANDSCAPE
THE RURAL POOR IN ENGLISH PAINTING 1730–1840
John Barrell

Focusing on the work of Gainsborough, Morland and Constable, this book shows why the rural poor began to interest eighteenth-century English painters, and examines the ways in which they could be represented so as to be an acceptable part of the decor of the salons of the rich.

'These essays are convincing, scrupulous, and original. They can be recommended to all students of the English eighteenth century and more generally, to all those interested in how class ideology produces cultural codes.' John Berger, *New Society*

BEN JONSON, DRAMATIST
Anne Barton

Anne Barton gives a reading of the plays which completely re-evaluates Jonson as a dramatist. Tragedies and comedies, especially *Volpone, Epicoene, The Alchemist*, and *Bartholemew Fair*, reveal a constant struggle, sometimes a delicate balance, between the classical principles of decorum and restraint Jonson espoused and the irregular, romantic Elizabethan tradition to which he was temperamentally drawn. Anne Barton argues that these plays mediate between his brilliant, if limited Elizabethan manner and such unjustly neglected Caroline comedies as *The New Inn* and *A Tale of a Tub*, where Jonson ironically turns back to the idiom of his former friend and rival, Shakespeare.

SELECTED ESSAYS

John Bayley

One of the best known literary critics of today, John Bayley has an unusually wide range – Shakespeare, the Romantics, the novel in England and Europe, Pushkin and the great Russians, contemporary Soviet writers, and modern American and English poetry. Many of these compelling and authoritative essays have been recognised since their first appearance as defining a new approach to the author or topic concerned, and their publication in book form will be welcome to a wide range of readers.

'Subtle, provoking and wonderfully idiosyncratic . . . '

P. N. Furbank, *The Listener*